LONG SHADOWS, HIGH HOPES

The Life and Times of
MATT JOHNSON &
THE THE

KU-347-183

for Mum and Dad

LONG SHADOWS, HIGH HOPES

The Life and Times of
MATT JOHNSON &
THE THE

NEIL FRASER

OMNIBUS PRESS
London / New York / Paris / Sydney / Copenhagen / Berlin / Madrid / Tokyo

Copyright © 2018 Omnibus Press
(A Division of Music Sales Limited)

Cover designed by Amazing15
Picture research by the author and Matt Johnson

ISBN: 978.1.78558.230.1
Order No: OP56870

The Author hereby asserts his right to be identified as the author of this work in accordance with Sections 77 to 78 of the Copyright, Designs and Patents Act 1988.

All rights reserved. No part of this book may be reproduced in any form or by any electronic or mechanical means, including information storage or retrieval systems, without permission in writing from the publisher, except by a reviewer who may quote brief passages.

Exclusive Distributors
Music Sales Limited
14/15 Berners Street
London, W1T 3LJ

Music Sales Pty. Ltd
(Australia and New Zealand)
Level 4, 30–32 Carrington Street
Sydney
NSW 2000
Australia

Every effort has been made to trace the copyright holders of the photographs in this book but one or two were unreachable. We would be grateful if the photographers concerned would contact us.

Typesetting by Evolution Design & Digital Ltd (Kent)
Printed in Malta.

A catalogue record for this book is available from the British Library.

Visit Omnibus Press on the web at www.omnibuspress.com

CONTENTS

CONTENTS

PERMISSIONS

'Angels Of Deception'
Words & Music by Matt Johnson
© Copyright 1986 Complete Music Limited.
All Rights Reserved. International Copyright Secured.

'Another Boy Drowning'
Words & Music by Matt Johnson
© Copyright 1981 Complete Music Limited.
All Rights Reserved. International Copyright Secured.

'August And September'
Words & Music by Matt Johnson
© Copyright 1989 Lazarus Music Limited.
Sony/ATV Music Publishing.
All Rights Reserved. International Copyright Secured.

'Beyond Love'
Words & Music by Matt Johnson
© Copyright 1989 Lazarus Music Limited.
Sony/ATV Music Publishing.
All Rights Reserved. International Copyright Secured.

PERMISSIONS

'Bugle Boy'
Words & Music by Matt Johnson
© Copyright 1981Complete Music Limited.
All Rights Reserved. International Copyright Secured.

'Dogs Of Lust'
Words & Music by Matt Johnson
© Copyright 1992 Lazarus Music Limited.
Sony/ATV Music Publishing.
All Rights Reserved. International Copyright Secured.

'Good Morning Beautiful'
Words & Music by Matt Johnson
© Copyright 1989 Lazarus Music Limited.
Sony/ATV Music Publishing.
All Rights Reserved. International Copyright Secured.

'Heartland'
Words & Music by Matt Johnson
© Copyright 1986 Complete Music Limited.
All Rights Reserved. International Copyright Secured.

'I've Been Waiting For Tomorrow'
Words & Music by Matt Johnson
© Copyright 1983 Complete Music Limited.
All Rights Reserved. International Copyright Secured.

'Lonely Planet'
Words & Music by Matt Johnson
© Copyright 1992 Lazarus Music Limited.
Sony/ATV Music Publishing.
All Rights Reserved. International Copyright Secured.

'The Sinking Feeling'
© Copyright 1983 Complete Music Limited.
All Rights Reserved. International Copyright Secured.

'Slow Emotion Replay'
Words & Music by Matt Johnson
© Copyright 1992 Lazarus Music Limited.
Sony/ATV Music Publishing.
All Rights Reserved. International Copyright Secured.

'This Is The Night'
Words & Music by Matt Johnson
© Copyright 1992 Lazarus Music Limited.
Sony/ATV Music Publishing.
All Rights Reserved. International Copyright Secured.

'True Happiness This Way Lies'
Words & Music by Matt Johnson
© Copyright 1992 Sony/ATV Music Publishing.
All Rights Reserved. International Copyright Secured.

'Twilight Hour'
Words & Music by Matt Johnson
© Copyright 1983 Complete Music Limited.
All Rights Reserved. International Copyright Secured.

'Uncertain Smile'
Words & Music by Matt Johnson
© Copyright 1982 Complete Music Limited.
All Rights Reserved. International Copyright Secured.

ACKNOWLEDGEMENTS

It goes without saying that nothing can be achieved alone. It has been a pleasure to meet and talk, and work with everyone involved in the coming together of this book.

Firstly, thanks to Matt Johnson who agreed to this project in the first place, granted me a lot of his time and hospitality as well as access to his archives. As well as many interviews we had many conversations that informed the book right up to the last moment. Thanks also to Eddie Johnson and Gerard Johnson for answering questions and queries between interviews, and who were very supportive throughout. Eddie was particularly helpful in furnishing me with details of the Johnson family history and kindly gave me permission to quote from his own book, *Tales from the Two Puddings*. Andrew Johnson's illness and sad passing meant we were unable to meet in person, but we shared emails, and Andrew answered questions, and sent me several anecdotes and photographs as well as messages of encouragement – all appreciated.

I would like to thank the following people for interviews, in person or over the phone or via Skype: Peter Ashworth, Rob Collins, Roger Cramer, James Eller, Marc Geiger, Ronnie Harris, Gerald Jenkins, Tom Johnston, Lee Kavanagh, Brad Lochore, Warne Livesey, Stephen Mallinder, Zeke Manyika, Johnny Marr, Denis Masi, David Palmer, Tim Pope, Lucy Rogers, Alessandra

ACKNOWLEDGEMENTS

Sartore, Eric Schermerhorn, Fiona Skinner, Johanna St Michaels, Jim Thirlwell, Ian Tregoning, and Paul Webb. Some of these interviews were lengthy, many entertaining and I would like to thank people for giving up their time, and in some cases, making me welcome in their home. Many other people allowed me to conduct email interviews, some of which were quite extensive. Thanks then to: Abdi Assadi, Colin Barlow, Charles Blackburn, Tom Bright, Nichola Bruce, Cally, Spencer Campbell, Justine Chiara, DC Collard, Mark Curtis, Anna Delory, Tom Doyle, Helen Edwards, Willy Ehman, Jim Fitting, Nick Freeston, Brett Giddings, David Gottlieb, Earl Harvin, Toby Hogarth, Liz Horsman, Keith Joyner, John Kennedy, Meja Kullersten, Bruce Lampcov, Thomas Leer, Colin Lloyd-Tucker, Jo Murray, Jared Nickerson, Steve Parry, Steve Pyke, Philip Richardson, Thierry Sommers, Mike Thorne, John Tottenham, Ivo Watts-Russell, and Chris Whitten.

Thanks again to John Tottenham, this time for allowing me to quote from *The Inertia Variations*. Thanks to Mark Wallinger who was happy for me to see his written memories of Andrew Johnson. Thanks to Jane Rolink for a brief, but amusing, chat on the phone; it's a real shame we couldn't follow up.

Thanks to Peter Ashworth, and Keith Joyner for showing me photographs from their personal collections, and to Fiona Skinner who was very generous with her time, showing me photographs as well as original sketches of her The The logo and various items from her personal archive. Thank you to Willy Lehman who sent scans of his The The tour passes, and Ian Tregoning for scans of a variety of elements from his archive. Particular thanks must go to Robin Kennedy who generously sent me many things from his collection of The The memorabilia, including many live recordings, interviews and television appearances, some of which proved very useful. Thanks to Steve Parry for sharing details of personal correspondence between himself and Matt Johnson from the early days and who kept in touch throughout the duration of the book, with useful details and support. Thanks to all of the above who wished me well with the book.

Many thanks must go to Scott Pack for his hard work, and perseverance in seeing the book through from its early days, through two publishers before finding it a permanent home at Omnibus Press. Thanks too for all the advice about the book and publishing along the way, as well as the excellent editing skills and suggestions. Thank you, Alexandra Cox, for helping out with scanning documents from Matt Johnson's archives.

A big thank you to David Barraclough at Omnibus, for his patience, flexibility and trust. Thank you to assistant editors, Sophie Scott and Imogen Gordon Clark, to Catherine Best for proofreading, and Martin Stiff for the cover design. Thank you to Debra Geddes for handling the publicity and Matthew O'Donoghue for marketing duties. Thanks also to Nick Jones for the copyediting and putting up with my attempt at a world record for different spellings of the same name! To all the above who made sure this book made its way into print, cheers for making it such a hassle-free experience.

Finally, thanks to all the people who asked me "How's the book going?" It was nice to eventually say, "I finished it." It's taken a long time and so a huge thank you goes to my family; for Suki and her endless patience and Eva and Louis for playing quietly when the need arose, and for brightening up my mood when the tiredness set in. My family, as always, are my inspiration.

FOREWORD

Matt Johnson grew up in pubs in the East End of London, surrounded by music and colourful characters with the city pulsing through his veins.

Unlike the global cosmopolis it is today, the London I moved to from Melbourne in 1978 was still a post-World War II city. Bomb sites pockmarked the East End, and the South Bank was full of empty Victorian warehouses that looked like they could be the domain of Jack The Ripper. It was still possible to live in a bedsit or a squat and get by cheaply. The punk movement had energised a new generation and spawned DIY labels and bands. Doors were opened and people were picking up their instruments for the first time and inventing new ways to play them, and forming a new community.

Matt and I didn't know each other, but we used to go to the same shows. Throbbing Gristle at the Centro Iberico, Cabaret Voltaire at the YMCA, Joy Division at the Electric Ballroom. This was the environment in which I first discovered Matt's group, The The. I saw them open for Wire and saw The Birthday Party open for them. The The were experimental and even a little psychedelic. At the climax of their set they took to abusing their instruments and effects, creating a frenzy of sound. The first single, 'Controversial Subject' / 'Black and White', came out on my friend Ivo's label 4AD. The two songs on the single had been shrouded in an oblique gauze of effects by producers Graham Lewis and Bruce Gilbert, creating an anti-musical mystery that almost invoked my heroes The Residents, and I was impressed.

I remember visiting Matt when he was living in Highbury back in about 1982, and his instruments and equipment engulfed the living room floor, so his roommates had to play hopscotch through the array of tape machines and stomp boxes. Similarly, when I was recently in his cocoon-like studio in Shoreditch he had a maze on the floor of dozens of interconnected effects pedals as his musical processing centre. He spends countless hours crafting songs and honing them to perfection. His music has profound resonance with his audience and endured with their universal themes. Matt's songs are burned into his listener's hearts. He's also a seeker. On one of my favourite songs of his, 'Slow Emotion Replay', he sings *Everybody knows what's going wrong with the world/But I don't even know what's going on in myself.* It took me many more years to concur with his statement *The more I see/The less I know.*

Matt is a complex and warm guy, and a devoted family person. He is also a jokester and a trouble maker. He's caught me more than once in his wind-ups. Once I visited him in a very expensive recording studio and he was mid-hi jinx, chasing the engineer around the mixing desk. And he's an agitator. Matt's passion about world affairs, injustices in society and social and personal politics bleeds through his lyrics. He has a passionate interest in local politics and is fiercely protective of his neighbourhood of Shoreditch. I have bothered him for years to host a TV show called Johnson's London, where he would talk about the changing landscape of the capital, of which he has a profound knowledge. He's a great story teller, and the rich history of the buildings seem to be embedded in his DNA.

I recently ran into my Brooklyn council representative at a rally for an amendment to a Housing Bill, and the first thing he blurted out was, "I didn't realise you played percussion on that The The album." He admitted he was a recent convert to The The. Matt Johnson's ideas and art continue to ripple and spread and his universal music is still seeping into hearts and minds. He's the real deal and I love him deeply.

JG Thirlwell, 2018

SIDE ONE
(INTRO – MURDERING SUCCESS)

MATT JOHNSON AND STEVO WERE ON THE ROAD. IT WAS foggy. It was raining. It was a big American car. It was a long way to Detroit. They wanted to go there because, in the parlance of the future, Johnson wanted to *keep it real.* The lyrics to 'Perfect' just wouldn't work for him until he got down on the street, in the dirt, in Iggytown, and actually felt it. This was the kind of thing De Niro would have done had he been a musician and not an actor. Become as one with your subject.

It felt like Hunter S. Thompson's mad car ride with Raoul; only Thompson had been on assignment and was going to write it all up, turn it into a book, whereas he, Matt Johnson, was running *away* from his assignment. He was supposed to be in Media Sound studios in New York, recording a single, but he had upped and left, gone AWOL, fucked off, leaving producer Mike Thorne drumming his fingers on the mixing desk, wondering where his wayward client was; it was getting *very* late and he would have to phone someone at CBS to say that Matt Johnson and his manager hadn't turned up for work. And whoever it was who answered in England would roll their eyes and be thinking one thing: Stevo!

But it was worse than that because Stevo was driving, and it was getting dark. And now he had his foot to the floor like he was trying to push the accelerator through the bottom of the car, roaring with laughter the faster they went, the roadside features just a blur to left and right. Johnson was getting a bit worried now but the last thing he could do was admit this to his manager – he would just put his foot down even more, if that was even possible. Then Stevo got all confessional, admitted that he didn't have a driving licence, he had never passed his test and in a manner of speaking couldn't really drive. But here he was behind the wheel with one foot on the accelerator and a system still reeling with drugs, speeding towards Detroit. Johnson wanted to shut his eyes but was worried that Stevo would notice and do the same, or something even more crazy. So he sat there, trying to stay calm, not think of the car accidents he had already been in, like the one where the driver of the other car was slumped forward, his head covered in blood, nodding like some grotesque clockwork toy. The trick was to not show any fear, like you tried when you were a kid in front of a big growling dog, cos they could smell it.

Although what they had done would appear to be a bad career move, they both knew that, in fact, Johnson's career was about to take off. It was like this mad road trip was a way to celebrate it, to celebrate being young, arriving, getting away with it. But now Johnson tried not to think about the fact that he might not live to see this career unfold, or might end up hospitalised, the life he had dreamed of turning instead to a nightmare. If Stevo went any faster even his old job at Walrond & Scarman might have started to look like a decent alternative. So he willed himself to show no fear and hope Stevo got bored of hurtling this chunk of metal at such velocity down the highway.

"And that's the sort of person he was." Matt Johnson is telling me the story some thirty-five years later. "He would do anything for either a dare or to push things over the edge. I've never known anyone that fucking insane. Did you ever see that film *Trains, Planes and Automobiles*? It was like that scene where the car gets squashed between two juggernauts. I was like, 'Please, God! Make him stop!' And of course the more scared I got, the faster he went, so I had to pretend... I don't know how I did it. I tried to talk him down, as in, 'Well, keep driving if you want, but...' It was terrifying. And there was... well, we'll talk about it another day."

But he doesn't, and it doesn't really matter. All you need to know is that once upon a time things were different. Two working-class lads, barely out of their teens, used their talent and chutzpah to enter the rarefied world of the pop industry and pretty much dictate their own terms. Give or take the odd contractual slip-up.

Oh, if only it wasn't for these. Hasty signatures on dotted lines that should be mere footnotes, but are in fact tiny points in time that cannot be undone and have cost Johnson a fortune. Sign in haste; repent at leisure. It's not like he was the only young musician who made this mistake but knowing this doesn't help. You just have to stop. Thinking. About. It. As a man who regularly practises meditation he knows that letting go of past mistakes is the only way to be rid of their weight. It is the only way to get that point of time moving again. But it is damned hard all the same, this battle in the mind.

John Kennedy was the CBS lawyer when Matt Johnson signed to the label. The two became friends, and Kennedy would later leave CBS and set up his own firm, representing Johnson. But even he couldn't undo a binding contract. It might not have been signed in blood but the effect was similar. The contract that would remain a thorn in Johnson's side was the publishing one he signed for Cherry Red. This was disastrous. His contract with CBS would also prove problematic. "I think the deal with CBS was with Some Bizzare, for the services of Matt," says Kennedy. And Some Bizzare was basically Stevo. "Stevo was one of the most interesting people I met in my thirty-nine years in the music industry – bright, talented, innovative – he walked the highest corridors of the music industry with none of us knowing he couldn't read or write." Or drive legally.

The ink was still drying on this contract as the two young men arrived in Detroit, somewhat amazingly, in one piece. Nobody knew where they were. In the days before mobile phones, a time long before we were all connected to the online world 24-7, they were as gone as gone could be. Sure, Mike Thorne knew they were gone, he contacted CBS to tell them. But he couldn't tell them where they had gone *to*. Matt Johnson's girlfriend was blissfully unaware of this vanishing trick until he phoned her from a call box. She was expecting him to tell her he was at the airport, ready to catch a flight home, but instead he held the phone to the air and asked her to listen. All she could hear was some kind of hissing noise; he explained excitedly that the noise was the roar of Niagara Falls. "Niagara Falls? What the hell are you doing there?" Blowing the cobwebs away.

Years later he did another disappearing act, only this time it went on and on. This time people knew where he was, more or less. It was now the age of being permanently plugged in to the web so no detective skills were necessary. At first nobody noticed because they were used to gaps of a few years between albums. But the years went by and there was still nothing. The music scene changed and changed again. At some point it was no secret. He had just stopped doing music. After a while no one but his fans noticed he was gone, and he was probably aware of this, and it probably got him thinking, because he had a tendency not just to think, but to overthink. His fans waited patiently. Then he did some music but it was for a soundtrack and in the world of pop music soundtracks barely count. He did more. Three were released on his own Cineola label. The fans felt like they were being given a knife and fork but where was the meal? Where was the manic pop thrill? Where were the lyrics on politics and the frailties of human relationships? They would send emails that simply said 'Tour!!' and nothing else. But he didn't feel like singing or writing songs, or getting on stage, and he certainly didn't feel like engaging with the music industry. There were a lot of things he was sorting out, and over time most of them were sorted but he remained mostly silent and he was aware that those patient fans were always asking the same question, or making the same commands. Tour! When is there going to be a new The The album? They would ask this of each other on Internet forums, and in the comments sections of The The videos on YouTube. It must have got a bit unnerving – like being behind the stage curtain with the audience sitting on the other side, patiently, but restlessly, waiting for him. Just waiting.

For another The The album. Another tour. They weren't all like this of course. Most weren't rude or demanding. In 2015 he was ready to release his third soundtrack album. "We put a notice on Facebook about *Hyena* and there were some nice comments," he tells me. "But also people saying things like, 'We want a proper album.'" It was frustrating. But also obvious to those who knew him that things were moving again, because for a while they had ground to a halt. One person who knew this was the mother of his first son, ex-partner Johanna St Michaels. She was in the middle of making a documentary about this whole thing, called *The Inertia Variations*.

Jake Riviera, the boss of Stiff Records, once had some promotional clocks made out of 12-inch vinyl discs with a slogan in white letters. Stiff were good with slogans. This one read: 'When You Kill Time, You Murder Success'.

Was this what Matt Johnson had been doing? Kind of. I mean, it seemed like he had a career within a career that just dealt with avoiding success in some way – initially refusing to tour, then after he had relented and toured America a couple of times, and was in a position to break through to the next level, deciding not to tour again. To distract himself, and procrastinate. To turn down offers of big money in return for his songs appearing in films or advertisements. And then finally, just stopping altogether with music. Of course it was more complicated than that. In 2002, sick of the music industry, and no longer with a record label or publisher he found himself in exactly the place he wanted to be, only at exactly the wrong time. "There was a sense of freedom," he explained thirteen years later, "but fear too. 'What am I going to do now? Do I want to be with another record company again?

What is the alternative?' It would have been easy to sign up to another record company, there were plenty of record companies that wanted me to sign for them, but what was the point? I couldn't put my heart in it… to be with someone for another ten years and then not get any royalties? So I felt in limbo."

Actually it was even more complicated – but some details can wait. The important thing at this point is that he stopped. He found himself free but it was negative freedom and he was in no fit state to turn it to his advantage. So between 2003 and 2009 he did nothing. He didn't even pick up a guitar for seven years. Inertia was his reaction to the impact of events in his life, and this sudden paralysing freedom of things he had little or no control over; something that gave him more control than he could then deal with.

St Michaels had an inside view of his tendency to procrastinate when the pair lived in New York for much of the nineties, but she found it strangely fascinating that after his performance at the David Bowie-curated Meltdown Festival in 2002, he should entirely stop doing what he was best at. The film she made tells only part of his story, but the film itself is a part of his story. Though *The Inertia Variations* was essentially about Matt Johnson's inertia, it became part of the process by which Johnson was able to start moving in the right direction again.

A poem about inertia, by John Tottenham, that gave the film its title, somehow snapped Matt Johnson out of his own. The poem described his problem, could almost have been written about him. It was like seeing the inert Matt Johnson for the first time and recognising himself. By observing himself he was able to end his state of limbo. The poem said to him, 'Wake up! Move. Do something!' And if he didn't know how, well, it was at least a start. The overwhelming burden of freedom seemed less onerous all of a sudden. After all, as the line in 'Me and Bobby McGee' suggests, when you have nothing left to lose, it's a kind of freedom.

All he had to do was get over his fears and do something. After all, the only things he could lose were illusory. There was a stanza in the Tottenham poem that particularly resonated with him:

You would think by now that people would know better
Than to ask me what I have been doing with my time.
And you would think by now that I would have come up
With an answer that would silence them. But I still stumble,
Crumble and quail when faced with this thankless enquiry.

And he knew that the only way to answer the constant queries, the only way to silence them, was to do what he had spent the first twenty-three years of his adult life doing: make another The The album. Get back up on stage and sing. Tour! That wasn't so hard, was it?

1

SONGS FROM UNDER
THE FLOORBOARDS

THE SOUND OF MUSIC WOULD DRIFT UP THROUGH THE
floorboards at night, a muffled but insistent four-to-the-floor
beat. Occasionally the door to the flat would open and the sounds
would inflate themselves and clarify into the thud of drum skins
and splashing of cymbals. Over the top would ride guitars and
vocals swollen by the power of electricity. The door would close
again and, as Eddie or Shirley ascended the stairs, the music would
quieten once more, sounding like it was under water. But it was
there; every weekend the entire building seemed to vibrate.

The young Matt Johnson, and his older brother Andrew,
didn't know it then, and wouldn't have cared, but sometimes
these sounds were being made by the likes of The Kinks, John
Lee Hooker, The Small Faces or The Who. Some nights it was
merely a covers band and, if they were doing a two-nighter, they
would leave their equipment behind and the boys would sneak
downstairs in the afternoon, after the pub had closed, and play
with the instruments. Flicking the rocker switch of an amp, wincing
at the sharp electronic pop – and making sure the volume dial was
turned down low – they would dare to strum their fingers over the

taut metal strings. The brightly lacquered guitars and pearlescent drum shells brought a glimpse of glamour and excitement to the somewhat drab daytime surroundings of the pub. Johnson's memories are still vivid. "There was one band, I don't know if it was Screaming Lord Sutch or someone else, who had this skull. I think it had red jewelled eyes or something like that, and we would sneakily remove it from its velvet-lined case. And then you would see the electric guitar... it was so exotic." This was a different life, one their school friends were not aware existed. It wasn't just that they lived above a pub, but that the pub, the Two Puddings on Stratford Broadway, was one of the premier venues for live music in east London in the sixties.

One afternoon Andrew came home from school and got to see some of the men who were using the dance hall, where the nightly discos took place, as a rehearsal room. "As I was trudging up three flights of stairs to our living quarters, dragging my duffel bag behind me, I became aware of loud music coming from the first floor dance hall – known as the Devil's Kitchen, on account of the lurid fluorescent paintings of monsters all over the walls. 'Go and have a look, but don't disturb them,' said my mum. I opened the door carefully and saw a small group of young men in the hall surrounded by their large PA system. The evident leader, calling the shots, wore a cheesecloth shirt and a battered broad-brimmed straw hat. He was Steve Marriott, and they were the Small Faces. To be honest I'd never heard of them, and I don't think most of the world outside Manor Park had at that point."

The closest Matt got to seeing anything was on nights when there was a dance on in the ballroom of the Town Hall. At the back of the pub was a tiny balcony which looked out over a waste patch of ground and onto the ballroom. Through the tall windows he would see lights playing against the walls and ceiling, and hear the sounds of whatever band was on stage, with applause, cheers and whistles in between well-received numbers. And like any kid he imagined what it might be like to be in there amid all that excitement, maybe even what it would be like to be responsible for all that glorious noise. These nights, like most of the music nights and discos in the pub, were mostly down to the efforts of Uncle Kenny.

Kenny Johnson, four years younger than Matt's father, Eddie, was something of a pioneer when it came to music at the dawn of the rock and pop era. He was pretty much up to his neck in it, responsible for putting on dances all over the UK. In fact, in a roundabout way it was these music nights that led to Matt Johnson growing up above the pub – but we're getting ahead of ourselves. If we want to get under the skin of our hero we need to go back and look at the DNA of his pre-history, both physical and cultural. He is, after all, just another link in that chain, coming from a working-class background, part of what Raymond Williams called 'The Long Revolution', born at a time in history when he could benefit from the blossoming of literacy, the cultural and political changes and the 'white heat of technology' that was shaping a new era of modernity.

When you think of the sixties, and of London, it is the West End: Chelsea and the Kings Road, Carnaby Street and Soho. East London barely gets a look-in in popular consciousness, aside perhaps from the Kray twins who, along with the Beatles and Stones, became cultural icons, thanks to the photography of another East End boy, David Bailey. But in swinging terms it all seemed to happen up West and when we think of the East we conjure up instead an altogether less groovy picture.

The East End of London, perhaps more than any other urban area of comparable size, inhabits an almost mythical space in the imagination. Its cast of characters includes such notables and rogues as Jack the Ripper Annie Besant, and the aforementioned Kray twins. It takes in Chinese opium dens, Jewish tailors, fights against fascists, pioneers of women's suffrage, and the battle of Cable Street. It weathered the Blitz and sang around upright pianos in corner pubs where men and women, who would eat jellied eels, pie and mash and beigels, were the salt of the earth; and at its heart lay the docks, a small window onto the riches of the world's largest Empire.

It was here that Matt Johnson's paternal grandparents, George and Jane, were born and grew up, on the eastern edge of what locals considered the East End proper – starting at Aldgate and ending at Bow Bridge. When George and Jane had both entered this world, in 1905, the area wasn't a great deal better off than it had been during the murderous spree of Jack the Ripper. George Johnson left school when he was 11, or maybe it was 12, as if an extra twelve months was going to make any difference to the prospects of a young East End boy in the middle of a war. He drove a horse and cart for a while and by the time he was 15 the war, which had claimed the life of his father, was over and he had graduated to a lorry. At some point he met Jane Bennett, who worked as a 'box-maker' until the couple got married, and George, being of the old school, took on the role of sole breadwinner while Jane took on the role of housewife and mother. Though these were the names they were christened with, everyone would always refer to them as Charlie and Jinny. Charlie was a resourceful chap and one way or another he was able to make ends meet, even if the two ends often seemed like strangers to one another. Life was a mix of hard work and sniffing out opportunity. It wasn't much use being a grafter if you couldn't also live by your wits.

Jinny Johnson gave birth to their first child in the Commercial Road Maternity Hospital, Limehouse on May 18, 1932. The proud parents christened him Edward Charles Johnson and they began their life as a family in their home on Cadogan Terrace, opposite Victoria Park. Four years later a second son, Kenneth, was born and they had moved to nearby Lamprell Street. By the time their first daughter, Doreen, arrived in 1940, another war had started and it wasn't until it was over that their fourth and final child, Michael, was born. This was in 1948, following the infamously cold winter of 1947. Whether or not Michael was a result of efforts to keep warm is not recorded.

Charlie Johnson, too young to fight in the First World War, missed out on the dubious honour of being able to fight in the second on account of having only one eye; this, according to family lore, the result of being kicked by a horse when he was younger. He was, however, a proud member of the Home Guard and spent many a night putting out incendiaries. He would sometimes visit Eddie and Kenny whenever they had been evacuated, impressing them with his uniform and tales of the larks that he and his friends got up to on duty. There were sad tales too, of little girls killed and the like, so the narrative would fluctuate between comedy and tragedy as the young boys listened with keen ears. Eddie especially. Whether contained in the form of books, film, radio shows or the oral storytelling of family members, nothing gripped Eddie quite like a good story.

Sandwiched in between the bombs and the rockets of the latter years of the conflict, Eddie passed his 'scholarship' and moved up to Central School, Morpeth Street, Bethnal Green. His experience of the war, like most London children lucky enough to survive, was a mix of the carefree and the miserable – just like any childhood, albeit under the ever-present shadow of fear and tragedy. He and his pals would play football and cricket in streets still free of traffic, and games like 'High Jimmy Nacker'. But they would also be climbing the bombed and blasted houses, risking life and limb walking along the narrow parapets of the rooftops, live cables rising out of the ground like snakes that would flash and fizzle and crack when hit with a stick. At night, if they weren't at home listening to the Home Service or Light Programme on the wireless, they would be in the shelters listening to the bombs falling, or doodlebugs buzzing overhead. They would carry their bedding back home at dawn, wondering if their house would still be there. And, just like any urban kids of their generation, war or no war, they would stare at things they couldn't afford in shop windows and suffer sadistic teachers who would cane their hands as if attempting to break their fingers.

The end of the war wasn't a surprise, more a gradual unfolding. The reports, as the Allies advanced on all fronts, were that Germany was crumbling, and the bombs and V2 rockets ceased for some time. The promised ringing of church bells across the land never happened.

"We had a big street party with huge bonfires on the debris," Eddie recalls. "There was plenty to burn, I went to bed and, the following morning, when I looked out of my window overlooking the debris most of the grown-ups were still sitting round the fire."

As the post-war era began, things probably felt much the same for the inhabitants of east London. Rationing was still in place and so was most of the damage of the Blitz. In fact, such was the financial impact of the war on Britain, some areas of London would have to wait two or three decades to be rebuilt. The new Empire was now America, with Britain its subservient ally, and this fact would later lodge itself like a splinter in the mind of Eddie Johnson's second son. But that was forty years into the future.

The teenage Eddie Johnson inhabited a tougher but more straightforward world than his son would; one of outside toilets and no central heating, which in the winter of 1947 was no laughing matter. But despite it being the coldest winter of the century, despite a lack of decent clothing, and rationing that was as severe, if not more so, than the war years themselves – despite all this people got by. A Labour government was in power and in the process of unfurling the welfare state – there was hope in the air. Things weren't so bad, really, and by the time the country had properly thawed, Eddie, at age 14, had left school.

After a variety of low-paid jobs, none of which were remotely enjoyable, he visited the local Labour Exchange in an effort to improve his fortunes. He told the man behind the desk that he wanted to be a journalist and after being told that he stood no chance of becoming one, the bearer of this blunt news softened. He told Eddie to go to 92 Fleet Street to an office below *Boxing News* where he would find a man called Stanley Clarke who needed some help with his press news service. And so Eddie, who could type a little bit, joined this one-man band, and each day would be given a pile of magazines to look through with the aim of finding an interesting story or two.

"He was a very mean man, terribly mean, gave me thirty bob a week, but I didn't mind because I enjoyed the work. He used to say to me, 'When the carbon paper runs out, heat it up in front of the fire so you can use it a bit longer.' I used to go to every newspaper in Fleet Street and Farringdon Road, delivering these stories. If I got a story published he used to give me half a crown."

Next, Eddie got a job with the writer Theo Lang and found himself north of the border working on a project called 'The King's Scotland'. This interesting, but low-paid, venture was in turn cut short by National Service, during which he found himself in London, Catterick, Colchester, Tripoli, Tobruk and Malta. When his two years in the army was up he returned to east London and, his writing ambitions temporarily shelved, was content to spend his free time going out drinking with his mates and, in his own words, being "a bit of a hooligan". By now his parents had moved further east to the leafy surroundings of Forest Gate. It was less than two miles from the area he had grown up in, but in such a tightly packed city two miles was practically another country, and though the Johnsons now found themselves in a bigger house among 'select' folk, as Jinny referred to them, they missed the close-knit community they had left behind in Bow. Upward social mobility might have brought its comforts but for all the gains there were losses too. Eddie just kept going back to his old stomping grounds.

"I used to get the bus to Bethnal Green and the Repton Club for Boys and Girls. There I'd meet friends and, once again, feel at home. One of the older lads was called Reggie Baker. He started taking me to all the well-known pubs, the main ones being the London Hospital Tavern in Whitechapel and the Two Puddings in Stratford. Both live-music pubs."

The Two Puddings, which stood at 27 Broadway, next to Stratford Town Hall, earned its unusual moniker thanks to an earlier kind-hearted licensee who would put two huge Christmas puddings outside the pub on a table during the festive season, and give free platefuls of food to the local poor. Some suggested that it wasn't the tiles on the walls that earned it the nickname of the 'Butchers' Shop' but the odd spot of violent bother. Still, that wouldn't have made it much different from a lot of pubs in the

East End and elsewhere in London, and it certainly didn't stop the place filling at the weekends. Above the bar, on the first floor, was a restaurant and it didn't take Eddie too long to see its potential.

"I ran a one-off dance on the first floor with a friend, Peter Aldridge, in 1953. It met its demise in complete disarray involving the police and arrests. The band never got paid, nor did the licensee, Harold Stark. As such, I avoided the place until Stark left. Harry Alden took the licence afterwards and ran the pub with his wife Flo. It was during his tenure that Kenny started the 'Big Beat Club' on the first floor and I started helping him out there on a regular basis."

The same year that Bill Hailey's 'Rock Around The Clock' was to cause such a fuss, Eddie was to meet his future wife, Shirley, during an eventful night that began with an altercation at the Lyceum. The doorman happened to mention that some Americans had made a joke about the speed of the British retreat from Dunkirk. This didn't go down well with Eddie and in the ensuing melee he was stabbed. At the time, perhaps due to the adrenaline, he didn't realise how serious his wound was and patched himself up so the night could continue. He had known Shirley for a long time, admiring her good looks, but hadn't seen her for a number of years, so when he met her in a pub that evening, the fact that he had been stabbed seemed to recede in importance. They went back to east London and had a bit of a party before the extent of his injury became difficult to ignore and he got himself to the hospital, where he was stitched up and then sent home in a taxi. "I went back the next day in agony. They kept me in hospital as I was quite critical."

Shirley was the second child of Josiah and Sue Ferdinando, arriving four years after her sister Josephine and just one year before brother Peter. Her younger sister, Susie, was born after the war and the two became best friends. According to family research, Josiah, or Joe as everyone would call him, had Portuguese Sephardic roots, which might explain how he came to be born in the East End of London. A builder by trade, finances were often rather precarious, though he was generous when he was flush and popular with the neighbours and local shopkeepers. Shirley took after her mother and could be just as stubborn. They once worked in the same factory and after a falling-out didn't talk to each other for a year, passing each other in silence on the factory floor each day. Like many women in the area, Shirley worked in more than one local factory, including Clarnico's, Bryant & May and Tate & Lyle. Other jobs included a stint at a record shop next to the King Edward pub on Stratford Broadway, and as an orderly at Forest Gate Maternity Hospital.

When he was fit enough, Eddie returned home and he and Shirley began dating. It had been peculiar circumstances that had brought them together but once they were it soon became obvious that they were fated to remain so, and on July 19, 1958 they married and moved to a small flat in Wood Street, Walthamstow.

By the time Shirley and Eddie had tied the knot a seismic event in popular culture had occurred, and it was one that was to have a hefty impact on the fortunes of the Johnson family – including ones not yet born. Years of rationing and austerity had created a generation ripe for some sense of excitement and glamour. Rock'n'roll, when it came, found not only fertile ground in the United Kingdom, but a growing mass media that was able to spread the message far and wide at great speed. In much the same way that the printing press took the Bible and Christianity to the masses, so television, radio and tabloid newspapers did the same for rock'n'roll. A huge increase in the number of jukeboxes in the country made sure that this devil's music found the ears of a hungry youth. It was this marriage of mass communication, new technology and new music that many canny operators were to seize upon, including Eddie's brother Kenny, who was to kick-start his own little music empire at around the same time that his older brother was settling down with his new wife, awaiting the birth of their first child. Andrew Johnson duly arrived on January 6, 1959, born in Thorpe Coombe Maternity Hospital, just a stone's throw from the flat in Wood Street where he would spend the first four years of his life.

Eddie and Kenny were, like most young people, taken by the exciting new music, but Kenny also saw it as a financial opportunity. He astutely saw how new technology – in this instance modern, lightweight record decks that played the latest 7-inch discs at the new speed of 45 revolutions per minute – could radically reshape the landscape of nightlife for the young generation who were, fortuitously, about to live through an era of prosperity, almost full employment, and increased opportunity and social mobility.

"My brother, Kenny, had an idea so simple; like many great ideas, it was incredible that no one had ever thought of it before. In all the dance halls, town halls, halls above pubs, club halls, and wedding functions, when people ran a dance they used a band. The stuff they played was limited, repetitious, and often very boring. Kenny's idea was that he would get someone to play the latest Top 20 records over a large sound system. As far as I am aware, he was the very first to do it and, although some dispute this, *that* is how disco was born."

Some *would* dispute this but they would be missing the point. The fact is that Kenny was, like others, in the right place at the right time with a revolutionary idea. Before the use of records and record decks it wasn't unknown for some venues to employ reel-to-reel tape recorders to play music, but these were expensive and limited in terms of available music and couldn't hope to cater to the fast pace of the ever-changing pop charts. One such venue was the Earlham Grove Dance Academy in Forest Gate, a venue that Kenny, who lived on the very same street, had his eye on. First though, he returned to the Two Puddings in Stratford. The dance hall above the pub was just what he needed. Arthur Taylor was employed to install a good sound system and an old mate called Bernie became the DJ – though in these early days this meant one deck and the announcement of each song title and artist. The set-up sounds rudimentary now, but it proved to be a local sensation. It was known as the Big Beat Club.

Eddie didn't need much convincing when Kenny asked him to help out with the new venture after a friend dropped out, and so he teamed up with his brother, brother-in-law Peter Ferdinando and Johnny Bruce. With Shirley now expecting their second child, this was a welcome opportunity and he doubled his money in short order. Kenny, meanwhile, bought the large property on Earlham Grove, where he started the Jive Dive around 1960. The ground floor was converted into a bar complete with tiki-style bamboo and fake plants, while the basement was to become the dance hall. It was a family affair, with Shirley and her sister-in-law working behind the bar, Jinny on cloakroom duties and Charlie upstairs on babysitting duties, no doubt itching to be downstairs with a pint and a fag.

A new decade was just around the corner and life was looking a bit rosier for Eddie. He had been recommended for an OST ticket by Canadian Pacific Steamships, the shipping container company, and further recommended by a friend, Stevie Hegarty, who already worked on the docks. This ticket secured his employ as an Overside Ships Tally Clerk, checking cargo being loaded or discharged. Getting into the docks without family connections had been a lengthy procedure but, now that it was over, it brought with it a welcome level of economic security. Having got in himself he soon got Kenny and Peter to follow, and so, docks by day and dance hall by night, life remained a family affair. Shirley, meanwhile, had stopped working at the Jive Dive as she was entering the final stages of her third trimester. Andrew, now two and a half years old, was soon to get a baby brother.

* * *

Eddie had invited his pal, Stevie Hegarty, over to the flat on Wood Street so the two of them could go out for a drink. He looked out the window at the darkening sky and wondered whether this announced the approach of a storm. Sure enough, by the time Stevie was knocking on the door the first claps of thunder were reverberating over Walthamstow, and the rain was bouncing off the pavements. Stevie looked like he needed warming up. He said hello to Shirley, asked her how she was? The two men were heading towards the kitchen, to make the tea and have a chat, catch up on the news, when Shirley was struck by lightning. Well, not exactly, but lightning did strike the steel fire-escape and Shirley had been standing feet away from it, watching the rain. She ended up across the other side of the room, almost getting there before Eddie and Stevie, who picked her up, dusted her down and asked if she was okay. She looked pretty shaken and the two men had to go to the nearby pub ahead of schedule and bang on the doors till the landlord opened them – two men standing on his doorstep in a thunderstorm asking if they could get some brandy, a large one, something about someone being hit by lightning. He duly obliged. So there you go… a few more feet and Matt Johnson may not have made it into this life. It's a good story, told by Eddie, who loves a good story. It's a true one though.

Zap! What might that explosive pulse of energy have done? What did it do to a baby in the womb to be presented with enough electrical force in the atmosphere to send its mother violently across the room? Who knows? Shirley didn't. By the time Eddie and Stevie got back from the pub she had gathered her senses and then gratefully necked the brandy. Soon they were laughing it off. It was a close one all right. A bit of a scare, but no damage done. Shirley felt her belly perhaps, rubbed it, checking to see if the baby was okay in there, feeling with a cupped palm, wanting a kick inside for reassurance but it would be a few weeks before she could expect that. No more standing near the fire escape in a thunderstorm, that's for sure.

They had been living in the tiny flat for three years, paying £4 a week for the privilege. Eddie would describe it as cosy, putting a positive spin on its size. At first it had been a bit of a struggle. "I remember we'd been so poor at one time that, in the winter, when it was dark, I'd climb over the high wall to the local coal yard with a couple of stout bags and fill them up with handfuls of coal, so we could keep warm." Things improved financially when Eddie secured more regular work at the docks and there was good money on the side from promoting dances with Kenny. Of an evening, with Andrew tucked up in his cot, Eddie and Shirley would sit in a pair of comfortable armchairs watching the television set they paid Universal Rentals 9/6d a week for. Some evenings Eddie would sit there, smoking a Player's, drinking a glass of R. White's lemonade and feel… well, content.

Shirley might have felt content with married life, and indeed with their flat, but she was more practical than her husband. Cramped as it was now, especially since Andrew had started walking, it was going to seem even smaller when their second child arrived. They both thought about a future for themselves that was more comfortable and secure, but Eddie was a dreamer, while Shirley had a steely pragmatism. Eddie had taken to reading *The Observer* and was particularly fond of the restaurant reviews, which were not at all common at that time. Soon he was buying the *Good Food Guide*, marvelling at the florid descriptions of food and wine, a world of mystery for a working-class man at the start of the sixties. This was a level of aspiration that his father's generation would have found ridiculous – like dreaming of flying to the moon.

For Shirley, who aspired to the finer things in life as much as Eddie did, practicalities came first. The delights of the French chateau vineyards would have to wait. With Shirley entering the final stages of her pregnancy, the Johnson family fortunes were poised on the cusp of change. Their aspirations weren't a delusion, rather a realisation, however subliminal, that this new decade promised real opportunities for improving one's lot. Social mobility might have been a phrase unfamiliar outside of university Sociology departments, but events were about to propel them into a new world of change.

On August 15, 1961, Eddie was working down the docks when a workmate told him that a friend had been picked up and was now ensconced at Her Majesty's pleasure. Did Eddie want to come and visit him? He said yes, and off they went to Brixton, or maybe it was the Scrubs, or even Pentonville – he can't remember now. Suffice to say that none of these prisons was near Walthamstow.

"He'd been nicked because there had been a few shootings in and around Canning Town at that time – it was quite a well-known feud going on. But when I got back to the flat on Wood Street there was a note on the table. *You're never here when I want you!* Shirley had already gone to the hospital. I felt terrible. Men weren't expected to witness the birth in those days, but I should have been there when she went into hospital."

Eddie rushed down to the end of Wood Street and round the corner onto Forest Road, where Thorpe Coombe Maternity Hospital was situated. A severe-looking nurse was waiting for him with a pronounced frown on her face. "Mr Johnson, this way," she said curtly and took him onto the ward. "All the nurses were laughing, Shirley was laughing and Matthew was in her arms – the perfect little baby. The nurse had been winding me up." That night there was a nice jolly-up in the pub to wet the baby's head. While Shirley may have wondered how they were going to fare in the flat now there was an extra person, Eddie drank to Matthew William Johnson. As the jolly-up got more jolly it perhaps crossed his mind that he had work in the morning and would be nursing a sizeable hangover, little realising that in a few months he would be off work for three whole months, without pay.

A routine X-ray at the docks indicated a possible problem; a follow-up at the hospital after Christmas revealed he had contracted tuberculosis. He was admitted immediately and would remain there for eleven weeks, beating the boredom by reading. He had enough time to get through *War and Peace*, and tackle Karl Marx's *Das Kapital*. Though Eddie was in tune with his political philosophy, Marx was no writer in comparison to Tolstoy, so he gave up halfway through. His reading habits were less unusual than they might appear, working as he did in a fiercely left-wing environment.

"I've always been a voracious reader, but when I worked in the docks I was staggered at how many self-educated and literate men worked as stevedores, dockers and tally clerks. The bible for many of them was *The Ragged-Trousered Philanthropist*. Karl Marx was another favourite. One docker would recite and quote Congreve, Dante, Byron, whole poems and complete quotations; another man was fond of the Greek philosophers; others would talk of Proust, Kafka and Joyce. Some of the most enjoyable moments of my life were spent working in the docks, talking of life, politics and the infamy of the ruling class. It broadened my reading horizons, and I read Camus, Tolstoy, Dickens, Hemingway, Mark Twain, Mailer, Kingsley Amis, Sillitoe, Stan Barstow and others. But my real hero was George Orwell."

It was this healthy interest in politics and good literature that Eddie would pass on to his sons, all of whom would demonstrate creative talents and a social conscience. For Matt, the positive influences of his parents would reveal themselves later in life, but an event of significance had happened when he was just five months old. Eddie's spell in hospital with TB brought home to Shirley how precarious their existence could be, and she saw with clarity that they needed to seize whatever opportunity came their way. Eddie, who was loving his life down on the docks, might not have made the move when it came, if it wasn't for Shirley. And perhaps Kenny. For want of a nail and all that.

Patsy and Jimmy Quill had decided to relinquish their role as the 'governors' of the Two Puddings in Stratford, and just a few months after leaving hospital Eddie and Kenny were asked if they were interested in taking on the job. The pair had been running their Big Beat Club nights upstairs at the pub for some time and handling trouble in a manner that convinced the Quills that either would make a good option for the brewery as landlord. Kenny, however, couldn't accept the offer, as his successful operation over in Forest Gate at the Jive Dive had taken one below the belt when an undercover cop, posing as a thirsty punter, managed to get someone to serve him an alcoholic drink after hours, resulting in a court case and no possibility of Kenny being able to hold a licence.

Eddie wasn't sure. Kenny pointed out that a new governor at the Puddings could potentially put an end to their dance nights upstairs, and after the Jive Dive sting they could be out of pocket twice over. Eddie mulled it over. But Shirley didn't need to think twice, as her husband tells it: "My wife, although a full-time mum and housewife, was keener than me to move into the pub trade; Shirley was practical and saw it as a way out of the poverty trap in which working-class people seemed to remain stuck. No more scrimping and saving. This, as far as she was concerned, was a way out of Wood Street."

To all of which Matthew Johnson, naturally, at just ten months old, remained oblivious. But, as a result of this chain of events, he was to end up living above one of east London's busiest music venues, and the sound of all this music would travel up through the floorboards and become part of the ambience of his early years, along with the sounds of the pub, and of the streets outside. So as early as the age of 4 he would tell any adult who asked him what he wanted to do when he grew up – that he wanted to be a singer. Of course he wanted to be musical. From the age of one upwards, every weekend, he would lie in bed and the whole building that he lived in would vibrate with the sound of music. It oscillated its way into his very bones, you could say.

It was October 5, 1962 when he moved there, a year to the day before The Beatles released their first single. He can't remember the early days, of course, though perhaps his bones can. It was hard work for Eddie and Shirley in those first few months and they relied on family and friends to look after the two boys as they busied themselves with their new career as landlords. Maybe they were too busy to notice the new pop sounds in the charts. Eddie was partial to singing Paul Robeson songs in a booming voice round the flat above the pub, so perhaps *Love Me Do* wouldn't have floated his boat. It wouldn't be long, though, before Kenny's ears would prick up, and soon the new Mersey beat was added to the playlist at the Big Beat Club. Before long, young Matthew and Andrew would be fans and have Beatles wigs and Beatles wallpaper in their bedroom.

2

LONDON BOY

AS MATT JOHNSON RECALLS: "THERE WAS A DUMB WAITER in the flat which went all the way down to the dance hall, and then down to the pub itself. Of course, the sounds and smells would funnel up through there, so it wasn't just the sound of people having a good time, it was the music as well, and the cigarette smoke and perfume pouring up. It was almost like an umbilical cord between us, in the flat above, and what was going on downstairs. Often, of a night, Mum would be upstairs with us, but our dad would be downstairs – we couldn't see him, but we would hear all the sounds of the pub and I liked that sound, of people laughing and enjoying themselves. It was reassuring, sort of comforting."

Whereas most kids would creep to the top of the stairs at night to listen to the sounds of the television their parents were watching downstairs, the Johnson brothers would be listening to the noises of the pub, and of music, live or on the jukebox, or the discos in the dance hall above the main bar. Matt remembers hearing things like "'Mellow Yellow' by Donovan, 'Needles And Pins' by The Searchers… The Beatles, Tamla Motown, The Who, Kinks, Rolling Stones… all the classic singles that made the charts really. It was an odd experience, because you weren't really allowed in the pub when it was open. We would sit on the stairs and watch during the daytime but at night time you weren't allowed down there at all. You would hear it, you would smell it, you would sense it."

The living quarters of the pub were on the second floor, and offered a view over the Broadway, a four-lane highway that ran through the heart of Stratford. This in turn became the High Street, which continued like a ribbon towards Bow, and Eddie's old stomping grounds. The two boys, who weren't allowed out of the flat to play on account of those four lanes of traffic, would stare out at the lights of the Broadway, thinking that the song, made famous by The Drifters, was about this very stretch of road, Matt blissfully unaware that one day in the future he would be living on the real thing in New York. There was plenty of activity to see out of those windows, all the hustle and bustle of what amounted to a town centre and a road carrying traffic into and out of the heart of London. Almost opposite the pub was the entrance to Angel Lane, home to smaller shops, many locally owned, and host to a lively market. It stretched all the way up to the station and halfway down was abutted by Salway Road, on the corner of which stood the Theatre Royal, at that time home to Joan Littlewood's maverick Theatre Workshop. Matt saw *A Christmas Carol* performed at the theatre and seems to remember Harry H. Corbett playing Scrooge.

Stratford, though it could be friendly and accommodating, like most poor inner-city areas was frequently violent. The week before Matt had been born in Wood Street, the *Stratford Express* reported that one of the many guns handed in during a three-month amnesty was a Czechoslovakian 9mm sub-machine gun. The amnesty was called in response to a rise in armed robberies and the killing of two police officers by John Hall on Tennyson Road the previous June. The Situations Vacant pages of the same newspaper were dominated by adverts for manual work, and with virtual full employment on the horizon there were an awful lot of young people who worked hard, wanted to play hard and had money burning a hole in their pockets. A lot of that money would be spent in the Two Puddings, where the new sounds of the sixties could be heard at full blast, upstairs and down.

Matthew Johnson, in his pre-school years, was blissfully unaware that this cultural revolution was going on around him, and underneath the floorboards. He just heard its sound, which fed its way into his being by vibration. While Andrew was at school he would read his *Teddy Bear* comic; perhaps inspired by a character within it – Paddy Paws the Puppy – he began to bark like a dog instead of talking. He would walk down Angel Lane and Salway Place with Eddie or Shirley to pick up Andrew from school, and if anyone stopped to talk and asked him a question he would bark. He even took to eating food from a plate on the floor. With more time to himself, now that Andrew was at school, his imagination would fill the solitude in strange and interesting ways – like days of the week becoming colours and such.

"Tuesday was a sponge, Wednesday was an orange… I just used to have weird associations. Friday was a frying pan. Cars would have personalities based on how they looked, the way the lights were, for example, or the radiator grilles. Many Hillman models, for instance, seemed to be either smiling or frowning. I was spending more time by myself, and would look out the windows and even the chimney pots had personalities. I just created this weird world where inanimate objects had these personalities." Not being allowed out onto the busy streets of Stratford shrunk his world, so, as if to compensate, everything within the pub and flat above it, everything he could see out of the windows, everything in earshot became alive. And sound in particular seemed to resonate more vitally in his ears. If he was in the front room he would listen to the traffic outside.

"On sunny summer days the sound would seem to reverberate around the Broadway. In those days the sound of cars was quite different to those of today, and many of them had unique-sounding engines. The sound of an MG couldn't be confused with another car, likewise a Morris Minor or Jaguar MK 2, for example. And some trucks had distinct sounds; some whining as the gears changed, others with a low throbbing rumble." All this listening to things that couldn't be seen made for keen ears. All these sound waves travelled into these ears, and left a residue in his memory, adding fuel to his imagination. Years later the resonance of all this sound would surface in the textures of his music on his first album, *Burning Blue Soul*, and would be present, albeit more subtly, in all his ensuing albums.

This time alone with sounds for company, and a world of inanimate objects to bend to his will, would, like it does for many children who are given the luxury of entertaining themselves, engender a creative impulse that was allowed to flourish. Though the boys were somewhat restricted in their physical environment, they were free to explore to the fullest extent their vivid inner worlds. Eddie, who was really a frustrated writer, and Shirley, who would have loved to have been a fashion, or interior, designer or something along those lines, didn't push their children in any direction, but instead provided an environment where music was a constant, stories were treasured, books were valued, films were enjoyed, trips to museums were the norm and the street theatre of the old East End was an everyday part of most weekends. But most of all Matt and Andrew had the time to amuse themselves, either alone or together.

"Because of the confinement of having just the pub and the yard, Andrew and I created these sort of fantasy worlds. Limitations are not necessarily a bad thing, they stimulate certain types of creativity. Our parents really had their hands full running the pub so we just had to get on with it." Of course, when the pub was closed – and licensing hours then meant that pubs were not open all day – the space the two brothers had to explore suddenly became much bigger, and even more fun when Eddie and Shirley were enjoying a well-earned breather in the flat. "Mum and Dad would be upstairs, and Andrew and I would be running amok downstairs... robbing the blind box, which was a terrible thing to do, and going to spend the money on comics and sweets from the shop next door. Or helping ourselves to packets of crisps and bottles of Coke from behind the bar. But the most exciting thing would be if there was gear left on the stage." Lead guitars, bass guitars, drum kits. That kind of gear. The instruments, lying idle in the room that was normally so noisy and active, held a kind of magic and power, responsible as they were for the music that made the building shake. They struck young Matt's imagination like he was a tuning fork.

So it was a strange upbringing compared to that of their peers, this hermetic existence in this semi-notorious pub, with four levels and all these little rooms, and nooks and crannies in which to play, hide in or just sit and listen to the noises all around them. Sound, ambience, music. Young Matthew Johnson's future.

It wasn't just the music and the pub that was exciting. In May 1964, West Ham United won the FA Cup for the first time. On the day of the victory parade Matt and Andrew spent hours on the roof of the Puddings with Eddie, Kenny and Grandad Charlie, waiting for the coach to arrive with the team and the trophy. When the coach was finally in sight, Kenny grabbed Andrew, Eddie grabbed Matt and the two of them went out onto the street and waded through the crowd with the boys on their shoulders to see Bobby Moore holding the cup aloft. For Andrew, who thought it bizarre that men were on top of traffic lights, the memory of the day remained clear. "Normal rules seemed suspended and anything appeared suddenly permissible. West Ham were on top of the world and everyone seemed happy. And that's how you begin a lifetime of footballing disappointment..." This was a fate that Matt evaded (if one ignores most of the seventies and eighties) by opting to follow Manchester United in an early bout of sibling rivalry.

Two years later, of course, Moore was holding aloft the World Cup; in the early evening of the very day they won it, Jack Charlton, on his way to meet a mate from Leytonstone, stopped off for a quiet pint in the Puddings, the unassuming way that he stood at the bar with his ale totally at odds with the momentous occasion he had been part of just hours before. Barman Norman Baptiste had been so stunned to see him walk in that he couldn't pluck up the courage to congratulate him. Eddie, who had been on a rare night out with Shirley, could barely believe it himself when Norman told him later, and the following morning he related the news to Matt and Andrew, who no doubt would have preferred it to have been Bobby Charlton or Bobby Moore. They took all this for granted – that below where they played with their toys and games, World Cup winners came to drink, or pop stars like Roger Daltrey or Clyde McPhatter. Or villains like the Kray twins. It was the peak of the swinging sixties and every now and then it would swing round to Stratford and appear in their mum and dad's pub.

By now Matt had joined Andrew at the Grove School on Salway Place, housed within a large Victorian building and, in many ways, still possessed of a Victorian mentality. The dying embers of Empire were still being fanned by certain institutions while pop stars raided its dressing-up box and films like *Zulu* were compellingly symbolic of its last stand. This film was a favourite in the Johnson household and John Barry's musical score made a big impact on Matt who, years later, would write soundtrack music of his own. In fact one of his strongest memories of school was the screening of a film in the assembly hall, a common occurrence in the pre-digital age when all schools had their own 16mm projectors and, as well as showing short educational films, would occasionally get hold of an old feature film and screen it at the end of term. One Christmas the pupils of Grove School were treated to *North West Frontier*, starring Kenneth More and Lauren Bacall.

In truth he had been dreading school. There was a reason that Wednesday was an orange, even if he can no longer recall what the reason was. But school? Now that felt like a trap, like opportunity being restricted. The imposing Victorian building probably didn't help matters, nor did the change in his older brother who would, as older brothers are wont to do, occasionally take his frustrations out on him. Perhaps it was the explosion of noise that he had witnessed while waiting with Eddie or Shirley outside the school gates, as he saw a swarm of bigger children bursting out of the school doors, a riot of kinetic energy. *Freedom*, they seemed to be crying – *freedom!*

So yeah, Matthew William Johnson, who had been a significant planet in the centre of his own universe, was not looking forward to being swallowed up by this institution called school.

Luckily for him his first teacher softened the blow of this potential trauma, letting the air out of puffed-up fears, managing the transition with her wise ways. Before long he had adjusted to this new universe and, though Monday to Friday was never as good as the weekend, he was happy enough. Like many kids of his generation, the real disaffection with the education system would arrive with secondary school. Primary school was a gentler, more benign experience. Primary school was where you still sometimes called the teacher Mum by mistake, drawing giggles from the rest of the class but not derision – for they had all done it, and deep down they knew why. Matt's memories of primary school begin, then, with this first surrogate mother. "My first teacher, Mrs Bhattacharya, was this lovely lady, a Hindu. She had a bindi on her forehead, and I remember her having these vibrantly coloured silks and robes. She would tell us stories, and bought us little presents when it came to Christmas, and was really my first experience of multicultural Britain." The fact that this woman is the only teacher he can recall vividly and for positive reasons suggests that her influence was keen, if subtle.

At home, Matt and Andrew were avid watchers of programmes like *Doctor Who*, *The Avengers*, *Danger Man*, *The Saint*, *The Prisoner*, *Captain Scarlet* and *Thunderbirds*. Matt sees the music of television and film as being equally as important as the pop songs he heard on the radio and coming from the pub. "I loved television theme music, particularly the Gerry Anderson stuff. I would say that is where my love of soundtrack comes from, right from the television. It made a huge impression on me." Soundtrack music was also part of the soundtrack of the flat above the pub. "We had a nice radiogram, a GEC G971, and the radio section pulled outwards. When switched on it would take a few minutes for the valves to warm up and a small green light would slowly appear and expand on the illuminated radio dial to tell you it was ready to go. Maybe because there was so much music in the pub day and night there was only a modest record collection in the small album rack built into it. I remember Maurice Jarre's *Lawrence of Arabia* soundtrack, the *Fantasia* soundtrack, *Porgy and Bess*, *Peter and the Wolf*, and a Wally Whyton album on multicoloured vinyl that was presumably for kids. But the one that dominated all the others for Andrew and I was The Beatles' *White Album*. Over the years that is probably the album I have played more than any other. Even as a little boy I found it mind-blowing. The strangest record though was an acetate that formed part of an alarm system that would have been connected to Scotland Yard and had belonged to the previous tenants of the pub. All it consisted of was a strange man's voice repeating over and over again, 'Calling Scotland Yard. This is the Two Puddings public house in Stratford. There has been a burglary,' or words to that effect. It used to freak my brother and me out."

The two boys would also go on regular trips to the cinema, visiting the Odeon in Forest Gate. One of their uncles, Allan Jones, was an occasional bit-part actor and sometimes they would go and see a film he was in. Trying to spot him became a game. Once he was a triffid in *The Day of the Triffids*, which caused much argument as to which particular triffid he had actually been. "You would go and get a Jamboree bag and there would be two or three films, a cartoon, a B-movie and then the main film. My dad would drop us off, go and see one of his siblings or friends, then come and pick us up afterwards. I loved *Zulu*, and a weird Japanese one called *King Kong Escapes* where the real King Kong fights a metal King Kong."

And just like all their friends they would have a running battle with the British cuisine of the day, particularly when it came to school dinners and the dreaded Mrs Mac, who would stand over the suffering children and demand that they "Eat it! Eat it!" One day Matt heaved so much he threw up onto his plate and then received a severe telling-off. "I could not stand it. We devised little techniques – all the kids would do it – like putting food in your pocket and then pretend to be eating when she walked past. It was like a little concentration camp or something. She would march up and down, and knew who did what, who ate what, who didn't eat what. So school dinners were unpleasant to say the least." Such was the lasting spectre of Mrs Mac and her looming shadow that some forty years later he wrote a song about her, releasing it online.

There were regular trips to museums, and to the 'Lanes' – Brick Lane and Petticoat Lane; the heart of the East End. The markets then were working markets for the local community, unlike the tourist destinations of today. This was the era when the East End was still run-down and half derelict, the scene of Don McCullin's famous photographs of homeless Irish men with blackened faces containing more hard-earned lines than an ordnance survey map. Men who could sleep standing up, reeking of booze, and fags, and piss. Eddie would take the boys on a Sunday morning. "I used to take them down the Lane, which was much busier than it is now. Brick Lane was always busy, and Petticoat Lane. I used to go down there and get beigels. An old Jewish lady used to serve them from a big hessian sack. We used to get pickled herrings from out of a barrel, wrapped in newspaper so you would have to be careful it didn't soak through onto your clothes. And we would go to Marks' Deli, and Mr Marks, a talkative man in his sixties, would always serve me himself."

For all his love of The Beatles, Matt has no recollection of the cold but sunny Sunday of February 5, 1967 when the Fab Four were actually in Stratford to shoot a promotional film for 'Penny Lane'. Based in the Salway Arms for the day, filming took place on Angel Lane and Stratford Broadway between midday and four in the afternoon, finishing with a shot of Lennon meeting the others outside the Theatre Royal. Their unannounced arrival caused a minor commotion among the local children who crowded round the stars as they mounted white horses in the car park behind Angel Lane in preparation for filming. Eddie was alerted to their presence by pal Tommy Morrison, and they and others rushed out of the Puddings and down Angel Lane, only to see the four Beatles and their entourage disappear into the rival pub.

There were holidays – in Ireland, and Scotland, but mostly Wales – and it always seemed to rain. Andrew used to get car sick so they would tie a belt to the rear bumper and swore that this worked in alleviating the nausea. The first car Matt remembers Eddie having was a white Vauxhall Victor estate with a mustard roof. A white Zephyr Six estate followed this, and then a succession of second-hand Mercedes – an exotic motor for the time. All these cars were constantly breaking down. Eddie would curse, gripping on to the steering wheel like he was trying to strangle it. And then it would rain, and the drops of rain would pock-pock on the metal and the windscreen. The boys would watch the drops begin to obscure the view and then as the rain got harder the windscreen wipers would be switched on and they would all be trapped there with rain pinging off the roof and the wipers beating out a clunking rhythm, punctuated by rubbery squeaks, waiting for the AA to arrive.

And it wasn't just the car trouble and the rain that would cause their dad to come to the boil. Matt can readily bring to mind other things that tipped him over. "Because our dad had a bit of a ferocious temper, what would sometimes happen on these trips was that there would be altercations, and Andrew and I used to find them very funny. One time we were in a hotel cafe and the guy serving us kept looking at us, muttering under his breath. At some point my dad just exploded. 'You fucking what?' and grabbed hold of the bloke round the neck. These sort of things happened a few times. I remember once a car went into the side of ours and our dad had lifted the bloke up by his shirt neck with his legs off the floor, and we used to think it was hilarious, but looking back, it wasn't hilarious, it was terrible."

On June 10, 1965, Eugene Johnson was born and the two brothers became three. In an attempt to escape the rain that plagued their holidays at home, when he was still a small baby they all went on a holiday to Portugal, a somewhat exotic sojourn for a working-class family at that time. Matt had already been abroad, to Brittany, where Eddie and Shirley bought him a sou'wester and boots, suggesting that this first venture overseas was just as wet as holidays at home.

The trip to Portugal saw yet another episode of car trouble. The five Johnsons loaded themselves into Eddie's white Ford Zephyr and drove down to Tilbury, where they boarded a ferry for a leisurely three-day sail to Lisbon, enough time for everyone to get their sea legs, while somewhere inside the car, down in the belly of the boat, the gremlins were at work. "It was only six months old," Eddie recalls. "I'd had it serviced by Gates's and told them I was going abroad, got all the way over there, the car was unloaded and halfway to Cascais it broke down."

They finally got to the small *pension* in Cascais, only to find that most of the food on offer was fish, which at the time none of them was particularly partial to – British taste in food not having quite caught up with the distance they had actually travelled. Still, it was an adventure when compared to the likes of Margate, Clacton or Norfolk, where most of their contemporaries might have ventured. One day they asked the maid if she wouldn't mind staying in the room with little Eugene, who was just six months old, while they went downstairs to eat in the tiny dining room. "We were having our food," Eddie remembers, "and we could see into the kitchen where all these Portuguese women were working round a big table, and they had a little baby in there and were feeding it bits of fish, and I said, 'Look at that baby. Ain't it like Eugene?' And everyone looked up and stared into the kitchen before Matthew piped up, 'That *is* Eugene!'"

Matt was 4 years old and has vague memories of how much he liked the little *pension*, and looking out over the balcony at the scene outside. One day there was a violent thunderstorm, which he found exciting. Maybe there was some strange connection for him, but Shirley stayed away from the window, mindful of the lightning.

At around the same time the family were enjoying these early jaunts abroad in the mid-sixties, and as if to mark the cultural paradigm shift, Eddie decided to spruce up the pub in order to give it a bit of pizzazz, make it more modern. Upstairs the disco had been rebranded the Devil's Kitchen. Devils and monsters were painted on the dark walls in day-glo colours. King Kong was on the wall behind the raised DJ booth. UV lighting was installed – a real novelty for the time. In the suitably hot and crowded atmosphere – all the boys lining the walls, watching the girls dancing, waiting to make their moves – faces looked ghoulish and drinks glowed like something from a Hammer House of Horror film, while flecks of hitherto invisible dust looked like a bad case of dandruff on the shoulders of the men who hadn't taken off their suit jackets. Tailor-made suits, thank you. This was the mod sixties and this was the East End, which was full of Jewish tailors who made a good penny out of the fashion-conscious youth. Upstairs at the Puddings, then, the atmosphere was often electric. As Eddie has written, "The music of that time was not just part of the magic – it *was* the magic. The very pavements seemed to pulse; the blood in our veins seemed to race." And young Matthew Johnson was soaking it all up like a sponge.

3

ROADSTAR

SO HAVING SOAKED UP ALL THIS MUSIC AND AMBIENT
noise, when did it start working on Matt Johnson; when did he start
projecting it outwards? The man himself has it thus: "The music
thing only came for me when I was about 10, when we moved to a
place called Ongar, which I didn't particularly like. Nick Freeston,
a close friend from school said, 'Shall we form a band?' I'd played
around on pianos in the pub so I thought, 'Yeah, why not?' But I
think that the interest had seeped into me, just hearing music every
day. Even when I was 4 or 5 customers in the pub would ask me
what I wanted to be when I grew up and I would say I want to be
a singer." But Ongar was three years away.

Wanting to take a break from the dirt and noise of Stratford and
the aggravation of the Puddings, Eddie and Shirley had decided
in the summer of 1968 to start looking for alternatives. They
found a cottage in Great Wratting, and after plenty of visits, and
discussions to convince themselves this was the right thing to do,
they exchanged contracts. As if to confirm they had made the right
choice, the very weekend before they were due to move, in March
1969, two men, evicted from the pub for fighting, returned in a car
and shot at the windows. When plain-clothes detectives arrived
soon after, they in turn were shot at.

Matt Johnson has no recollection of this incident, so maybe the noise and commotion didn't disturb the two boys asleep in the back of the flat. It wasn't that they were oblivious to this aspect of the world. As Andrew Johnson writes in a foreword to Eddie's memoirs, *Tales from the Two Puddings*, you couldn't expect to run a pub in the East End of London without having to deal with some very unpleasant characters, and survival meant being able to handle their bad behaviour in a way that discouraged any more of it.

"There were always weapons around, though mainly hand arms, such as police truncheons, pick-axe handles, baseball bats, lengths of chain, rubber tubes weighted with lead, a vicious-looking docker's hook, and a nasty butcher's boning knife. Whether these were ever used in battle or if they were simply taken off others and then left on display in the office as trophies was never apparent to us as children. I remember seeing a small revolver being wrapped in a cloth bank bag and placed in one of the safes. With a wink I was told that I must never tell anyone about it."

Andrew, being older, probably noticed much more than his younger brother. Two years is a lot at that age. But Matt certainly remembers hearing his uncles talk about different fights they had had. "There was a sort of glamorisation of violence, perhaps, but the word *violence* was never used. The language was designed to minimise, it was, 'havin' a row', or 'give 'im a slap'. It seemed, not exactly benign, but it wasn't just a slap of course – they sometimes beat people unconscious." On one occasion Kenny happened to arrive in the middle of a potentially tricky row and also happened to have a hammer in his briefcase, which he decided might be of assistance. Luckily, perhaps, for all involved, the head of the hammer flew off the wooden shaft on the backstroke; all that was missing was an accompanying slide-whistle sound effect as the offending article disappeared up the street.

So, like it is for many people in the inner city, violence was in the air around them, only more so because of the pub and because it was the East End. The contrast with Great Wratting, a small village in Suffolk where the only violent thing appeared to be the odd red sky at night, was somewhat stark. The boys suddenly had a garden to play in instead of a yard, and beyond the garden was the green and pleasant land – a far cry from the mean streets of east London. Eddie didn't give up the Puddings, but did hand over management to his brother-in-law, Peter Ferdinando, and his wife Kay.

The initial culture shock of the transition was somewhat troubling for a young boy. Children, being nearer the ground, closer to nature and their own senses, adapt to change well, but in the initial stages things can be a bit overwhelming, as was the case for Matt. "I remember the first night sleeping in the cottage, and being freaked out because it was so quiet outside. Cars would travel down the country roads at night and their headlights would come in through the bedroom window long before the sound of the car caught up, so I was convinced that someone was outside with a torch, and I was like, 'Oh my God, who's out there? What's going on here?'"

These slices of light moving up the bedroom walls ironically made this quiet rural village seem much more threatening than the rough streets he had left behind. The muscles of his young imagination were suddenly being stretched in new and vivid ways. "I had been given a present, a little lantern-like torch with a red flashing top. I would shine it at the ceiling and walls, creating all these shadows. It was very eerie – the smell of a new place, different carpets, lots of old wood, and leaded windows. It was very, very quiet, and at first I don't think I liked it all. I missed the Puddings. I had been happy there." Very quiet. No music coming up through the floorboards. So quiet at night that any noises had a clarity, all the more alarming when they were unidentifiable. It was the same thing as being in the pub – lying there immersed in sound, but these sounds were minimal and isolated, a far cry from the chaotic symphony of Stratford Broadway. In the morning they would hear birds, not traffic. The boys were free to go outside and explore, and instead of an overgrown back yard they had a half-acre garden with a willow tree and a copper birch, as well as enough lawn for running around or playing football on. The small school, in nearby Haverhill, was good and holds pleasant memories, though when Matt first started they made him and another new boy, from Birmingham, stand up and talk to highlight different dialects across Britain. "Of course I had a very strong Cockney accent, and Douglas, the boy from Birmingham, had a very strong Midlands accent, whereas everyone else spoke *loike thaart*. It was a bit disconcerting because I thought I spoke normally and what was the big deal?"

Meanwhile, Eddie and Shirley had familiarised themselves with the local pub, the Red Lion, enjoying being on the opposite side of the bar for a change. The landlord, Stan, said to Eddie, "Tell your Matthew to stay away from that Gordon Bremner. He's a bad lot." But it was too late because the pair had already teamed up. Free at last to play wherever he wanted, Johnson would spend hours with his new pal, playing among the hay bales and exploring the fields under the big Suffolk sky, not going home until the light was fading. One afternoon the two boys were out in one of the fields and happened to have a box of matches with them.

"We set the field alight. We were playing with the matches, to see what would happen, and the straw started to catch. We tried stamping it out but couldn't – there was just the smell of burning rubber from our wellies and a fire that was spreading, and getting out of control. So we panicked. I ran home, and Gordon ran home. Then the fire brigade came down, and the farmer told us off."

Johnson got off lightly thanks to Gordon Bremner's reputation. In the Red Lion, Stan told Eddie, "Of course, your boy was led astray by that Gordon." The rest of the locals supping their pints seemed to agree. Eddie had questioned his son, but despite his blackened face he denied everything. He was warned not to hang out with Gordon in future but ignored this advice. The pair would often try the well-worn trick of taking empty beer bottles back to the pub off-licence in return for the deposit. Not a lot per bottle, but given an armful of bottles the loose change was more than enough to buy sweets, drinks and crisps. The fact that they had crept round the back of the pub and into the bottle shed to purloin the empties in the first place was a bit of enterprise that Stan never seemed to cotton-on to.

There were frequent day trips to the surrounding countryside and villages, and shopping trips to Cambridge. Friends and family would often come and visit. Eddie and Shirley would take them to Newmarket for the races. The boys would ride around on their bikes and go fishing. Skirts got longer. The Tories replaced Labour. Money turned decimal. Eddie joined the golf club, while Shirley took up pottery. They frequented antique auctions and became regular faces in the saloon bar of the Red Lion. When last orders were called there they would retreat to a neighbour's house for supper, more drinks and James Last on the stereo. It was a case of country-living and easy-listening as the sixties turned into the seventies. But it didn't last all that long. Eddie, despite his attempts to look the part of a country gent – all tweeds and a trilby with a feather in it – was growing restless. Beneath the contentment there was something missing. He had been going back to the Puddings every Friday and occasional Saturdays, to keep his hand in. Every Monday he would be there to do the books in the office and meet Kenny for business discussions. Often he would take the boys.

This routine went on for three years until Eddie said to Shirley one day, "Do you realise we're in the Red Lion nearly every night spending? We could do that in our own pub and earn money." Although they were going out to lovely restaurants and taking nice holidays, Eddie was getting bored. And money was running short. So he started to look for another pub.

Great Wratting seems like a calm interlude in the early life of Matt Johnson. This is what he says about it: "I lived there between the ages of 7 and 10. Out of all the places I lived in growing up, that was probably the nicest." It was as idyllic as it sounds. A real rural retreat in Constable land. But what of music? With all this outdoors playing and mischief, village fetes and fishing nets, you would be forgiven for thinking that music mattered less. And perhaps in a way it did. But one Thursday in March 1971, Johnson was watching

Top of the Pops when a singer with a glitter teardrop on his cheek, a silky black top and yellow trousers, sang a song he had heard on the radio. Now, however, the sight of Marc Bolan in his glam pomp was being transmitted into the living room of the cottage. There was Johnson in an oak-beamed building that breathed Olde England and here on the television was a man surrounded by pretty young girls in hot pants, swaying their hips and clapping their hands in time to the beat of 'Hot Love'. Compared to his surroundings the vision on the screen before him could have been transmitting live from Mars. And then, just as the infectious *la-la-la* chorus kicked in, the scantily clad dancers of Pan's People sashayed across the front of the stage. Hot Love indeed. Young Johnson was transfixed. Guitars, electric music, pretty girls. It was one of the most iconic performances on the famous BBC pop show, and along with David Bowie's performance of 'Starman' a year later, responsible for encouraging more youth than can be counted to go out, get a guitar and dream of becoming a pop star. Johnson might have delayed the practicalities, but to all intents and purposes, this was the moment that mattered. It wasn't a vague answer to a question from a relative about what he wanted to be when he grew up. He looked at the television screen and thought to himself, 'I wanna be like him!' And back in the spring of 1971, who wouldn't?

It usually took a certain amount of boredom and angst to convert dreams of a career in music into reality for working-class youth and Johnson was to feel enough of both over the next few years. If Great Wratting had been a tranquil and picturesque experience for the Johnsons, then their next port of call ending up pleasing no one.

Ongar was created as a parish in the Epping Forest district of Essex in 1965. Up until 1994 it was served by the Central Line into London, twenty-one miles to the south-west. "I didn't like Ongar," Eddie would later say, and the rest of the family would pretty much concur, Matt in particular. "None of us liked it." It's just that it seemed like a good idea at the time. Eddie, on his regular journeys back and forth between the cottage and the Puddings, would often drive through it and in doing so pass the King's Head pub on the high street.

"I knew Harry Alden who owned it. He and his wife had been landlords of the Puddings before us and the Quills. I used to drive past and when it came up for sale I put in for it and got it. It was very run down by then. Harry had passed it on to an old fella called Colonel Wilkinson, who I think had been a colonel in the catering corps. He was the sort of bloke who never knew your name, and he let the locals pour their own drinks. Naturally, everyone liked him, but the trade was terrible." Eddie tried to rectify this by getting rid of the Freemasons, who had their weekly meeting in a back room called the Tudor Lounge, and who as well as being secretive were rather parsimonious. He turned the room into a restaurant and, when that failed to bring enough turnover, started promoting folk music nights, booking the likes of Jake Thackray, Ralph McTell and Sean Buckley. Some acts, if they were performing a residency, would leave their equipment behind, and so for Matt Johnson it was just like old times.

The King's Head was a grade II listed building, dating back to 1679. Inside the pub were ghosts. And their presence was most definitely felt, as Johnson remembers. "I used to spend a lot of time on my own plonking around on the pub piano, in the afternoon or late at night, and I would often get a strong sense that I was being watched, that I wasn't alone. Another time Andrew and I were playing in the Tudor Lounge and he thought he saw me run across the room, but then noticed I was on the other side of the room, and I thought I had seen *him* run across the room. So he was thinking, 'If you're over there, who the hell was that?' And I was thinking exactly the same thing. It wasn't just us. One time when our Nanny Sue came to stay, she said, 'There's something weird in this place.' She woke up one night and saw this green mist around the door. She thought it was Eddie playing one of his practical jokes but it wasn't and about a year later a book, called *Haunted East Anglia*, was published, and people who had previously owned the King's Head had described this exact same thing my Nan had seen, this green light… strange things went on there. It was a very strange place, a very old place. There was a portrait of King Charles above the door outside my bedroom that had been left behind and they had decorated around it, wouldn't take it with them."

Eddie too found the place eerie. "I went upstairs to the attic bedroom once and couldn't get in. Nobody was in there and yet it was locked, which was impossible. I ended up breaking the door down and found that the mirror in the room was cracked. There was a story in the newspaper, and the woman from the baker's said, 'You've got a poltergeist,' and told me to lay out three elements: soil, fire and water. I don't really believe in anything like this but I took it seriously that time and did as she told me." The poltergeist was one of three children who haunted the top floor of the pub, according to an article in the *Ongar Gazette*, and another ghost, that of an older man, haunted one of the rooms downstairs.

Take it how you will. There was a strange atmosphere about the place according to a succession of landlords and perhaps this had an influence on an act of vandalism that occurred in the summer of 1972, just before Johnson started at Ongar Comprehensive school. He had quickly befriended a boy called Francis Armes, who lived opposite the pub above his parents' newsagents. This was also haunted, according to legend, by the ghost of a child called Geoffrey who busied himself scaring the paper boys and the Armes family. Francis's mum, Delyth, was quoted in the local paper. "Sometimes things go missing and you get strange senses. You just get a feeling that he is about. When strange things happen, we normally blame Geoffrey." Lucky Francis.

Francis, seeing that a new family had moved into the pub, went over the road to introduce himself, and not long after mischief reared its head. "Francis, Eugene and I went exploring" Matt says. The King's Head had lots of old out-houses, which were formerly stables as it had been an inn in the seventeenth century. So we went out back and one of these big old stables was locked. We broke in and found all these vintage cars. Obviously someone had been renting it from the previous owners and they had been doing up these beautiful old cars, some of which were fully restored, others halfway there. God knows what possessed us, but Eugene, Francis and I got a load of Coke bottles and bricks, and went around smashing these cars up. It was awful. I feel so ashamed of myself now, thinking about it."

Seems as if the owners of the cars had rented the stable-cum-garage from the colonel; one day someone turned up at the pub to see about continuing this arrangement with the new landlord. Naturally, while they were there, they decided to check on the cars, which is when they discovered not only that the garage had been broken into but that the cars were looking a bit more vintage than they had previously. Johnson, in the way that only the young can manage, had assumed that in the passing of time all potential repercussions had evaporated. He, Eugene and Francis hadn't actually forgotten what they had done, but they hadn't considered that at some point they might have to face the music.

"They turned up to check on the vehicles, and were aghast. There's been a break-in and their cars have been vandalised. I don't know how we got found out, but we did, and this chap Tony Cook confronted my dad about it. And I think my dad did his usual thing — picked him up, feet dangling, and shook him. 'Don't you call my son…' Kicked him out. 'And you can take your fucking cars with you!' Something like that I imagine. We got a real bollocking. He wouldn't have anyone call us cheats or vandals or whatever, that was his prerogative."

And a telling-off from Eddie wasn't to be taken lightly, especially when it looked like you had led your younger brother astray. Still – it was done now and that, he expected, was the last he would see of Tony Cooke. Soon after this incident the summer holiday ended and it was time to start school, in this case, Ongar Comprehensive. Going from primary school to secondary school is always a bit of a shock for any kid, especially when the school has a couple of thousand pupils. He had been there a week and was beginning to find his feet when the first timetabled music lesson came around.

"Francis and I are in the classroom together when Tony Cooke walks in. He's the bloody music teacher! He looked at us and just said, 'I think we've met before somewhere haven't we?' Gave us this awful look. The sad thing is, he was a lovely bloke. I really wish I could go back in time and apologise. So I could never really concentrate properly in his music classes because I felt so guilty I could barely stand to be there. He was a really good music teacher. He used to play all kinds of progressive albums and try and get us interested in music, recommend we listen to Radio 3 or Radio 4. He was in a band. Loved his real ale. And restoring old cars…"

Matt still isn't sure where this mindless impulse to vandalise came from. Boys will be boys and they will egg each other on. For the thrill of it, the adrenaline rush. Same as he got from climbing onto the roofs of tall buildings, or from breaking into places. Not to steal anything. Just to do it. Rather than being stuck in some stuffy classroom listening to some teacher drone on and on about whatever it was – he didn't know because he wasn't even listening any more. A lucky few would find an ally or two in the guise of sympathetic teachers who recognised keen minds, but Matt Johnson wasn't one of them.

"If I look back on my school days I can't think of any teachers that took any interest in me. The only teacher I remember with any affection is Mrs Bhattacharya, but that was primary school. Beyond that I can't think of a single one who showed any interest, or tried to encourage me. Not one. There were a few I didn't mind, they were usually left wing, liked their pints of real ale, but no one particularly inspiring. I can remember plenty of horrible teachers."

School became something to endure, and when they couldn't endure it, the boys would bunk off. "Sometimes we would go to a den we had made in the local woods, but other times we would spend an entire lesson hiding in the school toilets, feet up, reading a book. We used to go to the chippy a lot. Some of the teachers would patrol the area, because we weren't supposed to go out, and we would end up being chased by them through the back streets, running as fast as we could, chip butty in pocket, teachers in their little Ford Anglias or Escorts flying around the streets after us. We would run like crazy, climbing over fences and through gardens. I was a chronic truant."

As he got older he got bolder, and by the time he was in the fifth form he and his fellow gang of skivers were catching the bus to places like Romford, Brentford and Chelmsford, where there was a lot more to do. "It was mainly Romford we would go to. I looked a lot younger than some of my mates so when we went into a pub they would get alcoholic drinks but I couldn't. One time we were in a pub in Ongar called the Two Brewers, which was considered a bit of a soft touch. I guess I would have been around 15 at the time – my voice hadn't even broken. When it was my turn I went up to the bar and asked for a pint of lager, and the barman said, 'Don't you mean a pint of lemonade, sonny Jim?'"

So, school didn't start well – what with Tony Cook being the music teacher – and didn't really improve. At home, in the King's Head, things hadn't got off to a great start either. Trade was particularly slow, certainly compared to the experience of the Puddings. In an effort to bring in more punters, Eddie brought in a DJ. Things began to pick up and, once again, the sound of music would drift up through the floorboards. In 1972, the big sound in the British pop charts was dubbed glam rock, a somewhat catch-all term that lumped together pop artists and those with more serious pretensions. Thus Gary Glitter, The Sweet and Slade found themselves, for the time being at least, in the same musical boat as David Bowie, Roxy Music and the act who started it all, T.Rex. Singles by all these acts made a big impression on the charts and all of them appeared regularly on *Top of the Pops*. With urgent guitar riffs and a stomping, hand-clapping beat that was almost a mirror of the noise heard on the packed terraces of football grounds up and down the country every Saturday afternoon, this was a scene that appealed to the working classes, and because of its pop sensibilities they could enjoy it from a very young age. Pretty much everyone liked one or more of the above-mentioned acts, and Matt Johnson was no exception. The first record he bought was T.Rex's 'Ride A White Swan', and Uncle Kenny bought him the *Stardust* soundtrack LP one Christmas on a cassette. He also bought *Snowflakes Are Dancing*, the album of electronic soundscapes by Japanese artist Tomita.

The month he started at Ongar Comprehensive, the following records all appeared in the Top 40: 'Children Of The Revolution' (T.Rex); 'Virginia Plain' (Roxy Music); 'Mama Weer All Crazee Now' (Slade); 'Wig-Wam Bam' (The Sweet); 'All The Young Dudes' (Mott The Hoople); 'School's Out' (Alice Cooper); 'Rock And Roll Parts 1 And 2' (Gary Glitter), and a month later, 'John, I'm Only Dancing' (David Bowie). In the flat above the King's Head many of these songs would be blasted out of Eddie Johnson's old radiogram on a Friday or Saturday night, as Matt Johnson and his two brothers, having changed the lightbulb to a red or green one, jumped around the room, tennis racquets serving as guitars. It was around this time that Matt met Nick Freeston.

Freeston had lived in Ongar all his life. The two boys met each other outside the King's Head one boring Sunday afternoon in the summer of 1972, and hit it off straight away, sharing a love of football, and more importantly, music. While Eddie and Shirley were working downstairs behind the bar of the pub, perhaps serving Freeston's parents, who would frequently drink there, the two boys would often be listening to music upstairs, sometimes joined by Andrew. Being older, Andrew's tastes were more sophisticated; it was he who introduced them to David Bowie, in the shape of the *Hunky Dory* album. And it was Freeston, according to Johnson, who suggested they do more than jump around with tennis racquets.

Wanting to form a band was a fairly unusual ambition for a pair of 11-year-olds back in 1972, but rather than just talk and daydream, rather than just stick to brandishing wooden tennis racquets, they actually did something about it. The first problem, Johnson remembers, concerned the resources necessary for making the requisite noise in the first place. "We didn't have much equipment. Nick eventually got a drum kit for Christmas and I think it was a Bontempi organ, which might have been his brother's. From somewhere came an old acoustic guitar, and I appropriated the family reel-to-reel tape recorder. You could set it up so that the microphone would go through the speaker, so I would put the microphone in the guitar, twang around, and use the tape recorder as an amp.

"So it started off as me and Nick and our first performance was in a place called Budworth Hall. We didn't actually have a drum kit at this stage, or even guitars. Boxes served as drums and tissue boxes with elastic bands round them were guitars. It was busking really. We just turned up and started making a racket while old people were sat there drinking their cups of tea, and after about fifteen minutes someone threw us out. 'C'mon boys, you can't make that row all day long, off you go.'"

After the impromptu Budworth Hall performance the pair decided to take things a bit more seriously, and started getting together some equipment. They also decided to recruit another member, Russell Ball, who Johnson remembers they called The Professor, or Prof. This was either because of his wild hair and glasses or on account of him being a bit of a swot at school. "His claim to fame was that his dad was a teacher and he had taught Roger Taylor from Queen. He was quite straight, not really one of our friends at school, and was well-spoken compared to Nick and me, but he had a guitar and knew some chords. We used to play songs from The Beatles' *Help* album, but Russell wasn't very rock'n'roll, so we got another guy in called Jim, and he wasn't right either. We would have been about 12 at this point and we played a couple of gigs in Nick's garage, charged about five pence to get in, provided crisps and orange juice. We used to rehearse in the garage as well. Nick's parents were very easy-going about it. Nick's brother, Russell, would use my tape recorder to record us."

It was 1973 and the exciting boom years of the sixties seemed long distant. The headlong spin into a brave new modern world was soon to collide with the realities of the OPEC crisis; before long there would be another state of emergency, all kinds of doom-laden public announcements about energy and power, a three-day week, more power cuts and a snap election that saw Harold Wilson and Labour back in power. At the beginning of this eventful year, as Johnson and Freeston practised in the garage and named their outfit – Roadstar – Shirley Johnson gave birth to her fourth son, Gerard, in St Margaret's Hospital, Epping. And it really was the beginning of the year when Gerard appeared. In fact, according to a report on television show *Nationwide*, Gerard beat everyone else to it. January 1, 1973 was the day that Britain officially entered the Common Market, and the television cameras were at the hospital to record a short feature on the first EU baby born in Britain. Presenter Michael Barratt, in the studio, spoke via live link-up to the proud parents of "baby Johnson", with Eddie sporting a rather fetching Zapata-style moustache and uncharacteristically long hair.

It was a marvellous moment for Europe. Well, that is what Barratt suggested, playing to his script. Britain's entry into the Common Market had been long and protracted, and public support had never been overwhelming. Foreign holidays were still in their infancy for the average family, after all. He asked them what name they had chosen for their son and Shirley, sitting propped up by pillows in her hospital bed, holding said infant in her arms, listened as Eddie told the nation that this future film director was called Gerard. Barratt, not one to miss the opportunity of putting some pro-Europe spin on the story, pointed out that this could be pronounced the French way and asked which pronunciation they had decided upon. Shirley said – in a French way – Gerard, while Eddie suggested – in an English way – Gerard, or maybe just Gerry.

So here was a new year, and now there were six folk living above the pub, and nine hands on the back of the new 50 pence piece. At the top of the UK singles chart when Gerard Johnson was born was Jimmy Osmond with a song so awful most dare not speak its name. Bowie, having released *Aladdin Sane*, was about to kill off Ziggy Stardust and re-emerge with a more gloomy persona. T.Rex and Slade had peaked and the remaining bands had descended into parody. Pop culture was in decline, the England football team – world champions just seven years previously – had been dumped out of the World Cup by Poland, the already bumpy economy was about to hit the skids thanks to the oil crisis, and all of this was being endured in the frosty environs of the King's Head.

By the time 1974 arrived, a gloomy outlook had descended. A year to the day since Gerard's birth, the threatened three-day week began. This coincided with a strange lull in the music scene – one that mirrored the economic gloom. In the pop charts the creative lights went out. The resulting boredom was something the nascent punks would soon exploit to their own ends. It was around this time that Johnson's grandma had seen the spooky green mist, and the family had got to know all about the hauntings, the broken mirrors and impossibly locked doors. Spooky Ongar. This wasn't any easier to come to terms with when the lights would flicker and go dim as a power cut would suddenly kick in, plunging the bewitched rooms into darkness. Walking round, floorboards creaking underfoot, with a candle or a storm lantern wasn't much better, as shadows loomed large on the walls and leapt up and down like something from German Expressionist cinema. On nights like these the local boozers supped their ale by the light of a flame, while Eddie rattled the collection tin for the striking miners. In order to add some defiance to his support, he got hold of a huge ex-army generator which took eight people to haul round to the back of the pub. This enabled him to keep the lights on when the government were asking people to conserve electricity, but though the generator worked after a fashion, the power flow did unusual things to the DJ equipment, so the music would suddenly sound rather weird, with notes elongated and unearthly, just to add to the general haunted ambience of the pub. Roadstar meanwhile, not unduly hindered by power cuts (public notices in the press revealed that four hours of colour television watching consumed a unit of electricity, whereas you could get twenty-four hours playing a record player), were ready to ditch Jim in favour of a younger kid they had heard about.

"I can't remember exactly when it was, but Nick and I heard about this kid called Brett Giddings who was in the year below us at school. We liked him, and his older brother was in a band so this seemed more promising than the people we had tried previously. He had long hair, wore faded denims and patchouli, and he turned us on to Led Zeppelin."

Giddings was in the year below Matt and Nick. He lived with his parents and siblings in a farmhouse just outside Ongar, which came complete with barns. In one of these, Brett's eldest brother, Darryl, already playing in bands, had set up a music room complete with guitars, amps, drums and PA. Darryl's band had also played at Budworth Hall, but unlike the early Roadstar effort in the cafe they had played in the main hall. Coming from a music-loving family (his other brother – also called Matt – was a competent drummer) meant it was easy for Brett to see that being in a band could be more than just messing about, and his inclusion made Roadstar a more serious venture all of a sudden, bringing musical competence, new influences and the all-important practice room full of gear. Matt Johnson remembers it as a new world opening up.

Tricks or no tricks, these are the details of the times. Here was a young teenager with an older brother in a band, in a farmhouse that rocked to Led Zeppelin and the Stones. He had long hair, faded denims and 4-inch sunburst platform shoes. It was heavy rock with hippy overtones. Matt and Nick, meanwhile, were all glam and football terrace (Nick was a big West Ham fan) with cherry red DM boots like Bowie sported on the back cover of *The Rise And Fall Of Ziggy Stardust*. They met in the middle with *The White Album*. For a trio of boys only just into their teenage years they had most avenues covered.

"It was fantastic. I don't really remember his parents being around much, but we had the run of the place. And we thought Brett was fantastic, cos he played a Cherry Red Gibson SG copy, and he had a Sound City 120 amp. With Brett we went from playing these really weedy acoustic versions of Beatles songs to playing things like 'Smoke On The Water', 'Black Knight' and 'Rebel Rebel', and thinking 'This is great!'"

Sometime in the summer of '74, Eddie's bad luck with cars was to continue in a most serious manner when the family were involved in a distressing crash. It was probably his long-time preference for German engineering that saved any of the family from being seriously hurt. Eddie, not surprisingly, has a clear memory of the day. "We drove along a country road and I stopped a little bit short at the junction to a main road, which must have affected my timing, as I pulled out thinking I had time to avoid a car that was tearing down the main road. Instead of stopping I put my foot down, and he crashed right into my door. The car finished up on the verge on the other side of the road. Luckily everyone seemed okay, though Eugene had hurt his head, which was bleeding. I got out the car but Matthew, brave little soul that he was, had jumped out before me and was trying to open the door of the other car and help the driver who was slumped, unconscious at the wheel. My car was a write-off."

Matt's recollection is even more vivid. "We were pulling out of the junction and I remember my mum shouting, 'Eddie! Look out!' She screamed and everything went into slow motion, and semi-darkness, and started to spin round and round. It was awful. And the car came to a stop. It was a tremendous impact. I got out and I saw the driver in the other car which was in a real state because it had hit us head-on. He was unconscious, but his nervous system must have been working in some way, because his body kept throbbing, and jerking forward, and blood was spurting everywhere. I was saying, 'It's all right mister, it's all right mister, I'll get you out,' and was trying to get him out of the car. I would only have been 13 or 14 at the time. I couldn't get him out of the car.

I must have known my own family was okay, or else why would I have been trying to help this man? I'd never experienced that sense of shock before. We ended up at the hospital and Eugene had to have some minor plastic surgery, because he had hit the windscreen. My dad had got broken ribs, Andrew had hurt his ankle and legs and had a bloody nose, and my face was covered in blood. Miraculously, mum and Gerard were okay – not a scratch on them. Eugene stayed overnight. The other driver was in there, in a coma, and I remember people talking to him... 'David. David. Can you hear us, David?' He did recover."

If the Johnsons' time in Ongar was beginning to seem cursed, at least music was keeping Matt's spirit buoyant. By now Roadstar were a four-piece outfit, with the addition of Mark Bratby on bass. "We started writing our own songs. In fact I've still got some of the handwritten lyrics, and somewhere I've got old tapes of our rehearsals. We were usually so skint we would have to tape over existing tapes. I would make little cassette covers, put photos on them and fantasize about having my own record label." While Brett's memory lacks the clarity of Johnson's, he remembers the band playing live. "We did a gig in North Weald, and I'm pretty sure that we did one in High Ongar. I know we only had around five songs we could play – including 'Rebel Rebel' – so we played them all twice."

Giddings remembers trips to Gants Hill Odeon in the summer of '75 to see *Tommy* and *Stardust*. "On the way back we decided to write our very own rock opera, entitled, 'What Do You Expect For Sixpence?' I don't remember much about it but the name has stuck with me." Johnson himself doesn't have much more recollection, other than they discussed the idea for some time and probably got round to writing some lyrics, if not music to go with them. Around this time another group had come to the attention of the boys, and they were local lads. Hailing from Essex, Flintlock were a pop band who rose to some level of prominence via appearing on television programmes such as *Pauline's Quirkes* and *You Must Be Joking*. "We used to joke that Flintlock were our rivals," Johnson remembers.

"They were on television and we were still playing in village halls, but the thought that we might get a break and appear on television like them kept us going."

If this dream indicates the naivety of youth, then a more important indicator of how music was beginning to dominate his attentions was the fact that he was spending more and more time on the pub piano. Before long his incessant hammering of the keys was driving his old man round the twist. "I would be playing it daily and would hear my dad's voice booming down the dumb waiter. 'Shut that bloody noise, I'm trying to sleep up here!' Basically I would be playing the same thing again and again, trying to work things out. So my dad said, 'Look, I'll send you to piano lessons.' So I went to this lady in Theydon Bois. She was a bit of a hippy, used to sit there smoking, trying to teach me Scott Joplin. After about two weeks trying to play *The Sting* I decided I wasn't into that at all, and so suggested that she let me play what I wanted instead. I think she just gave up, and so she would sit there smoking cigarettes, or maybe it was grass, staring out of her window and let me play on her piano and that was it."

"Bloody used to charge enough as well," Eddie recalls, so we can assume that it wasn't long before the lessons stopped.

The summer of 1975, with the boys in Roadstar dreaming of a big break, was the dull calm before the storm. Unless you had access to the sort of records coming out of Germany by Neu! or Kraftwerk, or out of Jamaica, or the ghettoes of New York, then the music scene was about as uninspiring for a young rebel as it had ever been. Only Bowie offered a flicker of interest. The country itself was still in recession and economically in as precarious a position as it had been since the immediate post-war period. It was so bad that the Labour government had to go begging to the IMF for a bail-out. In fact it was worse; not only was America the new global empire, but Britain was flailing in the wake of both Germany and Japan. As unemployment figures steadily rose and the two main political parties pulled apart like a cracker to far left and far right, Britain was looking like the sick man of Europe. The Troubles in Northern

Ireland were into their sixth year, secretive far right groups were plotting to overthrow Harold Wilson's government, and all that popular culture could manage to throw up in resistance, it would seem, was the Bay City Rollers or ABBA.

Of course, we are blessed with hindsight and know what lay ahead. We know that John Lydon had auditioned for the Sex Pistols via the jukebox in Malcolm McLaren's shop. We know (or some of us do) that Cabaret Voltaire had long been experimenting with tape recorders and dusty old synthesizers in an attic in Sheffield, and COUM Transmissions were in the process of morphing from a subversive performance art group into subversive art rock group Throbbing Gristle. While the Pistols led the important punk explosion that blew away the cultural cobwebs, it was the latter two bands who would be more important to Matt Johnson and others who, like him, had been born a couple of years too late to really benefit from the Spirit of '76. Our future pop star – if we can call him that – was oblivious to all of this. Even older brother Andrew, who would be one of the few who saw the Sex Pistols play at the 100 Club, was unknowing at this time. In the summer of 1975, then, there wasn't much more on Matt's mind than those vague dreams of emulating the success of Flintlock, because aside from playing covers in local pubs and halls, what else was there to aspire to? Rock music had become so bloated, self-indulgent and remote that the idea of breaking into the world of prog rock superstardom was even more absurd than getting a gig on Pauline Quirke's television show. So Flintlock it was. Punk hadn't happened yet.

What had happened, though, is that Eddie had gone to the travel agents and booked a four-week holiday in America. For Matt Johnson, the trip holds strong memories. "It was an amazing holiday. We are very Americanised in this country now, but back then there was a huge cultural gap. We spoke the same language but it was still a bit like being on a different planet." From the flight out on a Pan-Am 747, everything was just bigger and better. They saw Petula Clark crossing the road in San Francisco, said hello to Tommy Cooper when they saw him at a Universal Studios tour, and got a trademark Cooper "heh-heh" in reply. They visited Disneyland, where it struck Eddie that Americans weren't just big, they were huge, and when they encountered the size of the food portions he could see why. They went into McDonald's, which at the time was yet to begin its global invasion. It was very different to Wimpy bars in England, where you sat down to eat a beef burger on a china plate, milkshake was the actual consistency of milk, and chips were fat. And in America, if you took the food away with you it actually did come in a brown paper bag, just like on *Kojak* or *Starsky & Hutch*. There was no rain for once, no bickering whilst waiting for the AA to arrive, not even any kind of car trouble apart from the stress for Eddie of steering the monstrous mobile home down through California and towards New Mexico. For Johnson it was the start of a fascination with America that was to become something of a love-hate affair. "Now we know the dark side of America, of course, but back then we were innocent. That visit had such a strong impact on me as a kid that it's probably why I went to live in America later. The big blue skies, the sense of possibilities. Everything seemed different and like it was in widescreen. That for me was the best family holiday we ever had."

If America broadened his horizons and offered tantalising glimpses of a world much bigger than England could offer, let alone a sleepy backwater like Ongar, there was little a 14-year-old could do to force any palpable change in circumstances. Roadstar beavered away, rehearsing in the barn at the farmhouse, or in Freeston's garage, and occasional live performances took place. Both Matt and Nick began their fourth year at Ongar Comprehensive, and truanting was still on the timetable. Though Eddie and Shirley weren't aware of the extent of his unauthorised absences, it is fair to say that by this time academic expectations for their second-eldest child were not particularly high. One day some of the teachers from the school were drinking in the King's Head and one of them was served by Shirley at the bar. "How's Matthew, is he any better?" she asked. Shirley pulled a quizzical expression. "What do you mean?"

"Well, he hasn't been in school for weeks," the teacher replied, perhaps with some relish – who knows. Quite why our truant didn't think he would be rumbled sooner or later is rather remarkable and can only be put down to the misfiring neurones of a youthful nervous system that failed to take into account the fact that his parents' pub was the local for many of the teachers at his school. There was only going to be one outcome. *Matthew!* Grounded.

Back to Ongar – back to boredom. Every Monday morning the dustbin lorry would park outside the King's Head, beneath Johnson's bedroom window, and he would wake to the sound of it crunching and crushing the rubbish, all metallic groans, piston hisses and broken glass. It would be the signal for another tedious week at school. If truanting wasn't on the menu then it would be hours of sitting at the back of the class, staring out the window, scratching things on the desk, doodling, perhaps falling asleep. One evening at home, in an attempt to poke a hole into all this boredom, he decided to shave his eyebrows off. Nothing to do with David Bowie. Just because. When he woke the next morning he had forgotten about his now hairless brows. "My mum's parents were staying, and we were sat round the breakfast table in the King's Head when my dad suddenly exclaimed, 'Matthew looks different, what's going... oh my God, he's got no eyebrows!' At which point I remembered, and I was embarrassed, so I said, 'Oh yeah, they fell off.' My dad said, 'Fell off? He's got to go to the hospital!' Mum said, 'Oh don't be stupid, he's just shaved them off.' I got told off but then my nan had to draw some eyebrows on for me and off I went to school." So there he was, the Man Who Fell To Ongar, sitting in the back row at school with drawn-on eyebrows, wondering when the slow torture of the education system would end. The only thing that kept him going was Roadstar.

"Unquestionably that was my first band. That was a really important part of my life, and they were great guys – there was great camaraderie. The band was a wonderful creative outlet. I was lucky to find it."

4

SOHO

SOMETIME IN 1977 MATTHEW JOHNSON WAS TAKEN UP into a spacecraft by some beings that he describes as energies. He couldn't see their faces. They took him all over the world, showing him things, letting him know, by some mysterious form of communication, that everything was going to be just fine. The sensation he felt during the journey was one of overwhelming love. He loved his family and certainly never wished for another one, but it was suddenly as if *this* was his real family.

"The only thing I can compare it to is being on ecstasy, but this is years before I tried that. It was a sense of pure, unconditional love. I remember waking up from the dream and sobbing, because I wanted to go back. It was as if I had woken up in the wrong place and needed to be back with them, because they were my real family. This dream heralded a period of change for me. It gave me a sense of real optimism about the future, and about what I was going to do with my life, where I was going to go. Getting the job at De Wolfe was a fantastic thing, a wonderful escape, because all that was on offer according to the careers officers, and even my parents, was just fucking grim, and grimmer, and even grimmer."

What was the grimness that he was escaping from via a job at De Wolfe and dreams of pure love and aliens? How bad were things for a bored teenager in the middle of 1970s Britain?

In December 1975, Jon Savage, then 22 years old, wrote in his diary about London suburbia, about a boredom and cynicism that threatened to spill over into violence. He worried about the creeping influence of the far right, led by Margaret Thatcher. And, finally... *"Fuck London for its dullness, the English people for their pusillanimity and the weather for its coldness and darkness."*

Luckily for him, within a few months the weather would turn very hot and stay gloriously so for a whole memorable summer. Luckily for him, and many others, the Sex Pistols were already on their way to the rescue. Unluckily for most of us, there was nothing to be done about the rise of Thatcher, but two out of three wasn't bad. Unluckily for Matt Johnson, he lived in the very outer suburbs. Ongar was hanging on to Greater London by its fingertips at the eastern end of the Central Line and, though this umbilical cord led into the heart of the city, where any excitement and culture resided, it was far enough away to seem like its own little island of tedium and sterility. Though Andrew would discover and revel in punk, Matt was perhaps too young. He would enjoy some of the records Andrew would later play him, but these tended to be by American acts, like Television, Patti Smith and Pere Ubu. He would remain fairly indifferent to the English punk sound. For him, 1976 wasn't year zero, although it would prove to be a turning point of some sort, if not in a way that seemed positive or ripe with possibilities.

The year sort of drifted by in a heat haze. After a couple of months of this unrelenting sunshine, the effervescent mood of Radio 1 disc-jockeys emanating from the radio over breakfast, interrupting the beginning, ends and sometimes even middle of records – none of which improved his demeanour – Matt watched his beloved Manchester United lose improbably to second division Southampton in the FA Cup final. Andrew, whose own team had won this trophy the year before, didn't miss out on the opportunity to taunt his younger brother. The clock of teenage angst and frustration ticked relentlessly away. Only a couple more months of the school year to go before summer and then he would thankfully be entering his fifth and final year at Ongar Comprehensive. It didn't take Nostradamus to figure that this would be the end of the line for his formal education. He couldn't wait to leave.

What he also couldn't wait for was a motorbike. Well, not so much a motorbike as a moped – of sorts. What he wanted was not O-levels but a Fizzie. A Yamaha FS1E. Shirley put her foot down and said no. This was the era, after all, when television adverts depicted eggs being smashed with hammers to indicate what it might be like should a car sideswipe a motorbike at a junction. *Think Once, Think Twice, Think Bike!* went a memorable slogan for one particular safety film. "Think again!" went Shirley, every time her son asked her for a bike.

"I think it might have been Francis who got hold of a Puch Maxi, and we would take it up to the fields where we used to play truant. There were these long muddy runs, and we created ditches to ride over, just spent hours driving around on it. But I wasn't allowed to have a bike, so I got a bit cut off as Nick, Francis… all of them really, got their bikes – Fizzies and Kwakies – and off they would go from village to village, leaving me marooned."

The muddy runs were of course bone dry that summer and the bike buzzed around like a wasp, kicking up clouds of dust, Johnson desperate for his turn, knowing he wasn't going to get one of his own, growing more and more despondent as one by one his mates became proud owners of 49cc machines and sped off into the sunset leaving him behind. More pleading to Shirley. *No!* Childhood was rapidly disappearing like the last dregs of sand through an egg-timer and his friends seemed to be heading towards another world without him. Things didn't improve elsewhere either.

Roadstar continued to practise and occasionally play live in village halls, youth clubs and at birthday parties, but their chances of stardom were extinguished in October when Brett Giddings left

Ongar, relocating some thirty miles away. The days of Roadstar were over. That summer, Flintlock, the group they had hoped to emulate, had their only Top 30 hit and promptly disappeared beneath a tidal wave of change.

The final year of school was a slow descent towards failure, while out in the bigger world the dole queues were getting longer and longer. Andrew was immersing himself in punk and exploring the world of illustration and cartoons. Before long he was contributing his own illustrations to *Record Mirror*. Matt, however, was caught in a hiatus. Sure, he liked the Sex Pistols, particularly the song 'Submission' from the *Spunk* bootleg, but not enough for them to shake him free of his torpor. He still wanted his Fizzie. Eddie and Shirley still kept saying no. He felt left out and left behind, an echo of being a child in bed and hearing a party going on downstairs in the pub that he wasn't invited to. Maybe there was a strand of loneliness there all along. One of the songs that he and Brett had worked on was even called 'Maybe I'm A Loner'. The handwritten lyrics in blue biro on lined paper indicate that the pair were responsible for the music but Johnson alone wrote the lyrics. *Well maybe I'm a loner/But it doesn't concern you/I know I'm a loner/ It's all I want to do/Ma-a-ay be-e-e I-I/Want to live before I die.* Standard teenage angst for sure, but not bad for a 12-year-old, and certainly a clue as to how he was feeling at the time.

As the end of his final year at school drew closer and closer, the weight of an uncertain future bore down on him. His prospects were looking decidedly bleak. One by one his friends got jobs: Roadstar bass player, Mark Bratby, at electronics firm Plessey, in Chelmsford; Nick Freeston with the family green-grocery business in Witham; others at various local offices or factories. When they knocked off work they would be on their bikes, fizzing around until the day came when they could take their first driving lessons and graduate to a four-wheel vehicle. They got girlfriends. Soon they would be thinking of getting married, having kids, settling down. For Matt, none of these kinds of jobs filled him with anything other than a hollow fear, and settling down out here in the sticks was the stuff of his worst nightmares. He was a London boy at heart and had never liked Ongar. Now he was becoming isolated from his friends. What if the Sex Pistols were right? What if there really was no future for him?

It certainly didn't help that around this time he had taken to reading Eddie's papers. Being a man with a love of the written word, his father didn't just settle for the left-wing *The Guardian* but, in order to get a balance, took in *The Times* also. Whenever Johnson picked this up, the first thing he would turn to was defence correspondent Henry Stanhope's column. Before long the spectre of nuclear war had entered his mind, as it was to do with increasing frequency for increasing numbers of young people over the next few years. "I got very worried about that," he recalls. "It was part of the awkward journey from childhood to adulthood. Suddenly this realisation struck me, that the world is dangling by a thread, and I got depressed about it the more I read."

Looking back, he realises that much of the Cold War rhetoric was probably propaganda, but the fear at the time was real and felt by many. The realisation that the adult world was full of lies, and not to be trusted, was a rite of passage for those willing to question things, or unfortunate enough to have the reality thrust upon them. Better to have it illustrated in the abstract than closer to home, of course, but to a teenager suffering from angst and confusion this would have been no consolation. The tried and tested retreat to one's own room was employed, though Johnson took to this with more gusto than some, not even leaving at meal times. Instead, his father or mother would bring his dinner on a tray up to his room and leave it outside the door. Sometimes Shirley would venture inside and talk to her son. She would sit and ask him what was wrong but, like countless teenagers before and since, he didn't know. He was rapidly losing touch with his friends and the wider world seemed overshadowed by the threat of nuclear annihilation. Maybe that was what was wrong. Or maybe it was just Ongar.

He entered a period of what he now calls melancholia. What didn't help was a tragic accident that happened in one of the outbuildings behind the pub. Gerard was playing with a young friend called Christopher. He was a very young child and the memory of what happened has left an indelible mark. Gerard recalls this event. "Christopher and I went into one of the outbuildings looking for a place to hide and he said something like 'what about here?' I heard a horrible noise and a massive marble slab had just come down right on top of him, crushing him instantly. I had to step on the slab to get out and I just remember pools and pools of blood and his little boots sticking out of the slab. I screamed and screamed until my mum, quickly followed by everyone in the pub, came running out to see what had happened. I had nightmares for a long time afterwards."

Some of the locals blamed Eddie, perhaps in a vain attempt to make some sense of such a cruel act of fate. He received some glares at the funeral. The boy's parents didn't blame him, but the incident was perhaps the final straw for the Johnsons and Ongar, and Eddie decided it was time to move on. The brewery offered to find him another pub, but in the event he would find one himself. For Matt Johnson there was the added problem of what he was going to do after school. He remembers his mum being more sympathetic than his dad. "My school reports were terrible, so bad that sometimes I wouldn't even bring them home. And my parents were worried, because the careers officer was like, 'We don't know what is going to happen with Matthew, he's going to have no qualifications, and he's not interested…'"

Eddie remembers the solution. "I said, 'Why don't you go into catering?' and he seemed to agree with me and we went back up to the school to fill in the forms for catering college. So I thought he was going to be a chef, but he had other things on his mind."

What was on his mind was what had mostly been on his mind for years – music. This time he found a helping hand from two members of the family: Andrew, and cousin Jackie. Though there were still occasional punch-ups between the pair, Andrew would often give his younger brother pep talks, try and nudge him out of his state of inertia, try and open a window into a future he could believe in. One day Jackie came to visit and they sat and talked. Her approach, gentler perhaps, more pragmatic for sure, was to boil the problem down to manageable portions. What are you doing with your life? What is it you want to do? What is it you like doing?

When it became clear that the answer to most questions was 'music', Jackie came to the logical conclusion. "Why not get a job in the music business?"

"How?"

"There must be a book about it."

There was. It was written by Tony Hatch, and was called, *So you want to be in the music business.* It was as if Tony had been listening in and was addressing him personally. Andrew lent him the 30 pence to buy a copy. Tony was on the cover, smiling. His ex-wife, the singer Jackie Trent, had performed at the Two Puddings and the pair had written the song for Robert Maxwell's 'Buy British' campaign of the sixties, with a lyric that promised that 'the good times are blowing our way'.

The book was full of information, some chapters more useful than others, but the key thing was the list of record companies and music businesses at the back, complete with contact addresses. If you want to be in the music business, Jackie was saying, then start here. The rest is advice, but here is the door. Start knocking. Get a job as a tea boy and work your way up.

Johnson didn't tell his parents any of this. Eddie still thought his son was destined for catering college. Instead, he busied himself writing letters. "I wrote God knows how many letters. I think I started at A and worked my way through the alphabet, just wrote and wrote. I got some nice replies back." The first was from Red Lightning, a small label based in Ilford, run by Peter Shertser, who had been releasing blues recordings since the late sixties and had been an integral member of a psychedelic mod gang called The Firm. Maybe Shertser felt some kind of kinship towards a youth from the Eastern outreaches of London – a fellow rebel perhaps; enough to pen some encouraging words, and keep a flame burning. "I used to carry that letter around with me. I got loads of rejection letters, and I got one interview – with De Wolfe. And I got the job. It was like someone had lowered an escape ladder to get away from these awful job prospects."

There were around one hundred record labels listed in the back of Tony Hatch's book with a London address, starting with Amberlee Records Ltd, which gives not just an indication of the writer's cramp this might have induced for a 15-year-old, but also the healthy nature of the music industry during this era. Also listed were forty-five London recording studios. Clearly, if you wanted a job in the music business, then the seventies was the right time to be looking, and London the right place. So, despite having no qualifications, a letter from De Wolfe Ltd arrived like the last helicopter out of Vietnam and young Matthew Johnson clung on and escaped, not the dole queue so much as the sterile, suburban future of his nightmares. And when this act of fortune didn't seem enough, the loving aliens of his dreams came to tell him that it was all going to be okay.

He travelled into London with Eddie for the interview. "I put on my little suit, jacket and shirt, and I went in there for my interview with a chap called Gary Thomas, and he gave me the job. It was fantastic for me, absolutely fantastic. I went from being written off by school, and the careers officers, trying to be persuaded to go and do something I wasn't interested in, like catering college. After the interview my dad took me to a little Jewish delicatessen, called Tafgood's, on the corner of Wardour Street and St Anne's Court, and we had potato latkes. When I got the job they were very excited. It was a big deal for me. It was £18 a week. £10 a week went on travel, £5 to my mum for 'keep', and £3 left over for me to go wild with."

De Wolfe Ltd began life in 1909, established by Meyer de Wolfe, who had come to London from the Netherlands some nine years previously. Initially providing the accompanying sheet music for silent films, with the advent of 'talkies' they began what was the world's pioneering music production library, furnishing first film, then television, with incidental music and soundtrack themes and sound effects.

By the time Matt Johnson was ready to start his first day of employment, Meyer's son, James de Wolfe, had been steering the ship for eleven years at the Wardour Street premises in Soho, spread over two floors and including a small but very well-equipped 8-track studio.

It was a hot day on Monday July 4, 1977, and being stuck on tube trains for nearly two hours on the journey from Ongar to Tottenham Court Road wasn't helping. A few weeks before, he had enjoyed watching Manchester United beat Liverpool in the FA Cup final and now, excited and nervous about his first day in his new job, he was reading the news on the back page of newspapers held aloft by passengers sitting opposite, about the team's manager, Tommy Docherty, who had been sacked, following the revelation of an affair with the club's physio. Other people fanned themselves with folded copies of the same newspapers. The thin windows that opened in each carriage let in welcome air but when the train descended underground at Stratford, all that they let in was roaring, echoing noise. The next day was going to be the hottest of the year.

Also travelling in from the east that day – Upminster, to be precise – was Steve Rosie. Having joined the previous summer, he was looking forward to the first day in a new role himself, now that this new kid was starting, taking over as tea boy. Years later, and still at De Wolfe, he remembers the arrival of the new boy. "He was quiet when he first started, as I suppose you would be... everyone else knows each other, and you're the new guy trying to find your feet. What I do recall about his early days is that we used to have instruments hanging around the building, a piano, an electric organ outside one of the offices, and he would sit there and play little things, and he used to play so fast, nothing was mid-tempo, or slow, everything was frantic."

Soho in 1977 was still the centre of the film industry and the sex industry. Music too was an important part of the mix. The Marquee Club was next door to De Wolfe, and Trident Studios was round the corner in St Anne's Court. On nearby Dean Street was

Crackers, the venue of choice for jazz-funk aficionados. On certain nights the club would rebrand itself as the Vortex, second only to The Roxy in punk significance or legend. Sex, movies and music was certainly a heady mix for most 15-year-olds and tailor-made, it would seem, for catapulting oneself towards adulthood.

And so it went. Waking up in the distant suburbs where nothing happened, stepping onto the tube at Ongar, changing at Epping and contemplating life during the long journey westwards. Disembark at Tottenham Court Road, the arse end of Oxford Street – the bit for the locals rather than the tourists – and either a walk up to the top end of Wardour Street, or zigzag through the Soho streets and alleys to the same destination, emerging from St Anne's Court, home to Trident, a couple of brothels, and the sci-fi book and comic shop Dark They Were and Golden Eyed, owned and run by Derek 'Bram' Stokes and his wife Diana. Originally in Berwick Street, it had moved to larger premises and was frequently visited by Andrew Johnson, who recalls that the hippies employed there were usually so stoned that shoplifting was almost obligatory. This short passage between Wardour Street and Dean Street would also, a few years into Johnson's future, host the offices of Some Bizzare.

Up the road was The Ship, a pub so full of musicians that, in De Wolfe lore, if you needed a horn section for a recording session at short notice all you had to do was walk a couple of hundred yards to said drinking establishment and pull them out. As Steve Rosie remembers, "all the film industry used to meet in the pub at lunchtimes". And they could be long lunchtimes, particularly on a Friday. Hell, Fridays were so slack people could get away with disappearing from work and going down to the afternoon session at Crackers, should their tastes be soul, disco, jazz and funk. If not, a favourite watering hole would suffice, be it The Ship, The Crown and Two Chairmen, Dog and Duck or Intrepid Fox – all regular haunts of De Wolfe staff. It was a different era; people smoked everywhere for a start, even at work and in the smoking carriages of the tube trains. Five a day was more likely to be whiskies than portions of fruit or vegetables. And despite the jail sentences handed out to the likes of Kenneth Drury and Bill Moody of the 'Dirty Squad', the sex industry was at its neon-lit sleazy peak. Paul Raymond was still busy buying up any Soho building he could. Such a saturated atmosphere was bound to have an impact on anyone, and Matt Johnson was no exception. Though his sense of isolation was to continue, it was slowly morphing from melancholia to something else.

First of all, he had something he didn't want to run away from for once. It might not have been exciting at first but it was better than school, or truanting. It was routine, but a routine that was getting him somewhere. As tea boy he spent most of his time in the Transfer Bay, watching the older members of staff, like Steve Rosie and Fitzroy Blake, observing how things were done. Thousands of reels of quarter-inch tape lined the walls, containing the De Wolfe library of music and sound effects. It was here that transfers were made from master copies, using the half-dozen Ampex tape machines. As well as making tea and coffee for anyone who wanted it – staff or client – he would run errands, including the usual fool's errands. A De Wolfe favourite was being sent for a bag of sprocket holes, which Steve Rosie remembers falling for.

"I was sent round to PEC in Dean Street for a bag of sprocket holes. 'We need a bag of sprocket holes for the film machines.' I was like, 'yeah, yeah,' but they said, 'No, we really do.' Gary Thomas actually wrote out an order for PEC – 3 bags of sprocket holes – scribbled it out, tore it off and handed it to me. As soon as I was out the door he was on the phone to them, 'There's a guy coming round for a bag of sprocket holes. Do the usual.' Everyone had that baptism. Tartan paint, left-handed hammer, that kind of stuff."

But then there was the useful stuff, beginning with the nuts and bolts of tape editing, which in those days involved using a chinagraph pencil, a blade and a cutting block. Johnson was a quick learner. He watched people closely, saw how they did things. He watched how the others found desired points of recordings that they wanted to edit, scrubbing the tape backwards and forwards, listening for the exact point where a drum hit ended, or the silence between two words, then mark on the tape with the pencil, careful not to leave too much residue. He watched how they would pull the quarter-inch tape and lay it flat into position on the cutting point, then take a razor blade and use the 45-degree cutting slot to slice through the tape and join it to the other half of the tape reel at the desired point, using a piece of joining tape, careful to align everything exactly. There was all kinds of sonic fun and games to be had this way – reversing tape, or copying sections to repeat them. Messing about with time itself. Sometimes there would be bits of tape hanging everywhere, ready to be spliced in, and if you weren't careful you could get in a right pickle. But this would come later. First steps first. Pretty soon he was doing simple cuts and edits himself, having been taught on an ancient EMI tape machine by chief engineer, Les Saunders. These, he realised, were skills worth knowing. He was being inducted into the black arts of sound recording and editing, and this would open up a whole world of possibilities. It was one thing learning how to play an instrument, but if you knew your way around a recording studio, with all its alchemy, then that power could be put to good use. Even if he wasn't quite sure how he might put such knowledge to use, other people were soon going to show him just what could be done. He was restless from day one.

He became part of the team right away, as Steve Rosie remembers: "He'd be learning, as I did, first of all doing the tea and coffee, and editing, lining up the machines, de-magging them, lining up all the stock for the week. And then we would start our working day doing transfers for the music librarians. Film editors, producers and directors would come in to a listening room and would say what styles of music they wanted to hear. At the time there was John Hyde, Rosalind Druce and Alan Howe, and they would find tracks that were suitable. We would then go and find either the mono or stereo copy and make transfers. That's all we did, day in, day out."

Most of the others at De Wolfe, with all the skills they had learnt, were content to limit their use to the confines of the company and the job. It was a great job after all, and a laid-back family-run company, so much so that many of those there when Johnson started are still there now. Looking back, with the benefit of hindsight and maturity, from the cold corporate world of today, he can see the blessings of such a set-up, but to his teenage self in 1977 he found the atmosphere somewhat stifling. The majority of the older employees had very middle-of-the-road tastes, and though this was the decade of musical revolution it is worth remembering that for most people in the music business, adult-oriented rock and progressive rock was still the order of the day.

For Johnson, music like this was the enemy which he had to suffer at the regular lunchtime record clubs. During these, people would take turns to play a record they had brought in for everyone else's edification. Whilst many of those present would marvel at the dexterity of a keyboard or guitar player, or the pristine quality of a 24-track recording, Johnson would grit his teeth and endure it, like a tedious lesson at school, only in more comfortable surroundings. Luckily for him, there was a soul mate on board, one who had been at De Wolfe for a couple of years and, liking this newcomer from Essex, decided to take him under his wing.

Colin Lloyd Tucker was born in Harrow, north-west London, in 1958. Like Johnson, he left school at 15 with no qualifications. Like Johnson, he got his job at De Wolfe through writing letters to recording studios in London, though he had been given the addresses by an exasperated careers officer. Unlike Johnson, he didn't do this himself, instead coaxing his two sisters into undertaking the task. They obviously did a good job as by the time they got to 'D' he had received an interview request from De Wolfe.

By 1977 he had made it into the studio, first as Tape-Op, then as engineer. More importantly perhaps, he was also entrusted on occasion with the keys to the building, which opened up a world of opportunity for using studio 'down-time'. Life at De Wolfe was becoming very interesting for Lloyd Tucker and he sensed a kindred spirit in Johnson. "I liked Matt straight away. Like all of us he was quiet and shy at first but before long he began to display a rather wicked, mischievous sense of humour. He was very curious, and I was impressed by his ability to grasp the technology. He was also inquisitive about music, and in particular the more off-the-wall stuff."

During one of the lunchtime record club sessions, Colin would play him one of these off-the-wall records. After the diet of slickly produced but bland recordings that had assaulted his ears during these lunch breaks, what he heard was a revelation. So it was that Matt Johnson had his Velvet Underground baptism. It might seem hard to grasp in our musically saturated age, where the history of rock'n'roll resembles some kind of supermarket, but in 1977 The Velvet Underground were still as obscure as the latter half of their name would indicate. The music world was still recovering from the loss seven years earlier of The Beatles, and in August the king himself, Elvis Presley, died. These were the twin pillars of popular music. Just beneath them in the pantheon were the likes of The Rolling Stones, Bob Dylan, Led Zeppelin, Pink Floyd and The Who. It would take another decade before the importance of the New York quartet was fully acknowledged. The roll-call of bands and artists who would claim them as a vital influence would pretty much constitute a history of rock and pop from the mid-seventies onwards.

But in 1977 they were a secret. They never got played on the radio, were never on television or performing live. The only way you got to hear The Velvet Underground was through your own curiosity – piqued perhaps by Andy Warhol's famous banana sleeve for the debut album – or word of mouth. More often than not, somebody would play you one of their records. If this happened to be accompanied by some mind-bending substances of one kind or another you were likely to be converted instantly. There were other cult finds, such as Neu!, but the Velvets were the de-facto revelation, the Road to Damascus moment for hip music fans everywhere. As Colin Lloyd Tucker succinctly puts it, "I played him the first Velvet Underground album and he took to it straight away."

Before that, however, Johnson remembers Colin playing a track from their eponymously titled album from 1969.

"Normally people would put on stuff like Stevie Nicks, Fleetwood Mac or Tom Petty, and it would be like, 'Oh God, I've got to endure this.' At the time I was getting into stuff like Throbbing Gristle, and the guys at De Wolfe were pretty straight generally, apart from Colin. He put on the first Velvet Underground track I heard – 'What Goes On'. Somebody rolled a joint, maybe Colin, and we sat round listening. It was the first time I smoked grass. I've never been a big fan really but that was the best-tasting joint I've ever smoked, it really tasted good. And then I was listening to this guitar solo... I couldn't figure out where the guitar was and where the organ was... it was just Doug Yule and Lou Reed together as one, for ages, and I was thinking, 'This music is fucking fantastic!'"

The contrast with life back in Ongar was acute. Here the sense of isolation now felt more pronounced, as if being up west in the day was the high, and being back home the comedown. "I became extremely introspective, and would go for long walks by myself." After a time, perhaps when the possibilities in his job were beginning to manifest themselves, he started to take a portable Amex tape recorder and a small Kodak Instamatic camera on these long walks; in the tradition of writers and artists through the ages, these solitary ramblings allowed him the peace required to explore his inner space.

"I started to sense things and see things that I'd never noticed before. I started deepening myself emotionally, started to have extremely vivid dreams, colours became more intense and I could hear things I couldn't previously hear. It remains one of the most important periods in my life and was the making of me really. I started listening to more underground music, more esoteric stuff, partly inspired by Andrew. So I had two people who were turning me on to good music, Andrew at home and Colin at work, and that inspired me to go and discover other bands for myself and that's how I got into The Residents and Pere Ubu. So I went from melancholia into this world where the colours and sounds were suddenly a lot brighter."

Andrew by this time had his own band called Camera 3 and Matt would sometimes record them practising. His older brother, perhaps infused with some of the energy of the initial punk explosion of 1976, was in the middle of a frantic burst of creative activity, as Matt remembers. "He had a little Gestetner duplicator and was very industrious, producing his fanzines in a little room in the King's Head that he made his office. He was up the West End all the time and used to go to all these comic conventions. People would send him cartoons. Duplicators used stencils and he would produce stencils for the pictures and the type. When he had finished with the room Nick and I tried to build some kind of studio in there, which was ridiculous really as the ceiling was so low. We lined the walls with egg boxes."

So, in between punch-ups the two brothers were busy being inspired and helping each other out. At De Wolfe, meanwhile, Lloyd Tucker and Johnson would play each other tapes and records, sharing new discoveries and broadening sonic horizons. Soho was exciting and Johnson was learning, about tape loops for example. It was Lloyd Tucker who demonstrated to him the magic of this studio standard, and with so many machines they could run multiple loops and combine them.

By the late summer punk was effectively dead, co-opted by the music business and reduced to a minimal palette of knee-jerk tropes, while a safer, poppier version dubbed new wave was hoisted chart-wards. But as one thing was lost something else, less easy to pigeonhole, was already replacing it. New acts emerged, like The Residents, Throbbing Gristle, This Heat and a host of others, and it was these that Johnson was interested in. Cabaret Voltaire, The Human League and other pioneers of new synthesizer and recording technology came closer to redefining what music could be. Sonically they were far more radical. For all the hysterical anti-establishment threat that the Pistols promised, they were always tied to the establishment via record deals with EMI, A&M and Virgin. Buzzcocks had demonstrated the alternative with their independently released debut single, something that left a big impression on a young Scot, Thomas Leer, who would prove just what was possible with the minimum of equipment when he recorded 'Private Plane' in 1978. This was accomplished using nothing more than a TEAC A3440 4-track recorder, and a small Alice mixing board. FX were added via a Watkins Copicat tape echo unit, Electro Harmonix Dr Q filter, an old Roland drum machine and a Stylophone 350S. It was an important record, something Jim Thirlwell, who worked in the Virgin Records shop on Oxford Street, and who enters the story later, spotted straight away. "I had that immediately when it came out. That was a classic."

The Johnson family had upped sticks once again by the time that Leer's debut appeared on his own Oblique Records label. Eddie and Shirley had never been happy running the pub in Ongar, and while the hauntings could be tolerated, the tragic accident involving Gerard's young friend proved too much. The chance to relocate to Loughton, several stops closer to London on the Central Line, arose and they jumped at it, taking over a more modern pub, called The Crown. As far as they could tell, this one wasn't haunted. Eddie thought Loughton was okay. "Some nice people used to come into the pub and there were some nice shops on the high street. Shirley liked Loughton." Her second son, however, didn't concur.

"I didn't like Ongar, but Loughton I liked even less, as I didn't have any friends or connections there. The accommodation above the pub was much smaller so Andrew and I had to share a room, and Eugene and Gerard shared another. The window frames were metal so it would get very cold and there would be terrible condensation. It was a better pub for my parents. It was busier so there was more money coming in. Around this time though, in and after the summer of 1978, I was getting to know a lot more people and building a social life in London, and I spent less time at home."

Johnson felt more at home in Soho. He and Colin got to know all the call girls and strippers – not through any kind of transactions, but because they would see them every day and there was always banter to be had. Still only 16, this kind of atmosphere was rather thrilling. The working girls of the day were certainly more visible than in current times, including one orange-haired woman who would hang out of the window of the Golden Girl club on Meard Street, next door to Gossips nightclub. But it wasn't all sleaze and night-time economy, as Colin Lloyd Tucker recalls.

"In amongst the porn shops, pubs, cinemas and strip joints were also old family-run delicatessens, a primary school, pubs, and most of the British film industry of the time. In fact, opposite De Wolfe was the huge head office of Hammer films. Trident Studios was still there, and the Marquee had a studio attached. There were lots of film sound dubbing places too, one of the largest being De Lane Lea on Dean Street."

The De Wolfe boys would often lunch over the road in the Pick & Chews cafe, or Mr Natural's burger bar on Peter Street. Johnson would frequently head up to Tafgoods for his latkes, and, when it was his turn, be sent to Jolson's to buy a catering-size tin of Nescafe for the office. Cigarettes and sweets would be bought in a tiny shop called The Hobbit. All of these places are now gone or under new owners with new names or purposes, the Soho of Matt Johnson's youth having been reduced to nothing but memory. But if the evenings back then were increasingly spent in pubs or the Marquee, then lunchtimes were reserved for window shopping in and around Denmark Street, on the eastern edges of Soho. Once Britain's own Tin Pan Alley, it was host to a cornucopia of music shops, and the impression of Matt Johnson's nose would often be left behind on their display windows.

"I was always round at Denmark Street. There were certain bits of gear that I would fantasize about. Of course what I really wanted was a Revox, but that was way out of my range, so I got an Akai 4000DS Mk2. It cost £147 which in those days was a hell of a lot of money, particularly when you are on £18 a week, but I saved up for it and by the time we were living in The Crown it was mine. Then I started getting cheap bits of equipment, like a Colorsound Tremolo, some Electro-harmonix fuzzboxes, like the Small Stone Phaser; the cheaper stuff. There were these Russian 4-track machines called

Dokorder, kind of the Eastern Bloc equivalent of a Teac, and one of the shops on Denmark Street had them in the window, so I would stand there, salivating at the sight of all these bits of equipment and guitars and keyboards. I would get *Exchange & Mart* every week and they had small adverts for a Crumar Roadrunner electric piano. It was about £150 and I couldn't quite afford it. I found a second-hand one but it was the previous model, and I bought that for £115 and a little stand for it."

Though he didn't like Loughton, and sharing a room with his brother led to more arguments than usual, the move to The Crown was serendipitous for one reason – it had a huge cellar. "The cellar had quite a high ceiling. At one end was my dad's office; round the corner Andrew set up his art studio and I set up a small recording studio. I would come home from De Wolfe and maybe have some dinner, but other times just go straight down to the cellar, and spend the whole night down there while they were working, and after the pub closed, my dad would shout down, 'Matthew? Are you still down there?' What he didn't realise was that Andrew and I were eating into the profits. We would be working and get a bit thirsty and just reach over for a can of Fosters or a bottle of beer. Maybe grab a packet of Dunhill cigarettes."

Having this workable space to set up a rudimentary studio came at the perfect time. Here he was, working in the heart of Soho, learning the tricks of the trade, with the best music shops in the country all within arm's reach and some money in his pocket. Okay, so there wasn't much of the latter, not after the travel costs and keep for Shirley, but there was decent gear to be had if you could save diligently. If the likes of Teac, Moog and Rhodes were out of reach, then Akai, EDP and Crumar filled the gap for those on a budget.

"So, during lunchtimes we would look in the music shops, or do a bit of our own work. I remember Colin doing this stuff with flanging, the original way with two machines that you would start together, but speed up or slow down one of them. We were messing around with tape loops as well, creating them at different lengths, two or three of them going at once. De Wolfe had this big old graphic equaliser, and we would run things through that and learn about EQ. I would be working on stuff at home, then bringing it into work."

So the ambitious pair would busily work on their own projects, and as these progressed the confines of De Wolfe began to seem limiting in the longer term. With free studio down-time, however, neither was thinking of making any rash moves in the summer of 1978. The template provided by Thomas Leer and his home-made single had filled their heads with a whole new set of possibilities.

"I heard 'Private Plane' by Thomas Leer, which he did all by himself, all the playing and writing, *everything*. That was the big turning point for me because it introduced me to a whole new form of music. Leer had all these drum machines and loops and totally different instrumentation, and listening to his atmospheric experimentation a whole new world opened up. I realised then that I didn't have to make songs that sounded like everybody else. People could put out a record they had made in their bedroom. That was really inspiring."

Leer was ahead of the curve. It was one thing for Buzzcocks to release their own *Spiral Scratch* EP at the beginning of the previous year, but Leer made four men with guitars and drums look like an anachronism. Here was just one man, with a modest collection of equipment – a kind of futuristic one-man band it might have seemed at the time. He wasn't the only person messing around with oscillators and the cheaper end of electronic music technology – Cabaret Voltaire, Throbbing Gristle, Suicide, Daniel Miller and The Human League were all doing the same – but there was something about the texture of Leer's music that appealed to Johnson.

Synthesizers had been around for a long time and had been used in popular music since the late sixties. Back then, they tended to be huge and cost incredible amounts of money. When Bob Moog introduced the scaled-down and portable Minimoog in 1970 it was still out of financial reach for most – even at the end of the decade. Instead it was English company Electronic Dream Plant, with the Wasp, and Japanese manufacturers Roland and Korg, who gave cheaper synthesizers to the masses and thus were to enable the imminent synth-pop era. Tony Hatch, in his 1976 book, Matt's copy now well read and dog-eared, had this to say about synthesizers:

They can produce an almost endless variety of sounds and I'm sure it's only the beginning of an era as far as the synthesiser [sic] *is concerned.*

When he had first read the book it might have seemed overly technical and mysterious, but twelve months later he was exploring fully the world of recorded sound and benefiting hugely from what would have been out of reach had he not been working at De Wolfe. In our present-day era, when all aspiring musicians have their own home-recording set-up, this may seem like no great shakes, but in the late seventies it was a brave new world. And not only did Johnson realise that he could do things his way with all this technology at his disposal, but that essentially he could do it alone, as Leer had done. It wasn't that he didn't want to get a band together, or work with others, but the independence really appealed to him. He could be in complete control. It was always an option. And it was an option he would return to.

Having no social life in Loughton meant that his company, family aside, was mostly the old Bell piano from the King's Head, now painted green, upon which he would spend hours practising. Or his guitar, down in the cellar with his electronic gadgets and the newly acquired Akai. From here on, that's what it was. Practice, practice, practice. Every day. Like all those who eventually make it, he was obsessed.

Steve Rosie felt that Matt was always working towards getting out there. He was always talking about it, seemed to have an inner strength for it. "I would say he had a steely determination. He knew what he wanted to do, and he was going to make it happen. He was savvy. I think his dad having the pub and hiring bands… growing up in that environment, he wasn't green like a lot of people. He knew what he was doing. When we were young we all wanted to make it in the industry with a band, and become a pop star, rock star. Matt definitely wanted to make it."

5

"HOW ABOUT 'THE THE'?"

MATT JOHNSON HAD WASTED NO TIME IN FURTHERING HIS ambitions. As early as November 1977 he had placed his first advert in the music press. Charles Blackburn, staying in London at his cousin's flat, was reading through the musicians wanted adverts of the *NME*. Amongst the wall-to-wall requests for musicians, or budding musicians, into the Pistols or The Clash, he spied one that was different. *Looking for a bass/lead guitarist into Velvets/Syd Barrett.* Being a bit of a Barrett and early Pink Floyd obsessive his attention was immediately grabbed and he spent the next hour walking up and down wondering whether or not to reply. After all, he was supposed to be returning to Hull in two weeks, and he didn't even have a proper guitar.

Johnson, meanwhile, had met a few people already before the visiting Northerner finally made up his mind and contacted him. "Most people were really straight in those days – the underground was really small – and so it was really hard to meet people who were off the beaten track. People would reply to the ads who were into things like jazz-funk, and I used to think, 'Oh, for fuck's sake,' and Charlie was the first person that actually replied who was a bit interesting; and the Syd Barrett connection was good enough for me to give him the benefit of doubt. He was a year older than me. I liked him."

They met in The Ship on Wardour Street in December; Johnson was somewhat taken aback when Blackburn arrived with his dad and step-mum, who listened to the pair talk through their rock dreams before declaring, 'It's all a bit pie in the sky.' Despite this rather definite-sounding reservation, his dad decided to treat Charles to his first present in two years and gave him the £70 needed to purchase an Ivor Mairants Telecaster copy. He persuaded his cousin to let him stay another two months, and when his time there ran out Blackburn moved to a hostel for overseas students in King's Cross. The pair managed to get together several times in the first two months of the new year. In his diary entry for Sunday, February 12, 1978 he wrote the following: *Went to Matt's. Can't seem to get his songs done. He's annoyed. Then do mine. AUTOMATON. It is great. We record it spontaneously (v.good). Enthusiasm revived.* Johnson's frustration was an early indicator that things weren't going to work out, but the pair nevertheless enjoyed each other's company and would spend many an hour in the pub, drinking pints while talking incessantly about music. They might not have been quite walking the walk, but the talk was doing fine, and for two teenagers in the big city this wasn't such a bad state of affairs. It didn't last long, however, as Blackburn ran out of places to crash and had to return home. For the next few months he kept in touch as dreams of stardom were put on hold.

Colin Lloyd Tucker was having better luck getting his musical ambitions airborne, with the help of work colleague, John Hyde. "We wrote a track called 'I Am A', and put a band together with drummer Tim Broughton." 'I Am A' was recorded at the De Wolfe studio in late 1977, under the name Plain Characters, but wouldn't see the light of day until the following year when it was released on the company's own Rouge Music imprint. They managed to secure a lot of support slots at venues in and around London and various members of the De Wolfe gang would go along, Johnson included. Steve Rosie would sometimes drive people to these shows. "There

Grandad Joe, Nanny Jinny, Nanny Sue, Grandad Charlie – 1963. Photo: Johnson Family Archive.

Eddie and Shirley clubbing – 1950s.
Photo: Johnson Family Archive.

Two Puddings – Stratford 1960s. Photo: Getty Images / Steve Lewis.

Uncle Peter (far left), Grandad Charlie, Shirley (centre) and friends – Two Puddings 1960s. Photo: Alf Sheed.

Andrew and Matthew – Stratford 1963. Photo: Johnson Family Archive.

Uncle Kenny (far right) and friends – Two Puddings 1960s. Photo: Alf Sheed.

Eddie and Matthew – Stratford 1966. Photo: Johnson Family Archive.

Shirley and Matthew – Corsica 1964. Photo: Johnson Family Archive.

Matt – Roadstar 1974. Photo: Johnson Family Archive.

Nicky Freeston –
Roadstar 1974.

Matthew, Andrew, Eugene, Gerard, Shirley – California 1976. Photo: Johnson Family Archive.

The Crown 1970s. Photo: Johnson Family Archive.

Keith Laws and Matt Johnson supporting Wire – Notre Dame Hall 1979. Photo: Anne Weight.

Matt Johnson and Tom Johnston – The Bridge House, Canning Town 1980. Photo: Alessandra Sartore.

was one gig at a pub in West Kensington where Matt was doing the lights. Colin and the band were on stage, and there was a bit where one of the lyrics went, 'Let there be light!' and Matt switched the lights off, plunging us all into darkness."

The music of Colin's that had impressed John Hyde was the beginnings of what would eventually be *Toybox* – an album that was started as early as 1976 but wouldn't be finished until the following decade and then would remain on the shelf until its eventual release in 1984. "I was just staying back after work and doing the odd track. This went on for a couple of years before I had a whole album's worth of stuff." As well as valuable studio time during working hours he was able to take advantage of studio down-time at night. Electronic music was developing along very interesting lines, and the technology to indulge was being delivered in scaled-down units, at scaled-down prices, making it an even more intriguing proposition, as Colin remembers. "The first portable synths were appearing, and De Wolfe owned a Minimoog. Brian Eno was using synths and tape manipulation on his early albums, which Matt and I loved. We were also aware of Kraftwerk and, in 1977, David Bowie's *Low* appeared, so it was a pioneering time. When I got the keys to the studio I would often remain there all night recording my own songs, overdubbing all the instruments myself. It was natural for me to use the studio as a writing tool."

Johnson listened with interest to what Colin was doing and would appear as a guest vocalist on the track 'Casey's Last Trip', a title that gave away the pair's continuing fascination with the music of the previous decade. While Colin was working on *Toybox* in the De Wolfe studio, Johnson had begun working on music in the basement of The Crown, the results of which he would sometimes transfer to tape at work in order to take advantage of the superior equipment. By now he had the Crumar keyboard to add to his guitar, effects pedals and the Akai reel-to-reel. The ambition that Steve Rosie had picked up on so quickly was already manifesting itself and before long Johnson began work on a collection of tracks – a whole album's worth no less – which he called *See Without Being*

Seen and would copy from the quarter-inch masters onto standard C-30 cassettes that he bought from Woolworths.

With Blackburn back in Hull, he put another ad in the *NME*, which caught the attention of Steve Parry, then calling himself Stefan Jadd. Parry, born three years earlier than Matt in Pontypool, South Wales, had spent a few years in Harrogate with his family, and, finding the small northern town somewhat limiting for his ambitions, beat the well-worn path down to London in 1978. He phoned the number in the advert and spoke to a youthful cockney voice at the other end of the line – good-humoured and confident – who explained that there had been a rather negative response thus far. This fact clearly wasn't getting him down, as he promised musical revolution. Parry himself had also replied to another ad, placed by Derek Morris, in *Melody Maker*, but Johnson's enthusiasm and talk intrigued him enough to agree to a meeting. "I think it was in this little cafe in or around Stratford Broadway. Matt was shy, yet cocky at the same time. We were both being a bit cagey about things, with it being our first meeting. Matt was dressed in army surplus and looked really young. He seemed frustrated with things, but he was a likeable chap with a sense of humour. He had a vulnerable side but at the same time appeared to be a wise old bird. I don't remember talking about music much, other than professing a liking for David Bowie and The Velvet Underground, but Matt said he would send me a tape he'd recorded at home, apologising in advance about the quality."

Though the pair didn't team up to form a band, they would meet again – in the Two Puddings in one instance – and were like-minded enough to want to stay in touch. Parry returned to his south London base in Upper Norwood where his live-in landlady, Toni, was the ex-wife of producer Eddy Offord, who worked at Advision Studios. Parry, having already hooked up with Derek Morris and Steve Sherlock, decided this was a more viable and practical avenue for his ambitions. "I don't recall ever discussing with Matt forming a band together. At the time I considered Matt a solo artist living in east London – whereas Steve and Derek were keen on forming a band together, and we all lived conveniently in south London."

Though they were both going in the same direction, and would even end up on the same record label, they were coming from somewhat divergent paths. Parry's tastes were perhaps more fully formed at this stage than those of Johnson, who was a couple of years younger and still soaking up influences and inspirations like the proverbial sponge. For Johnson, this included American avant-garde music group The Residents, who he discovered via their *Duck Stab!* EP released that year. Parry, Morris and Sherlock would become Neu Electrikk. Johnson and Parry would exchange letters and phone calls and weave in and out of each other's social lives for the next few years. The following May, both Parry and Charles Blackburn would be in the crowd for the debut live performance of The The.

Blackburn returned to London in October 1978, securing a job at Selfridges. He and Johnson would meet after work in a pub called The Blue Posts. "We used to meet up every week on a Tuesday at six in a beaten-up old shack on Tottenham Court Road. The pub was really scruffy, and the lighting was low, so you couldn't see the filthy seats and carpets. For two teenagers talking incessantly about music for four or five hours it was perfect, and we could always get a booth to ourselves. Matt and I couldn't agree on a name for the band. He wanted Insect Fear, and I wanted it to be The Lucifer Sam. Finally, he saw an album in a record shop – Nico's, *The Marble Index* – and that stuck." This time round they decided to draft in two more people – Martin (Sanderson, a friend from Essex) on bass, and Martin (Brand, a colleague from De Wolfe) on drums. Once again nothing much came of this. "We had a couple of rehearsals in the winter of 1978, but at Christmas agreed to call it a day."

Blackburn would go on to form his own band, taking the Marble Index name. If Blackburn got the name then Johnson was to get something a bit more useful, other than all the beer and chat. "The biggest contribution Charlie made to my life and career was a guitar. He had a Telecaster copy, a Japanese copy I think. We had some rehearsals in the cellar studio at The Crown. Charlie said, 'Do you mind if I leave my guitar here?' So I said, 'Yeah, but can you show me a chord?' He said, 'This is a good one to play,' and showed me a barre chord – the E-shape, and said, 'You keep it all the way along the fretboard.' And it was from this chord shape that I wrote 'Uncertain Smile', because that is just the same shape in four different positions."

Blackburn too remembers this, but adds some detail. "Matt wanted to borrow my Ivor Mairants, as I had my Fender Telecaster, though I didn't think it would be forever! The open tuning was my 'special' version; unlike a normal 'Keef' open D or G at the 'nut', I tuned the top E down to the second string, then the third string is tuned up to the second, creating a drone/sitar-like effect. Matt didn't bother tuning the third string up, I believe, when he recorded 'Cold Spell Ahead'." Johnson says Blackburn is inaccurate about the tunings here as both 'Cold Spell Ahead' and 'Uncertain Smile' were recorded in the standard guitar tuning of EADGBE. Though the musical alliance never materialised, they continued to socialise and enjoy each other's company. Johnson remembers a different pub and a larger intake of ale. "Charlie and I used to go out drinking quite a lot. We used to go to a pub in Fitzrovia called the Valiant Trooper. We used to drink six or seven pints of lager a night. There was lots of talk, but no real connection when it came to playing the music – it just didn't click."

Another cul-de-sac. Still, they were young and full of enthusiasm and energy at a time when the capital city was some kind of musical melting pot, with various factions of what was in reality a fairly small crowd of people, about to launch themselves in different directions, depending on their view of how the lost spark of punk might be rekindled. For Johnson and Blackburn there was beer and talking, endlessly talking, about music and bands and records. In November, Thomas Leer had released his home-grown debut, and though it caused nary a ripple in the consciousness of the typical Radio 1 listener, its impact resonated under the surface. On Christmas Day, 1978, John Lydon's new group, Public Image Ltd, played their debut gig at the Rainbow in Finsbury Park and Johnson and his old mates from Ongar were there. "We met John Lydon's dad by the stage door and had a long chat with him. There was a big punch-up; there were skinhead elements in there who started on everybody. It was quite intense."

Nick Freeston had hooked up with Gavin Gritton and Ian 'Haggis' Haggerty and started a punk band called Cardiac Arrest. For a while Matt was employed on bass duties, though this wasn't a long-term arrangement. Under the name Anti-Establishment, and with Matt now replaced by Colin Little, they would record two singles, produced by Rat Scabies. Though he wasn't fond enough of the brand of punk they were playing to stick around on bass duties, he enjoyed being back in touch with his old school friends, and by now they had all progressed from two-wheel transport to four. "I moved to Loughton but kept in touch and used to socialise with them, used to spend a lot of time over at Gavin's place, get a bus there or Dad would give me a lift. It was Chigwell Row, or Lambourne End. Nick learnt to drive before I did because he was older. They all got cars before me. Nick had this Pink Panther-mobile, a bright pink Ford Escort van with shagpile carpet; it was hilarious. Haggis had a little Wolseley Hornet, which was my favourite. I loved that little thing. The four of us would squeeze into it and go to gigs; we used to go and see a band called 999 a lot, and after the gig we would have a chat. They were really friendly. We would drive around the West End and go to places in this little Wolseley Hornet, or in Nick's work van."

Johnson, however, was less interested in the dying punk scene than many of his contemporaries. Speaking to Kevin Foakes at Rough Trade East in 2014, he recalled the beginnings of the post-punk scene.

"De Wolfe was on Wardour Street next to the old Marquee Club so I was in there all the time. There were a lot of interesting underground venues – I remember seeing Throbbing Gristle in a place called The Crypt, beneath a church. These were the venues I really liked, there was a real sense of the counterculture."

The gig in question, on November 11, 1978, was notable for the fact that lead singer Genesis P-Orridge had taken an overdose beforehand, and his erratic behaviour during the set – he played guitar with his foot, and blinded the audience with spotlights – was probably overlooked by the majority of the crowd, who no doubt saw it as a typical Throbbing Gristle performance. With a background in rather extreme performance art, this was an act far removed from the cartoonish image of punk that the tabloids were comfortable with. Likewise, The Residents were light years away from bands like The Clash or Sham 69 – both sonically and philosophically. As Johnson, and others, have often stated, it was artists like these, and Thomas Leer, who truly offered what punk had promised but failed to deliver – new sounds, ideas and an independent and challenging ethos

But it wasn't just the music scene that was changing. The political mood was about to undergo a profound and long-lasting shift, and if the young Johnson wasn't yet clear about its implications, he would soon catch up.

* * *

The Sex Pistols may have been consigned to history but their soundbites continued to echo. By the long, cold winter of 1978–9 it was as though they had telegraphed messages of doom straight to Tory Party HQ. John Lydon's famous cry of anarchy possibly coming sometime soon to the UK was repeated by Margaret Thatcher in the Conservative political broadcast of January 17, 1979. The punk-for-dummies slogans of anarchy and chaos were like a subliminal message running behind news items on the latest round of strikes, and when a strike by refuse workers saw rubbish piling up on the streets, most famously in London's Leicester Square, the Tories capitalised. This was just the thing for the right wing; an image to contain their message – this was what anarchy looked like. This was chaos, and it could happen next winter, and the winter after too. Margaret Thatcher thus posed the Conservatives as the party that would bring order by ending this chaos, true to the Masonic motto. Only they could save the country from further descent into the abyss caused by the red menace of Labour and its striking workers. Ironically she also mentioned the natural riches that Britain possessed, including the coal beneath our feet. But that would be another story.

Thatcher talked straight to the watching nation, hiding party intent by suggesting that politics had nothing to do with her plea to moderates from both sides to come together, in much the same way that David Cameron would do decades later when he saw fit to use socialist rhetoric and suggest we were all in it together. And once Thatcher had the viewers' hearts she would set to work on their minds, switching from fear to greed.

Growing up with a father who had rubbed shoulders with Communist Party members on the docks, and had shared a platform with Vanessa Redgrave when she gave a speech in front of Jack Dash's strike committee, it is hardly surprising that Johnson would lean to the political left, but at 17 years of age his political awareness of the paradigm shift that was taking place was still forming. One incident, one that was to give his political sensibilities a good shake, sticks in his mind.

"At De Wolfe, most of the guys were fairly middle class, and if they weren't Tory they were fairly apolitical. But there was one person who was firmly left wing, a retired postman called Joe Cutler. I liked Joe, he was a real old-school character. Just before the election he stood in the transfer bay and said, 'You will rue the day!' It was the first time I'd ever heard the word used. He stood there, jabbing the air with his finger. 'You will rue the day that woman got elected! You will rue the day. It will be a disaster for this country.' I was in agreement but didn't realise just what was in store, just felt on an instinctive level that this wouldn't be a good thing, and Joe was standing there, deadly serious... 'You will rue the day!'"

The sense that Great Britain was a country in severe decline was palpable by 1979. Thatcher was to ramp up the pressure on the beleaguered Labour government by continually pointing out just how far we had fallen behind the rest of Europe. Knowing just what buttons to press, she appealed to the jingoism of a fading Empire by suggesting that even Italy was facing up to the global recession better than ourselves. It wasn't a difficult sell in reality. As Jon Savage remembers it, "England wasn't free and easy: it was repressed and horrible." Although Johnson's own perceptions were yet to gain the focus that comes with adulthood, he too remembers a country that, in retrospect, was a long way from the technicolour swing of the sixties. "In terms of the general atmosphere of that time Britain was a pretty dull and dreary place. One obvious difference was the food. You had fish and chips, cafes, cheap and cheerful Italian restaurants or takeaway places, but high-street boutique food and chain coffee bars were a long way off. If you wanted proper coffee you had to go to Soho, to places like Bar Italia. And it seemed colder back then because not everyone had central heating. There would be draughts coming through the floorboards and as a kid you would have layers of blankets, eiderdowns and those candlewick bed-spreads, before the continental quilt took over. The smell of cigarette smoke was everywhere; obviously in the pub, but people would smoke when they came round to your house, at gigs, in restaurants, on the underground and on buses. Everywhere smelt of cigarettes."

Though it was freezing cold and rubbish lined the streets, London still seemed to be brimming with opportunity for anyone young and into music. Matt Johnson, though still broke despite working, was generally less concerned with the state of a decaying nation than what new band he could discover and what was in the pages of the *NME* gig guide each week. It was in its pages that he placed his second advert seeking interested musicians, this time name-dropping The Residents and Throbbing Gristle, a sign either that the influences in his first advert hadn't brought forth the right candidates, or that his own musical tastes were beginning to take on a more solid identity that separated him from the tastes of his older brother, and pointed to the future rather than the past. This time, despite the usual calls from jazz-funk drummers who once again ignored the musical clues in the ad, he saw fit to meet with three hopefuls one day in The Ship in Wardour Street. The trio were Janice Higgs, Peter Fenton H Jones and, most significantly, Keith Laws. Higgs would only last for one rehearsal but would later team up briefly with Charlie Blackburn, when the pair met at The The's first gig. Fenton-Jones would play at that gig but Johnson, finding his posh sensibilities incompatible with his own more grounded outlook on life, would dispense with his musical services soon after. With Laws, however, he clicked straight away.

"As soon as I met Keith I liked him. We had a lot in common, both being from east London, having similar musical tastes and a shared sense of humour. We both had bad acne at the time as well and I think he was also a Manchester United supporter." Laws was a big fan of German music and introduced Johnson to Neu! and Faust, among others.

"We really hit it off and became good friends, spending a lot of time together. His family were really nice. I would spend a lot of time round there. His dad, Eric, had a huge record collection of old music, like Bobby Darin, and his one day for listening to it seemed to be Sunday. He would pull a record out of its sleeve, clean it, put it on, and just sit there listening, while Keith's mum was making the roast dinner, and I was always welcome to stay. It was quite a long way back to Loughton at night so I used to stay round his quite a lot, especially if we had been to see bands playing, and we would stay up late into the night talking."

What was just as promising for Johnson's ambitions was that Laws had his own equipment – a Wasp synthesizer, which he would later upgrade to a Korg MS10, and an Akai 4000DS. With two reel-to-reel tape recorders, two keyboards, Charlie Blackburn's guitar, and a motley selection of cheap effects pedals, here was the makings of an outfit that could hit the stage – the logical next step for Johnson after months and months of experimentation and recording in the basement of his parents' pub and, surreptitiously, De Wolfe studios. The fruits of these recordings had made their way onto various formats, one of which was a C-30 cassette that he would try and offload at gigs he went to. This came complete with a home-made card insert bearing the text: *Matt Johnson. Demo. See Without Being Seen.* The tracks were recorded on his trusty Akai in late 1978 and early 1979. In March 1979, Johnson transferred them to quarter-inch tape at De Wolfe, where he could take advantage of the vintage graphic equaliser to finesse the sound. The track-listing reads: 'Troops', 'Homa's Coma', 'Planetarium', 'Spaceship In My Barn', 'Insect Children', 'My Vymura', and 'Window Ledge'. The only copy of the cassette left in existence, apart from Johnson's own, belongs to Steve Parry.

Johnson sent a copy of the cassette to Parry in south London. In the accompanying letter he wrote, *The project which I'm working on at the moment (which the cassette is/was part of) is See Without Being Seen – which deals with you or I (or anyone whose listening to the songs) as a spectator seeing abstract views of life be it of people or situations or how people react to various situations and pressures.*

He apologised for the rudimentary nature of the music on the tape, explaining that having only his Crumar keyboard, a guitar and a selection of cheap effects pedals, it wasn't as experimental as he wanted it to be. Already he felt detached from the recordings but did think that two of the songs had potential. He added a postscript to the letter advising the listener to plug their cassette player into a large amp, turn up the bass, mid and treble, and add a touch of reverb.

Whether Parry did so or not, he thought that *See Without Being Seen* was an impressive piece of work for someone who had started recording it at the age of 16. Thirty-four years later he would write about the cassette on his website, describing the music as "experimental, complex and rich", though "naive at times". More significantly, as Johnson had imparted in his letter, was the prospect of performing. *I've met three people (all at the same time which was quite nice) and we all seemed to get on well and have the same interests, and we decided to get a gig in early May (after a rehearsal or two).* As one of these people, Janice Higgs, didn't last beyond the first rehearsal we can safely say that the foursome had yet to rehearse, an assumption supported by the fact that the letter also asked if Parry knew of any rehearsal rooms or warehouses where they could practise and safely leave their gear afterwards. The letter also included addresses for Genesis P-Orridge of Throbbing Gristle, Rough Trade records and concert promoters Final Solution, indicating that Johnson, galvanised by the response to his advert, was thinking much further ahead than mere rehearsals.

If things were suddenly moving quickly then the catalyst was Tom Johnston, a cartoonist who shared an office with Kipper Williams and David Austin in Covent Garden. It was this area, separated from Soho by Charing Cross Road, that was to become crucial to Matt's musical geography. Soho had the Marquee, the Vortex and Gossips, while Covent Garden could boast The Roxy (closed by this time), Blitz (soon to open) and the Rock Garden. If you want to get a sense of what Covent Garden was like at the end of the 1970s then you could do worse than watch Alfred Hitchcock's *Frenzy*, which was filmed there in 1973 during the dying days of the fruit and vegetable market. When this was closed in 1974 the Greater London Council had been planning to go ahead with outlandish plans for demolition and gentrification that at one time included four-lane roads, towering office blocks and raised pedestrian walkways. Needless to say there was huge opposition, not only from local residents but also figures such as the MP Anthony Crosland, and the original plans were effectively stymied by Geoffrey Rippon. What was left was a deserted market surrounded by hoardings and streets left empty of the hustle and bustle that the market had once caused.

Whilst the GLC pondered how to continue with redevelopment, and local community projects created their own shared spaces and protests, rents remained cheap and old warehouse spaces that had once served the market stallholders were filled with new tenants, many of them from the creative industries. By 1979 it was something of a hub for those who worked for small printing presses or in the worlds of music, fashion or photography, and so several of the people who would play a part in Johnson's career worked in the area. Filmmaker Tim Pope recalls a place far removed from that of today. "In those days the tube didn't stop at Covent Garden on a Saturday, so if I had to go to work at the weekend I had to get off at Leicester Square and walk. Because no one got off there at the weekend it was dead. On Neal Street, where I worked, there is now a big block of flats and shops, but I remember when it was an old bomb-site, which it was until the seventies when it was turned into a community Japanese Garden. It was at the junction of Earlham Street and Neal Street. That was what I looked out onto."

Just round the corner from Neal Street was James Street. It was on this street, which led down to the now boarded-up market, that Tom Johnston had his office. Born in Belfast in 1951, he had moved to England to study, first at Leeds College of Art, then at the University of London, where a Masters degree in Education led to a job teaching art at Leyton Girls Senior High School. In 1977, after two years teaching, he became a freelance cartoonist; his early work appeared in *Time Out*, *Private Eye* and the music paper *SOUNDS*, the office of which, above the tube station, was a few doors down from his own.

He too remembers the more dilapidated days of the area fondly. "Covent Garden was beautiful. It wasn't as commercial as it is now. The council still hadn't done anything with Covent Garden. They wrote to me and everyone else who was a tenant, asking if we had any ideas of what to do with the market? We all wrote back – 'How about a fruit and veg market?' Back then there were still quite a lot of working-class families living there, and there were lots of small cafes and stuff."

Johnston's neighbour at this time on James Street was Andy Czezowski, who had been the manager of The Roxy club, which lasted barely a year on Neal Street. "He got a couple of the buildings on James Street and he was hiring them out – he shouldn't really have been sub-letting, but he was hiring them out to the other managers and whoever, and he opened the bottom of the building as a shop – PX – which was I suppose the beginning of the New Romantic stuff. His girlfriend, Susan, was a fashion designer, and she was designing that kind of stuff. Steve Strange was the shop assistant in there."

Neither Tom nor Matt Johnson can recall exactly how they first met but the meeting came about through a chance encounter with Keith Laws and his younger brother, Darren. "I think Keith's brother knew me because of my cartoons in SOUNDS. There was some sort of street festival one day in Covent Garden which was right outside my door and I was walking through it when Keith's brother started talking to me for some reason. I'm not sure if I had met him before or not, but I do remember Keith was with him, though it was his brother who did most of the talking, and he gave me a tape which was of Matt playing meandering synth music. I could tell that there was some talent there and so from that we ended up meeting."

Though he can't recall the exact details of their meeting, Matt Johnson does remember how significant it was. Meeting the trio who replied to his advert was one thing, but meeting someone who had a bit more life experience and a number of useful connections so soon after was fortuitous. "Tom was a very important person because he was extremely encouraging. He was about ten years older than me, and seemed quite sophisticated. He used to wear his long mac, a trilby hat, and smoke cheroots. Meeting Tom was very significant because he gave me a lot of self-belief. He said, 'I think it's brilliant what you're doing,' and was the first person who had ever said that to me. It gave me such a lift. I played him all the demos and bits and pieces, and he really believed in us. We would rehearse at Tom's office, and sometimes sleep there. I remember this damp mattress in the basement… I would sleep anywhere in those days."

It was Tom who had arranged the gig that was to see the debut live performance of The The. Round the corner from his office, on King Street, was The Africa Centre, which had been opened as an arts centre in 1964 by President Kaunda of Zambia. By 1979 it was hosting an eclectic variety of events, music and otherwise, and Tom Johnston managed to hire the concert space for May 9, 1979. "I'm promoting a gig," he told the teenager he had decided to take under his wing, "and I'd like to put you on." They would be third on the bill, below Scritti Politti and PragVEC.

Keith knew a woman called Anne Weight who lived in East Ham; it was at her house that they prepared for The Africa Centre gig. "The rehearsals would have been at Anne's flat. There was a horrible thing that Keith and I did once when she was out. She had a cat and we gaffer-taped it spread-eagled to the wall, but we heard her coming back so we pulled it down. The cat was in a foul mood by then."

Perhaps it was the gig that led to discussions about a name for the band. Johnson was having difficulties coming up with a suitable moniker. "I was really having trouble thinking of names, but one day Keith phoned me up and said, 'I've got an idea – The The.' I thought it was perfect because apart from the take on the idea of The Who, The Beatles, The whoever, it didn't pigeonhole us as punk or anything. It was very much a blank canvas. I just liked everything about it, and whilst I was mulling the name over I ran it by a friend, a Bohemian, hippy'-ish girl who explained that 'the the' were the last two words from one of her favourite poems by Wallace Stevens, 'The Man On The Dump', and after reading it there really was no hesitation about the name. But apparently Keith had got the name through Tom. Tom had these badges made with 'The The' on them, which was exactly Tom's sort of humour, to wear the name of a joke band, and Keith had seen it, and then claimed it was his idea." Tom acknowledges that he had made a badge with 'The The' written on it, for the exact reasons that Matt remembers. "I'm not sure what the timing was. I thought that Keith had seen my badge, but I don't really care who gets the credit. We also found out that at the time there was another The The in New York, though I think they disappeared pretty quickly." Though no one can agree who should take the credit, the important thing was that Tom Johnston could now name the band he was putting on the bill. In the wider world, meanwhile, Joe Cutler's worst nightmare was about to unfold.

On May 4 the Conservatives were returned to government with a clear majority. In her victory speech outside Number 10, Margaret Thatcher quoted her famous lines borrowed from a poem: "Where there is discord, may we bring harmony." Aside from using a line that doesn't exist in the original, she mistakenly credited St Francis of Assisi as author. The poem was in fact discovered written on the back of a painting in 1912, and attributed to him, erroneously, 712 years after his death. What is more revealing than her lack of accuracy is the choice of lines she chose to use. It was perhaps an obvious choice for her to invent the line quoted above, another echo of *ordo ab chao*, but she studiously ignored "Where there is hatred, let me sow love," or "Where there is darkness, (let me) bring light." If you view the poem in its entirety you will see that its message is a far cry from what Thatcher's government, primed by the ideologies of Friedrich Hayek and then Milton Friedman, was about to unleash on the country.

With Cutler's words no doubt resonating, Matt Johnson nonetheless had more pressing concerns, with the debut performance of his band a week hence. The spirit of the times may still have allowed you to just get up on stage with three chords and play, but this didn't make the reality any less daunting. The practicalities, rehearsals at Anne Weight's flat aside, involved recording backing tracks, which Johnson was able to do at De Wolfe. By now his career at the company had stalled and newcomers were being promoted above him. Both Johnson and Colin Lloyd Tucker had become, in more modern parlance, slackers. They would both come into work late, mess around and spend an inordinate amount of time working on their own music, rather than the jobs required by clients. Johnson had even been given his own small studio at the top of the building. Ostensibly to help motivate him, this move backfired twice over as it enabled him to operate unseen, a factor he exploited to the full – and, as it was also accessible via a staircase at the rear of the building, it meant his slack approach often went unnoticed. But not always, as the first of a series of letters warning about his time-keeping and behaviour attested to when it was sent towards the end of the year.

On the way to the gig Johnson was understandably excited. "I hadn't felt that sense of excitement in years. It was the first gig I'd done since the days of Roadstar. We were in a taxi with our instruments and the adrenaline was pumping. There was a sense that something good was about to happen." Only a few months before, he and Keith had been in the audience at Scritti Politti's first gig and would now be supporting them. This rapid progress no doubt heightened his self-belief. For Tom Johnston the concerns were mostly confined to finances. "I can remember, because of Scritti Politti most likely, there were crowds of people trying to get in. I thought we would make some money back on the gig but then we were told we could only have two hundred people in, so I lost something like £70. I think Scritti Politti cost something like seventy quid and PragVEC cost thirty." The The presumably cost nought and received the same, but then Keith and Matt probably didn't care.

With the two Akai reel-to-reel machines behind them, the trio blasted out their short set with Johnson on guitar and vocals, Laws on his Wasp synth and Peter Fenton Jones, in his one and only performance, on guitar, violin and vocals. Memories of all concerned after such a length of time are understandably scant, but Johnson recalls that with the drum machines and bass lines pre-recorded and ready to roll, "We just played over the top of those. There are some recordings of The Africa Centre... a real mess, ranting and shouting..." Steve Parry was on the guest list and remembers the night "being a rather surreal affair because as the bands played upstairs there was an Afro-Caribbean event taking place at the same time down in the basement, and as The The played, the throb of African music permeated through the floor. Matt was dressed head to toe in khaki and Keith wore a red T-shirt and black leather jacket. I really liked the abstract sound of early The The. Their music was a hybrid of electronic drum beats, effected guitar, synth, slabs of noise and distorted vocals."

Johnson's undoubted high may have been crashed by the result of the FA Cup Final the following day, when Arsenal defeated Manchester United, but any dismay over that would have been short-lived, as it wasn't long before The The were to hit the stage again, now as a duo. This time the connection was partner-in-crime at De Wolfe, Lloyd Tucker. Plain Characters had recorded a second single, 'Man In The Railings', more synth-based than their debut, and to help promote it were playing at Acklam Hall, under the Westway, on June 14. They invited The The to support and gave a free copy of their single to the first fifty people through the door.

By this time Johnson had made acquaintance with Bruce Gilbert and Graham Lewis of Wire, through Tom Johnston. Wire had formed in late 1976 and though they were present and correct at the vanguard of the punk movement had always stood apart. More avant-garde than most of their contemporaries, it wouldn't be a stretch to say that the seeds of post-punk lay in their musical ethos, and they were about to become the next significant part of Johnson's trajectory, a role that would culminate three years later when their producer, Mike Thorne, would man the controls at two recording sessions for The The in New York, and their engineer, Paul Hardiman, would subsequently work on *Soul Mining*.

The White Lion was the pub of choice for many of the people who worked in and around James Street. Where once it had been packed with market porters, now it was photographers, journalists, musicians and other creative souls. Johnson's initial contact with the Wire duo was purely social but, with Tom Johnston's input, the pair were made aware of the talents and ambitions of this blond-haired youth who didn't look old enough to be in the pub in the first place, let alone have the fruits of his musical endeavours on various self-produced demo tapes. It wasn't long before the talk turned to action and Gilbert and Lewis offered The The two support slots on their forthcoming tour to promote their third album, *154*. Both dates were at the Notre Dame Hall, just off Leicester Square.

Having played only two gigs prior to this, some proper rehearsal time was deemed by all concerned a wise move, and the members of the band This Heat kindly offered their time and space at their Cold Storage facility in Acre Lane, Brixton. Here Johnson and Laws rehearsed and recorded their backing tapes. This Heat, like Wire, were very much on the avant-garde end of the musical spectrum and had modelled their rehearsal rooms on Can's Inner Space, another indicator of the underlying importance of the 1970s German music scene on the punk and post-punk environment of England. When Johnson and Laws weren't practising they would sometimes just hang around, and Johnson acknowledges his good fortune in being part of their orbit. "They were a brilliant band, lovely guys and extremely encouraging and generous with their advice. They used to let us watch them rehearse and I found it quite inspiring as these guys really knew their instruments but were very experimental. I was lucky to be taken under the wing somewhat by two of the most creative bands of that era."

Being a much bigger deal than the first two concerts, the forthcoming dates with Wire led to a certain amount of anxiety; Johnson's way of dealing with this was to take his mind off it with something equally stressful. "I was very nervous about this gig; it was a big deal for Keith and me. Around this time I was taking driving lessons and so when my driving instructor asked me when I wanted to take my test I chose the day of our first gig with Wire, so I had two things to worry about and they kind of cancelled each other out." Doubling up on his stressors seemed to work as on Thursday July 19, 1979 Matt Johnson, aged 17, passed his driving test at the first time of asking. The thrill of success had the hoped-for effect of calming him for the gig.

Third on the bill behind Vice Versa, The The received their first critical exposure in the music press, thanks to a review by Chris Westwood in *Record Mirror*, who chose the end of his piece to bring them into print. "Supports Vice Versa and The The depict the state of modern electronics, dropping sounds over pre-recorded rhythm patterns. Both have problems in that they lack diversity and variation, and in that their current formula tends to flirt with the one-dimensional." After pointing out that Vice Versa were destined to be compared to fellow Sheffield mavericks Cabaret Voltaire and The Human League, he suggested The The would encourage similar comparisons, but that both bands had "the facilities to become progressive. After all, the possibilities of electronics are obvious, the problem comes when reliance on all that equipment overshadows, then strangles, the ability to recognise those possibilities." With Tubeway Army at the top of the UK singles chart at this time with 'Are "Friends" Electric?' it is not surprising that the music press were considering that the increasing use of synthesizers might lead to the downfall of musical imagination as they knew it, but in reality Westwood had nothing to worry about when it came to the two support acts who would both soon move away from pure electronics, Vice Versa reinventing themselves as ABC.

Though Westwood's review was the first printed opinion of the duo, they had in fact appeared in the 'inkies' the week before when their support slot with Wire made the gig news pages, accompanied by a photograph of Matt and Keith with guitar and keyboard respectively. This came from a shoot with photographer Peter Ashworth, yet another figure from the James Street axis, who was working in a studio in Cubitt's Yard that would later become the home of Peter Fluck and Roger Law and their Spitting Image project. The session involved the pair lying on a black groundsheet with their instruments. Of the two, Keith had the trickiest pose, having to 'sit' on a chair that was on its side on the floor, whilst somehow balancing his Korg synth on his knees. The intention was to have the duo appear as if they were floating in mid-air with their instruments.

Though still living with his parents above the pub in Loughton, Johnson was spending most of his time up West or out and about with old school pals, something facilitated by the fact that he could now drive. His dad bought him an old Vauxhall Viva from a car auction his Uncle Freddie took him to, and he enjoyed the freedom it brought, no doubt making up for the disappointment he had faced when Shirley vetoed the motorbike. It wasn't long, however, before he wrote off the Viva and it was replaced by a Ford Escort, which he also wrote off, suggesting that car trouble might have been genetic in the Johnson family. This being the era when drink-driving was more common and wearing of seat belts was yet to be made law, it is perhaps surprising that he didn't come to harm when driving round the roads of Essex, but like nearly everyone before and after him, having a car was a rite of passage that marked a significant step towards independence. With his work and social life up West he was a typical teenager using home as one of many places in which to crash for the night, and so younger brother Gerard's memories of him during this time were of an intermittent presence.

Many of his evenings were spent going to gigs, most often with Keith in tow, sometimes with Charles Blackburn. The one that sticks in his memory the most was the four-night festival of bands at the YMCA, off Tottenham Court Road, at the beginning of August, boasting a line-up that included Joy Division, Echo & The Bunnymen, The Fall, Throbbing Gristle, Cabaret Voltaire and Teardrop Explodes, among others. Promoted by Final Solution it was a clear signal that the music scene had taken a decisive turn away from the three-chord thrash of punk.

Not having a girlfriend at the time meant that he was out with his friends constantly. "It was a very male-dominated period of my life. There weren't many women around really. We would see girls and lust after them but I was too shy when it came to women so I would never get to talk to them. I remember Tom Johnston never seemed to have trouble with women at all, he always seemed to have lots of ladies around him. I remember him giving me some advice, telling me to just be myself and talk to girls as if they were friends. It was no big deal." As sound as the advice was, it would be a while before Matt overcame this teenage shyness when it came to the opposite sex, so for now, life was all about the music.

6

EITHER YOU EAT LIFE, OR IT EATS YOU

IN JANUARY 1980 IT WOULD HAVE BEEN DIFFICULT FOR MATT Johnson to see what was ahead, both personally and artistically. World events that would later become artistic concerns were equally hiding what surprises they had in store. The Soviet intrusion into Afghanistan was, to most observers, a straightforward story of aggression by a major power. In January 1980 it was seemingly about the desires of Leonid Brezhnev; who was to know about the desires of Zbigniew Brzezinski?

Yet there it was… a deployment of Soviet troops in December 1979 that would register as a blip on Matt Johnson's mental radar but years later would grow into something that would infuse his artistic dreams. That Christmas he had more pressing concerns, the main one of which being how to break the news to his parents that he no longer had a job. His solution, for the time being, was to ignore the problem, and just not tell them. To his credit, this tactic was looking fairly successful throughout most of January, but eventually Eddie Johnson's curiosity over the length of his son's Christmas holiday got the better of him and he asked him when he was due to return to work at De Wolfe. With unemployment figures steadily rising it wasn't the best of times to admit that he had walked out of a steady job. He tried to justify his decision by saying that he was doing his music now and would have more time to focus on that. Eddie and Shirley were having none of it. Even if he had played a concert supporting Wire, whoever they were, the money wasn't exactly rolling in, was it? Not even creeping in.

"It'll be fine," Johnson said, but this less than robust argument disintegrated on impact from the withering looks on his parents' faces. Shirley, though she didn't exactly drag her son by the ear to the Job Centre, made it clear that the expectation was that he get a job. For his parents, who had grown up with a work ethic typical of their class, the idea of signing on was not very welcome. For Johnson, and many teenagers like him, being unemployed was seen as a kind of unofficial arts grant, an opportunity to pursue creative ambitions, particularly those involving music. If it hadn't been for art colleges and the dole, then it is reasonable to suggest popular music might never have existed in the expansive and inventive form that it did.

Devoid, for the time being at least, of any other responsibility other than signing his name once every two weeks, he was free to continue pursuing his musical ambitions. As he didn't know anyone in the area, and had little inclination to rectify this, he would spend most of his time in his makeshift studio in The Crown's cellar, surrounded by cheap effects pedals, a few instruments and his reel-to-reel. In this subterranean world he would spend hours experimenting, creating drum loops, Indian drone-like sounds and psychedelic soundscapes that were closer to musique concrete than post-punk. Often Andrew would be down there too, working on his painting or drawing. Inevitably they would spend time just talking, swapping ideas maybe, eating into Eddie's profits by taking plentiful advantage of the stocks of beer and cigarettes that were within easy reach. From the perspective of someone who was still a teenager, life looked pretty good. There was all the time in the world to make music, an unlimited supply of free beer and fags, and a home to treat like a hotel. Some days the pair did nothing much at all, as Matt admits. "Andrew and I would often be horizontal on the sofas in the flat above the pub nursing hangovers whilst watching daytime TV or films on VHS. Our dad might come upstairs and shout and holler about what lazy bastards we were and Andrew and I would just look at each other, shrug and wonder what his problem was. Eugene on the other hand was a much bigger help to our parents. He was so energetic, kind and thoughtful and would be tidying up and trying to make things nice for our parents."

If he wasn't in his studio, or perfecting the art of loafing around on the sofa, Johnson was reading, in an attempt to educate himself based on a curriculum of his own devising. "During this time I really began in earnest my journey of self-improvement, as I now began to feel a certain stigma of having left school at 15 with zero qualifications. I bought numerous self-help books to teach myself how to become more disciplined and orderly in my thinking and in my life generally. I began reading voraciously. I started borrowing books from my dad's collection at his recommendation; Somerset Maugham, Siegfried Sassoon, Evelyn Waugh and Kingsley Amis I really enjoyed, but Graham Greene, Ernest Hemingway and George Orwell resonated even more. Then I started heading off into bookshops by myself and exploring the works of André Gide and Jean-Paul Sartre amongst others. Of particular inspiration at this time was also the American nineteenth-century New Thought movement and writers like William Walker Atkinson and Ralph Waldo Emerson. I also determined that my life's learning would be mainly based upon a philosophy of first-hand experience and to 'eat life before it ate me'."

Gigs were intermittent and not always particularly memorable, such as the occasion they played at Toyah Wilcox's birthday party – a night Johnson remembers as happening in a loft space, possibly in south London, but any other detail of which he is unable to recall. A performance at Metropolitan Wharf in Wapping sticks in his mind a bit better. He was familiar with the area, thanks to visits with Eddie, when father would tell son all about the days he worked on the docks. Wapping at the turn of the decade was one of many zones of the capital that remained in limbo, the industry of its past having deserted it and gentrification yet to take place. Warehouses that in the eighties would be turned into luxury apartments, gallery spaces and shops were mostly empty. The Anarchist Ball was just one of many events in such spaces round London where large buildings had been re-appropriated by squatters who recognised they were ideal for putting on events and performances – warehouse parties.

"There wasn't a stage, it was just a huge room with our gear set up in the middle, and everyone standing around us in a circle. I don't remember what the set would have been, but we used to improvise a lot in those days. We would have had a backing tape of some sort, we didn't really have song forms; it was more experimental, improvised, using our guitars, keyboards, effects pedals." The line-up on this occasion seems to have been Johnson, Keith Laws and Steve Parry. At one point Nag and Bendle, of DIY band The Door & The Window, joined the trio onstage. Parry's memory of the evening is still fairly vivid.

"It was chaotic and noisy because there had been no rehearsal – we literally turned up and played. I recall we played a pretty loose and improvised version of 'God Save The Queen' by the Sex Pistols. People were getting high on the music and became pretty agitated. At one point a fire broke out at the far side of the room and there was acrid smoke in the air. Buckets of water were being thrown at anything and everything. Members of the audience threw bottles and anything else for that matter at us. It all got rather nasty. I recall us all madly attempting to get our precious music equipment down flights of stone stairs outside to my Volkswagen Beetle parked in the street. I felt like I'd survived a war zone!"

Though live performances might have been thin on the ground, Johnson's first appearance on vinyl came in March 1980, thanks to the recordings he had made the previous summer with Colin Lloyd Tucker and John Hyde as The Gadgets. Colin Faver and Kevin Millens, aka concert promoters Final Solution, decided to start up a record label and Johnson introduced them to Lloyd Tucker and Hyde. They released the Plain Characters' second single, 'Man In The Railings', the cover of which depicted Bert Ashing, one of the accountants at De Wolfe. The first album on the short-lived label was The Gadgets' debut, *Gadgetree*.

With The The his main concern at this time it is perhaps understandable that Johnson's interest in The Gadgets was not particularly great. Decades later his interest in this small corner of his music career is even less, perhaps tainted by the behaviour of John Hyde, who would later re-release recordings without the permission of the other two and with a sticker on the CD that took advantage of his fame as The The. The album, however, is more than just a curiosity. Colin Lloyd Tucker recalls it with more fondness. "Unlike later records we were all in the room at the same time, taking it in turns to come up with a song or groove. I recall that Matt's songs were fully formed from the off, the lyrics all pre-written. We worked very quickly. Once we had a rhythm track, usually a drum machine, we would add synths or sometimes guitars, all heavily treated. Then Matt or me would sing. I can remember Matt with his scrap of paper reading and singing."

The recordings were done at De Wolfe studios, using down-time in exchange for publishing rights; the pressing was financed by money Hyde received for music he had recorded for a Marmite advertisement – the sound of which you no doubt either loved or hated – and was done in August 1979, with mixing a month later. A photo session took place on the roof of the De Wolfe building, with the trio looking out over the Soho skyline. The front cover, like most punk and post-punk releases of the time, didn't have a picture of the band on it; instead there was a small picture of a tree festooned with pans, cutlery and what looked like other kitchen gadgets. Johnson remembers using the De Wolfe Minimoog and Simon Park's Prophet 5, which he stored at De Wolfe, a revolutionary synth at the time owing to its polyphony. They also employed a Roland rhythm box, amongst other equipment, the sound of the eighteen tracks being for the most part minimal electronics. Guitars were heavily treated, as were some vocals. In comparison to output of the same time by someone like The Human League, it was certainly less polished or fleshed out – due to a far lower budget as much as anything else – but the results were certainly interesting and might even sound more impressive in retrospect than they did at the time.

In its review the *NME* picked out inspirations in the shape of Bowie, David Byrne and the film *Eraserhead*, presumably a reference to the 'Lady In The Radiator' song. The film was a staple of the late night cinema circuit and Matt probably saw it on one of many sojourns to the all-nighter screenings at the Scala Cinema, then on Charlotte Street, and managed by Stephen Woolley who, years later, would produce Gerard Johnson's *Hyena*, for which Johnson would write and produce the soundtrack.

New Music News were also quietly positive in their review, declaring at the outset "Yes, very good" and comparing them to Young Marble Giants: "*Gadgetree* is insidiously listenable and quite funny in an 'interesting' sort of way."

The Residents were name-checked by Johnson in an interview for the fanzine *In The City*. "I really like their approach, it's so sort of free from the music press and if they get criticised, well nobody can touch them really because no one knows who they are. It's great because they can just do whatever they want." So smitten was he that he wanted his music to appear on The Residents' own Ralph Records label; though unsuccessful in his approach he did receive a letter of encouragement by way of reply, which he has to this day.

The way that The Residents were unknowable, hiding as they did behind masks, clearly appealed to him. Not being a natural born show-off there was a large element of *look-at-me-don't-look-at-me* when it came to being in the spotlight, a curious affliction for a surprising number of performers who are equal parts drawn like moths to the glare of public attention and repelled by the very experience. Maybe it was self-consciousness, or just the post-punk disdain for stardom, for being seen as a sell-out. Maybe it was just fear of getting up on stage and laying yourself bare.

In this he certainly wasn't alone. Nor was he when it came to the typical solution of getting fortified for the occasion with alcohol, which would inevitably lead to problems if the intake outweighed the nerves. Live performance inevitably becomes somewhat shambolic under these conditions. Easy, then, to see the appeal in being anonymous, hidden behind a mask. If Johnson was self-conscious when out of his comfort zone then another ambitious teenager, also from east London, was having no such problems with being the centre of attention. As the seventies morphed into the eighties, Steve Pearce, otherwise known as Stevo, was like a small planet entering a solar system with a gravitational pull that would in short order suck a number of young, talented mavericks into its orbit.

Stevo had grown up in Dagenham, a bleak sprawl at the arse-end of east London, famous for nothing more glamorous than the A13 and the Ford car plant. A predictably rough part of town, its geographical isolation didn't do it any favours, and if you were young it was easy to fall victim to a state of inertia. Joe Pearce, Stevo's older brother, like others, sought solace in far-right ideology and, inspired by Blackpool 'punk' band Skrewdriver, became a prominent member of the National Front. Stevo didn't agree with his brother's views and his reaction to being stuck in such an entropic environment was to go West.

Like Johnson, he left school with no qualifications. He suffered from severe dyslexia but this was at a time when little was known about the disorder; it is highly probable that he received no support at school for it, other than being labelled a slow learner. Dyslexics often have trouble following things in a linear fashion, but by way of compensation can be very adept at following patterns. This might be a good way of describing the 17-year-old Stevo. He certainly wasn't linear in his approach to life and he was definitely seeing patterns emerging in the changing landscape of music in the post-punk era. Armed with a mobile disco unit that his mother had bought on HP, he launched himself as far as he could from Dagenham and ended up in the fashionable environs of the Kings Road, as stark a contrast as you could hope to invent. The Chelsea Drug Store, a fashionable three-storey emporium that had appeared in a scene in Stanley Kubrick's *A Clockwork Orange*, was where Stevo landed, as a DJ playing an eclectic mix of music that he could see would fit into a coherent whole. Much of it was electronic, and thus more forward thinking than the traditional instrumentation of most punk and even post-punk music. A poster advertising his night for March 17, 1980, promised music from 'Cabaret Voltaire, Human League, Numan, Foxx, Devo, Orchestral Manoeuvres, Ultravox, Kraftwerk, T. Gristle, Bowie'. He saw this music as the future, so it was easy to use words like *futurist* when promoting his events.

In those days punters might only notice the DJ if they went up to the decks and requested a particular record. It was a long way from the celebrity status of later years. Stevo, however, was having none of this and would draw attention to himself by wearing outrageous outfits, even on one occasion performing naked. Making surreal announcements on the microphone or mixing Disney records at half-speed into something like Cabaret Voltaire was also part of his approach to the job in hand, so, not surprisingly, his reputation grew.

Seeing patterns convinced Stevo that some kind of scene was emerging and it was his job to pull the disparate elements together somehow. The nascent New Romantic scene was also soundtracking its club nights with old and new electronic music, where the synthesizer was the weapon of choice over the guitar and the resulting textures made for a sound that often seemed – there was no other word for it – futuristic. And being of the future, so to speak, there wasn't quite enough of it to go round. While the New Romantics were happy to pad things out with large dollops of David Bowie and Roxy Music, as much for the respective fashion statements as the music of each, Stevo was increasingly looking towards totally electronic music, something not romantic but industrial. He guessed that while some such music was making its way onto vinyl, there was probably a lot more out there that was yet to break out from the confines of live performances or demo tapes. So he started to track it down, often visiting the Virgin Records shop on Oxford Street where Jim Thirlwell worked. "He would come down wearing this blue, kind of jumpsuit-type thing. He was younger than me. Sometimes he would buy records; we had a really great singles department because we had a lot of weird German imports and stuff you just couldn't get anywhere else." Thirlwell, who had come to London two years before from Australia, would eventually provide Stevo with music of his own, rather than German imports; he was also, unknown to Johnson at this point, attending most of the few gigs that The The played. Stevo now turned his attentions towards performance as well, branching out into promoting live acts.

He was a year younger than Johnson, so what he was about to achieve, from the ground up, was quite remarkable. Having secured the services of Cabaret Voltaire he needed another act to support them at a gig he was promoting at the Retford Porterhouse, and turned to The The. "Stevo kept phoning up. There was an old cream-coloured GPO phone at The Crown and it had little buttons with lights on it so you could put it through to the upstairs or downstairs, so the phone would ring and then there would be a buzz and it would be my dad, 'Oh it's for you again! Some bloke ending in "O".' Stevo called up about three or four times, begging us to play this gig, and I kept saying no. I had heard from people that he was trouble, maybe from Tony Mayo, who was in Naked Lunch. But he just seemed a bit odd, saying, 'Will you do this gig?' I said, 'How much?' but he said there was no money in it. I thought, 'fuck that', I'm not going all the way up there for no money. In the end we did it for a crate of beer. We travelled up in a transit van with a couple of skinheads, nice blokes they were, who were connected to Stevo somehow and roadied for the event. Whether we got the crate of beer or not I can't remember."

Neither can he remember anything about the gig, which took place on May 30, while the only lasting impression for Mal Mallinder of Cabaret Voltaire was of sartorial matters. "Stevo had a shirt on that I think he'd made himself with a Throbbing Gristle flash on it, and me and Matt were taking the piss out of it, going on about his 'Throbbing Sherman' because it was like a shit Ben Sherman but with a Throbbing Gristle flash on it." At the gig, Steve Hovington of B-Movie handed Stevo a tape, and he phoned the following day offering them a gig at The Bridge House in Canning Town, supporting Blancmange.

So by the summer of 1980 things were beginning to happen in a bit of a rush for both Johnson and Stevo, the only fly in the ointment of all this excitement for the former being the fact that he now, despite his best efforts, found himself employed. Eddie Johnson remembers that it was his insistence, more than Shirley's, that Matt get a job, but between them they put an end to a stint on the dole that had lasted several months. In the same building block as the pub were the offices of an insurance company called Walrond & Scarman and a fair number of employees would have a drink in The Crown after work. Shirley, taking advantage of this fact, asked to be kept informed of any vacancies in the future. One day a job as post boy came up and that was it; Matt Johnson didn't stand a chance.

The job entailed twice-monthly trips from Loughton to the City Document Exchange; his first day gave him a sinking feeling. "I was taken up to Liverpool Street on the train by the guy who was showing me the ropes. He was pleasant enough; grey hair, grey moustache, grey suit and a grey face, but I remember him saying, 'Oh you'll like this company. I've been here for forty years,' or something like that and I just thought, 'Oh my God, you've got to be fucking joking?'" With all those years stretching out in his mind like a life sentence he decided from the very beginning to get the sack. One man in particular, Mr Robinson, had it in for him. Perhaps it was a family thing, as he was to learn that Uncle Kenny had also worked for the company, many years before, and Kenny confirmed that Mr Robinson had been a bit of a rotter in his day too, or words to that effect. Robinson was the sort of man who would save all his outgoing mail, hide it even; then just as young

Johnson was hoping to leave for home would hand over this huge hidden stash that would then have to be sorted, addressed and put through the franking machine. No doubt while Johnson was doing all this he would see Robinson putting on his coat and leaving. That sort of bloke. Getting the sack, however, wasn't as easy as he had hoped and even when he later gave his superiors enough reason to dispense with his services it was a delicate decision for them, drinking as they habitually did in his parents' pub.

Outside of work, things were moving in the right direction. He had already been touting his own demos, recorded either in his makeshift studio in the cellar of The Crown or the small studio at De Wolfe. "I was hanging around at a lot of the independent record companies – Rough Trade, Cherry Red, 4AD – I regularly did the rounds. It was a bit more relaxed in those days. I was at gigs all the time and everybody knew each other, it was a very small scene. You would always see people… Daniel Miller, Ivo, Geoff Travis, Mike Alway… they were all at the gigs, so you would chat with them, have a beer with them, ask if you could come and play your demos, whatever, and that's what I used to do. I had about three meetings with Geoff Travis at Rough Trade. He was very nice, would sit and talk to me, listen to my demos and say, 'You're not quite there Matt, you're nearly there, keep going.'"

Another voice of encouragement belonged to Rod Pearce of Fetish Records. "I remember meeting him at a gig at the Marquee when I was selling copies of *See Without Being Seen*. And he was so encouraging to me it really put a spring in my step."

Kind words of encouragement were one thing but, like any aspiring musician, it was actual endorsement in the shape of a record contract that was the goal. Getting your own music pressed on a piece of 7-inch plastic that you could hold in your hand. That's what it was all about. So when Tom Johnston decided that The The needed to get into a studio and get some songs down onto tape he enlisted the help of his mates Graham Lewis and Bruce Gilbert. The pair were embarking on their own Wire offshoots in the guises of Dome and Cupol, recording at Blackwing Studios

127

with engineer Eric Radcliffe. The first Dome album was recorded there in March and April 1980; it was probably around this time that the pair took Keith and Matt into Blackwing to lay down two tracks, 'Controversial Subject' and 'Black And White'. Radcliffe engineered and Gilbert and Lewis produced. The session was paid for by Tom Johnston. For Matt, who had been schooled by De Wolfe in the ways of the studio, it was inspiring to see a different way of working. Maybe the experimental sound that the Wire duo had produced for their own recent Cupol output bled into the session, as the resulting two tracks, though more urgent and spiky, had more than a hint of the sound that had been realised on 'Like This For Ages' and 'Kluba Cupol', due for a 12-inch release on 4AD that July.

The 4AD office was above the Beggars Banquet shop in Earls Court, and this is where Tom Johnston took a cassette copy of the two songs Gilbert and Lewis had produced for The The. The fledgling label was being run by Ivo Watts-Russell and Peter Kent. Ivo was the first to hear the tape and was suitably impressed. "It was the overall sound as much as the songs that piqued my interest. I couldn't really find a point of reference, which is always a good thing." He told Johnston that he would like to release the two tracks as a single, but would have to let Peter Kent hear them first. Kent listened just once and gave his approval, so Ivo suggested that it might be a good idea to meet Johnson. "I met him in a pub near the shop, to confirm things. He was rather shy, awkward in himself, and decidedly more interested in the football being shown on the pub's television than anything I had to say."

It was Tom who had broken the news of 4AD's interest, and while Johnson might not have given away any signs of excitement in the pub with Ivo, by the time he and Laws were in the label office they didn't even bother to ask for a lawyer to check the contract, such was their desire to sign on the dotted line and confirm their status as recording artists – even if the home to their musical efforts was something of an unknown quantity, yet to establish its own identity. The fact that Gilbert and Lewis recommended them was a good enough endorsement and Johnson liked both Ivo and Peter Kent, so signing didn't really take a second thought.

'Controversial Subject' was released in August, 1980. In between recording it and releasing it The The had doubled in size. Tom Johnston was added on bass guitar and Peter Ashworth replaced the drum machine with a real kit. Exactly when the pair became members of the band isn't clear. Johnson concedes that Tom contributed to the lyrics of 'Controversial Subject', and Tom Johnston recalls that he and Peter Ashworth contributed percussive sounds in the shape of stones taken from a nearby building site that they rattled in bags. Whatever their contribution, Johnson decided that, as members of the band, they should appear on the record's label and thus they were both given a songwriting credit. In fact Tom Johnston should perhaps get more than just credit as, being the person who paid for the recording sessions, it was he, technically, who owned the rights to 'Controversial Subject' and not 4AD.

Tom, earning his bread and butter as a cartoonist, wouldn't have had the temerity to consider himself a musician, but nevertheless had a good enough grasp of the bass to perform with Graham and Bruce. He remembers less about being on stage with The The than he does about rehearsals, or the lack of them. "We never rehearsed. Well, I think Matt and I rehearsed, maybe we did have one small rehearsal." This laissez-faire attitude to playing live would lead to a number of shambolic performances. Peter Ashworth, like Tom Johnston, was pursuing a career outside of music. He had taken the first publicity shots of Johnson and Laws and would go on to be one of the most successful rock and pop photographers of the eighties. He had, however, been playing drums for over a decade, teaching himself by listening to Ginger Baker, Mitch Mitchell and Jaki Liebezeit. He had seen The The play – either on stage or in a rehearsal space – so already had an idea of where he might fit in.

"When Matt was playing with Keith it was quite an art-show I think. I liked their weirdness. I liked the fact that they wanted to be out there; I liked the fact that they didn't want to be pop stars or anything like that. It was challenging stuff, and Matt was already playing with tape-loops. He didn't sing in the way that most singers would so his vocal instrument was quite unusual. His subject matter was unusual. There was this layering of jangling guitars that was more akin to chaotic bell-ringing. It was interesting, but unfocused. It suggested to me, as a drummer, that what wasn't in the group was a solid background, so I could see a place for myself."

Ashworth's memory of rehearsals contradicts Tom Johnston's. "We would always rehearse seriously before gigs. Actually getting a gig may have been the prod needed to get rehearsing, which may not have happened otherwise. Matt would often come in with some sort of idea; he would play through something. Keith would sort of interject, trying to find some chords to fit in – almost like a rhythm guitarist – and I would try and play some sort of pattern. Andy Czezowski, who ran the Fridge, had a rehearsal studio by London Bridge, or Borough Market, and we used to rehearse there, and I was the only one with a car, so I was the one who had to drive everyone and the gear around."

The The were now a four-piece of Johnson, Laws, Johnston and Ashworth, with rehearsals taking place after a fashion, and a single to their name. The contrast between the life Johnson was leading as a musician and the one he had to endure from Monday to Friday at Walrond & Scarman was sharp. Tom Johnston knew just how much he hated this nine-to-five role, and not long after he had met him had even tried to ease Eddie and Shirley's doubts about their son's musical ambitions. "Matt's parents were worried about him going into the music scene. Matt's mother wanted him to go into insurance, and I remember her ringing me up and asking me, was I really, really sure that it was a good idea for him to be doing this? And I told her it definitely was. And what was funny was, I didn't see her for a few years, but then next time I saw her Matt had invited me along to the premiere of the *Infected* movie at the Electric Cinema in Notting Hill or somewhere, and his mum turned up and she had become a rock'n'roll mum with a big cowboy hat and stuff. She was very sweet. I got on really well with her and Eddie."

For now there was no cowboy hat in Shirley's wardrobe, but each morning Johnson would leave the house feeling uncomfortable in his suit and mac and go to work. The occasional forays to the City Document Exchange were the only respite. "They had an office at 36 Spital Square, in Spitalfields. I would try and get my work done sharpish so I could then go off on my own. Around that time Spitalfields was like it was in those Don McCullin photographs, full of dossers and really derelict. I used to walk round there and up to Shoreditch." Tom Johnston felt sorry for him, but he sensed this job wasn't going to last. While it was lasting, though, being a post boy turned out to have at least one perk: Johnson used the post-room facilities to send out copies of 'Controversial Subject'.

One of the first performances of the expanded line-up was a few weeks before the single was released, at the 101 Club in Clapham. Matt's memory of the evening is rather hazy but certain details stay in focus. "I remember Keith in a pyjama top he used to wear. He got really drunk, grabbed the microphone and shouted something like, 'We're from the East End ain't we.' I think that was the last time I got so drunk on stage. I was so bad I couldn't get the jack-lead into the guitar. It was a horrible feeling, being completely out of control, but then again that was part of it; you would drink when you were rehearsing, you would drink on stage, you would drink before you were playing, when you were playing, after you played. But that was the gig where I thought, 'I can't do this any more.'

Being so drunk it is not surprising that he has no real memory of the performance that night, but one can guess it wasn't exactly controlled. Neither were things afterwards when the band had a row with the venue manager and some of them jumped up and down on the roof of his car. Not surprisingly they were banned from playing there again but luckily none of this appeared to put off Ivo, who had been in the audience with Peter Kent. He only recalls seeing the band perform a couple of times, once as a duo –

Johnson and Peter Ashworth – in a pub in Richmond, which Mike Alway arranged. Johnson thinks it is the only time they played as a duo. "We did not play very well and both of us felt a bit depressed about it afterwards." Ivo does recall the live experience of the band as being somewhat unprofessional. "I think the kindest thing one might say is that their performances were diabolically under-rehearsed."

They played at the Rock Garden twice in quick succession, the first time being at the end of July, when they were supported by Dance Chapter. One reviewer of this gig offers perhaps the best description available in print of what The The were like as a live act at this early stage. "They played a short, but quite incredible set. From the opener, 'Controversial Subject', which I believe is their single, we were well and truly treated. With coloured slides projecting onto them as they hovered in the blackness, it was rather like watching something quite unnatural playing. Matt, their guitarist, didn't so much play his guitar as try to pull the strings off the fretboard. More than a ghost of Syd Barrett lurked around on this stage. Even Triash, the drummer, looked uncannily like him, sitting whirling like a chained-up dervish over his drum-kit, whilst Tom Johnston held down the axis with some extremely imaginative bass. You could have almost called it psychedelic but they certainly didn't waste as much space as those of that particular ilk. True, the vocals could have been stronger and little things need polishing, but ultimately they were the best band of the evening and with more time and experience, could be an interesting option."

The single got encouraging rather than glowing reviews, but it did well in the independent charts, the barometer of cool for all serious fans of music, a generation of whom had taken punk's antipathy towards selling out to heart. John Peel liked 'Controversial Subject' enough to play it on his show, and this being the jungle-drums of the underground scene, it meant that The The were being heard by the arbiters of taste and fans of tasteful music in towns and cities across the land.

August was a busy month for Johnson. Though he no longer worked there, he was back at De Wolfe to make use of their studio and record some tracks for an album project with the working title of *Spirits*. With Colin Lloyd Tucker engineering, 'What Stanley Saw', 'Perspectives And Distortions' and 'Ex Mar Boo' were all laid down to tape. To support their single, The The played again at Covent Garden's Rock Garden for a 4AD evening, with The Birthday Party. The two bands were photographed at the rehearsal rooms on Clink Street the day before by Ashworth.

Attending this gig was Alessandra Sartore, who had decided that London was more exciting than her native Italy and had ditched the idea of going to university, to the dismay of her parents. Working in low-paid jobs like hotel maid and waitress, she began contributing, without pay, gig reviews, interviews and photographs to Italian magazines such as *Rockerilla* and *The Wild Bunch*. One night she had travelled as far as Canning Town, to The Bridge House, a mock Tudor affair nestled amid the flyovers and concrete wasteland of this unloved part of the capital. There was no tube here, you had to get the bus, unless you got off a tube at West Ham and walked down Manor Road, but that wouldn't have been a good move at night for a stranger to these parts. Alessandra looked at the dismal scenery from the top deck of the bus and felt like she was travelling to the end of the world. "I can't remember what band I went to see but I think Plain Characters were on the bill and that is why Matt was there. At that time I was going round reviewing anything that caught my eye so I could write about something new. I just remember that I was standing by a pillar, and this eager, curly-haired boy comes over and says, 'Who do you write for?' And I said, 'If you think I write for *NME* or *SOUNDS*, I'm afraid not, it's an Italian magazine, more like a fanzine,' and we carried on chatting. Phone numbers must have been exchanged. I was living in Highbury and he came to visit. He was working for some insurance company, a job his mum found for him, and had to wear awful clothes – a suit and beige mac. He was so ill at ease, but at the same time rather cocky."

Through this meeting, Alessandra, who referred to herself as Alex, found herself taking photographs at the Rock Garden gig. She can't remember who did what – can't even remember The Birthday Party, even though she was a fan – but there was some trouble. Drunken trouble that saw Johnson attack the PA in a fit of frustration with the performance and the poor sound, or maybe the audience, which, according to Sartore, was thin on the ground. Equally frustrated, perhaps by the sound quality, the audience took to flinging glasses at the stage; the upshot was Johnson taking things out on what he considered the source of the problem, introducing his guitar with some violence to the PA system.

Peter Ashworth remembers the tension ramping up before gigs. "It was always nerve-racking. Matt and Keith both had bad skin at the time and that might have made them feel self-conscious on top of nervous. It was amazing that we got on a stage at all quite frankly. Matt had more nerve, I think, whereas Keith seemed like he would have preferred being at the back, which is where I was. Matt was the one out front with the microphone, singing out of tune and not giving a fucking monkey's. We would sometimes clear a room when we played because people didn't have a clue what they were going to get, and they weren't sure they liked it when they got it. It was more a time for us to try stuff out in a different space to a rehearsal room. We weren't doing it for the audience, we were doing this more for ourselves. Which was quite an interesting thing for me to do, because I had been playing in bands up till then where the aim was to impress people and get a girlfriend. We started getting really interesting hangers-on, people like Betty Page, who wrote for SOUNDS. There was a whole bunch of interesting people beginning to be attracted, and beginning to turn up."

One thing does stick in Johnson's mind about the evening, more than the PA incident. "What I do remember about that gig was that we ended up getting very drunk with The Birthday Party. I had these bizarre silver wrestling boots at the time which didn't have a proper sole on them, so I used to slip over when the streets were wet from rain. I used to go to the Lonsdale shop in Beak Street during lunchtime, when I worked at De Wolfe. There was a boxer who served us called Roy Gumbs, and who went on to become a British champion. Me and my friend Martin Brand from De Wolfe were always down there, buying our Lonsdale T-shirts, boots and stuff; this is before they were fashionable, and there were these bizarre silver wrestling boots that I bought and used to wear on stage.

"I ended up back at the squat where The Birthday Party were living. The guys from The Birthday Party woke up, came downstairs, and all they saw was a blanket with a pair of silver wrestling boots poking out the end, and that was me. I didn't know where I was. I just remember there being newspapers everywhere; maybe they were using old newspapers as wallpaper." Thirlwell, who lived at the flat, was on his way to work at Virgin Records, and spotted Johnson on the sofa as he left, but didn't know who he was. He soon would.

The The were then banned from the Rock Garden. In fact, they would soon have a rap sheet somewhat at odds with their image. As well as the Covent Garden venue they were also banned by the 101 Club, Bridge House, Clarendon Hotel and Acklam Hall. They seemingly only had to turn up and play and something would happen that resulted in a ban – damaging a support band's van, wrecking the house PA, drunk and disorderly behaviour and even 'borrowing' a bouncer's cardigan which just happened to contain the keys to the venue.

More positively, all the hanging out in record label offices was beginning to bear fruit. Cherry Red were producing a compilation album and looking for tracks to fill it. Johnson, who had been bringing in his demos, was thus in the right place at the right time. "At Cherry Red there was Theo Chalmers, who later signed me to a publishing deal, Mike Alway, and Ian McNay, the owner, who used to go and study with the Baghwan, the Orange People in Oregon, before the Baghwan was unmasked as a serial philanderer and crook. Ian wasn't unfriendly, he would smile and say hello, but he was sort of aloof. Mike Alway was a very enthusiastic person. I used to go up there and play my demos, and *Perspectives And Distortion* was a title I took from one of Andrew's paintings. They said could they license the title off me, gave me ten quid or whatever. The only recording they wanted to license and include on the compilation was 'What Stanley Saw', but the album also had my – or rather Andrew's – title."

Perspectives And Distortion wouldn't be released until early the following year, and would barely be noticed, but by then Johnson's career was continuing on a steep upward curve and the fact that this song got lost in the rush was hardly any kind of setback. Final Solution, meanwhile, were wasting no time in getting more Gadgets product out there. A second album, *Love, Curiosity, Freckles & Doubt*, was released only a matter of months after the debut. As prolific as the trio were, a close look at the writing credits reveals a less cohesive effort. Matt has sole songwriting credit for only two numbers and joint credit on a further two. His songs, 'Checking To Make Sure' and 'She's Queen Of Toyland', sound like his heart wasn't really in it, and the best work belongs to Colin Lloyd Tucker. The other thing of note about the album is that film director Peter Greenaway provided the words for the song 'Happy Enido'. The Gadgets were clearly spending less time together in the studio and had only been a side project for Johnson. His keenness to be in the studio and work on music had led to his involvement, but his own project was now taking off and was the obvious priority. Added to this was the deterioration in his relationship with John Hyde that would come to a head with the third album the following year.

His efforts to get sacked from Walrond & Scarman, meanwhile, revolved around turning up late for work and behaving in an increasingly surly way. This campaign paid dividends and escape from the straitjacket of low-paid conformity came six months after he had started. All he had to show for his efforts there was an intimate knowledge of the streets around Spitalfields, Shoreditch and the City, and an antipathy for Mr Robinson. He now gleefully seized the opportunity to exact some kind of revenge for all those five-minutes-to-five mail-outs. For once he was happy for Mr Robinson to leave the building before him, because he had earlier gone to the staff car park at the rear of the building and jammed a potato in the exhaust of Robinson's pale blue Vauxhall Cavalier, before grabbing the windscreen wipers and bending them out of shape. "It was childish, I know, but I was a teenager and he had been really nasty to me the whole time I worked there." He watched from a window as his nemesis left work and went out to his car in the pouring rain. Robinson, of course, turned on his windscreen wipers and the buckled blades shuddered across the glass. "I think he even looked up at the windows, and I was peeping out the curtains." Perhaps, with perfect comic timing, as Robinson left his car to examine the damaged wipers and turned to shake a fist at the young tyke looking down at him laughing, the potato exploded from his exhaust.

Eddie and Shirley were naturally disappointed, but by now their son had a single in the independent charts and all his talk about a career in music was beginning to look a little less like teenage bluster. For Johnson, a return to days where he was free to do as he pleased meant more hanging out in record company offices or the associated shops that were usually on the floor beneath, thus anyone wanting to find him could try Rough Trade, Beggars Banquet or Cherry Red and have a reasonable chance of succeeding on any given day. In the evenings he could be anywhere, but more than likely it wasn't in the flat above The Crown.

Andrew was now studying Fine Art at Camberwell and had left home, while Matt's continuing aversion to the Essex suburbs led him to crash wherever he could in London, whenever he could. To him Loughton just meant his studio in the pub cellar, while London meant everything else that mattered, and what mattered most. London represented the future that he could feel was within his grasp and a constantly changing carousel of spare beds, sofas and squats within the city enabled him to keep himself plugged in to the small but growing scene. At one point he tried squatting, rather than just stopping over at one of the countless squats scattered around the streets of London, a result of post-war neglect and a slow exodus from the city that meant empty buildings were two-a-penny and many of them were very central.

"There was a friend of Tom Johnston's called Jez who was quite a character. He knew this couple who were junkies, though I didn't know it at the time. They were really nice and they had broken into this empty flat in Battersea and said there was another one above them and why didn't we move in? So Jez and I went over there with our stuff, bought some cheap furniture and one of those hippy lampshades made out of tissue paper. I think we painted the place as well. My mum and dad didn't want me to go but as it turns out things didn't really work out for me there and it wasn't very long before I was back home again."

Back home but hardly ever there, like many a teenager of the time. He would soon be gone again though, this time to move in with Alex, who he had struck up a friendship with. "Sometimes I would go with her to the all-night screenings at the Scala, or to gigs. She was living in Highbury and I would stay over now and then before I moved in with her." Alex herself recalls how moving into a different flat in Aubert Road, with her friend Akane, meant Matt could make the move to London that he craved. "I don't know how we stayed in touch after we first met at The Bridge House because in those days you always had to leave messages for people as they were usually never in when you phoned. I knew Matt wanted to leave, wanted to be in town. The flat Akane and I shared was the ground floor of a huge house. It consisted of two self-contained bedsits and there was a communal bathroom upstairs. I took the front room and the landlord had partitioned it so there was a further two rooms – one a kitchen and the other a kind of store cupboard. So knowing Matt was desperate to get away from Loughton I offered him this store cupboard room in exchange for some help with the rent. It was the size of a small bathroom but without a window. I think he had left the insurance job by then.

"Akane was probably in her flat all day making art or doing

another course at Sir John Cass and I was out all day and evenings waitressing in Old Brompton Road, so Matt was at home in my flat messing around, making music or whatever. He must have had his tape deck and guitar at least. I would come home late and be really tired but because he had got up late he was still full of energy and would want to talk or play me a song. To get in and out of his store cupboard he had to go through my room, so sometimes I would never get any peace. My bed was just a mattress on the floor and one night he rode Akane's bike over my bed with me in it, just to get me up so he had someone to talk to."

Meanwhile Stevo had expanded his operations and was now DJing and promoting at places other than the Chelsea Drug Store. Music paper *SOUNDS* was now printing his 'Futurist Chart', which soon afterwards would also appear in the pages of *Record Mirror*. In the summer he took over from Rusty Egan as the DJ at Billy's. One night he, Matt and Keith Laws watched Charlie Blackburn performing with Marble Index, only their second gig. Stevo had big plans for B-Movie and had also started managing another group, an electronic duo from Leeds called Soft Cell. Talking to major labels with the chutzpah that perhaps only youth can bring, the A&R fraternity in London began to fall for his expansive confidence and increasingly flamboyant approach. This led to a licensing deal with Phonogram; now Stevo was busy building a roster of acts that could fill a compilation album that would be the vinyl equivalent of his Futurist Chart. All while still living at home in the tiny terrace on Rosedale Road, Dagenham with his parents.

Stevo was also very persistent and he wasn't going to give up on the idea of adding The The to his slowly expanding operation, despite Matt initially resisting his repeated advances. He would phone The Crown and Eddie would invariably pick up the phone. "At the time there was Ivo, Theo from Cherry Red and now Stevo, so my dad said, 'What is it with all these blokes called "O" who keep phoning you up? Is it a cult?' He would answer the phone and say, 'Who is it?' and it would be, 'It's Theo, it's Ivo, it's Stevo.' Anyway, Stevo kept on and on, like a dog with a bone and so eventually we agreed to appear on the compilation." At the same time Neu Electrikk were persuaded to join him, and Steve Parry recalls the tactics he employed. "Stevo rang and went into hyperbole – he was a DJ, manager and record promoter, and he was eager to manage Neu Electrikk. I asked him who he currently managed and he said, The The, which I thought was a coincidence, so being inquisitive I phoned Matt and asked him whether or not The The were managed by Stevo. To my surprise he responded by saying that Stevo had also been in contact with him and had pulled the same trick, this time saying he was the manager of Neu Electrikk."

Johnson and Laws decided to contribute a track that they had recorded earlier in the year at Elephant Studios in south London, recommended to them by Parry who had recorded there with Neu Electrikk. As well as booking the session, Parry also drove the pair and their gear to the studio, and so was witness to the rather unpleasant atmosphere created by the engineer, who made it abundantly clear he didn't like what his clients were doing. "The session was very difficult with the engineer clearly irritated by the music. I sat in the console room with him, watching Matt and Keith record their respective parts while the engineer protested, 'Who are these guys? They're crap!' I felt terrible because my friends were paying good money for the session but the engineer clearly didn't understand the music."

With the duo affected by the unprofessional and obstructive attitude of the engineer, the session was not surprisingly somewhat disjointed. To make it worse he wrote on the tape box after the mix-down, 'The Bollock Song'. Afterwards the trio drove to the house where Parry was living, in Upper Norwood. Laws and Johnson, most probably because they were drunk, left behind the tape they had recorded at the session. Sometime later Parry received a phone call from Keith explaining that they urgently needed it back because they had nothing else to offer Stevo for the album project.

The two bands would play together at The Bridge House on September 4, with The The headlining. The advert that appeared in the music press misspelled Parry's band's name and a rogue letter 'e' was added to the name of the man promoting the night, so readers could expect pre-gig entertainment from *Steveo's Electronic Disco*. Matt's memory of the evening is minimal but luckily Parry's recall is significantly better.

"There wasn't much of an audience – only a handful of fans and the pub regulars. Stevo was dressed in his usual DJ garb and I recall his face had some rather loud make-up. The The that night comprised of Matt, Keith Laws, Peter Ashworth and Tom Johnston, looking resplendent dressed in long dark macs." How the headliners went down with the sparse crowd isn't known, and Parry can't recall much about their set, as Neu Electrikk remained backstage for most of it, getting stoned and playing around on an old piano.

The Bridge House was run by Terry Murphy who, though Matt wasn't aware of it at the time, was a good mate of his father. Murphy didn't realise the singer of that night's headline was Eddie's son. It was just another band – one of many. Murphy's son had his own band, Wasted Youth, who would play in the pub and had built up a useful following. He had given Stevo a run of Thursday nights to promote his bands but was unimpressed when Stevo booked one of the same studios he regularly used – Stage One in Forest Gate – for some of the recordings for what would become the *Some Bizzare Album*, as this would include the first recording by Depeche Mode and Murphy felt Stevo had taken them from under his nose. In the end they would sign for Daniel Miller's Mute label.

It had been a good year for Matt Johnson, and the one to follow would be even better. Everything seemed to be slotting nicely into place. The music scene was changing. Post-punk was still going strong but many acts were now shying away from austere and serious noise towards something more frivolous, escapist and colourful. The New Romantic scene, though born of nostalgia, seemed to point to a future where the resolutely pop magazine *Smash Hits* – colourful and glossy – would take on the more serious-minded music papers. Adam & The Ants, for a seemingly perpetual cult band who had formed at the birth of punk and had been broken up by Malcolm McLaren, were now high in the charts and on their way to being the biggest act on the planet. Pop music was stretching out its history into a new era and on December 8 one of the giants of its past, John Lennon, was shot dead in New York. Lennon was the closest Matt Johnson had to a musical hero and his death knocked him sideways, as it did for so many. Something seemed to be over. Maybe, if only subconsciously, it was December 1980 when Johnson thought about Lennon's craft and his own aspirations as a songwriter. Up until now he had written obscure lyrics, partly because obscurity had a lot of credibility, and partly because deep down he was afraid of revealing too much of himself. Masking his feelings and thoughts in ambiguity was hardly a long-term strategy for anyone who wanted to take the craft of songwriting seriously, so he resolved to change this. He would take his hero's dictum to heart. From here on the aim would be to *tell the truth and make it rhyme.*

7

JUST SIGN HERE

HALFWAY THROUGH THE LONG HOT SUMMER OF 1981, England went up in flames. The dark, brooding tension that had been simmering under the surface for the best part of two years suddenly erupted in Brixton in London, Toxteth in Liverpool, Moss Side in Manchester and other towns and cities all over England. If Thatcher had been elected on the back of the Winter of Discontent then, two years into her first term, came the Summer of Rage.

There was even a riot, of sorts, in Loughton, though on a scale that hardly troubled the local paper, never mind the national ones. Matt Johnson, however, being a local lad, at least on the increasingly rare occasions he was sleeping at home, was aware of it. Enough to reflect on how the discontent might have been manipulated by people who benefit from shaping the forces of disaffected, but naive youth. Interviewed by journalist Helen Fitzgerald at the time he said, "It really annoyed me – there were kids of 11 and 12 being egged on by extremist organisations who were capitalising on local unrest."

Fitzgerald was interviewing him on the strength of the album *Burning Blue Soul*, which had just been released by 4AD. The article quoted lines from the song 'Another Boy Drowning': *There's people on the streets throwing rocks at themselves/Coz they ain't got no money and they're living in hell/But there's animals down the road adding fuel to this heat/It never did take much guts to be a sheep.*

The local disturbance had offered a close-up view of the wider malaise. Thatcher had promised to bring order and harmony, and instead there was chaos and discord. Perhaps the stabbing finger of Joe Cutler and his warning that people would "rue the day... rue the day!" that this woman got into office, was resonating somewhere in his mind when he sat down to pen the lyrics to this track. Whatever it was that inspired his choice of words and influenced his pen, 'Another Boy Drowning' represented a turning point in his career. Looking back thirty-five years later he considered it to be the first time he was happy with a lyric, and the moment that he felt ready as a songwriter who was in charge of both words and music. *Burning Blue Soul* was released under his own name rather than that of The The, and it was here, after several years or more working in studio environments, and two years into what can only be described as a fluid band line-up, that Matt Johnson found his voice. The next step would be working out what to do with it and where to take it. So while England seemed to burn that summer, Matt Johnson was also about to catch fire, artistically speaking. The title of the album may have been a coincidence but in hindsight it certainly appears fitting.

Like all serious fans of music he was open to new listening experiences. One day Tom had invited Johnson and Keith Laws round to his flat in Walthamstow, and played them an Erik Satie record – perhaps *Gymnopédies*. It was a late summer afternoon and the room was full of plants that cast impressionistic shadows, while the shadows of trees outside also shimmered on the walls – a perfect environment, then, to hear the gentle music of Satie for the first time. "Have you guys heard this?" Tom asked, holding up the record sleeve. No doubt Johnson and Laws pulled puzzled faces as Tom took the vinyl from its sleeve and put it on the turntable. The younger pair heard the hiss and crackle of the stylus hitting the grooves and then the music transported them. Johnson thought what he heard was "just fantastic".

He was equally blown away by the music of Can. "Peter turned me on to Can, he made me cassettes and they really blew me away. I loved them; particularly Michael Karoli's guitar playing and Jaki Liebezeit's drumming. I was just like 'Woah!' My little Ford Escort didn't have a sound system, I just used a portable cassette machine. I would put it on the passenger seat or dashboard and listen to it while I was driving. I remember playing that Can tape over and over thinking, 'This is fantastic!' Can had an impact on me similar to The Velvet Underground a few years before, and The Beatles' *White Album* a few years before that."

Both Can and Satie made music with a lot of space. It was a world away from The Residents, who crammed as much sonic information into their grooves as possible, and compressed time, cut it into tiny pieces in the way future artists would do with samplers. Can and Satie was all about stretching time, or even suspending it. The influence of something like Satie was much more subtle and took longer to reveal itself in Johnson's music, while the methods and sounds of Can's ethnic forgeries and The Residents would colour the demos he was working on as the year began.

The experimental approach of Gilbert and Lewis also had an impact, though this could sometimes lead up a blind alley, as it appeared to when another recording session with the pair had been financed by 4AD after the success of 'Controversial Subject'. The band line-up, usually in a state of flux, had now reduced itself to two again, only this time it was Johnson and Peter Ashworth. Ashworth has painful memories of the session.

"It was an utter bloody disaster and I remember I burst into tears at one point because the drum kit I had wasn't good enough for recording. It shook a lot and things were ringing and making all kinds of noises. I think Wire weren't necessarily great sound recordists and were perhaps being impatient. But as I was self-taught I hadn't really been shown how to get my drum kit apart and together. I used to work in a little triangle with my snare and two toms – one was a big floor tom. I used to like a machine-like groove. They asked me to take my kit apart and play my piece bit by bit on individual drums. Of course, I couldn't do it. I'd never done anything like this in fifteen years and so it wasn't a good time to start learning, really. I was put on the spot and realised I didn't have the ability to play this way. The two guys out of Wire and Matt were sitting there expectantly. I could play my normal way confidently, was great at doing it, creating a machine-like backing for Matt's jangly guitar, but to break it down into little bits? You can't really know how hard to hit the drum if you haven't been hitting the other drums naturally before it. One by one? It just seemed to take it away from my body and I couldn't do it. I was thoroughly blamed for wasting the money on the recording. Matt probably felt quite let down by it, and I probably felt let down by Matt not supporting me somehow. That incident pained me because there was something that I felt I was really good at and suddenly I was made to feel a real fool, with no ability in the professional world. And maybe that's why I put my drums away. I fell out of love with playing music."

According to Johnson, Peter Ashworth and Graham Lewis "just didn't like each other", and so whether it was an Eno-esque attempt at studio experimentation or just a rattling drum kit is perhaps a moot point. Not being at the blunt end of their whim made it easier for Johnson to admire their methodology. "I thought it was very interesting working with them, and learnt quite a lot from them. They were lateral thinkers, and they would take our basic idea and say, 'Well why don't we try this? Or try doing this?' Graham, I think, had his little aluminium briefcase with his effects pedals, his chorus and delay, and he would bring it out and start putting things through them, distorting things… I found them very creative in the studio. It was a bit of an eye-opener. It was different to my approach, but very inspiring, very thoughtful. They liked to dismantle things, and reconfigure."

With Ashworth's confidence as a drummer thus dismantled it was obvious to him that his role as a member of The The was soon going to become less permanent. He would find himself floating out of the band and then floating back in again. He kept his hand in when it came to music but his Hasselblad was now more important to him than his drum kit. Matt's resolve when it came to music was, by contrast, unwavering. "He'd obviously been dabbling in music from a young age," Ashworth surmises. "He'd been going to bed as a kid listening to bands playing in his dad's pub downstairs, just like I had gone to bed and heard my dad playing his jazz records. Matt was hearing real bands and some of the best bands of the day playing downstairs. It has an amazing effect on you as a child. It becomes the norm. You can't believe that not everyone is experiencing it. I heard at some point that Matt used to listen to a lot of long-wave radio at night back in those days. You get the crackle, and the sound coming in and out, phasing and so on. And he was also making notes about what was being said, as he got more political. But I don't really pay attention to words when I listen to music so I never really knew what he was singing about."

Any disappointment over the unproductive recording session was tempered by events that saw progress on more than one front. Johnson was considered within the scene as something of a boy wonder, so it was no surprise that there was more than one interested party. Though 4AD had released the first The The single, the label's ideology concerning artists and contracts was only one step up from the looseness employed by Factory Records in Manchester. Ivo preferred one-off contracts, which inevitably gave the artist a lot of freedom. Stevo had already been making his moves and the track Matt and Keith had recorded in Elephant Studios was set to make a public appearance in January 1981 on the *Some Bizzare* compilation. Not taken with the surly engineer's suggestion of 'The Bollock Song' as a title they opted for a simple 'Untitled'. At Cherry Red, meanwhile, Theo Chalmers had been tasked with signing acts to the publishing arm. It is this side of the business that secured ownership of compositions, as opposed to the actual recordings of songs. With Matt hanging around the offices so often with his demos it was an obvious decision to persuade him to sign on the dotted line, which he duly did;

like so many before him and since, it was a signature that took a couple of seconds to write and a lifetime to regret. At the time it had seemed so good. In reality, however, they now had him by the balls. Forever. Which, when he looked it up later, was what 'in perpetuity' actually meant.

"I remember my dad being shocked that I got a cheque for £1,500. I'd been on the dole and he didn't believe it. I signed that deal because there was a guitar that I wanted that Steve Rosie was selling, the John Birch. I was stupid. I didn't take legal advice, and I didn't know what 'in perpetuity' meant. It was a disaster for me, and now Universal own those songs and I get a shit fucking royalty. But that gave me a bit of money at least. And the John Birch." As well as the guitar, he also bought Rosie's 2-12 combo Arbiter amp and a couple of extension cabs. The whole lot for around £250.

To be fair, it was a lot of money back in 1980, especially for a 19-year-old on the dole who was living in a glorified cupboard. If Johnson had known what the deal actually meant, would he have done any different? After all, it was a bit like selling your soul, this 'in perpetuity' business. But on the other hand, £1,500 was the equivalent of a quarter of a year's average wage, and that was before tax deductions. For a teenager who had been drawing £18.50 a week unemployment benefit, this represented a tidy sum, particularly when the country as a whole was in a deep recession as a result of the early failings of Thatcherite economic policies. Then there was the whole ambition thing; a publishing deal whispered things in your ear, "You've made it son! Welcome aboard."

Though he would later come to regret signing the publishing deal with Cherry Red, at the time it was all part of the ride, and at the time everything seemed good. Ivo was unperturbed by the failed recording session and simply suggested that Johnson send him some more demos, so before long a tape with four or five new tracks found its way to his desk. These may have been the same songs that Johnson had taken to Geoff Travis, but this time he was left to wait for any feedback, which led to a rather anxious few days. "I was in The Crown, probably down in my studio, and Ivo called. He was very complimentary about the demos and said, 'Look, why don't you do an album.' I thought he might be kidding at first but he just said, 'I think you're ready to do an album.' I was jumping for joy when I put the phone down... walking on air."

Recording of the album was spread out over a period of about six months, beginning in January 1981. This, more than anything else, was a budgetary issue – the whole recording only costing £1,800. Different studios, producers and engineers were employed, and though the final mix renders a sonic cohesion to the whole, it is easy enough to spot not just the different production but also the development of Matt Johnson at this stage, as he grew towards being a fully fledged songwriter rather than just an electronic and sonic experimenter.

Betty Page gave the *Some Bizzare Album* a fair to middling review in *SOUNDS*; of Matt and Keith's contribution she wrote, "The The might appear moody and gloomy on first hearing the creeping bass line but the word plays are the highlight." Which was a lot kinder than the review by Steve Taylor in *The Face*, who seemed to hate every minute of the album, and referred to The The, and others, as "awful noise-collages".

Johnson found himself back in Blackwing Studios with Bruce Gilbert and Graham Lewis, to record 'Time (Again) For The Golden Sunset' and 'The River Flows East In Spring'. On the latter, Gilbert contributed guitar, while Lewis added piano. The piano comes in just after the minute mark, along with some handclaps that have a gypsy-like rhythm. Initially they offer aural relief after a minute of ethnic chanting – no doubt one of the tape loops that Johnson prepared at De Wolfe – but the chopping rhythm that Lewis employs only sends the tension into a different place. Though he was learning from the Wire pair it is noticeable, when listening to the album as a whole, that he was expanding his horizons and stretching himself. The influence of Gilbert and Lewis's work as Dome and Cupol is evident, and other influences are present, such as Can and Faust, The Residents, Throbbing Gristle, Thomas Leer and Robert Rental, and in the use of tremolo and fuzz on guitars a definite nod to psyche and garage of the sixties. Throw in Syd Barrett, Tim Buckley and a bit of Lennon and you get a picture of what would have spent most time on the turntable in the room he shared with Andrew in the year or so leading up to recording. He had also recently discovered the work of electronic composer Tod Dockstader and had even been hearing about mythical organisations of avant-garde musicians: the Zodiac Free Arts Lab in Berlin and the San Francisco Tape Music Center. Both of these had long since ceased to exist but the idea of musical experimental collectives intrigued him.

Just as important as what he was listening to, though, was his reading material. A short tome, written by Terence Dwyer, called *Composing with Tape Recorders – Musique Concrete for Beginners*, had become his bible. The first chapter has a short section headed 'Collecting Sounds', wherein Dwyer writes: *I hope the reader will become more and more interested in the sounds he hears around him every day, and will eagerly examine them for their intrinsic interest and individual character.* For someone who had spent so many hours of his early years stuck indoors, making sense of the world through the sounds beneath the floorboards or beyond the walls, this barely needed stressing, and now, years later, armed with his own reel-to-reel tape recorder he could do just that.

With the book at his fingertips and the training he had received at De Wolfe, Johnson had the perfect opportunity to experiment, so when Ivo gave him the green light to do an album, his apprenticeship in recording techniques and tape manipulation could be put to the test.

Album opener 'Red Cinders In The Sand' was produced by Johnson and Peter Maben at Stage One in Forest Gate. It was a demo recording of this track that Ivo thinks convinced him to let Johnson make an album, and years later he still felt that "'Red Cinders In The Sand' is as good as anything that was being done by anyone at that time." Johnson came to some recording sessions armed with tape loops that he had prepared at De Wolfe. 'Red Cinders' begins with a muffled drum loop that spends a minute accompanied by flashes of noise stabs, the whole thus far being a good demonstration of how exposure to the studio had heightened his appreciation of the atmospherics he had discovered in film soundtracks as a boy. At one minute a guitar riff bursts into play and disappears almost at once to allow another, much funkier drum loop to take over, again with various noises put through various effects boxes. Around halfway things take a more industrial turn and the track continues in this vein. Although it is perhaps a minute too long it serves as a good introduction to the album, letting listeners know that they are going to be taken on a journey of some kind, something that the album cover probably gave away before the vinyl was put onto the turntable.

The design, a homage of sorts to The 13th Floor Elevators, was Keith Laws' idea. Andrew did the original drawing but it was rushed and Ivo, unhappy with it, asked Neville Brody to completely redo it. A painting Andrew had done of Johnson was used on the back of the sleeve and Keith's brother Darren took the photographs. It screamed psychedelia at a time when a number of bands had been linked together by the press, hinting at a psychedelic revival. After creating this tag the music papers wasted no time in shooting the idea down and this probably didn't help the album on release, though some reviewers were astute enough to mention that as far as psychedelia went, this was the nearest anyone had got to what you might consider the genuine article without falling into the trap of mere parody.

Peter Maben also co-produced and engineered the recording of 'Delirious' but the rest of the tracks were produced by Ivo and Johnson himself, Ivo's involvement coming about by happenstance.

"I'd been to Spaceward Studios in Cambridge to record the Modern English single 'Gathering Dust' and suggested it might be a good place for Matt to record. The deal at Spaceward was for a sixteen-hour session after which you would be forced to watch as the 2-inch multi-track tape you had just rented was erased! I remember the two or three trips we made there as something of an adventure. I would get up at the crack of dawn, pick up Matt and head off for a crazy and creative day and night in Cambridge. I think my only input was to help Matt feel relaxed and encouraged enough to explore whatever he felt like in the time allotted. We were both deeply in love with tape delay and backwards guitars. It did afford me the opportunity to witness someone writing on the spot for the first time in my life. With each song one got a whole new insight into what this 'boy' was capable of."

Johnson also recalls the sessions with fondness. "Ivo had a little blue Peugeot and he drove me up there and we had a couple of sleeping bags and slept on the floor, in this church where the studio was, in the live room. It was great. He was lovely, Ivo, very encouraging, very gentle. A very thoughtful, fair-minded person. We spent two days in there. They were probably the last sessions. I think we mixed it there as well. In those days you would play the mixing board, bringing things in… you'd have a delay line, and dub-style you would send things off to your delay line. And Ivo, he was credited as co-producer but he let me get on with it really and gave feedback when it was necessary, whereas with Bruce and Graham it was far more about being produced."

Though possessed of the cockiness of a young man who knew where he wanted to go in life, he was less sure of himself when he was out of his comfort zone. Being holed up in Spaceward for forty-eight hours with someone as introverted as Ivo no doubt led to a few awkward silences until they were able to find common conversational ground. "Both Matt and I were equally shy. I'm fairly sure we would've talked about Syd Barrett! I do remember telling him about something I'd seen on television that had scared the shit out of me and committed me to wearing a seat belt for the rest of my days. Within days Matt was involved in a rollover car accident he probably wouldn't have survived had he not heeded my warning and immediately started wearing his belt too." Though he survived the accident Johnson's 'passenger' came off badly. "I wrote off my little Ford Escort in a very bad accident down a deserted country lane in Suffolk. It destroyed the

John Birch guitar which was unprotected and in the boot as the flight case was too big to fit in. I cursed the Cherry Red publishing contract even more!"

With the Spaceward recordings in the can Matt had succeeded in capturing musical and lyrical ideas that had been swimming around in his mind for much longer than the six months it took to record the ten tracks. His magpie-like approach saw him adding lyrical touches culled from incidents that were happening around him, like the reference to the attempted assassinations of Ronald Reagan and Pope John Paul in 'Song Without An Ending'. Or the lines in 'Bugle Boy': *This strange little boy said/Mister play us your guitar/I said, No I can't/And put my guitar in the car.*

Interviewed by Pat Gilbert in 1993, when the album was reissued for a second time, he revealed the origin of the lyric. "That actually happened. I was walking out of the door of the pub I lived in, and some kid said it to me. And I said, 'No, I can't,' put my guitar in the car and drove off. But later I thought that I should've done really. If I considered myself a singer-songwriter I should have sat and played for him, but I didn't. I'm a bit shy." The track itself is introduced by an evocative 'sample' of what actually sounds like a hunting horn, something no doubt culled from the De Wolfe vaults, lending the track its title, and a phased twelve-string guitar riff. The vocal is heavily treated, a sign perhaps that, though his confidence as a singer and writer was developing apace, he still felt the need to bury himself deep into the mix. Or maybe it was just the irresistible temptation to indulge in all the sonic time-warping that an array of stomp boxes and a mixing desk can deliver, a temptation that recedes with more recording experience. Either way, though he would never release anything quite like *Burning Blue Soul* again, the first flashings of the later, more recognisable, The The sound are in evidence here – from the distinctive guitar play to the vocal delivery and an instinctive understanding of how abstract sound can be used to add atmosphere and ambience. These little flourishes would be employed to great effect throughout his career.

Though he was miffed that the album's release coincided with the brief psychedelic revival, there's no denying that it might have been the album of choice for anyone inclined to accompany their listening pleasure with a good smoke, or something more potent. With all the Eastern-sounding loops of chanting, Indian reed instruments and ethnic percussion, weaving in and out, swathed in echo and reverb, it is easy to see how it would have appealed to listeners of adventurous music. Only Eno and Byrne, who released *My Life In The Bush Of Ghosts* in the same year, were doing similar sound collages, and both albums essentially achieved what many acts would do a decade later with samplers for a whole new generation primed for ambience and trippiness by the post-rave comedown.

The reviews in the music press were generally positive, though more than one writer compared Johnson's voice to that of Jethro Tull's Ian Anderson, which may have sounded like a warning to the average fan of post-punk music. Many of the better reviews only came when the album was reissued, on the back of it appearing as the only modern record in cartoonist Ralph Steadman's 'Portrait of the Artist as a Consumer' in the *NME*, a feature that listed current tastes in music, films and literature of a different person each week. As Ivo recalled in 2015: "It seemed to take forever to be able to build up a few sheets of reviews for his biog. I'd say most journalists at the time were pretty private about their enthusiasm if they indeed felt any. Adam Sweeting was an exception. There was no one championing him at any of the weekly press, there was no band, or at least no band that would be a promotionally effective tool! It was incredibly frustrating. I'd hired Chris Carr as a publicist, one of the few people who also 'got' how broad Matt's talents were, and he was incredibly patient and diligent about spreading the word."

Matt Johnson was a slow-burner. The trouble for Ivo Watts-Russell was that by the time he ignited with a wider public he was on a different label. "I think I'd been on holiday in Crete for a couple of weeks when, upon my return, Matt told me he had taken on Stevo as manager and was fairly sure he would sign with a major. It seemed like the right thing for him to do." Though it is unlikely that Ivo gave up quite as easily as that, 4AD was set up in a way that didn't tie artists down to long deals, the whole ethos of the label being a far cry from most others at the time. Talking to Martin Aston, who wrote the definitive book about the label, Johnson remembered Ivo suggesting that CBS wasn't the right place at that time for him – advice he chose to ignore. He also recalled that Ivo was very gracious about his decision to jump ship, but ultimately his own ambition and the ambitions of Stevo meant that it was only going to end up one way.

The first move that Stevo made was to suggest that Some Bizzare release a The The single in a one-off deal. Thus, in the spring of 1981, Johnson and Laws went into the studio to record two tracks. These would become the second single released on Stevo's label, coming after 'Tainted Love', which had exceeded everyone's expectations, including Soft Cell themselves. This cover version of an old Northern Soul tune turned out to be a bona fide smash hit; in fact it smashed things to bits, selling worldwide and in the process launched not only the careers of Marc Almond and Dave Ball, but essentially that of Stevo and Some Bizzare too. With Stevo busy hustling Soft Cell back and forth between London and New York, and all over Europe, Johnson was free to work on the album for Ivo and 4AD as well as this one-off single.

The recording session for 'Cold Spell Ahead' was at Stage One studios in Forest Gate, situated over the road from the home of Johnson's maternal grandparents. Pete Maben again helped to engineer, and this production steered clear of the levels of reverb and echo that characterised *Burning Blue Soul*, resulting in the vocal being pushed much further forward in the mix. The song was in fact two songs stitched together, something that required a well-timed manoeuvre in the studio. As Johnson recalls, "It wasn't a tape splice, it was dropping-in, so what we would have done, maybe one of us would have pressed the drum machine, while the engineer pressed 'record'. So we were listening to the 'Uncertain

Smile' segment and then it was, 'One, two, three,' bang! over to the 'Touch Of Experience' section. It took us quite a few goes to get it and then there was overdubbing on the top of that." Though he remembers how they achieved the segue, he is less clear as to why the two songs became co-joined in the first place. "Why I did that I can't remember. I think I had the two songs; they were going to be two separate songs, and maybe I couldn't find a part to that outro? I've never done anything like that since, changing the tempo *and* key at the same time. I did want to turn that end section into its own song but never got round to it."

Though his vocal delivery was nowhere near as confident as it would be when the first half of the song was recorded again as 'Uncertain Smile', it is nonetheless significant as being the first time it had taken centre stage, where any vocal track belongs. The other thing that sets this recording apart from those that appear on *Burning Blue Soul*, considering that it was produced in the middle of the sessions for the album, is the rhythm track. The The had used drum machines from the beginning but the rhythm on 'Cold Spell Ahead' was bolder, more *motorik*, more confident. Maybe more expensive.

Maybe not even theirs. It sounds suspiciously like a Korg kr55, the same drum machine used by Depeche Mode on the version of 'Photographic' that appeared on the *Some Bizzare Album*. In fact it was Daniel Miller's machine. As Johnson readily points out, you took advantage of what happened to be lying around. "Daniel Miller's gear happened to be in there – it could even have been an Arp sequencer – so we were using that without him knowing, a bit like I later did when I borrowed John Foxx's gear. You did in those days, you used what you could find."

The rhythm track on 'Cold Spell Ahead' roots the track to the ground and steadies it, allowing for the guitars and vocals to sit where they should in the mix. Whether it was a Korg kr55 or indeed an Arp sequencer – the latter of which would explain the tightness of the overall rhythm, particularly if both had been employed, as Johnson suspects – is just a matter of detail. The fact of the matter is that 'Cold Spell Ahead' is significant for a number of reasons. Gone now is the looseness of *Burning Blue Soul*, or the murkiness of early The The recordings. From here to *Soul Mining*, via *The Pornography Of Despair*, is much less of a leap. It is also significant in terms of Johnson's lyric writing. While 'Another Boy Drowning' marks the moment he defines his birth as a lyricist, the first half of 'Cold Spell Ahead' reveals a new-found confidence in expression. Lastly, it marks the point from which he begins to move away from Ivo and 4AD and enters a relationship with Stevo and Some Bizzare. He was no doubt hoping that Stevo could accelerate his career and would, in due course, find himself being propelled into the mainstream – a progression that would trouble him as much as it excited him. It was a move that he would make without his sidekick. "When we recorded 'Cold Spell Ahead' Keith was doing less and less. I was pretty much writing and playing everything by this stage. Keith's interest lay elsewhere, I guess. He loved music, experimental music, but I don't think he was someone who sat at home practising, as a songwriter or whatever, so I was working in my own studio, and writing, and really coming on in leaps and bounds. I think all the instruments on 'Cold Spell Ahead' were played by me."

* * *

It's hard to say just when anyone left The The in these early days. No one got sacked, as such, they just sort of faded away, or as Peter Ashworth put it, floated away, and then on occasion floated back again. By all accounts available Keith Laws' interest did seem to fade. The more The The made inroads into the music scene the more Laws seemed to retreat into the background. Perhaps it was Johnson who was getting all the attention, and perhaps to Laws it seemed that his bandmate was the one earmarked for recognition and fame, but the decision to attribute *Burning Blue Soul* to Matt Johnson rather than The The must have spoken volumes. He recalls in a piece written for his Internet blog, spending many summer days driving around the Essex countryside with Johnson, smoking cigarettes and listening to early and final versions of songs from *Burning Blue Soul* on the portable cassette player. He also recalls these drives as being made seat belt-less, so perhaps Ivo's advice had not yet been taken on board. Johnson apparently was unsure about some of his songs and would discuss this with Laws, who then, as now, was of the opinion that he had nothing to worry about.

Though Laws was never at any of the writing or recording sessions for *Burning Blue Soul*, the title and sleeve design were his suggestions, and when he heard the tracks Johnson had recorded, he was positive with his feedback. Though Laws had become a peripheral figure, Johnson thinks, as far as this album goes, that he deserves to be considered a part of the process. He was also part of the process that would ultimately lead to *Soul Mining*.

"Keith was very encouraging despite the fact that I was pretty much now going off by myself. He would listen to stuff and really got what I was trying to do. I was playing all the instruments at this point, and we did some recordings at Phonogram – they used to have a demo studio off Bond Street, and we re-recorded 'Waiting For The Upturn' and 'Three Orange Kisses'. Keith had pretty much become a spectator really. Because I had my own studio I would have worked out all the parts and just knew what I was doing and it was quicker than showing him what to do – just doing it myself. He must have realised that this was not what he was going to be doing with his life and he would more or less sit at the back and have a cigarette and give encouraging feedback. But there was no real role for him by then."

Without the input of Laws himself, we, like Johnson, can only guess how he felt about being, and then not being, in The The. Tom Johnston remembers a very laid-back personality who was less driven than Johnson, so maybe he just sat back and watched his partner accelerate into the distance. Peter Ashworth also has it this way: "I remember Keith being a pretty laissez-faire kind of guy. I would suggest he try a different chord progression to one he had played and he would just be, 'Yeah, okay.' He was pretty casual about stuff. There wasn't a big ego thing with Keith about being in a band. I think he was quite shy." It was certainly clear to many that Johnson was sure of himself when it came to music, and many observers saw him as a person destined for bigger things. Tom Johnston, no longer part of the band in 1981, had pretty much left the pair to it and so has no idea just when Laws was no longer part of things, but their respective fates didn't surprise him. "I thought that Matt, right from the time I left would be going on by himself, so I just left them to it. He always had other musicians who wanted to play with him... The Gadgets and people like that. But I always thought he would be better by himself." Ivo Watts-Russell thinks that one possibility as to why *Burning Blue Soul* was released as a solo album was as a way of Johnson forcing himself to tell Laws he was no longer part of the band, but admits this might be false memory or conjecture and suggests an equally plausible explanation was that, with Stevo now involved, he wanted to keep his projects separate – thus for 4AD it was Matt Johnson and for Some Bizzare it was The The. Johnson says this latter explanation is more accurate, as he didn't force Laws out of the band and the two remained friends. For the first Some Bizzare release at least, Keith Laws was still a member of The The, with a songwriting credit for 'Hot Ice', on the B-side, a meandering jam that was most likely created in the studio.

After *Burning Blue Soul* was released in August, Martin Brooke, who worked with Charles Blackburn at Selfridges, suggested he and Matt go on a hitchhiking holiday to France. It was Brooke who introduced Johnson to the poetry of Sylvia Plath. Aside from one incident when they ended up in two different cars, the drivers of which proceeded to speed off in opposite directions through the French countryside before ejecting their respective English hitchers, it was a trouble-free trip. They eventually ended up staying with a girl Brooke had met the previous year when he had befriended her boyfriend. A year later she was single and Matt found himself falling for her Gallic charms. Despite neither of them speaking the other's language, they connected, played a lot of chess, whilst listening to Serge Gainsbourg, and though things never got beyond a bit of kissing and cuddling, it was no doubt a significant thing for someone as shy with the opposite sex as he was. Still suffering from acne and being in awe at the ease with which someone like Tom Johnston handled things when it came to women, a holiday romance was no doubt just the ticket when it came to boosting his own confidence in this regard.

All the trips to talk through the progress of *Burning Blue Soul* with Ivo meant that Matt would spend a lot of time in the Beggars Banquet record shop below the 4AD office. He got friendly with a young woman who worked there, called Nasrin, and would often stay at the squat she lived in on Formosa Street with her friend, Daisy. "It was quite a well-known squat and quite druggy. People like Nico and Steve New, who had been in The Rich Kids, stayed there a lot. It was a bit *Withnail & I* when I think about it; the Victorian rooms and bare floorboards and coal fires, tin baths and cold water. In the winter you had to sleep with layers and layers of blankets. I spent a lot of time there. It was sad because Steve New was struggling with heroin addiction. If I had stayed and the girls had gone out to work, I would be in the kitchen, having a bowl of cereal or whatever, and Steve would come down and sit by the coal fire and I would have a cup of tea with him, and tell him about my plans, and he said once, 'You're so fucking together and you're only a teenager.' He was a young guy himself, only a year older than me, and he said, 'I just can't get it together.' He once showed me his arms and back which had these huge welts from Chinese cupping therapy, and said, 'Look at all this.' He tried everything to kick the habit. And he got involved with Nico, which certainly didn't help. I really liked him though, he was a nice guy. He told me a funny story once, about how he enjoyed golden showers and how the woman doing it had to drink lots of water first so she was pissing clear liquid."

New's description of such practices was a bit of an eye-opener for the young and somewhat naive Johnson, causing him to gulp on the tea he was drinking. On the other hand, smack addiction, deviant sex and being in the same squat visited by Nico, one-time chanteuse for The Velvet Underground, were clear signs that he was a long way from the suburban existence he had found so stifling. The moth-like journey towards the flame at the centre of the big city was complete. Home was now more or less a place he would visit to change clothes. "I was living in Loughton but was barely there. I was crashing everywhere, and during this time Andrew and I had a couple of bad punch-ups. Twice, even though we were sharing a bedroom, we didn't speak for six months, which shows how pig-headed we could be, being in the same room and not talking to each other all that time. At this point I was getting into exercise as well, weight training and push-ups, things like that, so if Andrew tried attacking me I would fight back. I wasn't a little kid that could be bullied and punched any more."

Though licensing hours were more restrictive at that time, there were plenty of opportunities in a city like London to engage in after-hours entertainment, be it at gigs, clubs, secretive Soho drinking dens or all-nighters at the Scala. "I was out all the time. It was all very sociable. I used to spend a lot of time at the London Film-Maker's Co-Op in Camden Town and would often head off to all night parties with people I'd met there. I remember there were also these really opulent squats we'd go to all-night parties to and sleep in, these huge old John Nash-designed stuccoed terrace houses on Park Square between Regent's Park and Marylebone Road. The electricity was cut off so partying was strictly by candlelight and battery-powered ghetto blasters. It was incredibly atmospheric and like something from a 1960s Italian art film." All this socialising required some kind of fuel, and Johnson, like most teenagers, would sample a range of options. "Alcohol was the prime thing. In terms of drugs, the main thing was speed really, because at that point cocaine was too expensive. Sulphate was cheap and it would keep you going. I never really liked dope that much. I would always take a few tokes if it was passed around, though if it was too strong it would make me paranoid, or if I'd had too much alcohol it would make me feel a bit sick."

It was during a night out that Johnson met Pete Hunt, who was in London with a friend to check out the scene. They were looking for the Wag Club in Soho. Johnson said he was going there himself and so the trio ended up in the club together. Hunt was the manager of Discount Records in Altrincham, and talking into the early hours about music he learned that this affable young cockney had just released an album on 4AD. He suggested that Johnson might want to check out the scene in Manchester and that there was a young guitarist he would get along with called Johnny. His surname was Marr; Hunt had been plying him with classic sixties pop singles from his record shop and perhaps thought that the two lads might be able to work together. Johnson, finding Hunt friendly, good-humoured and clued-up about music and the scene in London, decided he would take him up on the offer. Manchester already had a reputation musically, and it was the home of Manchester United, so it wasn't hard to make the decision, especially at an age when all you want to do is expand your horizons. Off he duly trekked.

"So I was staying at Pete's place, and he said, 'You've got to meet our mate Johnny. You and him are gonna get on great, you're gonna love Johnny. Johnny's a star, you've got to meet him.'" Hunt took him to X-Clothes, the shop where Marr worked, where they chatted a while before agreeing to meet up later. They did so at Hunt's home, Marr bringing along his guitar, so the two of them could have a jam. Hunt had loaned Marr a copy of *Burning Blue Soul* and he had given it a very close inspection. He asked Johnson how he had played different tracks. They played and talked, and the more they talked the more they found they had in common. For Marr, it was as if they had known each other for ages. "It was just one of those times; within minutes you feel as though you've known each other all your lives. You've got so much in common. Sense of humour is a big part of it, ideology, and liking similar things in music. In our case that would be melody, the same kind of rhythms – a lot of that came out of glam rock; we were besotted by the music of the early seventies. And also an understanding of a certain kind of search in life beyond the senses, and beyond the three dimensions. That turned out to be a real quest for both of us, separately and together." The two fuelled their enthusiasm with beer and some speed, ending up in Legends nightclub, where Johnson tried amyl nitrate for the first, and possibly last time.

Though he was suitably impressed with Marr's obvious skills on the guitar and the fluency of his playing, it was obvious that the two were at different places music-wise, with Marr following up Hunt's prompting to delve into classic 1960s American and British pop, while Johnson was exploring much more left-field areas. He also saw himself at this point as a solo artist – even if other members of The The might not have been officially aware of this status. They did discuss the possibility of Marr joining The The but on a more practical level the pair lived at opposite ends of the country and realistically neither was going to relocate at this stage of their lives. Despite all this, they made a pact to work together, and if Johnson hadn't soon after secured a record deal with CBS, and if Marr hadn't very soon after met an ambitious chap called Morrissey, then, who knows, The Smiths might never have happened. A friendship was sealed, however – Cockney and Manc, north and south, Manchester and London, the two poles of a divided England. Johnson would visit Manchester several more times, Marr taking him out to clubs like the newly opened Hacienda, while Marr made the trip down to London a few times, meaning on some evenings Alex Sartore would finish her evening shift as a waitress, come back to the small flat and find Johnny Marr there with Matt Johnson, never realising just how big these two young men would become in the music scene of the ensuing years. She was still busy taking photographs at concerts, following bands like Echo & The Bunnymen and Psychedelic Furs, who had already made it. The two guys back at the flat were nice boys but nothing in comparison. Not then.

8

AWOL IN AMERICA

ANDREW JOHNSON WAS STUDYING FINE ART IN THE ERA of minimalism and post-modernism, firstly at Loughton College of Further Education, and then Camberwell School of Art. In the days when our culture was less saturated with imagery and the Young British Artists were all still in primary school, much of the modern art on display at the Tate Gallery would have seemed somewhat daunting for a working-class lad, belonging, as it did, to a world steeped in intellectual theory and laced with what some observers would gladly refer to as high pretension. Andrew recalled one trip organised by the college. "I remember seeing Michael Craig-Martin's 'This Is An Oak Tree' and being bewildered because all I could see was a glass of water on a glass shelf. I was determined to try and get to grips with all this and every month I bought art magazines and ploughed through acres of pretty turgid art criticism, trying to unlock the secrets to this new and fascinating world."

One writer he found relatively accessible was Peter Fuller, and it was in one of his pieces, critical of much contemporary art of the time, that he came across a phrase that stuck in his mind – 'pornography of despair'. When he wasn't puzzling over the mysteries of the art world, or hanging out with fellow Foundation art student, Mark Wallinger, at Loughton College, Andrew would be getting up at the crack of lunchtime, along with Matt, in the flat above The Crown and abusing the hospitality of the kitchen staff below by ordering up some hot food while they watched daytime television and talked about music, art, football and whatever else took their fancy. At some point Andrew did a painting and the title – 'Pornography of Despair' – was painted onto the canvas. Matt Johnson saw it and it immediately struck a chord.

With an album behind him and brimful of new ideas, Matt Johnson was already working on another project and 'pornography of despair' became the working title. Ultimately this new project wouldn't realise his artistic ambitions, but it would serve as the stepping stone to the album that did. Discovering his singer-songwriting voice with 'Another Boy Drowning' saw a significant shift in his methodology. Though he wouldn't totally abandon the tape manipulation techniques of his earlier work, the emphasis from now on would be on more traditional song structure to support his new-found lyrical confidence. His reading list around this time was expanding and included books such as Sartre's *Nausea*, Conrad's *Heart of Darkness*, Henry Miller's *Tropic of Cancer* and *The Bell Jar* by Sylvia Plath. It was natural, therefore, for him to start exploring how he could express himself in words as much as in music and sound. Though he wasn't going to retreat completely from the idea of the studio being another instrument, an increased interest in lyrical content naturally shifted the focus of composition towards instrumentation that supported this.

Performing live remained an infrequent habit and 1982 was a period of mostly abstinence. He continued to play fast and loose with band line-ups and was to perform two dates that saw The The as a threesome, teaming up with Colin Lloyd Tucker and Simon Fisher Turner. He had met Fisher Turner at the same Cherry Red Christmas party he met Jim Thirlwell, and soon after saw him again at an art show in an empty swimming pool. They got talking and the next day Johnson dropped into De Wolfe to tell Colin that the three of them should meet up. They invited Tucker to the Cherry Red offices one evening and thence to a pub. Turner had been a child actor and teen pop singer but had long since abandoned the Tin Pan Alley trappings of that period and was working on more serious music, having recorded the soundtrack for a Derek Jarman short film, *Sloane Square: A Room Of One's Own*, using a Revox tape recorder and whatever had been lying around his flat.

At the time, Turner was living in Egerton Gardens with his girlfriend, Melanie McDonald, who had a daughter, Fleur, from a previous relationship with Bowie manager Tony Defries. Lloyd Tucker remembers how the trio worked towards their stage incarnation.

"The flat's large front room with its big windows and upright piano made it an ideal place to get together, not least because of Melanie's enthusiasm and encouragement. She loved having music around the place. So Matt, Simon and myself would sit around with guitars playing each other our new songs, or simply strum through old Velvet Underground numbers for the fun of it. One evening we took our guitars up to the ICA on The Mall, and set up in the corner of the bar playing, amongst other things, an intolerably long version of The Velvets' 'What Goes On'. Emboldened by this Matt asked if we were up for doing a couple of The The dates. We played the Lyceum Ballroom and The Venue. Prior to the first show Matt thought we should all have very short haircuts. I had long hair at the time and Matt and Simon's was collar length. I mentioned that my mum could do it as she was in the hairdressing trade. The night before our performance we took a train to my parents' house in Harrow and sat in a row whilst my mum sheared her way along the line. There was a last-minute rehearsal before the first show, at Egerton Gardens beneath the big windows as the sun went down. The mood was very mellow, and the thought of facing a large audience in a few hours was somewhat surreal. It was a short cab ride to the venue, guitars in hand, and walking on stage in our all-denim outfits, someone shouted, 'It's bloody Woodstock!' to which Matt shouted, 'Shut your face.' After that I think our set was well received."

The gig at The Venue was supporting Colin Newman of Wire. With a favourable review in one of the music weeklies: "Scrambled into a remarkably low-key performance, so loose he made Orange Juice seem like Earth Wind and Fire, you could still detect the brilliant songs and ethereal voice of a real contender. Though he failed to do justice to his minor after-hours masterpiece, the solo 'Blue Eyed Burning Soul' [sic] LP, with only bass, guitar and flute as support The The still managed to capture fleeting moments of magic from that ridiculously obscure album."

This stripped-down line-up had forced Johnson to consider ways of composition that reflected his own musical tastes. His appreciation of the traditional alongside the innovative and experimental was now an aspiration and he now had the self-belief necessary to try and accomplish this. Perhaps as much as anything else, what brought on this new sense of conviction was the belief that if he could deliver the music, then someone else could make sure it was heard in all the right places. His artistic ambition was about to be given a piggyback by someone whose own ambitions were even more lofty.

When Stevo had managed to persuade Phonogram Records that if they really wanted to sign B-Movie then they would have to take Soft Cell as part of the deal, no one could have dreamt in their wildest dreams what the outcome would be.

So when Stevo was in Matt's ear about how he could make things really happen for him – not just in an indie label, *NME* kind of way, but a major label, *Smash Hits* kind of way – it was hard to ignore the fact that whereas not long ago Stevo had certainly talked the talk, he was now, undeniably, walking the walk. Exactly when Stevo first started proffering his services as a manager nobody really knows but he certainly would have thrown the idea up into the air around the time he had sent Matt and Keith into the studio to record 'Cold Spell Ahead'.

"Stevo started making these promises. He said, 'I'll get you a major label deal, you can have your own flat,' and he always used to knock on the wall when he said this. 'You will have your *own* flat...' *knock knock*. And remember, I was still on the dole, and as much as I loved Ivo, and the artistic freedom, there was no money, at all. I didn't get an advance, I didn't get royalties; I didn't get anything." Though he had received money from Cherry Red for the ill-advised publishing deal, he was still living in a glorified cupboard in Highbury. He also must have been cognisant of the fact that Marc Almond and Dave Ball were suddenly in a different world, shuttling back and forth across the Atlantic with their new boss. It was on one such transatlantic flight that Stevo popped a copy of *Burning Blue Soul* into his Walkman and as he was listening to it decided he had to bring Matt Johnson firmly into the Some Bizzare stable. Such was the effect of the music, or such was the effect of whatever Stevo had been imbibing, that he kept hearing 'Red Cinders In The Sand' even after he had removed the headphones. He found himself in the cramped airplane toilet slapping and pinching himself, and throwing water over his face in his efforts to stop the music circling around and around in his mind. Voices in his head spelt it out for him. "Sign Matt Johnson," they said.

'Cold Spell Ahead' had been a one-off deal that gave Stevo no managerial control. With the success of Soft Cell inflating his already robust sense of confidence in what he could achieve, he was now looking at expanding his empire. The carrot he was dangling in front of Johnson was looking increasingly juicy. As much as he loved the world of the independents and the music it fostered, Matt Johnson also admired people like John Lennon, Bob Dylan and Leonard Cohen, who had been signed to the big labels of this world, and this is what Stevo could deliver. The lack of critical response and publicity for *Burning Blue Soul* must have rankled. Now he wanted to move on from the experimental approach of his 4AD album. Having recorded a number of demo tracks for what he dubbed the *The Pornography Of Despair*, he gave Stevo a copy on cassette. Armed with this, Stevo started approaching record labels. One person who remembers this time better than most is Zeke Manyika, then drummer with Scottish band Orange Juice.

"I actually met Matt through Stevo. The band used to stay in the Columbia Hotel. So I used to come down to London on Sunday night, stay the week, either recording with Orange Juice or doing other work, and go back to Glasgow on Friday. Most of the eighties bands used to stay there. Even the ones that came from London; the record companies would put them there. There used to be musicians there, or the American military; a really strange combination. You would see musicians falling about, and then these really straight-backed military men. I met Stevo because he used to come in with the bands from outside of London, Cabaret Voltaire and people like that. Stevo played me Matt's demos, and I really liked them. One day he said, 'Do you fancy coming with me, I'm just going to talk to some record companies.' So I went around with Stevo while he was playing these demo tapes to record companies. And that's how I got to know Matt really. We got on like a house on fire. I used to think of him as like my little brother really."

Stevo at this time was practically living in the hotel, which from 1955 to 1975 had served as an American Officers club – hence the unlikely scenario of square-jawed military men under the same roof as pop stars flailing around on acid. Having taken the tape to various labels he decided to try someone he was already dealing with – Roger Ames, of Phonogram Records. In 1979 Polygram bought out Decca, who had owned London Records. It was this corner of the media giant that Roger Ames was tasked with looking after, with A&R assistance from Tracy Bennett. Armed with a demo tape and a Walkman, Stevo and Zeke approached Ames. "Roger Ames, who was the head of London Records, was moving house, and Stevo and I went to visit. We put headphones on him to let him listen to this demo. I remember him taking the headphones off and going, 'It sounds like Jethro Tull.' So we went, 'Nah, fuck off.' He said to me, 'What do you think?' and I said, 'It doesn't sound like Jethro Tull,' and he turned round to Stevo and said, 'Don't bring me your yes-men' – which was really insulting." Ames would later apologise to Manyika at a Phonogram Christmas party, admitting that he had been wrong, but in reality his opinion of Matt's music had changed shortly after the encounter and he was soon interested in The The. Stevo was going to persuade Phonogram Records to put some money where their mouth was – crucially, as it would later prove, without any written promises from either party.

Johnson was back in the studio, re-recording some of the demo tracks with Keith Laws but it was the existing 'Cold Spell Ahead' that really grabbed their attention, and it was decided to re-record it with an eye to releasing it as a single. Tracy Bennett contacted producer Mike Thorne in New York, who told him that though he had a tight schedule he could fit things in. It was Thorne who had produced 'Tainted Love' for Soft Cell the previous year. With all parties happy – Ames, Bennett, Thorne and Stevo – the cheque-book was duly opened. No paperwork, just a handshake. Matt Johnson flew to New York City in May. Regrets over the flimsiness of the handshake deal would come later.

Having spoken to Johnson on the phone before he flew over, Thorne, and his partner Leila, set about making him feel as welcome to the city as possible when he arrived. The Media Sound studios were on West 57th Street, and Johnson was booked into the Mayflower Hotel on Central Park. From the beginning the conjoined twins of 'Cold Spell Ahead' were separated. The first half of that track was the source material and the latter section was forgotten about. The job was to now transform the sound and effectively create a new song. Three key instruments made this possible. Firstly there was an upgrade in rhythm box. The Roland 808 drum machine was much more effective at creating a driving rhythm, its continuing use some three decades and more later testament to its qualities. Over its insistent groove came an equally rhythmic bass line, played by Matt on Thorne's electric Fender Precision bass guitar. It was also the first time he played on a Rickenbacker twelve-string, which he employed for the main rhythm and riff parts. With the rhythm in place the rest came easy and strings from Thorne's trusty Synclavier were brought in at intervals along with some sax and flute by Crispin Cioe of the Uptown Horns. The final, and what turned out to be winning element, was provided by an instrument that Matt had become transfixed with on a shopping trip to Manny's on 48th Street, New York's 'Music Row'.

It was a xylimba, a mallet percussion instrument, with wooden keys over a single box resonator. This was used to add another, much faster, rhythmic groove. The decision to open the track with this riff was a master-stroke. The first few bars of the finished ten-minute recording consist of the xylimba pattern and 808 hi-hat taps, with the 808 kick drum introduced for a few bars before a snare fill brings the guitar riff in and the song suddenly fills out in all its recognisable glory. By delaying the start of the song-proper in this way, Thorne provided club DJs with the sort of intro that could be used to mix from one track to another and, when the song was familiar, announce its presence in a way that was designed to get people onto the dance floor. No other song had a xylimba groove in it, so when you heard it in a nightclub it not only stood out but before long it was easily identifiable, even if you didn't know it was called 'Uncertain Smile'.

The pair got so into the groove that it ended up quite a bit longer than they had originally anticipated; as Thorne was to write twenty years after the session, "at the wrap, Matt and I were quite giddy". With both parties happy, Johnson returned to London with a copy of the final mix and his head turned by New York. With feel-good vibes surrounding him he was blissfully unaware of how events would quickly sour for certain parties, but was no doubt convinced that his life was soon to change. Bennett and Ames, on the other hand, were about to find out just what a handshake was worth. For Stevo, as soon as he heard 'Uncertain Smile', it was worth diddly-squat. He was to demonstrate that a gentleman's agreement served only to prove that, when it came to business, there were no real gentlemen. Though his resulting sleight of hand might have been decidedly un-cricket-like, it is hard to feel overly sorry for a major record label being outwitted. Here was ample evidence that Stevo, still only 20 years old, had the balls to take them on in a manner they wouldn't balk at themselves. Copies of the recording were duly touted to other labels. A major label deal had been the carrot Stevo had dangled before Matt and 'Uncertain Smile' was the carrot he was dangling before major labels. It was a streetwise manoeuvre and in terms of enticing more money to the table he was doing what a good manager should do. Phonogram were left to contemplate the fact that they had effectively paid for a very expensive demo they had no legal rights to. Bennett and Ames were furious, but what could they do except regret something they had failed to do? According to Martin Costello, who ran Cherry Red's publishing arm, they did try to buy the publishing rights to just this one song from Cherry Red in an attempt to sabotage the deal with CBS, who won the bidding war that Stevo created, but to no avail.

As Matt was to tell John Doran in 2014, it was an easy choice to make. "To be honest with you, I didn't really like London Records. I didn't find them that friendly. They were seen as more of a British pop label. CBS, to me, was more like Manchester United coming in to sign me. Suddenly it was Bob Dylan, Leonard Cohen, Johnny Cash, that's where I wanted to be. So I was delighted, to be honest. I got friendly with a lawyer from CBS, a man called John Kennedy, who later became my lawyer and a friend. He lived in Highbury and he would often give me a lift and he loved my stuff. So I thought, 'My God if the lawyer of CBS is this vibed up and friendly...'" Kennedy would play a part in persuading CBS to sign Johnson. "I lived in Highbury and Matt was a few roads away. I kept bumping into him much more than was logical. We would chat when I gave him lifts and we became friends. At the same time it was becoming clear Matt was one of the most extraordinary talents of his generation musically, lyrically and politically." Kennedy took the lead in getting Matt signed, despite resistance from some quarters, and Maurice Oberstein, head of CBS Europe, decided to take up the baton to ensure the label got their man. Mike Thorne duly delivered the master tape to CBS.

If side-stepping Phonogram demonstrated Stevo's business smarts, then the actual signing of artist to label was another example of his ability to generate publicity for something as mundane as a signature on a dotted line. Malcolm McLaren had famously done the same when arranging for the Sex Pistols to sign their short-lived deal with A&M Records outside Buckingham Palace. Stevo's approach was much more left of centre. Maurice Oberstein was no stranger to eccentricity, often bringing his dog to business meetings where he would ask it questions and bend his head down to 'listen' to its advice. At other times he would remove his hat, place it on the table and leave the room with the parting instruction to "talk to the hat". So he was perhaps ideally placed to deal with the eccentric requests of another maverick operator like Stevo, who had told Oberstein to meet him at midnight at a bus stop on Tottenham Court Road. Expecting that they were going to head somewhere indoors Oberstein instead found himself driving Stevo to Trafalgar Square, where he insisted that the negotiations to secure Johnson's signature take place astride the lions at the foot of Nelson's Column. Happy to go along, and no doubt realising the stunt would engender extra publicity for something as mundane as the waving of a pen, he duly agreed. After being asked to move on by the police, the deal, according to legend, was actually signed on the roof of Oberstein's car, after the latter discovered it had been slapped with a parking ticket in his absence, but seeing as he had just parted with £70,000 of CBS's money this was small potatoes. Matt Johnson now found himself in the big league with enough money to buy his own flat in Stoke Newington, with as much again left over.

For now, though, he was still living at the flat in Highbury, still riding his bike over Alessandra's bed to annoy her, and still playing pranks; like the time he called for a hooker but upon her arrival panicked and claimed ignorance. What he wasn't counting on was for her pimp to then turn up in a somewhat disagreeable mood. Alessandra recalls: "I don't think I opened the door but I didn't know what was going on, and he's hiding in the corner of the room." Another unexpected guest for her to contend with was the woman who Johnson had met at a club in New York when he had been there for the 'Uncertain Smile' sessions. "I met her at the infamous Mudd Club on my first ever night in New York. Stevo flew back to London the next morning and I moved into her Alphabet City apartment and left my room at the Mayflower unattended, apart from picking up clothes and messages occasionally." He had told her that any time she was ever in London she could look him up, probably not for a minute thinking she might actually get round to doing such a thing. But one day there she was. Not only did she enjoy an extended stay, she would phone the States daily. New Yorkers like to talk, so it's not hard to imagine the size of the phone bill that she left behind.

These weren't the only visitors that he inflicted on his flatmates. A constant stream of musicians passed through, from Thomas Leer and Jim Thirlwell to Johnny Marr, alone or with Pete Hunt as The Smiths worked out their deal with Rough Trade. They would fuel themselves with beer and sulphate, listening to demos that would become The Smiths' debut album, and demos of tracks meant for *The Pornography Of Despair* as well as some that would end up on *Soul Mining*. Johnson had his portastudio rigged up to a pair of huge Tannoy speakers and the music would usually be cranked up to the kind of volume that would lead to rows with people in the other flats. All in all things were looking up. Unless you lived above him.

* * *

Sometimes life accelerates, projecting you into your future at such a pace you hardly have time to wonder how it was you got there. Going to New York may have been the first sign of such a quickening, but once the ink was dry on the CBS deal Johnson was about to be launched headlong into the life he had been dreaming of ever since he had performed with Roadstar in Nick Freeston's garage.

Now he was with a major label there would come the requisite drive by said label to push their product out to market. Unlike independent labels, who often worked almost purely on the basis of a love of music and were thus sometimes unable or unwilling to enter fully into the publicity game, the established labels, as divisions of much larger corporations, were no strangers to the workings of capitalism. Music may be considered art but its prime purpose from a record label's perspective is its role as product. Annie Roseberry was tasked to direct this indie prospect towards some kind of pop stardom. Roseberry had previously worked in A&R at Island Records, and had played a part in luring a then unknown U2 to the label. She had also been there when the label rejected early The The demos, so having to work with Johnson now was perhaps in the first instance a bit awkward. She certainly knew how to do her job, though, and would later recommend a certain pianist during recording sessions for *Soul Mining*. Pat Stead, head of Epic's press department, was in charge of PR, and for Johnson this would mean a huge and sudden increase in exposure via not just the music press but also the pop pages of newspapers and, where possible, on television. In September he found himself on the cover of *SOUNDS*; in the two-page feature Helen Fitzgerald revealed that Johnson had let her hear a demo tape of his new album, "provisionally entitled *The Pornography Of Despair*". As well as attempting to describe this music Fitzgerald ended her piece by quoting lyrics to 'The Sinking Feeling', one of the songs on the demo.

He now had a whole team of people behind him. Jo Murray had met Johnson in The Ship on Wardour Street just after she started working for CBS in nearby Soho Square. After a short stint in the print-buying department she found herself in A&R as PA to Dave Novik and Annie Roseberry. "Stevo and Matt had made quite an impression on the bigwigs there – mainly Maurice

'Obie' Oberstein, who was obviously a fan of Matt's music, but who I think took a shine to 'character' and a general sense of causing chaos." Oberstein's willingness to embrace the chaos of Stevo was soon illustrated. "One particular day, I received a call to head up to the fifth floor, where all the executives had their offices. Upon entering, Obie's PA motioned for me to go straight into his office. There, I saw Stevo, Matt and Obie having a picnic on the conference table and was asked to join them, which I did, but being so new to the job, I was terrified I might get in trouble. I didn't of course."

Murray was also soon witness to Johnson's love of practical jokes. "Matt did a terrific impression of Obie and would sometimes prank call A&R, and one day, putting on Obie's voice, he asked for Colin Barlow, the new talent scout at that time, to see if he would like to go on a date." Barlow, now a successful operator in the music industry, takes up the story. "I was very young and naive and our Chairman was a very flamboyant man called Maurice Oberstein, Matt pretended to be him and rang me to say, 'Kid, you're coming with me to New York,' and then said what goes on tour stays on tour: I was to tell no one, and if I didn't agree to go I was fired. For me that was it; my record company career was done. I wasn't going. I came out of my office broken, only to see Matt and the entire A&R team waiting for me. Matt then did his Obie impersonation and I realised I'd been totally pranked!"

Before signing to CBS, indeed before the New York recording trip, Johnson had been interviewed by Ian Pye for *Melody Maker*. After giving the reader a sketch of Matt's background and career to this point, there is the briefest of mentions of a single, and a joint venture with Marc Almond. So without any product to promote as such he still found himself with a full-page spread in one of the big three music papers, and though he hadn't yet signed for a major label he told Pye that, "I realise now that I want to be successful. I was green enough before to think that it didn't matter." The feature also contained a tag line that would later prove useful: 'Ian Pye goes soul-mining with shy, introverted Matt Johnson.'

Another significant event had taken place earlier in the year. Soft Cell's 'Bedsitter' single had entered the charts and they were duly invited to perform on *Top of the Pops*. Marc Almond invited Johnson along and in the green room he met Fiona Skinner, who was there at the invite of Billy MacKenzie, lead singer of The Associates, whose single 'Party Fears Two' was also in the upper reaches of the charts. Skinner, who hailed from Dundee but had grown up in England and Cyprus among other places, had moved to London as a teenager and was working at Thames Television, utilising her skills in graphic design. She also did the occasional fashion shoot for magazines like *The Face* and was to appear on the cover of then street-fashion bible *i-D*. Although in a relationship of sorts with MacKenzie, she found herself drawn to the quiet intensity of this east London lad with badly bleached hair who was nervously pulling apart a polystyrene cup. Being equal parts confidence and shyness herself, his obvious nervousness appealed to her.

"We all reconvened later at Camden Palace. I was with Jane Rolink and Stevo came up and said, 'Oi, Jane, I wanna fuck your mate.' Jane said, 'She's not interested.' It might have been because of that we got talking, Matt apologising for Stevo's behaviour."

The Camden Palace was the hang-out of choice for the in-crowd in 1982, and the VIP section upstairs was the place where most of the gossip and bitching took place. At a time when licensing laws in England were still very restrictive, a nightclub was an opportunity to stay out after last orders, and even if Johnson never took to the dance floor himself he would soon have the opportunity of seeing others doing so to his own record. Pre-release copies of the 12-inch version of 'Uncertain Smile' were in the hands of select DJs and Paul Barney, writing in the October issue of *ZigZag* magazine, declared that "the hottest sound being played down the Camden Palace lately has been 'Uncertain Smile', a sad throbbing dance beat by The The. It's designed to pull at your heartstrings rather than get you moving…" It was an enthusiastic Rusty Egan who was playing it at Camden Palace, and anywhere else he was DJing. With release a month away there were more interviews to be done and another trip to New York to work once more with Mike Thorne. In the September 18 issue of *SOUNDS* Helen Fitzgerald described demos of a potential new album as more uptempo than *Burning Blue Soul* but with a similar mix of treated instruments and distorted sound. Quoting lyrics from two songs, 'Absolute Liberation' and 'Dumb As Death's Head', she inferred that they contained the sort of angst that the hipper-than-thou *NME* would gleefully pour scorn upon, though pointed out that in the flesh Johnson was not the person his lyrics might suggest.

Describing to Fitzgerald early The The gigs as drunken affairs he said, "I hate performing anyway, I'm more and more growing to believe that gigging is a pointless ritual." Hardly words to warm the hearts of his new employers. The fact remained that he was happiest in the studio and he told Fitzgerald that he was soon to be in New York again working with Mike Thorne, adding that the new single had originally been called 'Uncertain Emotions' and that he hoped to have his album out by the end of the year. This latter hope wasn't going to be realised but for a while at least *The Pornography Of Despair* still had a future. He told Simon Tebbutt, of the *Record Mirror*, that he was busy writing a new album, often locking himself away for seventeen or eighteen hours at a stretch. In the same article he reiterated his dislike for the rock'n'roll circus and record label expectations, including photo sessions. One such session, with Peter Ashworth behind the camera, resulted in the accompanying picture of Matt posing with his twelve-string guitar behind a wooden chair. On the chair is a plastic cup with the words 'Bring Me Coffee Or Tea' written in marker pen, a reference to the song by Can, of whom both subject and photographer were big fans.

With Pat Stead and Stevo behind him there was no shortage of press, and the latter would waste no opportunity to promote the idea of Some Bizzare as a kind of maverick organisation working within the belly of the beast. In a news feature in *Noise* magazine that September it was suggested that the master tapes of the forthcoming single were only secured from the clutches of Phonogram after Stevo handcuffed various members of staff to their desks. Whether this was actually true or not hardly mattered. What did was being under the Some Bizzare umbrella, which offered Johnson a degree of protection from the more naked capitalist instincts of the parent label. That and having the talent that allowed him to be considered as a prestige signing rather than the more usual cash cow. Not many artists fall into the former camp and this allowed him the luxury of pursuing his artistic ambitions without too much interference from the men in suits. It was a luxury he would often stretch to its limits and when weighed up against his publishing contract with Cherry Red represented the positive side of the win some, lose some adage.

It must have seemed like win, win, win in the autumn of 1982, but with all the sudden success, and personal milestones reached, came a certain amount of despair and angst. "I've been having weird dreams, almost nightmares lately," he told music journalist Chris Bohn, "now that everything's started going really well and all. The other night I was in my bedroom which is like a little coffin anyway, and I started dreaming I'd sold myself to the devil! I was thinking I was going to die, like all these other people who'd died young and they'd sold themselves to the devil too! Then the ceiling was coming down and I didn't know what to do." Familiar with the Robert Johnson crossroads myth he was now obsessing over the idea that there would be a price extracted from him in return for the good fortune that had come his way.

In a second interview with Ian Pye he again admitted his insecurities, but also revealed some angst over the amount of money that CBS had paid to secure his talents. He also bristled when Pye referred to 'ex-colleagues' who had been suggesting he had 'sold out'. Though it was six years since the birth of punk the idea that being on a major label was selling out was still a topic of heated debate in interviews with most bands who were coming through the ranks of the independent scene. Just who had been bad-mouthing Johnson in this way was not revealed but it was a bone of contention that cropped up in at least one other interview during this period, and another example of the inner struggle that was taking place. He expressed his frustration to Pye thus: "The majors see me as a real militant little git but the independent scene thinks I'm now supposedly a mercenary. I just can't win." He then went on to pour some scorn on the independent scene and suggest that he was ready to move on from what he saw as its angst-ridden world. Perhaps mindful that his words were a result of having his anger piqued, he backtracked slightly to say that he still liked the way 4AD operated. Amongst other things the article revealed that the collaboration with Marc Almond had turned into an album (though Johnson only contributed to two numbers) and the mooted next album was still *The Pornography Of Despair*.

The sell-out jibes weren't made any easier when he was faced with the kind of interviews that occasionally came with the new territory. A fluff piece for the *Evening Standard* in December made *Smash Hits* look chin-stroking by comparison; when asked about his love life he deliberately avoided mentioning anything about Fiona Skinner, instead talking of how his heart had broken when his pet goldfish died. Whether he was protecting his own privacy or hers, it was obvious that he wasn't comfortable giving a more straightforward answer. As 1982 drew to a close Johnson's life had irrevocably changed. Alessandra Sartore described this transformation over thirty years later: "All I remember is that one minute he is a kid who takes his washing home to his mum, and the perception is he hadn't had a girlfriend up until that point, and then, here we go, he's all coupled-up, he's got some success and he's just grown up."

It appears to have been one of those relationships that drifts into being somehow with neither party spelling out its actual start. Skinner was often unsure as to their status as a couple but sees the beginnings of their relationship as starting when he gave her a test pressing of his single. "He had just recorded 'Uncertain Smile', and I remember him giving me a copy; it must have been a first pressing. I went back to my flat and said to my friends, 'I really hope I like it, because I like him.' I remember my friends Alan and Nicola going, 'Oh, we like this,' and that was the start of it."

Reviews for 'Uncertain Smile' were generally very positive. *Smash Hits* and *Noise* loved it, the latter calling it "one of the best dance records to come out of this country for a long time". Dave Lewis in *SOUNDS* called it a "hypnotic recording that hooks deeper into you with its casual intrusiveness the more you hear it". This hypnotic feel was the result of the simple and repetitive riffs, and Mike Thorne's awareness of how to create an extended edit that allowed the riffs to work their magic, whether you heard it in a club or not. *Record Mirror*, the one music weekly that gave extensive coverage to dance music, was less impressed, deciding that it was "long and drawn out" and that the sound was laboured. Stacked up against some of the slick disco and boogie tracks of the day this might have been fair comment, but when measured against his contemporaries 'Uncertain Smile' did come across as a breath of fresh air, and the record was a staple for a few months in 'alternative' clubs where any kind of rhythmic sensibility stood out against the usual indie and goth fare. The B-side of the 12-inch release included two tracks that featured the flute and saxophone of Steve Sherlock, who had been in Neu Electrikk with Steve Parry. The 7-inch release only included one of these tracks, 'Three Orange Kisses From Kazan'. These two numbers were barely mentioned in any reviews, though many fans were to regard them with affection, perhaps because they represented the 'lost album' that *The Pornography Of Despair* would soon become. In reality they sound much closer to *Burning Blue Soul* than *Soul Mining*, with a muddy production that does them no favours, especially when compared to the production values demonstrated on the A-side.

Though critical reception for the single had been generally positive, the UK charts were barely troubled by its release. Registering for only four weeks it peaked at number sixty-eight in the second week of December. Its timing, coming as it did during the business end of the traditional rush for a Christmas number one, may not have helped but at least CBS had got their boy out into the world. Of more significance is what the song suggested about Johnson's progress. 'Uncertain Smile' is the first real sign of the lyrical qualities that he would rapidly develop. There is a new sophistication and an establishment of what would be recurrent lyrical themes, conscious and perhaps sometimes unconscious, namely relationships and the angst that attends, in this case, unrequited love, but in the future, love itself.

I've got you under my skin where the rain can't get in/But if the sweat pours out/I'll try to swim and pull you out. These are much more polished and poetic lines than those that had come before and as such made for a memorable refrain. The nature of his writing and depth of his emotional enquiry were something that belied his then tender years. He would soon add politics to his thematic handbook and develop a surgical precision for cutting into political undercurrents that would resonate for years, sometimes decades, afterwards. It is worth remembering, however, that the lyrics to 'Uncertain Smile' had been written some time before; it was with his next recording that he used his newly developed writing skills in a more controlled way. When it came to the words for 'Perfect' he had a set idea in mind and had to find the words to fit. Though not overtly political, the tone here was one of cynicism and his use of irony, though rendered with fairly broad brush-strokes, was a useful method for him to comment on something other than affairs of the heart or self-doubt. The decade was only two years old but the agenda of those in power on both sides of the Atlantic was, clearly, to present reality through a lens of distortion, and much pop music duly obliged with this tendency to escape from reality. Johnson, though, was having none of this nonsense.

CBS, happy with the results of the first sessions with Mike Thorne, asked for more of the same and in October sent Johnson back to New York. Significantly, it would turn out, Stevo, who had been urgently called back to London on the first day of the first trip, would be around for the duration of this one. Whereas the sessions earlier in the year had been a positive and productive experience, second time around things didn't run so smoothly and it wouldn't be long before they spiralled out of control. Johnson's idea for his lyric, which he had written in the Highbury flat on whatever scraps of paper came to hand, was to capture an idea that underneath the surface of the modern world there still existed the deprivation of past times, such as the Great Depression. To finesse this he wanted to have the harmonica parts of the song recorded by an old blues harp player. Whether or not such a person existed in a way that matched the image in his head, the idea was soon ditched because no such musician could be found. Thorne suggested instead the ex-New York Dolls singer David Johansen, who happened to be a very good harmonica player. It was clear, however, that things weren't quite right – not with the playing, but with the general atmosphere. Johnson described the studio vibe to Simon Tebbutt of *Record Mirror* that December as being sterile and like an "undertaker's parlour".

The first sign that things weren't going to run smoothly was when there was a disagreement as to what equipment was necessary, with Thorne keen to employ his Synclavier sampling system and Matt opting for a cheap, new piece of kit from Japan, called an Omnichord. The difference in price of these two pieces of technology was significant – one costing thousands of pounds, the other just a few hundred. The huge Synclavier also dwarfed the Omnichord, making it look like a toy. This led to a kind of Crocodile Dundee moment in reverse, as Johnson later related to Johnny Marr: "I brought a little Suzuki Omnichord with me. Mike looked at it and said, 'I've got a Synclavier, we're using that,' and I said, 'Well, no actually, we're using this.'"

Things got worse when Johnson began to doubt his ability to sing his lyrics with the necessary conviction. Having recently trousered a sizeable advance from CBS, he now doubted the authenticity of his voice when it came to singing about deprivation and despair. To get around this he hit upon the idea of immersing himself, albeit temporarily, in some of New York's then legendary lowlife by way of inspiration. When, at some point, he indulged in a joint of pure Hawaiian grass, much stronger than anything he was used to, things became more exotic than he could bear, and so began what he later described as a "three-day bad trip". Not being able to face going into the studio he turned to Stevo for help; with the logic of the young and foolhardy Stevo recommended an ecstasy pill. When this didn't have the desired results they resorted to some Quaaludes. This cocktail of drugs, though doing wonders for blowing away the sterility, was hardly conducive to any kind of productivity. Johnson was in a complete daze, walking into equipment, and it was clear to all that nothing useful was going to be accomplished. Johansen was somewhat taken aback by the drug-enhanced behaviour of Johnson and Stevo in the studio. He may have been in a band notorious in the past for the drug habits of some of its members but he nevertheless saw the attitude of the two young men from England as unprofessional. Thorne, who hasn't got much positive to say about these sessions, lays the blame mostly on Stevo who, he thought, as manager should have been setting some kind of example, rather than leading his young charge towards the subsequent trail of mayhem.

With the atmosphere in the studio having gone from awkward to unworkable, Stevo's solution to his and Johnson's frustrations was to indulge in that well-worn rock'n'roll habit of hotel destruction. They were sitting in their room and Stevo, upon finishing a call to England, said, "I've always wanted to do this," before ripping the phone off the wall. The pair then proceeded to go berserk, trashing the room, emptying some of its contents out of the window and racking up what would amount to a fairly hefty bill for CBS to subsequently deal with (perhaps not stopping to consider that CBS would just put it on Johnson's tab). But it didn't stop there. Throughout the sessions Johnson had been struggling with doubts about the authenticity of his artistic voice when it came to the lyrics of 'Perfect'. In a nutshell, how could he sing these words with convincing feeling when he had not experienced the requisite deprivation and alienation he was attempting to describe?

In pretty short order two ideas collided. Johnson felt he needed to immerse himself further in the underbelly of America. Stevo, meanwhile, thought that a road trip in the style of Hunter S. Thompson might be a jolly good laugh. Ignoring their obligation to record a single for CBS the pair went AWOL, heading off on the road trip to Detroit and Toronto.

In Canada the madness subsided and Johnson rediscovered himself. In hindsight it is easy to see that signing to CBS, and the sudden expectations this brought with it, had led to self-doubts, and all the stress that came with this. The road trip was the release of weeks, maybe months, of pressure that had built up with no time to reflect on the sudden and extreme changes that were occurring in his life.

He returned to London in time to take Skinner to Battersea Park for the November 5 firework display. A month later he was a cover star, sharing the cover of *Melody Maker* with Marc Almond. When Marc and the Mambas performed at the Theatre Royal on December 5, 1982 he joined them on stage to perform 'Angels', adding what the *Melody Maker* review called "blistering guitar and treated tapes". Johnson's contributions to Almond's album included co-writing the tracks 'Angels' and 'Untitled' and providing guitar to two others. Reviews were somewhat lukewarm and Almond himself has written about the album in a manner that suggests he looks back on it in a similar way.

It had certainly been a whirlwind year and though the second New York trip had been a disaster as far as recording goes, producing nothing more concrete than a hefty hotel bill, it had been a cleansing exercise of a sort. With a clearer head Johnson decided that Thorne wasn't the right man for production duties. Stevo had met Thorne's former engineer, Paul Hardiman, when he had worked on Soft Cell's 'Tainted Love' and thought that he would be the right man for Johnson. His instincts proved correct, and the timing was perfect. Though Johnson was in acknowledgement of Thorne's talent, and kindness as a person, he had come to the conclusion that working with established producers wasn't the way forward. "I had decided that from now on I would co-produce my albums. I knew my way around the recording studio and I also knew exactly how I wanted my songs to sound. In fact, when writing songs it wasn't just the music but also the sound that I'd be working out in my head. I needed a creative foil, though, rather than just an engineer for hire. I decided the ideal situation would be to find talented, ambitious engineers who I would offer a co-production credit to, rather than established producers, who were often set in their ways and quite controlling. Paul Hardiman, Warne Livesey, Roli Mosimann and Bruce Lampcov all fitted this bill." This was to prove a pivotal decision, and it was Hardiman entering into the picture that paved the way for aborting the problematic *The Pornography Of Despair* and making the creative leap towards *Soul Mining*.

9

NICE SPEAKERS, JOHN

JOHNSON'S BEHAVIOUR DURING THE 'PERFECT' SESSIONS
in New York might have been due to the stress of dealing with the
sudden rush of his career onto a different level, the waywardness
of his manager, or the cocktail of drugs – probably all three – but
the mad jaunt north was clearly cathartic and he indicated in at
least one interview that he "rediscovered" himself when he was in
Canada and Detroit. With the cobwebs duly blown away he was
ready to start working with Paul Hardiman.

Thus 1983 was to begin with the stability and financial benefits
that came with the backing of a major label, a new relationship
and the support of the growing crowd who were part of Some
Bizzare, and shared a gang mentality that came with outsider
status. The change in his circumstances led him to conclude that
The Pornography Of Despair project needed shelving. He had begun
this in a transitional period of his life and career and so much had
happened since that it, possibly, no longer seemed as relevant.
Certainly he was struggling to make the music work, hampered
by recordings that fell short of what he wanted. Though he knew
his way round a studio, he was astute enough to recognise he
needed someone with more skill to get the quality he now aspired

to. Some of the songs from *The Pornography Of Despair* were hastily re-recorded and released as B-sides and it is clear to the ear that they lack the sophistication of the A-sides, that they were stuck somewhere between the experimental sound of *Burning Blue Soul* and the fully realised sound he was able to achieve with *Soul Mining*.

Trends in popular music had also shifted considerably by 1983. The post-punk explosion that had seen all manner of radical and independent music in the charts had dried up when it came to the Top 40. In the third week of February, the rather bland, slightly funky pop of Kajagoogoo was number one and the charts were full of similar acts who were championed by magazines such as *Smash Hits* and marketed to a younger generation. The bulk of the rest of the chart was made up of well-established acts making 'safe' music and the regular flow of disco and soul from new and established artists alike. The highest chart position from anyone remotely connected to the independent scene was for Echo & The Bunnymen, who were at number thirty-two with 'The Cutter'. Johnson had no desire to make bland pop music. Equally he didn't want to be stuck in the indie ghetto, forever hitting the upper reaches of the independent chart but never reaching a wider audience. He was also determined to wield as much control as possible. This was no easy feat and the music industry is full of tales of artists who have fallen foul of the dictates of their label and contractual obligations. Johnson, however, had grown up with parents who were their own boss. This proud independence was therefore instilled in him from a young age, and no doubt the resilience needed to see it through. Though his relationship with CBS wasn't without hiccups, it is significant just how much he was able to call the shots, and a measure of how much key people at the label respected his talent.

Though the recording sessions in New York had been problematic there *was* an end product. Johnson, though, wasn't entirely happy, thinking the recording of 'Perfect' didn't exactly live up to its name. CBS therefore agreed that Paul Hardiman could do remixes for the release, re-recording the vocals and adding some overdubs, though because of a contractual detail Thorne was named as producer, much to Hardiman's annoyance. The job, as he was to remind Johnson years later, nearly cost him his marriage as he found himself in the studio on Christmas Eve. After promising his wife that he wouldn't be late, and that he would get back to Berkshire in plenty of time to help her get presents for their sons, he drove to London and set to work. Johnson sat in with him as they beefed up the drums and sped up the whole track, injecting a bit of life into the rather flat original. Time ticked away and kept on ticking. They finished at four o'clock in the morning. Christmas Day. Hardiman may have been pleased with the result but now he had a long drive home to face the music. "She didn't speak to me all of Christmas Day. We went to church, and I was going, 'Look... speak to me...'" Still, his client was happy with the result, though fans differed in their opinion over which mix was better. The 7-inch version, though it does sound lethargic, with a lumpy drum sound, does have its own wobbly charm, and a lush bass line, complete with the sound of fingers squeaking on the strings. The 12-inch version puts a real spring in its step, rendering the mood more positive. Though this was a good move sonically, it perhaps didn't fit so well with Johnson's lyric, but the bigger loss was the bass line, which all but disappeared into the mix. It was the 7-inch format that generated chart sales, however, and the record barely troubled the Top 40. What it did do was act as the bridge between one project and the next, from the rawer sound of his early recordings to the more polished and fully realised work that was to come. Lyrically, too, it is significantly less a song concerned with personal angst and more one concerned with the wider world. It would continue to cause problems for its creator when a version was added to the CD release of *Soul Mining* by CBS in America, something he would have to wait years to rectify.

There wasn't a clear-cut date when Johnson was working on the album that would become *Soul Mining*. Fiona Skinner recalls, "One night when there was a record company person coming over and Matt left all these cassettes lying around the room with *The Pornography Of Despair* written on them, so the record company would think there was another album. There was a constant writing flow and another narrative took over and that was *Soul Mining*." The enquiries from CBS as to what was happening regarding an album no doubt helped Johnson to make up his mind. Nobody was entirely happy with the recordings that had taken place thus far, Johnson included, so rather than struggle on with something that wasn't quite right it made more sense to start afresh. Though remnants of *The Pornography Of Despair* were reworked into tracks that appear on *Soul Mining*, this was effectively a new project.

What certainly helped the creative process was making use of Fiona Skinner's flat. It was here that he had more room to spread out and, as he always worked on the floor, the room would be littered with bits of paper covered with ideas and lyrics, and with various instruments and pieces of recording equipment. This was how Johnny Marr had found him one afternoon in the more cramped confines of the Highbury flat, crouched over with headphones on, surrounded by equipment. Back in 1983 this was unusual. Though some artists had home-recording set-ups they were generally those with considerable sums of money to do so. Technology was getting both smaller and cheaper at this time but Johnson was one of the few people working in this way. For Marr the process of getting a song to the demo stage involved rehearsal rooms and booking studio time, so the idea that one man could work on his own demos at home impressed him. It was a demo of The Smiths' 'Hand In Glove' that had brought him to London in the first place, and having succeeded in getting it into the hands of Geoff Travis at Rough Trade he had decided to hook up with Johnson instead of returning straight to Manchester. He wasn't expecting the woman who had been on the latest cover of *i-D* magazine to answer the door, so this and the home studio situation he saw gave him an instant appreciation of how things had developed for his friend since they had jammed together up north a year or so earlier.

Johnson had in fact just finished writing a song called 'This Is The Day' using the Suzuki Omnichord, that David of an instrument that had defeated Mike Thorne's Goliath, the Synclavier. The Omnichord was a curiosity, designed in Japan and released in late 1981. It had buttons that played major, minor or seventh chords and a touch plate that you could 'strum' using either your fingers or the supplied rubber plectrum. You could also use rotary dials to adjust sustain and release and there were accompanying, though basic, rhythm patterns available as well as a built-in speaker that meant you didn't even need an amplifier. Sometimes a new bit of music gear reaps instant dividends and the Omnichord more than paid for itself in this regard. The cascading tinkle of high notes at the beginning of 'This Is The Day', almost drowned out by accordion, highlights the lightness of touch it could bring sonically. Designed in part for home use by those who lacked the time or inclination to learn an instrument, like any piece of music technology it proved very effective in the right hands. Importantly, it was a distinctive sound, especially if you were one of the first people to use one on record, which Johnson was, employing it not just on this track, but also 'Perfect' and 'The Nature Of Virtue' from *The Pornography Of Despair*.

Marr, a guitarist of considerable talent already, no doubt got Johnson to show him how the instrument worked as they talked and caught up on each other's news. They were both at life-changing moments in a sense – Johnson working on the material that would establish his reputation, Marr hours away from hearing positive news from Geoff Travis concerning the demo he had left with him. The lyrics to the song Johnson had finished writing must have seemed pertinent to both. In fact this *was* the day that Marr's life would surely change. That evening the pair went out to a gig and heard 'Perfect' being played over the PA. Marr, a fan of harmonica, was duly impressed to hear it on Johnson's record, even more impressed to learn that it had been played by David Johansen, no doubt making a note to relay this information to Morrissey back in Manchester, his friend having written a book about the New York Dolls in 1981.

Writing and recording demos for what would become *Soul Mining* took place over several months, in the Highbury bedsit, and Skinner's flat at Braithwaite House with Johnson always working on the floor. He had invested in a Fostex 250 4-track cassette multi-track and a Roland TR-606 Drumatix drum machine to add to the Omnichord and his existing gear, which included the Crumar, a Yamaha CS01 employed for bass lines, and a Fender Strat. Hanging off all this kit was an array of Electro Harmonix pedals – a Memory Man delay, Small Stone phaser, Y-Triggered filter and Muff-Fuzz distortion plus a Colorsound Tremolo and a Crybaby Wah-Wah. When it came to writing 'GIANT' and 'Waiting For Tomorrow', inspired by his experience of using tape loops, he created short rhythmic phrases which, because he didn't have a sequencer, he would play over and over for as long as he could manage. With these loop-inspired recorded passages sometimes lasting as long as ten minutes it was no wonder that repeatedly playing them back at high volume through his Tannoy speakers didn't impress his neighbours.

Though not a fan of gigging – and in most interviews around this time he was negative or ambivalent about the idea – Johnson has never shied away from a challenge, and so it was that he booked a month-long residency at the Marquee on his old stomping ground of Wardour Street, starting on March 3. For four Thursday nights The The played live at the famous venue, but instead of a small band behind him he opted for something a bit more ambitious. Calling on friends old and new, including the growing pool of talent at Some Bizzare, an ever-shifting line-up saw a host of musicians perform. Zeke Manyika and Edwin Collins were recruited from Orange Juice, Mal Mallinder from Cabaret Voltaire, Marc Almond, Thomas Leer, Jim 'Foetus' Thirlwell, Simon Fisher Turner, Colin Lloyd Tucker, Steve James Sherlock and Jean Marc Lederman. Even Peter Ashworth accepted the invitation in what was to be the last time he played drums live. He remembers rehearsals "somewhere round Caledonian Road". It was almost certainly at John Henry's on Brewery Road, just off Caledonian Road. Manyika can't remember any rehearsals, though as he forgot to turn up for them this is hardly surprising. He would later demonstrate his legendary time-keeping skills for Paul Hardiman when he turned up a mere three days late for his first recording session on *Soul Mining*.

Fiona Skinner recalled years later, "Matt was quite a buzz then," so the gigs were packed with fans and industry insiders. Reviewers name-checked the likes of Virginia Astley, Glen Matlock and Nick Cave hanging out at the bar, along with members of German industrial act Liaisons Dangereuses, and Graham Lewis from Wire. Skinner remembers that "the gigs were fantastic, such a brilliant atmosphere. I bust a gut to get the backdrops done. Our printer at Thames Television got the logos printed in fluorescent pink. A set-designer friend of mine got hold of a load of black drapes and we were in the Marquee that day hanging them all."

Steve Sutherland, reviewing the first night for *Melody Maker*, was almost entirely negative, a trait that was rife among certain music journalists of the decade who only appeared to operate on a thumbs-up or thumbs-down principle; he seemed to have come to a thumbs-down conclusion purely on the basis of what Johnson was wearing. Other reviews were more constructive, commenting that the improvisation that was often taking place on stage – and included the sight of Thirlwell playing a kitchen sink that he and Johnson had found – left the crowd somewhat confused. During one performance, after Johnson had performed solo with backing tapes, band members returned to the stage in balaclavas and launched into chaotic wall-of-sound experimentation that the musicians found thrilling and challenging but some members of the audience found too much to take, such was the intensity of the noise. Manyika remembers the improvised sections well. "There wasn't really that much structure, it was very loose, someone would just kick off, normally Matt, and everyone just sort of reacted to it. I remember one particular gig where we almost had a riot because Marc Almond hit someone with a guitar. The sound that we were creating was just so intense, and then that happened.

The place was packed, everyone wearing black leather. It was buzzing."

What had provoked Almond was a series of bottles and glasses being thrown at the stage from the crowd. Johnson remembers the incident clearly, partly because in the hour of need, half the band scarpered leaving him, Thirlwell and Almond to deal with this sudden attack. Almond swung his guitar like a golf club at the audience and connected with at least one person. Unfortunately it wasn't one of the missile launchers and the victim, a Soft Cell fan, was not only physically hurt but couldn't believe his hero had done such a thing. Almond, who had calmed down by this point, offered profuse apologies, while Johnson made a mental note that the Soft Cell singer was definitely a good person to have in the trenches beside you when the going got tough.

Mal Mallinder of Cabaret Voltaire remembers how Johnson's desire for improvisation took everyone out of their comfort zone, which was as daunting as it was thrilling. "He was a twat, because it was the encore that I played on and Matt gave me a guitar, and just shoved me out saying, 'You're starting it.' So I'm stood on the stage at the Marquee on my own playing the guitar, with no plectrum. I had to use a penny or two-pence piece or whatever it would have been." Jim Thirlwell also remembers the improvised encores. "Each night it would end with a one-chord, repetitive... I hate to use the word jam, but it was a piece that revolved around one chord. This is when Glen Branca was coming into people's consciousness. I feel it was very much connected with that. And each night we had a different guest playing in that section. One night it was Mal, and I remember he was playing and he cut his hand open and he had blood all over his guitar, and another night it was Marc Almond. It was very krautrock. Krautrock meets Branca. Kind of like Neu!"

It was these gigs that were to help him decide which musicians might work best as collaborators in the studio. Having accepted that he couldn't do everything on his own, he needed to trust and respect those he chose to collaborate with. In the event he opted for Manyika, Thirlwell and Leer. The fact that he attempted the residency was an indication that the off-piste venture to Detroit and Canada really had given him a sense of equilibrium. He spoke to Dave Henderson of *SOUNDS* about how his confidence had grown as a result of the confidence others had in what he was doing. In an interview with Johnny Black of *More Music* he said: "Finding a girlfriend changed me a lot. When you're in love, everything seems much better, even if you haven't got any money." Now he had money too, at least more than he had ever had before. And then there was this collection of misfits, led by Stevo.

The social scene around Some Bizzare had two geographical centres – the offices in St Anne's Court, round the corner from De Wolfe, and the house in Hammersmith that Stevo bought thanks to the proceeds of Soft Cell's huge early success. The former was in the same building as Trident Studios and can best be described as ramshackle in both actuality and ethos. Rob Collins joined the operation in 1983 as *Soul Mining* was being prepared for its release. He had been working as a talent scout for Virgin Records and had signed Cabaret Voltaire to the label, which brought him into contact with Stevo and Jane Rolink, who was ensuring that, amid all the chaos, Some Bizzare ran with some measure of efficiency. He was offered a job and took it. The contrast with Virgin was stark to say the least. "We were in the Trident Studios building, on the second or third floor. It was like a building site. At some point Stevo decided to get what would now be dubbed astro-turf, as a carpet, but it was the stuff you used to get on fruit and vegetable stalls. He did the whole office out in this stuff. I don't ever remember a cleaner coming in. There were piles and piles of cables from the studio downstairs, and wood and... just loads of stuff. Stevo didn't have his own office. Jane and I had an office in the corner, and Marion who did the book-keeping had the other office. Stevo is not the sort of guy who kept regular hours, you didn't have to clock in and clock out. It was pretty wild, with all the artists coming in and all the stuff we used to get up to. Everyone was really good mates and really friendly and we did a lot of stuff together."

Peter Ashworth was now establishing himself as a photographer, and so whilst no longer a member of The The, was still part of this social crowd, doing photo shoots with many of the Some Bizzare artists. "The whole Some Bizzare thing was interesting. You had a recording studio in the basement and there were a couple of floors of offices above. The people that came into that place were Psychic TV, Marc Almond, Dave Ball, all sorts of people, and I was also working with them as a photographer. So everything started getting mixed up in all sorts of ways, we were all climbing inside each other's lives." The other people Ashworth refers to would have included Mal Mallinder, Zeke Manyika, Jim Thirlwell and members of Einstürzende Neubauten, Test Department and Swans. Thirlwell had been brought to Stevo's attention by Johnson, who brought his records over for his manager to listen to. He then signed to Some Bizzare on the proviso that Stevo also bring Neubauten on board. In terms of music, thought and outlook this was a pretty radical bunch of people, and though there were similarities – for example, industrial-sounding music – they were hard to pigeonhole and resistant to this very idea. This put them at odds with the music press who liked to label music and cultivate scenes that they could attach these labels to. Johnson was more mainstream than most of his stablemates; he appeared in a piece dubbed 'Young Londoners' in a May edition of the *Evening Standard*, alongside Gary Crowley – the sort of publicity that would not have been likely for Psychic TV or Jim 'Foetus' Thirlwell – and admitted he was a bit of an outsider amongst them, but nevertheless he belonged and felt at home.

One thing that helped grease the wheels of the Some Bizzare social scene, and enhance the sense that they were a band apart, was ecstasy. Some five or six years in advance of the 'discovery' of the drug by a group of DJs and clubbers in Ibiza, there was an even more exclusive coterie of people who had experienced it at a time when hardly anybody outside of America had heard of it. Johnson was initiated via Stevo and Marc Almond. "There was this girl who used to bring them in, Cindy Ecstasy was her name. You know those coat hangers that have that white cardboard strip on them, I suppose to stop the trousers getting creased? She would put the pills all the way along the inside of those, on all her clothes, taking a hell of a risk, and you would get a phone call, 'Cindy's in town', or 'Cindy's coming to town', and we'd all meet up in a friend's flat in Knightsbridge. It blew my mind the first time I took it, and I think it was a lot stronger back then, though everyone says that don't they. But it was powerful stuff and we got quite heavily into it, and so that influenced *Soul Mining*."

Cindy was one of the few people anywhere on the planet to have a connection to its source. Almond, Ball and their backing singers had developed a taste for the drug during recording sessions in New York, and back in England it was a taste they wanted to continue. Cindy was coming to England to sing on Soft Cell tracks, such as 'Torch', and perform on *Top of the Pops* or film videos, like the one for 'Seedy Films' where she and Almond are being driven round Soho by Dave Ball, clearly under the influence. There was therefore ample opportunity for the Some Bizzare crowd to be introduced to the drug and consequently stock up on supply. As well as indulging at people's homes it was also tempting to try it anytime, anyplace, anywhere and so it wasn't unusual for an office tea-break to turn into an MDMA-break. One wonders what any patrons of the Ship on Wardour Street, imbibing nothing stronger than alcohol, made of the wide-eyed loved-up people who had downed tools for the day in deference to that ecstasy feeling. This was the drug in its pure form, coming straight from the chemist. MDMA was still legal in America at this time and would remain so for a few years.

It wouldn't be until October 1985 that awareness outside this exclusive enclave started to spread, thanks in part to an article by Peter Nasmyth in *The Face*. Even as late as 1987 some people were still referring to it as Adam; it was the house scene that firmly established its nomenclature. Johnson continues: "There was just a small group of us doing it, here and in New York. I was spending quite a bit of time in New York at that stage as well. I overdid it once. I think I took about five or something ridiculous. I turned into this stream of water, pure consciousness. I don't know what I was getting up to in nightclubs. I don't know how I got there, how I got home. Obviously I was with a group of people, and Fiona, and it was so… out there. I would not want to go that far out there now. Yeah, it was odd because at the time no one had heard of it."

There were frequent parties in Knightsbridge, according to Fiona Skinner. "William Street, where Alex Kerr Williams lived, was the hang-out – we would all be partying there. Wham! used to hang out there. Alex, before she met Zeke, was going out with Adrian Thrills. There would always be a party. William Street was the road next to Harrods. It was a massive flat, but her Uncle Sparrow just happened to have a bedroom there and he had been there since the 1960s." The main hang-out soon became Stevo's house in Hammersmith. He would often work from home in the mornings and turn up at the office above Trident later in the day. Rob Collins certainly remembers Jane Rolink and himself being in the office much more than their boss. Finding the big house a bit lonely Stevo asked Zeke Manyika, who was tiring of travelling down constantly from Glasgow, if he wanted a room. "I moved in. He needed company, and he was really organised at that point – he was still Stevo, but he was very organised, and he was house-proud, because it was the first house he'd ever bought." Skinner concurs with this last observation. "He was incredibly house-proud and he was fun at first. One morning at about 3 a.m., after we had all been up on whatever, he started frying quail's eggs." But, as Manyika relates years later with a chuckle, "things deteriorated".

This, then, was the new world that Johnson found himself in by the spring of 1983. He was in love, loved-up, had a place of his own, and was hanging with possibly the coolest gang in town. Collins puts it well when describing what it was like to be involved with Some Bizzare at this time. "It felt like us against the world."

With CBS keen to see an album it was time to find a studio. Johnson found himself drawn back to the familiar environs of Shoreditch where John Foxx had designed and built a studio called

The Garden. Foxx had started his musical life as Dennis Leigh, forming a band called Tiger Lily in 1974. He changed the name to Ultravox! in 1976 but three years later decided to pursue a solo career and realised that having his own studio would give him greater artistic control. At the start of the decade this neglected part of London was completely different to the gentrified version so popular today, and was typical of the inner-city decay and neglect that was evident during the Thatcher years. The building that Foxx had found, six stories including the basement, was so unloved it had small saplings growing out of its upper-storey windows, and some of the nearby side streets had patches of grass growing on the roads. In between rush hours the place was quiet and at weekends it was a ghost town. If you knew where to look, however, there was plenty of life, as Foxx discovered when he, and friend Gareth Jones, visited the Knave of Clubs public house on Bethnal Green Road. "There was a pub near Brick Lane market where birds were sold. Gareth and I wandered in and had a drink. It was very smoky in there, and then suddenly you realised there were hundreds of birds flying around; it was a very high ceiling, and you would see a hand come out of the crowd and pick one out of the air, have a look at it, discuss it, then throw it back into the air. We went in there quite a lot after that because it was just so strange and so wonderful."

Though this way of life was fast disappearing, and though the demographic of the area was changing rapidly, this pocket of London still resonated deeply within Johnson's soul, which was part of The Garden's appeal. The other reason was that Foxx and studio designer Andy Monroe had built it with musicians in mind, and particularly a new breed of musician who wanted to spend as much time in the control room as possible. This, for Foxx, was the heart of the whole process, so he built one of the largest control rooms he could, much bigger than was then the norm. For Johnson, this was obviously appealing. The studio was fairly minimal but well designed, with a 24-channel Amek desk, some AMS delays and reverbs, Urie compressors, other well-chosen outboard and a decent microphone collection. The live room also appealed to Johnson, and he wasn't the only one interested in the studio. The Cure, Madness, Siouxsie & The Banshees and Depeche Mode had all recorded there. In fact it proved so popular that Foxx could never secure a slot for himself. Though other studios, such as the Townhouse, Advision and Genetic were used, it was the homely Garden where most of the magic took place. There was a relaxed atmosphere that meant even Fiona Skinner's two cats were welcome to hang around, and Foxx basically left Johnson and Hardiman the keys, letting them come and go as they pleased. Skinner herself was sometimes present, sitting on one of the sofas, sometimes falling asleep. Working in television meant she was familiar with a recording situation and knew when to keep quiet. With a small team of trusted friends to help Johnson with the music – Zeke Manyika, Thomas Leer and Jim Thirlwell – the convivial atmosphere led to a rewarding experience for all involved inside the studio, if not always beyond its walls. Hardiman, living in Berkshire, had a daily drive back and forth at unsocial hours. Parking wasn't a problem but local kids were, and when he found some of them sitting on his car one day he duly told them to "Fuck off." Emerging from the studio twelve hours later he discovered they had, as instructed, fucked off, but not before they had covered his car with paint stripper and white paint. Aside from this, and the frequent problem of locating anywhere nearby for food and drink, it was as good as it gets.

This was also no doubt due to the fact that there was less pressure on Johnson at this stage of his career. As most people were barely aware of *Burning Blue Soul* he had less to live up to. He was also at the start of his first creative peak – that moment when everything clicks for an artist, when the low-hanging fruits of inspiration are abundant and higher forces seem to be at work. A lot of the credit for the success with which Johnson was able to capture on wax what he wanted has to go to the crispness and luxurious warmth that Hardiman was able to bring to the sound. As interesting as the recordings with Thorne are it is only with *Soul Mining* that the essential sound of The The begins, one that combines the hard edges and experimentation of Johnson's early work with the polished sophistication that allowed it to sit comfortably with the new pop sensibilities that were beginning to dominate in the 1980s. There is also the vibrant sense of depth to the sound that would soon be diminished in the recording world, as the analogue equipment responsible was rapidly being replaced by digital technology.

Manyika credits both Hardiman's skills behind the desk and Johnson's ability to create the right atmosphere as being key to the success of the sessions. "He knew to take the vibe into the studio. He knew the right people. He knew exactly how to get that atmosphere. When I hear it, even now, I can feel that spirit. It was actually a rather easy album for him to make, considering how good it is. All the things in the universe were in balance. Sometimes you just get that." Thomas Leer has equally fond memories of working on the album. "Matt was great to work with. He had lots of ideas but was open to suggestions. I remember laying down my parts, peering over the top of my little Korg synthesizer at Paul Hardiman's quizzical face. He didn't get me at first and I didn't get him, but in the course of the sessions I really warmed to him and decided he should produce my own album later that year. It was also great just hanging out in the studio with Matt and Zeke. There was always a lot of laughs." Working in the basement meant that it was easy to lose track of time, day and night, and so all that remained was to submerge into the creative process and get lost in music. With minimal interference from his record label, despite being only 21 years of age, Johnson had the time and the space to record at a relaxed pace that was conducive to studio improvisation, which was to turn his demo material into the inspired collaborative result that made it to vinyl. The limited palette of instruments, rather than any kind of hindrance, became a strength and Johnson's skill in blending guitars and acoustic instruments with synthesizers blossomed. What helped was getting his hands on the versatile and punchy sounds of one of Roland's newest keyboards.

"John Foxx had just got a Juno 60, and he said, 'You can use anything, apart from my new Juno 60,' which was under lock and key in the cupboard. After about a couple of weeks – I was working down there for months I think – I couldn't resist it, so I sneaked the forbidden Juno out to try and thought, 'This is fantastic!' We did most of the album with it. And he came down one night – he was a lovely guy John – he came in, looked round, saw us using it… and just nodded. And that was it. We got away with it." Foxx, the man who couldn't get into the very studio he built, also dropped in late one night when Johnson and Hardiman were indulging in their usual post-session joint. The pair, confronted with his tall, calm presence were, all of a sudden, rendered somewhat paranoid and after a lengthy stoned silence could only muster a "Nice speakers, John," by way of any kind of conversation. Hardiman was a big fan of Foxx's studio. "The control room was great. It was big and the DI sound was great, so we did DI a lot of the guitars, but it sounded fantastic." This is a reference to plugging the guitar directly into the mixing desk, using the desk pre-amps, rather than placing a microphone in front of a guitar amplifier. He also loved the sound of the live room and a combination of his ear and the studio space and equipment gave *Soul Mining* a richness and warmth that Johnson was never able to emulate.

'I've Been Waiting For Tomorrow (All Of My Life)' opens the album with the number seven mysteriously missing from the sampled countdown at the beginning. The lyrics are seething with frustration and angst as Johnson not only refers to unrequitedness but to love itself as being like a cancer. One can only conclude that these lines were written before his relationship with Fiona Skinner began, but the anger then casts its net wider and he fumes about pretty much everything, including fate, rendering him in a permanent state of the present where the tomorrow wanted never comes. Ignoring the philosophical nuggets that this idea throws up it is clear to see that this lyric is Johnson's first overtly political one, as he rails against society and what he sees as the machinery that has created it. The lines, *I've been filled with useless information/ Spewed out by papers and radio stations*, about the subtle propaganda of the state, were written a few years before Margaret Thatcher was famously quoted, in a *Woman's Own* interview, as saying there was no such thing as society, intent as her government was on completely reshaping it.

With such anger in his words Johnson was clearly going to need the sound to match, and Zeke Manyika and Thomas Leer obliged with a blistering drum attack and delirious keyboards respectively. The track is one of Leer's favourites. "It was just a really exciting track to play on. I always get a thrill when I hear it." Though when writing it Johnson had employed a loop style and drum machines, the playing on the album version is live and shows off why The Garden was in such demand; not just for its laid-back atmosphere but for the sound of its live room. Certainly the most aggressive track on the album, sonically it points towards the sound of *Infected* with its emphasis on the attack of all the instrumentation, and Johnson's taste for industrial music informing the tone. This was aggressive music for aggressive times. It was less than two years since the riots, only a matter of months since the war in the Falklands, and slap bang in the middle of an escalation of the arms race which saw the arrival of American cruise missiles on British soil, an act that had some people lamenting that Britain was acting like a US aircraft carrier. The response to all this, and to Thatcher's monetarist policies was, for many people, anger, but for Johnson there was personal anger spilling out. Driven as he was to succeed he seemed to suggest that one of his weaknesses was the inability to actually do what needed to be done, singing, in self-accusation, *Another year older/and what have I done?* This was a theme he would return to. In fact it was something that would come to resemble a monkey on his back.

Another song reflecting on the state of the nation was 'The Sinking Feeling', which Johnson wrote in the bedsit in Highbury before the Falklands War. Here he expressed in full his views on the state of things now it was clear that the outcome of the conflict had given Thatcher and the Conservatives a mandate that just a year before had looked highly unlikely. The general election was then some way off but there is a sense of resignation, and despair in the anger displayed, that the result of this was inevitable (and the landslide victory for the Tories duly came in June 1983). He sings of being 'raped by progress' that was bringing with it a permanent state of affairs and he says that this despair and anger makes him *just a symptom of the moral decay/That's gnawing at the heart of the country*. And yet, as desperate as the words sound, the music itself is uplifting. There is nothing he can do except this. Music is his only weapon. He is the proverbial poor boy in a rock'n'roll band that The Rolling Stones sang about. Here Johnson hit upon something that very few people could manage – to sugar the pill of political and philosophical musings with the sort of melodies and rhythms that pop music generally reserved for more frivolous lyrical content, and this gave him an edge that separated him from nearly all of his contemporaries. He would refine this technique over time, with more overtly political messages married to ever sweeter melodies, and eventually this subversive quality to his work would cause him problems from certain sections of the music press.

Sandwiched between these two songs is an altogether different animal in the shape of 'This Is The Day', which is probably Johnson's most well-known and possibly most popular track. It is, for many, the best example of a bittersweet approach that enables him to present music that is melancholy and elevating in equal measure, the fine balance of which adds a discreet tension. At first glance we are in the familiar territory of regret and the battle with time, though instead of a tomorrow that won't come and fulfil his hopes, Johnson laments not being able to return to the past. The cascade of notes from the Omnichord that Johnny Marr heard in the demo version were now partially obscured by a breezy piece of accordion playing by Paul 'Wix' Wickens. Accompanying him with equal deftness is Paul Boyle on fiddle and it is surprising that these two folksy instruments somehow don't draw more attention to themselves.

Closing side one is 'Uncertain Smile' but the sound that Hardiman was delivering in the studio meant that the Mike Thorne version wouldn't sit right, so there was no option other than re-recording it. The new version was certainly more dynamic and cleaner, with the flute of the New York mix disappearing, but as often happens in the studio the protagonists sensed that something was missing and weren't sure what to do to fix it. Andy Duncan, who had worked with Linx and Wham!, had done a sterling job with his drum track but there was now an abundance of it in the second half of the recording with little else on top. Rather than cut the song short, Johnson and Hardiman decided that the length of the track was fine, it just needed something adding. After a serious amount of head-scratching and discussion it was decided that the beautiful-sounding Yamaha C3 baby grand piano sitting there in the live room might be the answer, and Annie Roseberry, who had made the suggestion, was asked if she knew of a good candidate. She suggested Jools Holland, who had tinkled the ivories with Squeeze until they had split the previous year, and was now better known as compere of Channel 4 music show *The Tube*. It proved to be an inspired choice, as Johnson was to relate to Kevin Foakes at an event to celebrate the reissued box set of *Soul Mining* some thirty-one years later. Holland had turned up on a sweltering hot day in his leathers having arrived on his motorbike, helmet in hand, ready for work. "Jools came down, very, very nice chap, very low key, and sat at the piano. 'Oh, this is nice,' he said, then put the headphones on and he played it through. He didn't play the whole song, he just played it for about two minutes, and realised it was the same four chords repeating to the end, and then he said, 'Okay, I'm ready to go for it now. Are we ready to go?' We said, 'Yeah, we're ready to go,' and put it in record and then as the song progressed and the piano solo progressed Paul Hardiman and I were just looking at each other going, 'Oh yes!' Because we just knew we had something special. It just built – crescendo upon crescendo. It was incredible.' Afterwards Holland said he was hungry, and with limited options in the area, the party walked to Bethnal Green Road to Gina's Cafe, as Hardiman recalled for one of Johnson's Radio Cineola broadcasts nearly three decades later. "We didn't know this but Miles Copeland was his manager, and it was a hundred quid, which was a serious amount of money then. Anyway, we set it up... five minutes, and Matt and I just look at each other and we're thinking, 'Did that really happen?' I think there was one drop-in we had to add. And then we went for something to eat down Bethnal Green Road, and all the way, Matt and I, *sotto voce*, were going, 'I ain't fucking paying for this. He's had a hundred quid for half an hour's work, he can pay for his own egg and chips. I ain't paying.' We were broke."

Side two begins with the minimal and atmospheric 'The Twilight Hour', an early indicator of Johnson's love of soundtracks. There is something moody about the music; it's on the verge of unsettling, suggesting hot summer nights and slowly building tension. The lyric is an extraordinary laying bare of the soul. After all those songs about the pain of unrequited love, now comes one about the anguish of finding love and the anxieties it brings. Fear of the relationship ending seems to fight a running emotional battle with the fear of opening up to another, as a tangled web of insecurities reveals itself in six minutes of self-confessional outpouring. The song starts with pattering percussion and keyboard stabs from the Juno 60. As the layers of instrumentation gradually build the tension, however, the awaited release never actually comes, only the increasing angst in Johnson's voice. The song then slowly fades as both vocal and backing vocal turn to a tone of resignation that suggests the author will never get over his doubts, will always have these inner demons to contend with.

There is no thematic respite with the album's title track that follows. With lines like *Someone captured your heart like a thief in the night/And squeezed all the juice out until it ran dry* we are back with the idea of love being a kind of agony rather than a kind of joy, and the beginning of the next verse spells out the author's fear of opening himself up, and not wanting to do it again. How much of this agony is real and how much imagined is hard to tell but the first line of the last verse offers a clue. *Something always goes wrong when things are going right* sounds like the pessimistic motto of someone who almost needs the security of self-prophesied failure. As he had only just begun what was his first proper relationship of the heart it is hard to see where Johnson's agonies were springing up from or what caused them, but they were real enough. By the standards of an era when laying bare your soul was permissible, Johnson was nevertheless going to attract more than the odd raised eyebrow with the intensity of emotions he was revealing, and one or two journalists started to sharpen their knives.

What saves side two from leaving the listener feeling too uneasy is the nine-and-a-half-minute track that bears the whole album on its sturdy shoulders. 'GIANT' is a glorious ending to the album. Johnson wanted something cinematic to close with, something huge – hence the title, emphasised by the capital letters. When he was writing it he employed methods that would much later be routinely used by dance and electronic musicians utilising computers and sequencers, but at the time were uncharted territory for almost anyone operating in the indie world. Working to a click track he laid down ten minutes of drum machine, then added the distinctive synth bass line, repeating the same tight riff over and over in metronomic fashion for ten minutes. Then he layered various keyboard parts over the top. It would have been recorded in the studio in much the same fashion, this time with Thomas Leer playing the synth bass line, layered over the bass provided by Central Line bass player Camelle Hinds, and so the track slowly builds.

Helping out were Zeke Manyika and Jim Thirlwell. Speaking to Kevin Foakes in 2014, Johnson recalled how the latter's contribution came about. "Jim listened to the track and said, 'Okay,' and he wandered off into the kitchen, and brought back trays, pots, pans, found some sticks… and we didn't realise what he was doing first of all, and then he said, 'Okay, just run me the track down,' because Jim's not really a musician… he's hard to describe really… he's a great producer, he's a conceptualist, he doesn't really play instruments, he plays a lot of samples and it's all up in his mind. And – overdubbing track after track – he built up this fantastic syncopated rhythm before our eyes and ears which fitted perfectly."

Listening back to the track, however, all concerned felt it needed something else and it was Manyika who came up with the missing ingredient of a tribal vocal chant. "That's an abiding memory for me, when we did 'GIANT'. 'Let's do this African chant thing.' So there was me, Matt, the engineer… Stevo was there as well, we did this chant and that was it – done. Normally when you do something, you go away and get anxious for a few days, wondering if it works. I never got that with 'GIANT'. I just knew we'd done it."

In fact Manyika feels like the whole recording experience was pretty much like this. "Sometimes when you are going into the studio you have all the preparation and lots of discussion, meeting each other and sending each other tapes… none of that happened. He would go, 'I've got this idea,' and play the drum machine and we would just go – bang! – we went in and then did it. Bang! Bang! Bang! It was so quick. There was a lot of joy doing that album."

Johnson's memories of Manyika's contribution to the album include many late-night conversations where Zeke would talk about what he dubbed 'African Science'; it was some of this science that he managed to infuse 'GIANT' with. The African connection made its way onto the front cover as well, a painting that Andrew Johnson had done of one of Fela Kuti's wives. Matt saw his brother working on the painting in his studio one day and fell in love with its colours and lines. The rear cover was another one of Andrew's paintings, this one of a screaming head, eyes screwed shut, lurching from the right while a hammer hovers in front of it, about to strike. The contrast of the aggressive image on the back cover and the chilled-out one on the front cover (she is smoking a spliff, after all) is perhaps a good visual representation of the musical content: aggression, angst and dynamic power blended with plenty of harmony, mellowness and ethnic sounds, a combination that made this a post-pill album six years or so in advance of such a concept. The bold images were set off with a hand-designed typeface that Fiona Skinner had painstakingly drawn up on vinyl, printed, then photocopied so that there were enough individual letters to make up the title of each song and the new The The logo, which was so striking that it has remained thus ever since.

SIDE TWO

(INTERLUDE – THE HUNGRY GHOST REALM)

HAVING RECENTLY FINISHED RECORDING *SOUL MINING*, MATT Johnson meets Leonard Cohen. The meeting comes about because they share the same lawyer, Marty Machat, who has asked Cohen to pass on some of his wisdom to the younger man. Johnson takes along Jim Thirlwell. Over dinner Cohen offers his guidance – such as forget about singing lessons and just sing from the heart. He also speaks about the mystical power of melody and of not being afraid to use it to help express some of life's deeper subjects, that gentleness in music (he looks at Johnson) can be just as powerful as aggression (he now looks at Thirlwell). He then warns Johnson about the laziness of music journalists, pointing out that once they force you into a little box you can never climb out of it – complaining that whenever his name was mentioned in any article the words "depressing" and "gloomy" were never far behind. Johnson accepts Cohen's advice, but of course is to suffer the very same fate when it comes to lazy journalists. It isn't long before he becomes Moody Matt. This will become a large part of his public image, a persona he only has limited control over, but the one through which almost everyone else connects with him. Everyone in the limelight has a public persona, of course, it comes with the territory, but if you make your private thoughts public, your ideas, say, on the human condition, or politics, or spiritual matters, then you open yourself up to an invasion of a sort. It isn't that he doesn't want success, and he certainly has no problems with the money, but the attention success carries with it will soon be causing him problems. He is in the first flushes of this success when Leonard Cohen passes on his hard-earned wisdom, but his next project will change this, and he will be conflicted by the notion of fame and celebrity to the extent that at times, consciously or otherwise, he will appear to self-sabotage, in an attempt to keep his private self intact.

Which makes 'disappearing' for a long spell at the start of the next century much easier to do. He has spent a career thus far hiding behind a band name that describes absolutely nothing, and that in the new online age acts as an invisibility cloak with Internet search engines. But wall-to-wall privacy soon makes him feel rudderless. He still wants to say things, just doesn't know how to go about it. He still feels passionately about politics, for example, but without his musical platform isn't sure how to go about expressing himself, until local events catch his eye and he notices that the manifestations of globalisation are suddenly springing up from the ground like the skeletons in the famous scene from *Jason and the Argonauts*. Here is a battle worth fighting right on his own doorstep. He gets involved with local campaigns, such as *Save Shoreditch*, that have grown in opposition to various property developments in this once unwanted part of London, and the thing is: nobody knows who Moody Matt is. He is just Matt Johnson, a local resident who is, just like themselves, ethically, and personally, affronted by the aggressive neoliberal project to destroy the physical past. Nothing moody about him. And if he is a bit serious then aren't they all; isn't this a serious business?

On April 3, 2014 Matt Johnson is accompanying Eva Hrela

to a Planning Sub-Committee Meeting at Hackney Town Hall. Ostensibly it is to object about the proposed installation of a two-storey-high shipping container structure at the rear of her business premises. The bigger picture is that this is just one of the early rounds in a battle that involves much bigger concerns, and the sort of money at stake that will ensure that whatever objections Miss Hrela, or anyone else, might raise are ultimately swatted aside. Eva's small locksmith's shop is in danger of being swallowed up by the looming behemoths of corporate architecture that will crush it like a small fishing boat caught between converging icebergs.

The councillor is dressed in jeans and a lumberjack-style checked shirt, no doubt thinking this marks him out as one of the people, the same as the people who have come here tonight to plead their case. Only he isn't anything of the sort, as he has the power and they have none. In due course he rejects everyone's appeal in favour of the money-men. One wonders what backhanders have been done, when and where, and how much trickled down to the ground. After a couple of hours the charade is done and everyone leaves as powerless as they had arrived, minus any sense of hope they might have been foolish enough to arrive with. Hope that change would happen. Change, after all, is just for poster campaigns for US presidents – a slogan – the only real change being the day that the same shit doth occur.

Johnson promises that this is the last such meeting he will bother attending (though it won't be). He has been engaged in battle for seven years, fighting property developers intent on changing the very fabric of the area that has been part of his life since he was born. But there is only so much that can be done in the face of such power and corruption. Before long Eva Hrela's business has quietly disappeared. This is the murky end of politics where backhanders buy silence and complicity at every level necessary, and where the law is rewritten as the charade of democracy is played out in public meetings that none but the concerned ever know about. This is all part of the machinery that Matt Johnson was famous for railing against, but there is only so much that can be done when you are constrained by a system that favours those in power. So Johnson is throwing his hand in. It is like getting a monkey off his back, he admits. "The odious development plans in this part of east London will proceed afoot but I just have to train my mind to blank it out. It will happen whether I am screaming from the rooftops about it or not and do I really want to use up my 'life force' on such negativity? Absolutely not. I've learned a lot and met some great people and local activists through all this but my life is best served creating things rather than trying to stop others demolishing them. Having battled countless property developers I have finally come to understand that they gain as much pleasure out of destroying an old building as I do creating a new song. They could not care less about local history."

Artist Brad Lochore, who lives nearby, met Johnson when they both found themselves in opposition to the proposed development of the Goodsyard, a wedge of land that straddles the council borders of Hackney and Tower Hamlets. More importantly, where this area was once neglected, unwanted and symbolic of the poverty that has blighted this compass point of the capital, it was also at the edge of the City of London, and this ancient square mile, with its own laws, has been creeping eastwards. The land used to be owned by the railways and by extension the public but they were privatised by Margaret Thatcher, sold off on the cheap and now the land has been sold off again at vast profit. Developers in turn increase their own profit by building upwards. Forty storeys or more is the plan.

Lochore explains the difference between late Victorian London and now. "The cruellest irony is the Boundary Estate. This was the Jago. It was the worst slum in London, a Victorian horror show, highest child mortality rates in Europe with grinding poverty. London County Council acquired the land, knocked the slum down, and commissioned their internal architects to produce something to cater for the same density of people but put light and air into it. They designed it so that all the windows see direct sunlight at some part of the year. So the shocking irony is that for six months of the year they will lose all their direct sunlight, thanks to these towers. You couldn't have a more shocking symbol than this, to put up these huge buildings, to do this to the very first public housing in the entire country... a Grade 1 listed estate. It's beyond me that they are able to propose something like this."

Power. Of the absolute, corrupted kind. Another irony, of course, is that when Matt Johnson released *Infected* in 1987, voicing the kind of anger that so many felt about the policies of Margaret Thatcher's government, it seemed like the worst of times. But it wasn't. It was just the beginning and in order to convince people otherwise the machinery of persuasion endlessly churned out the narrative that we were now going through the best of times. And when the global economy crashed in 2008 they just went into sheer denial – on everyone's behalf. So it seems like, if there is ever a time we need someone like Matt Johnson back as The The, then it is now. But, of course, so much has changed. He is older, like those who followed his career, and behind is a generation who grew up with Blair, not Thatcher. This is more of a Beaten Generation than the one Johnson sang about in 1989. They don't even know they've been defeated. The 'war' has seemingly been lost. Neoliberalism and neoconservatism have won. Privatisation has triumphed. We couldn't stop what was coming.

In the Buddhist Wheel of Life there are six realms. One of these is the Realm of the Hungry Ghosts. The hungry ghosts, trapped by an over-attachment to the world, are tormented by unfulfilled desire. They have huge bellies that they can never fill because of their tiny mouths. Looking at the triumph of neoliberalism it is hard to work out if we have entered the realm of the hungry ghosts or these hungry ghosts have invaded the human realm. Some people spend much of their lives in one realm, others flitting between them. Matt Johnson is familiar with the realm of the hungry ghost, of being unfulfilled by a seemingly perpetual pursuit of things outside oneself in a vain attempt to soothe an aching emptiness.

He even admitted this in interviews around the time of *Dusk*, and in the lyrics to 'True Happiness This Way Lies' demonstrated an understanding of the root of this problem.

In 1995 on the recommendation of a friend, he went to see acupuncturist and psychotherapist Abdi Assadi, himself a former addict. Having both experienced a fruitless quest for comfort they discussed Buddhist concepts of the twin traps of desire and attachment, and an uncomfortable, yet important, understanding that they had shared a trait with the enemy. And how can you square up to the enemy if you behave just like them? If your mouth, too, is like a pinhole? How can you hope to sing songs about the evils of global corporatism if within you is the same hunger that afflicts them?

The first stage of the fight, therefore, lies within. For Matt Johnson it would be a long process and it would be interrupted by inertia. And within this state of inertia he was fighting other inner demons. When he first read John Tottenham's poem about inertia, as funny as he found it, as uncanny as it seemed – like Tottenham had been peering into his life – there were lines that struck discordant chords. Like these, for instance:

I may as well face the fact
That I am no longer capable
Of doing what I once believed
I was capable of doing

There was a fear at work now, and the longer he went without doing anything, the harder it was to contemplate doing anything – 'anything', of course, meaning music. And at this point, the Matt Johnson of the past, in 1985 say, who was preparing another project – admittedly in his own sweet time – that was to demonstrate the sort of ambition that only huge confidence can bring… that Matt must have seemed like a stranger. Moody Matt. Serious Matt. Angry Matt. According to the lazy journalists. About to begin work on an album that, amongst other things, attacked the initial stirrings of the neoliberal catastrophe. Looking back on it, it seemed to be all about battles that would ultimately be lost. He had no doubts in 1985 about the power of music to change things, but now, after Thatcher, after Seattle, 9/11 and an illegal war against Iraq? Now he wasn't so sure.

10

A BAND OF OUTSIDERS

IAN TREGONING HAD BEEN COMING DOWN TO LONDON ON and off for four years until he moved permanently in 1978. He remembers seeing melting roads in the summer of '76 and traffic lights with all three lights on at once. The city was run down and insular in those days and he would often find himself walking back to his flat in the early hours because the night buses didn't actually run all night and cabs were either hard to find or too expensive. In 1979 he helped set up the Do It record label with Robin Scott of M, who had scored a number one hit single with 'Pop Muzik'. Do It would release the debut album of the original Adam & The Ants line-up, and early singles by Yello, amongst others. The label had folded by 1982, proving more trouble than it was worth, but with plenty of years in the music business under his belt Tregoning was an arbiter of good taste.

He met Matt Johnson at the Raymond Revue Bar in Soho at a precursor to the Comedy Club. During the interval he was at the bar: "I think it might have been Mal from the Cabs who introduced me to Matt and said, 'You guys will get on,' and it was funny, we didn't go back in to see the second half. We were just chatting and it was like – 'Wow! This guy's brilliant. I really like him.' He had a white label of *Soul Mining* with him, and said, 'This has just been pressed, check it out,' so I took it home. I was living in a house in Camden at the time with friends, and one by one they were going, 'What is that album? It's fantastic' and they all wanted it. I said it wasn't out yet, so they demanded I make cassette copies for them. We had the whole house listening to this album – they loved it."

It was released in October 1983, after a slight delay caused by the spine of the record sleeve being too thin to squeeze in the accompanying remix of 'Perfect' on a separate 12-inch disc. CBS had decided to release 'This Is The Day' in September, to help push the album, but although it got some decent reviews (apart from a dismissive *NME* one), and was an obvious choice for a single, it failed to trouble the Top 40. Some reviews mentioned the news that Johnson had been struck down by a mysterious illness that had caused temporary blindness. Though it was referred to in more than one subsequent interview it was never really explained as anything more than nervous exhaustion, but the effects were real enough and suggest that underneath all the positive vibes surrounding the recording and mixing of the album there had been an emotional intensity that had caused some kind of psychic damage. Talking to the *Daily Mail* he is quoted as saying, "My eyes are much better but they still ache. I think it's a nervous complaint, caused by having to do so much so fast. The way I feel now I am so ill I can't write. The LP has exhausted me."

He spent a week in the Maida Vale Hospital for Nervous Diseases, where he was wired up and had extensive tests, including a lumbar puncture. Results were inconclusive and the specialists were unsure if his symptoms were caused by excessive use of drugs like ecstasy or if he had picked up a virus on one of his trips to Africa with Stevo. The pair had been on many adventures abroad, becoming partners in crime. Sometimes they would be sitting in an airport, waiting for a flight back to the UK, when Stevo would suggest they fly off somewhere else instead, for the hell of it. Johnson remembers one such jaunt that resembled a sixties caper movie in its scope. "Within the space of just a few days we were standing on top of the Empire State Building, then standing in front of the Leaning Tower of Pisa, then in Rome climbing around the Coliseum and then, whilst waiting at the airport in Rome to fly back to London Stevo suddenly said, 'Hey, why don't we go to Egypt instead of England?' It seemed like a good idea to me so we quickly made a change of plans and jumped on the next flight to Cairo." Johnson phoned home to tell his parents that he wouldn't be home for tea as he was two thousand miles away. He and Stevo hired horses at dawn, and raced off on laps of the pyramids while the hapless owner chased after them. They even got to go into one of the pyramids and explored its hidden depths. It was around this time, when he was taking full advantage of CBS finances (though possibly not considering that he was essentially spending his own money), that the young Matt Johnson decided that he really did like this new life of his. Before the unwelcome effects of fame and celebrity arrived it all seemed like the best fun imaginable.

Reviews of the album, in contrast to those of the early single, were positive. Dave Henderson of *SOUNDS* gave it five stars, calling it "a classic slice of everyman's everyday music, ready for the radio, the dance floor and those thoughtful interludes late at night". A positive review in the *NME* noticed "rare literary flair" and wondered why Johnson wasn't much more successful than he had been, an opinion shared by other reviewers. Steve Sutherland probed the deepest, pointing out that the naked honesty on display might only appear too much because most other music was bland and ineffectual. He recognised that it was the "musical dexterity" of the album that infused it with a sense of hope to counterbalance the angst exposed in the lyrics. It was "great pop" according to Sutherland, who also suggested that with 'GIANT' "Matt Johnson may have touched on some state of abandonment", and "that if he is to go on, then survival lies through living more and contemplating less". In fact there would come a time when he would do a lot more 'living', though not at the expense of any contemplation. Before then, however, there would be a strange year-long lull when he would do very little, once the round of interviews to promote the album were over.

He told Sasha Stojanovic of *Juke* in December that there would be an album the next year, and some videos, and that "the next single 'Body Work' is going to be a total departure, musically and lyrically". Of course none of these things would come to pass in 1984. In the November 5 issue of the *NME* he talked about politics, amongst other things, with Leyla Sanai, expressing that the extremes of the left and right wing were as bad as each other, and that while a Labour government would "be a more humane option than Thatcher", it would "be a relief rather than a cure". He also appeared on the daytime television programme *Loose Talk* and told the audience to "Stop cruise" missiles.

The year had ended successfully with a more or less uniform appreciation of *Soul Mining* and sales that, while not spectacular, were respectable and would remain steady. On a musical level he was garnering a lot of plaudits in the music press while, as a person, thanks to writers basing their perceptions almost wholly on his lyrics, he was often portrayed as being depressive or full of angst, though many who interviewed him were surprised to find someone at odds with this persona, someone with a cheeky, sometimes cutting sense of humour. In a sense the music press weren't sure what to think. His band wasn't a band, with a name that was an anti-name. He was neither an indie cult nor a pop star but something in between. When it came to pigeonholing he was therefore an awkward customer for a media that seemingly wanted to label everything and everyone.

Melody Maker asked him for his 'Tracks of My Year' and in the Christmas Eve issue they printed a fairly eclectic list. The Smiths' 'This Charming Man' was present, perhaps a nod to his friend Johnny Marr. Marc Almond also made the list with his track 'Gloomy Sunday', and there was politics in the shape of Robert Wyatt's version of 'Shipbuilding'. Two dance tunes were also there – Rockers Revenge's 'Walking On Sunshine' and Flash & The Pan's 'Waiting For A Train' – no surprise perhaps when you listen to some of the tracks on *Soul Mining*, with their tight looping phrases and all that Juno 60. But the top two tracks listed were both by Tom Waits, from his *Swordfishtrombones* album, and he was increasingly dropping Waits's name into interviews as the man he found musically and lyrically the most interesting person around. It was an interest that he would try to take further in the near future. *NME* readers, meanwhile, voted him as joint ninth 'Best New Act' alongside Paul Young. The Smiths had topped the list.

Though it would seem to the record-buying public, as 1984 progressed, that he had pulled off some kind of disappearing act, in reality he had started writing *Infected*. He was also building his own 16-track home studio and spending a small fortune on gear for it, including a PPG Wave 2.2, which cost an eye-watering £5,000. He also got his hands on one of the first Emulator 2s in the UK, which set him back an even more eye-watering £9,000, but this would be used on both the writing and recording of *Infected* and as such turned out to be a shrewd purchase. Manufactured by EMU, it was probably the first, relatively – though barely – affordable sampling workstation. At the time the idea of sampling was still a real novelty and could be a source of fun as well as musical endeavour, as Fiona Skinner was to find one night at the Braithwaite House flat.

"I remember being asleep once, and he nudged me half awake and I said, 'I'm sleeping,' and he said, 'Just say your name,' and next thing all I could hear was *I'm sleeping – Fiona, Fiona – sleeping*, being played up and down the Emulator keyboard." Echoing, overlapping, sped up and slowed down, helium-voiced and low, rumbling demon-voiced, on and on, ricocheting round the walls of the cramped room *Fiona, Fiona, Sleeping, I'm sleeping*. "He found it really, really entertaining."

As well as playing around with this early sampling technology, the pair were able to spend time in New York; on Skinner's first visit they stayed with Fran Duffy, whom Johnson had met via Stevo. "Fran had this amazing loft apartment in Chelsea. It was enormous, with a really high ceiling… the first time I'd ever seen a proper American loft, and I just knew then, that's the way I wanted to live." New York at the time was the only city that never slept, a far cry from then-sleepy London. Duffy and his wife took the pair to clubs like Danceteria and the Limelight, and once, to a party at Grace Jones' apartment.

It was during this trip that Johnson visited the New York office of CBS and picked up a CD copy of *Soul Mining*. It had a different cover, the Americans not liking the idea of an African woman smoking a joint and, as he saw to his horror, an extra track – 'Perfect'. "Who the hell did this?" he asked. "Oh that was Bob," came the reply. Bob Feineigle. "Bob was a nice guy, but he had no business doing this." This version of 'Perfect' was a new recording, made during the *Soul Mining* sessions and featuring renowned jazz trumpeter Harry Beckett in place of the harmonica, which Johnson felt was rather flat compared to the New York version that he and Hardiman had remixed. 'GIANT' was the natural climax to a track list that he had programmed with deliberate care, and the addition of 'Perfect' made the whole thing imperfect. Fiona Skinner had seen how long he spent over track selection first-hand. "He would have tapes of all the songs and listen to them and see what order they worked in. He would take great pains over the order of tracks, because he was so into the idea of it being a journey." Johnson would have to wait years before he was able to get it removed, its continuing presence a lengthy and nagging irritant.

At a press conference in Manhattan to promote the US release of *Soul Mining* he was asked by Carol Anastasio if he would be touring the US. "I was planning to do a world tour this year, but if I do it'll probably just be in America. I plan to do that at the end of the summer. I'm not going to play anywhere else, because I have the album to do which I'm going to record in Bavaria in autumn." He went on to describe how it would be a three-piece band but that all the songs would have to be reworked as he felt it wouldn't be possible to reproduce the album live without relying on tapes, and he wanted to avoid this as it made live performance too rigid and sterile.

The tour never transpired and neither would the recording. He talked about doing duets, of African influences and gospel choirs, mentioned again that he wanted to work with Tom Waits, but also Holger Czukay and Brian Eno. But he also referred to a "big argument" in London. This "argument" boiled down to the fact that CBS wanted an album that year and so any recording – in Bavaria or elsewhere – would have to commence in July. In a *SOUNDS* article from April 14 Stevo was quoted as saying that Matt recorded "when he feels inspired, or when he feels the time is right and we record when, where and how we want". Annie Roseberry, however, said that without her agreement Matt couldn't have the studio time. Stevo went to see Maurice Oberstein but he opined that if they couldn't work with Annie then they couldn't work with CBS. Stevo then asked how much it would cost to buy out Matt's contract and after being told that it could be done for £60,000, phoned seven major record companies, who all claimed to be interested. When he got back to CBS they withdrew the offer of releasing Matt from his contract; Matt was then quoted as saying: "In view of the attitude of CBS I think it would be gentlemanly for them to honour their word regarding my release. My faith in their belief has been irreparably damaged. A label that is prepared to 'sell' me for £60,000 is a label I want no part of."

Oberstein refuted the idea that CBS had lost faith in their artist. "Recordings are planned and don't come down from heaven with manifestations from the Archangel Stevo. Managers manage and record companies record their artists. That's the situation and we'll be in the studio with Matt soon making a great record. This is Stevo trying to get his artist publicity between albums. We are grateful." Grateful or not, Oberstein would have to wait another two years before he got his album. The only recording that would see the light of day before then was a track called 'Flesh And Bones' that Paul Hardiman produced. It would appear on the second Some Bizzare compilation, released in 1985.

It was clear that, even at the very beginning of 1984, Johnson considered *Soul Mining* was behind him and that he was looking forward. He told Adrian Deevoy, of *International Musician*, that he was thinking of purchasing a Chroma Polaris keyboard because he could link it up to a computer. The idea of working with computers was appealing to him but he didn't want to abandon traditional instruments at their expense. He believed that computers would become ubiquitous in the future and wanted to get used to them, rather than struggle years later.

In the same interview he also said he had been thinking about getting a band together. "I'd quite like to hand pick a few people, although the people that I would like to play with always have other commitments." But at this stage he only saw a band as a temporary affair, to interpret live songs he had recorded without them. Working with others was still something that he found double-edged. He revealed that some of the lesser-known members of the 'super-group' who had played at the Marquee had asked to be paid, rather than do it for fun, as had been the original idea. Even collaborating on a remix had proved disappointing. Interviewed by Charles Neal for the book *Tape Delay*, he was asked if he was excited about the prospect of Arthur Baker remixing 'GIANT'. Baker was hot property at the time and had already worked with New Order on 'Confusion' but Johnson sounded frustrated. "I just wish he would get a move on because when I was over there recently he just couldn't get it together. I went up to his studio a couple of times and just messed about a little. He was listening to the multi-track and suggested a few things, but he just hasn't done it. So I wish he'd get on and do it basically. If he does it, great, but if he doesn't then..." He didn't. Not only that but CBS had sent the multi-tracks instead of copies and they were never seen again. Three years later Baker asked if he could remix something from *Infected*. Johnson politely declined. He also told Neal that he himself wasn't putting enough effort into things. Neal asked what it was that was holding him back and he replied "laziness". He then said how he could learn from the likes of then number one tennis stars Martina Navratilova and John McEnroe and, like them, strive for perfection. This answer was revealing, though, of just how much probably wasn't noted at the time, for it would be the desire for getting everything 'just right' coupled with a sense of what he would later refer to as 'inertia' that would come to define his progress from here on.

There were also a fair number of distractions. Moving into his own place in Carysfort Road was one of them, and the freedom to party was another. By this stage the goings-on at Stevo's house in Hammersmith were well on the way to getting out of control, as many of the participants are willing to testify. Mal Mallinder from Cabaret Voltaire remembers going round all the time. "Stevo's house in Hammersmith was like the gang headquarters. You couldn't be on Some Bizzare and not go round his house. You would go there before a night out, or you would end up there after you'd been on a night out." According to Skinner, "Stevo would make you listen to this dark industrial music on speakers the size of doors and you couldn't escape, you had to listen. He decided you were listening. And he would do this with journalists too, or record company heads." It was like Stevo, at some point, decided to throw a party and the thing just carried on, for days, weeks, months. It was relentless. Johnson's own recollections sum up the general vibe.

"We were round Stevo's house all the time. It was like one of those 1960s films you'd see of decadent parties and general excess. All the Some Bizzare artists and their partners would be round there much of the time and partying together through the night. The music was almost exclusively Some Bizzare, as Stevo would play us all each other's latest recordings – often at ear-splitting volume. Lots of music, endless drink and drugs. I remember Fiona and I would sometimes go round to a party there but immediately end up in one of the beds taking drugs, with other people wandering in and out of the room. For quite a while it was a really great atmosphere and everyone got along incredibly well. Inevitably things started to deteriorate as the drug-induced paranoia slowly set in."

Also living on Carysfort Road at this time was Paul Webb of Talk Talk. Though he had seen Johnson at parties he had never spoken

Matt Johnson – London 1983. Photo: AJ Barratt.

Fiona Skinner,
Stevo, Matt Johnson
– Promoting
Soul Mining –
Edinburgh 1983.

Another road trip, MJ heading to Mexico in a Cadillac Eldorado 1984. Photo: Johnson Family Archive.

JG Thirlwell and Matt Johnson – Carysfort Road 1985. Photo: Fiona Skinner.

Matt Johnson – Filming *Infected* – Peru 1986.

Brothers of infection –
Matt and Andy Johnson
– 1986.

Mind Bomb band –
James Eller, Johnny Marr,
Matt Johnson, David
Palmer – 1988. Photo:
Andrew Macpherson.

Eugene Johnson – Portugal 1988. Photo: Johnson Family Archive.

DC Collard (left) and Matt Johnson – Performing at the Tempodrom – Berlin 1989. Photo: Henrik Jordan.

Johnny Marr, Angie Marr, Matt Johnson, Fiona Skinner, David Palmer – Rockerfeller Centre, NYC 1988.

Fiona Skinner and Matt Johnson – Shoreditch 1993. Photo: Steve Pyke.

Matt Johnson – Filming the video for 'I Saw The Light' from *Hanky Panky* – 1995.

Lonely Planet World Tour – Jared Nickerson, Matt Johnson, David Palmer, D.C. Collard, Jim Fitting, Keith Joyner – New York 1993. Photo: Chris Buck.

Naked Self World Tour – Spencer Campbell, Eric Schermerhorn, Earl Harvin, Matt Johnson – New York 2000.

to him, but his girlfriend got talking to Fiona Skinner one night and then he decided to throw a party himself. "My girlfriend invited Fiona and Matt came along and that was the first time I ever talked to him. We got on like a house on fire. I remember the next day he phoned me up asking me to help him take his synthesizer to the shop to be fixed, and he was my neighbour – he lived down the road, so we just started hanging out quite quickly after that really. What I liked about him was that he wasn't a muso. He introduced me to things like Tom Waits, whose music I adored. But he was influenced by films too. He would talk more about films than music really."

Johnson's admiration for Waits was such that he was on a list of three people he decided he wanted to approach, in the hope that they would produce some tracks for his next album. Speaking to Michael Bonner, of *Uncut*, in 2016, he revealed how far he got with this aspiration. "I was a fan of Tom Waits and Holger Czukay, and thought it would be amazing to collaborate with them. I was very confident. I just reached out. I also contacted Brian Eno, who came back lukewarm. We didn't hear from Holger, but Tom Waits got back and said, 'Come over to New York, hang out and discuss it.' So we spent a week talking about it. We played a lot of pool – he thrashed me. He wasn't drinking at the time, just soda water and bitters. But he had a big thing going on. He just fired his manager, he was living in the Chelsea Hotel, just finishing off *Rain Dogs*. So it was a fantastic trip, but he said, 'I think you could produce yourself. I'd love to do it but I've got so many things going on, I just can't commit to you.'" Whether or not Waits would have got involved had he not been committed to work on Jim Jarmusch's *Down by Law* film we will never know. The results might have been interesting, though how the prolific Waits would have dealt with Johnson's talent for procrastination is anyone's guess.

The trip was both interesting and useful for Johnson, as Waits introduced him to his own world. "He introduced me to the great Robert Frank on this trip and I had coffee with the pair of them at the Chelsea Hotel. After our meeting I immediately went to my favourite bookstore, Strand Books, close to Union Square on Broadway to buy an old copy of *The Americans* and this triggered a lifelong love of photography. He took me to the old RCA studios where we were going to record *Infected*. We spent a couple of hours in there discussing old microphones and live rooms. I remember that at one point, to demonstrate one of the studio facilities, an engineer pressed a button in the control room and these huge baffles shifted into place to deaden the sound of the live room. We were both suitably impressed. Tom liked it because it was so old school and he was very much into old technology and atmospheric recording environments. He also took me to the Ear Inn, the second oldest bar in Manhattan, which, years later, became a second home to me. It was whilst sitting at the bar at the Ear that he gave me the most fruitful piece of advice. He pulled out of his pocket a tiny notepad and urged me to do the same as him and carry one on my person at all times. He said, 'This is your butterfly net. Without it the words may still come but they will just fly away again, lost forever.' I took his advice. When he came to realise he was just spread too thin with various personal and professional commitments he was very encouraging to me and said that my demos were so explicit that it was obvious I knew what I wanted and that I didn't really need a producer, just a good engineer and a good studio."

In a world where artists are expected and pushed by their record companies to have a continuous stream of product – an album every year, a tour, a couple of singles that help promote said album and all the obligatory television appearances and music press interviews – the long silence of Matt Johnson was unusual. Very few artists would have been given the luxury of a gap of almost three years between albums at such a critical moment in their career, especially one signed to a major label. Clearly enough people at CBS had faith in their man, but also of significance is the role of Stevo. His aggressive style of management, though often bluster, meant that he was able to protect Johnson from corporate pressures. As Mal Mallinder put it, "Stevo acted like a prophylactic between his artists and the music business itself." While Johnson couldn't get away from his obligation to promote *Soul Mining* he resisted the pressures of writing a 'Soul Mining 2'. Though he had released an album back in 1981, this was his first on a major label, and if we treat it as his first album, or the debut album by The The, then, in 1984, Johnson was facing the problem of what the industry referred to as the 'difficult second album'. He had literally been exhausted by *Soul Mining* and wanted to recover. He realised he had no new ideas and therefore needed time to let some grow. He was also, in a sense, in the process of turning from boy to man, and all these factors would play a part in what would look like a lengthy lay-off.

He was still promoting the album and racking up the air-miles in the process. At other times the travels were just for fun, like the time he and Stevo flew out to Kenya over Christmas. Judging by Johnson's recollection, Stevo, as seemed usual, was first to be visited by any trouble. "We landed in Mombasa and stayed there for a couple of days whilst en route to the small island of Lamu. We'd been warned in advance to be careful about drinking water from questionable sources. The night before we were leaving Mombasa we were wandering around some desolate, under-lit backstreets. We were both extremely thirsty when we came across this filthy little bar. I ordered a glass of beer or a cola – without ice – whilst Stevo insisted on ordering a pint of tap water *with* ice. I said, 'Stevo, I really don't think that's a good...' He just turned round and with his Cheshire cat grin, clinked his glass against mine, said 'Cheers!' and quickly guzzled the lot. A day later on Lamu Island Stevo was running awkwardly to the toilet every ten minutes, tears rolling down his face as he was crying out 'I've got dysentery!'"

Having lived out of bags since he left home, the chance to secure a more comfortable domestic surrounding was something of a relief and the CBS advance gave him the funds to do so. Once he had bought the flat on Carysfort Road it was understandable that he wanted to spend time there, both with Fiona and alone. Aside from the new-found comforts, it provided him with space to create a home 16-track studio, though getting down to new music wasn't first on his to-do list; as he was to admit to more than one interviewer querying his prolonged absence, the temptation to sit and watch Ceefax for far too long, to eat and drink too much, was hard to resist – after all there was no requirement to get up and go to work in the mornings. Johnson has described how the material comfort that came with the record deal led to a certain amount of decadence that was more or less inevitable at the age of 22. "You end up drinking more than you should and your internal state changes. You see, often it can take a songwriter years and years to make their first album and now I was onto my, what was it? Including unreleased albums, about my fifth I suppose. So you've got to take time to fill up on experiences again. Naturally one's focus changes, because you're moving away from childhood and adolescence and all the stuff that led up to those tricky years, the early twenties. So I just became more and more interested in politics and religious affairs. Trying to look outside of my own tiny orbit."

He was settled in a relationship, was a critical success and had the money that allowed his material wishes to be fulfilled, and while doubts remained, they were different ones. Sex would replace love, though his reflections on this would not be straightforward, and while angst was not completely eliminated he would begin to direct much of this outwards rather than inwards. He was done with eating himself up and was looking around for other targets. He didn't have to look far; just turn on the television or pick up the newspapers.

With policies that led to a growing divide in the population it is no surprise that Margaret Thatcher polarised opinion like no other prime minister before her. This was the start of the neoliberal experiment that had been road-tested in Chile. As Johnson was to tell Andy Dunkley in December 1986, the government was "forcing people who wouldn't normally be political to become more political". Simply put, it was hard to have no opinion on Thatcher. Growing up with Eddie's influence had given him a definite left-leaning perspective, though there was an element of mistrust of the party politics of the left – not necessarily an ideological one but a healthy working-class scepticism of the depth of belief and commitment behind the rhetoric of politicians who were distinctly middle class. As Paulo Freire might have put it, there was a tendency for members of the Labour Party to talk for the people without wanting to be of the people. Johnson's attitude to the Tories was much less ambiguous.

He had already made reference to the riots of 1981 on *Burning Blue Soul*, but the event that probably had most impact was the Falklands War. Like many of his generation, this played a significant role in his politicisation. The government, who just months before had been staring at almost certain defeat at the next election, used the conflict to drum up a jingoistic fervour and push the narrative that the embers of the dying Empire could be set aflame again. For those who saw through such obvious tactics, witnessing a majority around them who fell for such polemic was a dispiriting experience. A much clearer sign of Britain's status in the world was its subordinate position in relation to America, one manifestation of which was the siting of cruise missiles at the US airbase at Greenham Common. Johnson had been paying attention to the protesters there and his "Say no to cruise" on *Loose Talk* was as much in support of the women of Greenham, whom he admired, as it was an expression of his own mind. Fears of nuclear war were widespread throughout Europe at this time so when he stated his own he wasn't being unusual. His understanding of politics and political intrigue was developing quite keenly. It wasn't the fact that he was dismayed with the state of Britain (plenty had expressed their thoughts about social decay since the days of punk) that was going to fuel ideas for his next project, but the disconnection between the myth that Thatcher and her government were constructing and the reality. It was also an emotional response to this decay, lament rather than patriotism, and it would find its focus in what would become 'Heartland', the song that would serve as the taproot for his next album.

As well as searching for themes worth exploring with his lyrics, he was determined to develop a new sound, one that, while identifiable as The The, was sonically moving forward. At home he started listening to a lot of blues, reaching back to performers like John Lee Hooker, Muddy Waters, Robert Johnson and Howlin' Wolf. He made a mix tape of his favourite blues songs at one point and spent a whole week doing nothing more than listen to it whilst drinking vodka, trying to conjure up spirits perhaps, a feeling. The romance of the bluesman appealed to him. It was somewhat mythical of course, but there was a purity, he felt, about the man alone with his guitar, his bottle and a head full of lyrics that revealed the pain simmering beneath the surface of that subtle, or not so subtle, machismo. The blues also resonated because it represented the well from which sprang rock'n'roll. Though the influence of soul music isn't necessarily easy to discern in *Soul Mining* it is there, but now Johnson was turning from the sacred and looking towards the profane. It was time for songs of experience rather than songs of innocence and what he had to do now was transpose this into a new sound. All he knew at the early stage was that it was going to be harder and dirtier.

Along with finding his political voice came the recognition that he was in a position to project that voice. Whilst many young people were pissed off and angry, Johnson had the option of voicing this kind of anger on a hugely amplified scale, and being in a position to broadcast dissent was an enticing prospect, around which he would shape his new project. When seeking more specific inspiration he found himself wandering and reflecting, like he had once done in Ongar, round the east London streets of his childhood. On one such walk he passed the Forest Gate cinema where he used to go with Andrew. Being a nostalgic person, this brought a flood of memories and these memories, when projected onto the present, got him thinking about the myth of progress. This would find its way into the lyrics of 'Heartland'. Snatches of lyrics and ideas for lyrics would go into a notebook. Thus, bit by bit, the songs of *Infected* would take shape.

All this inspiration-seeking was obviously thirsty work as there seemed to be plenty of time given over to drinking and generally having fun, as Paul Webb points out: "It was the eighties. It was all Muswell's and Long Island Ice Teas, which were called 'Skylabs' at the time. I would go out with Matt and Ian quite a lot, or even out to dinner, because there were so many things to talk about with Matt. He liked the one-to-one conversations." If they weren't in a pub, club or restaurant then there were plenty of hours spent in snooker halls, an ideal pastime and ambience for conversation and after-hours alcohol.

When it wasn't drink, it was drugs, and being successful musicians gave them licence to indulge as much as they wanted. Johnson was smart enough not to overly abuse this privilege, but while there was a side of him that practised restraint he wasn't afraid to experiment and indulge in whatever was going round. "We once went to this party, six of us, three couples, on New Year's Eve and took, I think it was mescaline. We were in this taxi in Piccadilly on the way to the party in really bad traffic, and you know with hallucinogens it slows down time and we were all killing ourselves laughing because we felt like we'd been in this taxi for weeks, and we eventually got there, and the weird thing was, most of the people at the party were on ecstasy. We couldn't stop laughing cos we felt we were on a sort of higher level than them. Then there was this other group who I think were just smoking grass and we couldn't be around them either and it was such a weird thing… it's almost like it affects a certain frequency of the brain and you can only be around certain people. It was like a kind of tribalism, a group who couldn't be around another group. It was really strange."

But perhaps not as strange as what was going on at Stevo's house. Things got so bad that Zeke Manyika and Jane Rolink moved out and into a flat on the Edgware Road. "Marc Almond was having wild parties and bringing people round, and you had Psychic TV there all the time. Nobody could understand that Stevo's house was his escape. He wanted to escape and they just didn't get that, and he couldn't say no to them. I mean, it's his fault as well because when he was enjoying it he'd be, 'Oh, come round my house!' And we'd be doing all sorts of things, but it was every single day; you'd come back from the office, dealing with the same people and you'd come home, eat with the same people. Instead of actually dealing with it he decided to make it uncomfortable for everyone by removing the door from the toilet. Things just went downhill after that. Too much substance abuse; always something going on, parties to go to every night. The local cab company were rubbing their hands, always picking people up."

Manyika laughs at the memory but one suspects that the prospect of having no privacy whilst sitting on Stevo's toilet might not have had the instant effect that he intended. As a solution to his problem it was somewhat left-field and was the first clear signal that, domestically at least, he was losing control. As Manyika infers, things weren't to get any better and it wasn't long before Stevo solved his dilemma, in a roundabout fashion, by selling the house – a rather drastic way of getting rid of the unwanted guests crashing on the sofa.

11

INFECTED

ON APRIL 14, 1986, AMERICAN WARPLANES BOMBED LIBYA in retaliation for the bombing of a disco in West Berlin, apparently organised by Libyan agents. The attack was part of Ronald Reagan's attempt to destabilise Libya. Spain, Italy and France had been against the operation and had refused permission for the US warplanes to use their airspace. In contrast, the UK hosted the warplanes, at Upper Heyford airbase, in Oxfordshire.

On hearing about the raid, Matt Johnson pushed for CBS to rush-release a track he had recorded with Roli Mosimann. The label's reluctance to do so was hardly a surprise. They were, after all, merely a small part of a multinational corporation, and being American put them in direct opposition to the Libyan point of view. In an interview with *The Guardian*, Johnson told Rose Rouse that Special Branch had advised CBS to take down their American flag. 'Sweet Bird Of Truth', written at the tail-end of 1985 and recorded in January 1986, detailed the thoughts of an American pilot whose plane has been brought down over the Gulf of Arabia. There was no doubt a certain amount of unease amongst the CBS executives when they considered that the lyrics echoed reality somewhat, as during the raid on Libya, an American F-111 bomber had been shot down over the Gulf of Sidra, killing both pilots.

If truth be told, Johnson himself was somewhat spooked by fact following fiction so rapidly, though he was to point out to more than one journalist who interviewed him at this time that the gift of prophecy was hardly required, just a television set and an interest in the news. The words of the song had come in a sudden rush one night when he was on ecstasy. At first he feared he was going to have a bad time on the drug, even though he had taken it before, but his anxiety melted away and in its place came all the words, all the lines and they all made perfect sense. Though he had expressed fears about terrorism and fundamentalism in the recent past the main tilt of the lyric was religious hypocrisy. The pilot, who is the subject, is not religious but has found himself fighting a holy war. When his plane is shot down he then discovers a pressing need to find God. The pilot's hypocrisy, however, is nothing compared to that of the religious leaders and political leaders on both sides. Duplicity was to be a thematic thread running through much of the album, one that perhaps isn't acknowledged as much as it should be. Johnson was also railing against the fraudulent Victorian values espoused by Thatcher's government, whilst songs dealing with love and sex were full of deception and self-deception. The inner angst of *Soul Mining* looked rather tame in comparison as he now appeared instead to look into Pandora's Box. These were altogether more adult themes, suggesting that listening to all that blues music had rubbed off. Whether he was courting controversy or it came looking for him, the *Infected* project would be dogged by censorship from start to finish. 'Sweet Bird Of Truth' was just the first episode.

It had been recorded in Manhattan, with Roli Mosimann co-producing and mixing. Mosimann had been drummer in Swans and was introduced to Johnson by Jim Thirlwell. On backing vocals was Anna Delory, working under the name Anna Domino. "Working with him was delightful because he knew exactly what he wanted, which was pretty unusual. Once in the studio, I had all sorts of ideas I insisted on airing but he was very clear about the exact harmony and timing of the part he wanted me to sing."

With Stevo adding to the pressure in his own inimitable way, CBS appeared to relent and the single was released, but only as a 12-inch – a move guaranteed to torpedo a good chart run. To add insult to injury it was then deleted the very same day, such was the concern of the record label of attracting any unwanted attention. It did receive a positive review from the *NME* who went as far as proclaiming it "Single of the Year so far", though *Record Mirror* begged to differ, describing it as "rather ponderous and drawn out". CBS may have won this particular battle but there were more to come, between artist and label, and artist and censor. By the time this first ripple of controversy was over Johnson was well on his way to completing the recording of the album.

Paul Hardiman wasn't going to be involved. Though Johnson thinks, in retrospect, that he might not have been the right man for the job, it was nothing to do with his ability in the studio, or his likability as a person. "The truth of the matter is that Stevo did not get along at all with Paul's manager, who also happened to be his wife. It was all a real shame as I liked Paul a lot and regret not doing another album with him – although I also knew *Infected* was not really the right project for him. Stevo's negotiating skills were extremely bullish back then. He took no prisoners and often left a trail of destruction in his wake. Paul's wife, Eileen, could also be quite a tough negotiator herself and so when it came to working out a new deal for Paul at an improved royalty rate the two of them just locked horns and couldn't get along or agree upon anything."

Johnson had been working on the songs that would become *Infected* for some time when, in 1985, he met Warne Livesey in a small bar in Islington after another recommendation from Thirlwell. Livesey's recall of events is as clear as his production. "Jim suggested that I would be a good fit with Matt, and I guess Matt had heard those records and liked what we were doing. So Matt and I arranged a meeting and started getting to know each other. Matt was able to demo his songs at a good level prior to me even hearing them. He'd bought the Emulator 2 and had started to experiment with that. He came up with that guitar riff on 'Infected' by playing it on the keyboard and we worked from that idea and experimented with it when we were recording. We bought the Emulator drum machine [Drumulator] as well."

The first track on the album, as well as showcasing a much harder sound, also demonstrated how Johnson was more than ready to integrate the latest technology into his palette, utilising the sonic opportunities to enhance, rather than bury the sound of guitars, drums and analogue keyboards. Livesey was just as excited as Johnson to explore what could be done. "We were all over that thing. All that guitar riff stuff in the title track. There is some real guitar, but there's also sampled guitars going along with it. There was actually a drummer who played the drums on that song, but then we re-triggered the samples. We used Emulator sounds, triggered from what the drummer played, so the sounds were more souped-up, and processed-sounding. We got to the mix and felt that the kick drum pattern the drummer had played needed something to make it more frenetic, so we came up with this new beat; we replaced the original kick-drum part, which was a nightmare because in those early days getting things to sync together was very difficult. In the end we actually went through the whole track manually. It took a long time."

The drummer Livesey refers to was Dave Palmer, who had been connected to Johnson via mutual friends at CBS. "I'd actually met Matt many moons before when we all used to stay at the Columbia Hotel. Stevo would play me Matt's stuff – *Soul Mining* was out at the time. Then fast forward to 1985 and I got a call from CBS saying, 'Matt's recording and looking for a drummer, would you come down and play?'" Palmer ended up drumming on six of the eight tracks that made it to vinyl. Though there would be future problems, Johnson remembers the significance of the two being brought together. "Apart from establishing my relationship with Warne, working with Dave Palmer for the first time was one of the most exciting things to come out of recording *Infected*. Dave and I hit it off immediately and became close friends. He was a phenomenal drummer and really seemed to understand what I was trying to do. I would work out the parts in my head and he was able to play everything I threw at him."

Both musically and lyrically 'Infected' set the tone for the album. It has a strong driving beat and urgency, like the opener to *Soul Mining*, but the voice is more aggressive and the content more mature, more explicit. The introverted angst of his previous album is now thrust outwards towards the listener, and out into the world. Though many contemporary reviewers made the metaphorical link to AIDS, in relation to Johnson singing about being infected by love, fewer picked up on the more personal element, of the fear of intimacy, not from a sexual point of view but an emotional one; the male fear of opening up and the vulnerability that comes with it. After more than a minute of building instrumentation, Johnson's vocal comes in with the simmering energy of a boxer who has just stepped into the ring. What saves the song, however, from being a mere expression of the tortures of love is a chorus that bursts with soul, as in the sound of Detroit, and soars upwards with such a sudden rush it feels like being swept off one's feet. It bursts with energy and confidence of expression. Here was fully realised artistic ambition. Johnson knew his time had come and he was going to make every moment count.

Later, speaking about the videos that were made to accompany each track on the album, he talked about *Infected* meaning many things, including how the West infected the 'third world' with its ideologies and culture. Here he was talking about the album itself, rather than the song that opens side one. A couple of trips to Africa before he wrote the album were an inspiration regarding the Western economic colonisation, and when he then went to South America he saw first-hand both the old imprint of Spanish imperialism, and the modern US version epitomised by Coca-Cola. Other songs, 'Heartland' most obviously, implied that this Western empire was in decline and that in Britain this decline was accelerated. Topically this was a fairly big leap from *Soul Mining* and it needed a sound to match. Livesey and Mosimann were able to deliver this but the scope of Johnson's ideas and ambition was clearly boosted by the willingness of CBS to bankroll his project with a budget that raised more than a few eyebrows, indicating the faith of the label in their charge. Livesey, for one, found the leap in budget a personal eye-opener.

"I remember getting into one big argument, or discussion, with the label when we wanted to have a big string orchestra, and I got pulled by the A&R person who said, 'Can we go to lunch?' and I'm like, 'Sure we can go to lunch,' and then he's telling me stories, about this extravagant weekend conference they'd had for the label in a beautiful manor house, and how the CEO had hired a tiger, to walk on stage with when he gave his keynote address. So he's telling me all these stories and we're shooting the shit, then halfway through the meal he says, 'So, these strings... they're going to cost quite a lot of money aren't they? Do you think this is really necessary, spending all this money on strings?'

I said, 'Dude, you've just told me about your CEO hiring a tiger for a dinner party, and how much money you spent, and you're telling me that we can't have a real string section to make this record – that you are going to be selling – as good as it can be?'

And he said, 'Yeah okay. I think you've got a point.' And that was the only discussion I think that I ever had with the label at all. So there was never really a budget, we just got what we needed. I think it was close to £300,000 we spent, but that's a guess. We spent nearly a year in the studio on and off."

The two tracks that saw the benefit of these live strings ended up as the next two in the final running order of the album, both co-produced by Livesey. The first of these was 'Out Of The Blue (Into The Fire)', and again the contrast with the previous album was stark. Whereas before Johnson was singing about the tortures of unrequited love, now his angst was about the tortures of sexual relationships. Livesey putting the label in their place when it came to paying for live strings made a vital difference. 'Out Of The Blue' is another hard-edged track with some booming gated reverb accentuating the drums when they finally come in, but it is when the strings and honey-voiced backing vocal come in after three and a half minutes that the emotional content unfurls from what has begun as a cold, hard and aggressive-sounding piece of music. This contrast makes perfect sense if one considers the extraordinary lyric that tells of a visit to a prostitute in shocking and confessional detail. As a meditation on the nature of male sexual desire and its contradictions it is brutally forensic and offers no hope or redemption. Male and female listeners alike have nothing comfortable to grasp onto and the stark imagery makes it all the more difficult. Again, it is only the added sonic sweetness that makes this unflinching gaze into the darker side of human nature palatable, though even here it presents the listener with problems, as the swooning strings and chorus evoke an atmosphere of the lust that skews our moral compass.

The Astarti String Orchestra was also used on the album's next track, its undeniable centrepiece. 'Heartland' is a five-minute indictment of the state of Britain in the infancy of the neoliberalist project that Margaret Thatcher – inspired by Pinochet and Chicago School economists – had set in motion when elected in 1979. Seven years on, not only was the damage palpable, but the growing divide in the country, whether between north and south, haves and have-nots, was inescapable. In four verses Johnson paints a vivid picture of a country in decay, full of people with broken dreams and no voice. He refers to a press that won't write the truth about a divided nation and wars that are televised but never explained. As it builds to a close he aims a final potshot at the bankers who are *getting sweaty/beneath their white collars* ready to line their pockets. The punchline is the well-known refrain – *This is the 51st State of the USA* – a declaration that Britain is now merely a colony of the American Empire and that our foreign policy is, in reality, theirs.

'Heartland' is less abrasive sonically than the first two songs and the ending with its sweet-sounding backing vocals provides an upbeat musical contrast to the downbeat lyrics. It is this refrain at the end that sticks in the memory of most who hear the song, and this refrain is how most listeners identify it. The actual chorus goes almost unnoticed as a result. Again the pill is sugared by

239

those backing vocals but Johnson's words are unflinchingly bleak. *Here comes another winter/Of long shadows and high hopes/Here comes another winter/Waitin' for Utopia/Waitin' for hell to freeze over.* The winter is the future and the reality is that three decades later it would still be that same winter. 'Heartland' is a magnificent song and statement, as relevant today as it was in 1986. Thatcher may have been deposed but the disastrous economic philosophy she championed remains. The welfare state, then under attack, is now on its knees. The media is even more inclined to shield the population from the truth that matters, the bankers have taken all the money and we continue to march in lock-step with an American foreign policy that is the stuff of nightmares.

In an interview with Andy Strickland of *Record Mirror*, published just after 'Heartland' was released as a single, Johnson said, "I think it's the best song I've ever written, it sums up everything I'm saying… It sums up my feelings for this country, which although it frequently disgusts me, I still feel for it."

The song had been banned by Radio 1, for the use of the word 'piss', but as most intelligent observers noted, this was an accurate way of describing the sort of soulless shopping centres in the deprived heartlands of Britain. The moral arbiters of taste didn't see it that way and demanded that an edit of the track with the offending phrase removed was done before airplay could be granted. 'Heartland' may well be Johnson's greatest achievement. Historian and analyst of UK foreign policy, Mark Curtis, thinks so. "I heard *Infected* when I was a postgrad student at the LSE. It was probably 'Heartland' that really struck me first – just an extraordinary song and words. 'Heartland', I would say, is the greatest political lyric in British music."

The point about the reality of the 'special relationship' was perhaps made most directly in 'Angels Of Deception' where the lyrics refer to the devil arriving in town: *He's stuck his missiles in your gardens/And his theories down your throat.* The missiles in question were the cruise missiles at Greenham Common airbase. The theories were the economic ones of the Chicago School who strongly supported the ideas of Friedrich Hayek.

This track, which closed side one, was one of two produced by Gary Langan and mixed by Livesey. Roli Mosimann also co-produced two tracks, 'Sweet Bird Of Truth' and 'Twilight Of A Champion', the latter arranged with French horn, trombone and trumpet and coming across like a jazz-inspired soundtrack to an early sixties US cop show like *Dragnet*, complete with obligatory walking bass line. Interviewed by Betty Page at the end of 1986 Johnson revealed that the song was inspired by a painting of the Chicago skyline that Eddie and Shirley had hung above the bar fire in the front room, which he had spent a childhood looking at. "When I wrote that song, I created this scene where I was in the Chicago skyline at the top of a building and had become everything I'd wanted to become, but had sold my soul." Though he told Page that he didn't feel that he himself had sold his soul, but that plenty of people who achieve a certain amount of wealth and fame do, it seemed that the nagging fear of succumbing to the shallow delights of the ego, at the expense of personal integrity, nevertheless lingered. It was Dr Faustus meets Robert Johnson at the crossroads and it seemed to haunt him.

In the same interview he revealed that 'Mercy Beat' was inspired by an episode in New York where he felt like he was hanging on to his sanity by his fingertips, thinking he could converse with animals, such as cats and a lobster. "I don't know how I won this thing, but I did, and that was what that song was based on, a knife fight with the devil. I was scared then, I thought I was actually going to kill myself, I felt this overwhelming urge to jump off buildings, which was terrifying." This drug-induced descent into temporary madness was fuel for his own fire, the artist feeding merrily off his own excess and making something useful. Though the last two tracks on the album see the vitality and energy dip, the overall experience for the listener is fairly intense, both in sound and content. In comparison to other music that was making it into mainstream consciousness at this time, *Infected* was akin to a small bomb going off. It ripped through pleasantries in a manner that Public Enemy would do a year later and no matter how you viewed it musically speaking, it was hard to ignore.

Dave Palmer, who had performed drumming duties on most of the album, recalls listening to the finished product for the first time. "I was still living in Sheffield at the time. I would come in and play, then leave, come in and play, then leave, and that went on over the course of a year. Then Matt said, 'Hey Dave, do you want to listen to the record now?' I hadn't really heard the full production, they were very basic tracks, no lead vocal, they were just instrumentals. I came down and hung out at his flat in Stoke Newington. It was one of those moments. I heard it in its entirety and it just blew me away. It was a game changer, he'd taken it up another level. The urgency and the aggression of it... *Infected* was just balls-out; everything was out there. When I walked away from Matt's that night I said to him, 'You've made a fucking brilliant record here Matt. A really brilliant record.'"

From conception to realisation (and there was a visual element to the project yet to come) it was a defining moment in his career on a personal as well as public level. Johnson managed to collate a tangled mass of thoughts and feelings and articulate them in a way that wouldn't have been possible a year earlier. He had turned from boy to man and this was a work that reflected this maturity. Over a decade later he looked back at the period from which the album had sprung itself. "I was only 24 when I wrote it and I really wanted to write something extremely political. I was feeling really pissed off and dismayed by the Thatcher era. It was starting to grip hard and I was feeling pretty affected by all that. And her relationship with Ronald Reagan just drove me mad. The increasing demonisation of Islamic fundamentalists was also another interesting ingredient thrown into the mix. It was like a new holy war was starting. Also the sexual element is in there too of course and, I suppose, I was drinking a lot, mainly vodka, and probably doing other stuff I shouldn't be doing. There was a certain amount of aggression coming out; a lot of residual anger that I've carried within my bones since childhood. I'm a pretty angry person in many ways. I was trying to figure out what I was really angry about, and a convenient target for my anger was someone like Margaret Thatcher, of course, and more generally, what was happening to my country."

Fiona Skinner refers to it as the angry album. "I think there is an arrogance, an anger, a drive in *Infected*, whereas *Soul Mining* is more reflective." The anger was fuelled by a mix of passion, success and cocaine, by vodka and the demons buried within Johnson's psyche. Andrew Johnson's artwork for the album cover, and that of the singles, was much more abrasive than usual, and offered unambiguous clues as to what the listener might expect to hear. The cover chosen for the 'Infected' single release was a painting of the devil masturbating, complete with rubber glove on the hand of action, the sort of black humour that the Johnson brothers were entirely comfortable with. Needless to say, this depiction of diabolical onanism didn't go down too well. As Johnson recalls, "it was actually the ladies who worked on the production line at the CBS manufacturing plant who were outraged. A few copies were printed up and released initially but word soon reached us that they refused to manufacture any more unless it was cropped as the women at the plant were deeply offended by it."

'Slow Train To Dawn' is, perhaps, the most telling song on the album, a classic duet with the male and female voices telling a tale of a relationship in trouble. The music is pure soul, albeit a very eighties version, replete with blazing horns from John Thirkell and Jamie Talbot, but unlike many a classic soul song there is no satisfying conclusion to the dialogue. Neither party walks away but no resolution is found. Instead there is the seemingly perpetual 'slow train to dawn', a metaphor for all-night discussion leading to nowhere, the woman still waiting for the words she wants to hear that her man seems incapable of uttering. The tension thus remains. This was the gospel-like companion piece to the dirty blues of 'Out Of The Blue (Into The Fire)' and, if we discount the hysteria of the title track, the pair provide the album's quota of songs about relationships.

Johnson had been taken with the vocal performances of Neneh Cherry with Float Up CP and invited her to sing on the track, after a meeting at his flat where they drank so much vodka Cherry almost fell down the stairs. 'Slow Train To Dawn' is another troubled lyric about male sexuality and desire. Johnson sings *I'm just another Western guy/With desires that I can't satisfy*, the rejoinder, sung by Cherry, is the accusing and betrayed female voice wondering if her professed love means anything at all. The male voice appears to want his cake and eat it, as if by the mere fact of admitting his urges and probable infidelity he can be absolved. In an interview with Betty Page, published in *Record Mirror* that December, Johnson came on like a Catholic in the confession box, as he talked freely about the lyric and revealed clues about his personal life. "'Slow Train To Dawn' is about the psychological relationship between two people and the weakness of the male in that relationship, and infidelity, which is borne from insecurity and weakness; it was a difficult song to write. It's my girlfriend's favourite song now. She understands me and lets me get away with a lot, I suppose. She likes what I do so much that she's always said never to let her feelings get in the way of my artistic expression. Which is great because at first I always thought 'I can't do that', then thought I've got to… I know that all the people I care about most have given me total artistic licence to be a bastard."

He was speaking with some kind of hindsight but in between writing the song and talking to Page had come a trail of personal self-destruction in South America and New York, and if the chickens hadn't quite come home to roost at the time he spoke to her, their actual arrival was probably inevitable. The road to excess may very well lead to the palace of wisdom but it often stops off at ruin on the way. For now though, the music was done. Recorded at The Garden, Air and Livingstone studios, Livesey took charge of the whole mix at Comforts Place in Sussex and, that job admirably done, it was time to think about the next phase of the project.

* * *

Johnson's adventure on the road during the filming of *Infected – The Movie* was like an unstoppable train, with a plan to follow the path of madness trodden just a few years previously by German film director, Werner Herzog, when he filmed *Fitzcarraldo* in the Amazon. It was inevitable that things were going to get very messy, very quickly. He travelled to South America with a tiny crew that included Stevo, Peter 'Sleazy' Christopherson, and producer Aubrey 'Po' Powell, who worked with Sleazy at art design group Hipgnosis. The chances of this being a straightforward trip were nil. Christopherson, a member of Throbbing Gristle offshoot Psychic TV, was the man behind the camera of one of the earliest Sex Pistols photo shoots, the rent boy theme of which caused a certain amount of consternation as the ambiguous sexuality of early punk gave way to something more straight and strait-laced. Psychic TV was the ideal set-up for Christopherson to further his visual ambitions and he was by now working with film and video. Being signed to Some Bizzare brought him into Stevo's orbit, so he was perfectly placed to become involved in the film project that Johnson had in mind for *Infected*. Johnson and Stevo had somehow managed to persuade CBS to cough up even more money to realise this dream, a not inconsiderable sum of £350,000. For an artist of his stature this was unheard of, but with the album in the can, and unwilling to form a band to tour, the film was his alternative to performing live. CBS were reluctant but Johnson said he would also be prepared to embark on a worldwide promotional tour of interviews, an odyssey that proved almost as gruelling as touring with a band. Colin Barlow remembers Stevo being relentless in his pursuit of securing the funds. "He did an amazing job at rallying anyone he could to make this happen."

Johnson backs up Barlow's opinion. "The two key people in making *Infected – The Movie* happen were Stevo and Paul Russell, the MD at CBS at the time. Obie was the chairman but Paul Russell took care of the day-to-day running of the place and signing-off on projects like this. In fact, it was around this time that Obie 'retired' I think and then Russell took complete charge. Stevo made it his mission that every time he saw Russell he would hound him into supporting us with this project. Russell – an ex-lawyer – was himself a tough negotiator, but I think he was eventually worn down and convinced by Stevo's sheer enthusiasm."

Christopherson had already filmed in South America, not far from where Herzog had filmed, and suggested this as a possible location. A big fan of Herzog's films, Johnson didn't need much persuasion and it wasn't long before flights to Bolivia were booked. There was a three day stop-over in Jamaica where it is likely that the island's finest herbs were sampled. Any such indulgence may have set the tone for what was to follow. Suffice to say that when they got to South America things began to warp out of shape rather wildly. This was a travel experience in the proper sense, with hotels where, as Christopherson mentioned to one interviewer, you never knew what was going to crawl out from under the toilet seat. Johnson was particularly struck by the uneasy conflation of cultures where local Indians sporting Elvis haircuts and crucifixes guzzled Coca-Cola. Western corporate capitalism had, as Johnson saw it, infected the indigenous culture, as Catholicism had done centuries before. Thrown into this mix would be tribal witch doctors, communist rebels, drink and drugs. As they were in Bolivia, cocaine was hard to avoid, and of a purity that no one had experienced before. Strange local hallucinogenics were also on offer, and the strongest weed that any of those who indulged had ever smoked. Not to mention all kinds of potent booze. As if trying to evoke the drink-sodden spirit of Malcolm Lowry's *Under the Volcano* via Hunter S. Thompson, Johnson's desire to push himself physically and mentally to the limit, to inform his art, inevitably led to a state of mind that swiftly became somewhat unhinged.

Though much of what happened went unreported, and much will remain so, you can see the manifestation of all this carnage in the videos themselves. How else could you explain the spectacle of Matt Johnson strapped to a bizarre metal frame atop the deck of a boat travelling down the Amazon like some East End version of Klaus Kinski? Or more vividly in the finale of closing video 'Mercy Beat', the story behind which sums up the craziness of the whole adventure. That Johnson needed to escape himself through

246

drink and drugs in order to film some of this stuff is perhaps understandable – he was after all not an actor, and revealed years later that he didn't feel comfortable in his own skin at this time. He was also exploring and exorcising his own demons. "All the stuff that was going on in Britain at the time, I just felt angry about. I was a lot younger then. Life had changed a lot for me and I was trying to deal with all these residual feelings that are dragged forward from childhood, trying to rationalise them." In a television special about the making of the film he talked about the atmosphere on the shoot, which would impact his already charged mood. South America, understandably, seemed exotic compared to Europe and North America, and the sense of otherness served to push him further towards the fringes of rational behaviour. "You almost sense the spirits in the air, there's something magical about the place. But the thing was, the heat started getting to people, and also people were doing things they shouldn't have done I suppose; I'm not excluding myself from blame, but you kind of get a bit carried away, and everyone got up to things that you can't really talk about on TV, and started to get a bit paranoid."

Also part of the small crew was Philip Richardson, who had been working as assistant to Christopherson, and was invited onto the project from the beginning, working on pre-production duties like location scouting, casting, prop-sourcing and filming cutaway scenes. He had already worked on the 'Heartland' video, which had been filmed in Greenwich, supplying Matt with the iconic Hofner Committee guitar, which he had borrowed from a friend. Filming in South America was a touch more exotic than south London, however, particularly when the crew reached Peru. "In Iquitos we had a fixer called Fredy Valles who spoke English. He was rumoured to have made lots of money smuggling jaguar skins out of Peru. I spent a lot of time with him during pre-production. One day, with me on the back of his motorbike looking for a location on the banks of the Amazon, there was a beggar standing in the road. As we passed him, somehow Fredy ran him over. The man lay bleeding in the dust. Fredy slowly turned the bike round and drove back. He screamed at the poor chap still lying on the ground, flung a couple of notes at him and off we drove." Richardson avoided the cocaine, though did chew his way through a lot of coca leaves, which goes some way towards explaining why he can't remember eating anything for the entire trip. "One night Fredy took Stevo, Matt and myself out to a late-night rave in a jungle clearing. We were the only non-locals there. No one except Fredy spoke English. It was very dark, very noisy and very jungly." He doesn't remember too many details of what happened that night, though does recall strange conversations that he describes as 'physical', which may, or may not, help you understand just how strange a night the trio had in deepest, darkest Peru.

Iquitos is a small city and port so deep in the Peruvian jungle it is only accessible by plane or arduous boat journey. A square in the ghetto area was chosen as a location for the filming of 'Mercy Beat', which seemed to be some kind of climax to all this weirdness and tension, and it was as if all the clichés about South America suddenly descended upon the crew in a single day. The hot square was deserted when they arrived and started to set up, but as filming was about to start in the early evening a political rally of around two thousand Marxist Peruvians suddenly arrived and the scene and atmosphere was, quite literally, radically transformed. Naturally, the leaders of the rally wanted to know what a gringo film crew was doing in this sleepy part of town. Were they just another example of the capitalist West, come to exploit the peasants of a foreign land? In fact this possible contradiction had troubled Johnson. Was his attempt to highlight Western infection not, in some small way, guilty of the very same thing?

Not that those particular thoughts had much time to cross his mind in the heat of the moment. Speaking to Ian Pye of the *NME* at the end of the year he tried to convey the chaos that ensued. "When we did that shot on the bandstand in Iquitos, a communist rally came marching through. They wanted to burn down the houses of the rich people. Then they started shouting at us. 'Gringos, the exploiters!' The Indians stood around us and protected us. I was trying to hurl Stevo out into the crowd to film them. He's going, 'Get off, leave me alone.' Then the generator went dead and all the lights went out. Everybody was terrified. The communists' leader managed to climb onto the bandstand. He was screaming, going mad. But two of the crew managed to hurl him off. Although I don't think we really captured what went on down there I think you can see it's not just a performance. I virtually *lived* that song when I was there."

Though he says his memories of evening at the bandstand are not clear, Philip Richardson's version of events is still vivid. "By this time we had been in Iquitos for some time. It was a hot night, lit with flaming torches and we were deep in the jungle village. There was a snake and a vicious monkey. Matt was off his nut. We all were. The rally was so random. We heard the chanting first and then they all came down the track into the clearing. As I remember, we just went with it. There was no point in resisting. They swamped the whole area. A fellow with a megaphone stood on the bandstand and whipped up the crowd and then off they went to burn down some rich people's houses. After they left, we just carried on filming but it certainly ramped up the vibe." You couldn't really have made this up: a small film crew from England making a video for a pop star who was questioning Western democracy, when all of a sudden the *Sendero Luminoso* (Shining Path), who wanted to replace bourgeois democracy with a 'New Democracy', appear in the very same square. The two political viewpoints were on the same side of the fence but the protagonists were, in reality, worlds apart.

The pragmatic Christopherson, interviewed for the 'making-of' television special, explained how they were able to exploit the situation they found themselves in. "What you have to do is use those situations and make them work for the film, and I think that if you can do that, and if you have an artist who is prepared to take those risks, because a lot of rock musicians and creative musicians are not prepared to take any risks whatsoever, and that's one of the good things about Matt – he's prepared to stand up in the middle of a thousand people who are all completely out of their heads on cane alcohol or drugs or whatever, and, you know, go through that experience. And hopefully that intensity comes out in the films." Anyone who has seen the video can make their own mind up. The chaos captured was mostly un-choreographed. Johnson looks possessed, and who's to say he wasn't?

Though the craziness subsided, the remainder of the trip, if Richardson's recollections are anything to go by, was like the wreckage of a wild party. "I do remember on the plane going from Iquitos to La Paz we were all warned about the perils of drinking. High altitude will render you much drunker than you thought you would be. Stevo drank anyway. Got smashed. Fell down the steps onto the tarmac. Next day we were filming a busy scene with Matt in the chair being unloaded from a train. I can still picture Stevo sat alone on a bench at the end of the platform, plastic mask glued to his face, sucking on an oxygen tank. Not a word." For Johnson, who had accompanied Stevo on many an adventure, the sight of his pal suffering was, naturally, highly amusing. "It was hilarious. I also remember Stevo being warned explicitly before the plane even took off for La Paz not to drink alcohol as the effect would multiply in high altitude but he just gorged himself silly on champagne and brandy and for the entire flight laughed and made fun of everyone else for not drinking. Fast forward to visiting his hotel room later that day. Curtains drawn tight and in semi-darkness, horizontal and motionless on his bed, oxygen tank beside him and with a mask strapped over his face. I remember him whispering to me 'I'm dying... I'm dying'. I couldn't stop giggling."

And for the crew who weren't going on to America it didn't stop. "The craziness was unrelenting right to the very end," Richardson recounts. "Filming proper had finished in La Paz, and we were due to return to England the following day. Peter asked me to take the 'Mercy Beat' car out and do some cutaways. I went with the Spanish-speaking production assistant, Mark, who drove while I filmed. On the street we were accosted by a thin, casually dressed man in mirror shades and moustache. Although the conversation was in Spanish, I understood that he was asking Mark what we were doing, whether we had a permit, passports please, and take me to your hotel. On arrival, this not-so-secret policeman instructed that the whole crew were to be confined to the hotel until an investigation had been made and suitable fine agreed. Later, in the dead of night we gathered in the foyer, split into various cabs and drove swiftly to the airport.

"Unfortunately, on arrival at Heathrow, we were expected. Each crew member was intimately searched, the film cans were opened, etc. Nothing was found. Matt had left for New York and given me a wooden flute to bring back for him. As they searched me, a small package was detected jammed halfway up the flute. It took the customs officer an age to get it out while I cried inside. Turned out to be a piece of crumpled-up newspaper. I never did find out if Matt put it up there on purpose." Three decades on, the man himself professes innocence, though he does remember how Christopherson fared. "There's a very funny story Sleazy told me after he'd been strip-searched back at Heathrow upon his return. Anyone who knew him and his particular predilections and perversities knows it is probably true. He was stripped naked in a room with a couple of customs officers giving him a thorough inspection and after they'd donned the latex gloves and inspected a certain intimate cavity Sleazy then told them 'It's up there somewhere… you'll just have to search harder!'"

Johnson, meanwhile, had arrived in New York to work with Tim Pope, in a state of disrepair. This was a different Matt Johnson. Having survived some dangerous filming experiences, be it strapped to a boat, threatened by the Shining Path or kissing snakes, his self-belief had stretched like the skin of a balloon into a taught arrogance. Pope did not like this version of Matt Johnson that had arrived in New York. This was not cool.

"He arrived in New York and he was in a real state from South America. Frankly I did not like him very much. He was very difficult, dangerous even; he was into a state which, I'm sure he doesn't mind me saying, was of him bingeing, shall we say? And working out. So he was in a completely worn-out state, beyond exhaustion, and I remember he would go to the gym and really work himself out but then would drink like mad. He was really, really edgy. I mean, indescribably edgy, very difficult to work with. I would say I was much more the sensible half of that relationship."

There was certainly no love lost between the two at this juncture. Though they are now good friends, Johnson's view of Pope at this point was not much better than Pope's view of him. "Tim is not inaccurate in these recollections but there's always two sides to a story. Despite Sleazy's reputation and image as a member of Throbbing Gristle, Psychic TV and Coil, he was an absolute sweetheart and in all the time we spent working together we never had a cross word. Tim on the other hand was another matter. Although he and I have obviously gone on to become very close friends – going on holidays together and even becoming godfathers to each other's children – those early shoots were full of friction as although we respected each other creatively we didn't particularly like each other personally. I arrived into Manhattan from South America feeling emotionally and physically exhausted and was immediately thrown into yet another shoot.

"There was something about Tim's demeanour in those days that immediately started to grind my gears. I found him to be pompous, controlling and spoilt and – surrounded by his production team – someone who was obviously used to always getting his own way. Having this person then trying to order me about was like a red rag to a bull really, so I quickly made it my mission to rough him up and take him out of his comfort zone and into somewhere very dark. I wanted to ensure these shoots would be like nothing he'd ever worked on – before or since. I was exercising hard, guzzling vodka and all the while Stevo was feeding me cocaine on the sidelines. To his credit Tim went toe to toe with me the entire time and didn't moan too much. It was only when we got back to London that he complained how dangerous it was and how frightened he'd been during the shoot. The film he made for 'Out Of The Blue (Into The Fire)' is still my favourite even to this day. But we bonded through that experience and out of that a mutual respect and genuine affection and friendship grew."

Pope had got into film work when working for Hyvision in Covent Garden, a company set up by Stanley Hyland, an ex-head of current affairs at the BBC. The company was in the business of coaching politicians in the art of presenting themselves effectively on television, and were using video to assist this process. Filming the likes of Denis Healey in the daytime, he was moonlighting at night, filming live performances of up-and-coming bands, like The Specials, with the same camera. It wasn't long before Pope had found a way to get a foothold in the nascent industry of music video, and after blagging his way through an interview with Stevo, he found himself directing videos for Soft Cell, including a whole album's worth released on VHS as *Non-Stop Exotic Video Show*. He was, therefore, no stranger to excess, but half a decade on from the Soft Cell video project he was working with clients as big as Neil Young, and the somewhat toxic vibes emanating from Matt Johnson came as a bit of a shock. Not that this was to temper in any way the artistic decisions the pair made about the two films they were to make in New York. Pope, like all good filmmakers, was happy to embrace edginess and danger as it more often than not led to inspired results. By the mid-eighties the majority of music videos on MTV were safe, bland productions, stuffed to the gills with clichés such as petals falling in slow motion, billowing curtains, people running down corridors or splashing into swimming pools. They weren't typically filmed in a real-life brothel in New York.

'Out Of The Blue (Into The Fire)', Johnson's confessional about lust and infidelity, was filmed in glorious 35mm colour, the drink-sodden singer manifesting his guilt in a performance as far removed from the standard music video as it was possible to get. Rather than a fantasy vision, Pope was to present a slightly crazed, but far more honest depiction of where male sexual fantasy could lead than was being portrayed at the time in videos by the likes of Duran Duran.

"We started in the afternoon and shot the scenes in the apartment. We brought hundreds of cockroaches which we let loose, and I sometimes think of the poor sod who inherited that place; there's probably thousands of cockroaches walking around it now. We filmed that on the Bowery, or somewhere like that. And then we went up to Spanish Harlem. What we didn't know was, crack was just becoming a big thing, and we had chosen an area near the biggest crack dealer. It was very edgy. So we had police protection. I was standing on the sidewalk with my producer and all the crew were loading up the gear and this huge rat came out of this building site next to us and ran around our feet. I watched this rat roll onto its back, have an epileptic fit in front of us and die. And that was about the best fucking thing that happened that evening. From thereon it was downhill.

"Matt had by then drunk a bottle of vodka. A young lady was put into the car, and I didn't tell Matt but she had no knickers on, and she was writhing around, pushing her knees into his face. At some point the gangs had realised we were there. Suddenly we were being pursued up these streets by these gangs who were so heavy that the cops said they were pulling out of the situation. But I still had a few shots to do so we just carried on shooting without police protection. We went to the brothel around midnight, and it was a really hardcore place. I remember going into the loo and the toilet was filled with syringes. The whole place was incredibly dark."

By comparison the filming of the video for 'Twilight Of A Champion' was fairly straightforward, though not without its own troubles. "We went to CBS and said, 'Do you mind if we shoot this little sequence for this video we are making?' And next thing they know we have got guys with machine guns outside, opposite the Chrysler Building, and an old boy sliding down a glass window in his own blood. But we were being deliberately provocative. We clearly did it to piss off the label." It seemed to work in this regard, mostly because of a shot where Johnson puts a revolver in his mouth, which wasn't exactly MTV-friendly.

Returning to England the madness subsided but Johnson still pushed himself into uncomfortable situations for the benefit of his art, and Pope was willing to join him. The video for 'Slow Train To Dawn' was filmed on the Severn Valley Railway and involved that staple of silent cinema, a woman tied to a railway track. The woman in question was Neneh Cherry, wearing a figure-hugging Katharine Hamnett dress that left little to the imagination. This and the symbolism of the video would lead to accusations of sexism, which the knowing irony of the final shot of a tiny train bearing down on the damsel in distress instead of the huge steam train didn't manage to dispel. The shoot itself involved a steam engine passing over Johnson's head, and both he and Pope didn't go in for half-measures in order to get the footage required.

"I wanted to do a shot where Matt and I were in a pit underneath a moving steam train. We were in this ash pit which was about three foot deep, and they strapped me to this plank of wood which was rigged so I could look into the eyepiece of the camera, with my head just beneath the level of the rails. Matt was on the other side of this pit, and we were looking at each other. I remember seeing this great big steam train starting to come over us. I could see it behind Matt's head and I was shouting out stuff to provoke him, and we had the music cranked up really loud. I remember having all these perverse thoughts, like, will it fall sideways and collapse on top of us? There were steam jets underneath this train, so as it slowly went over us, the steam was going down my body and then this searing steam hit my ankles. Then we said, 'Let's do another take.'"

The remaining two videos were filmed by Mark Romanek and Alastair McIlwan. Romanek was tasked with helping Johnson visualise his ideas for 'Sweet Bird Of Truth', opting to load up on symbolism with angels, and fish falling from the sky. McIlwan meanwhile worked Andrew Johnson's striking graphics – an important visual part of the entire project – into his video for 'Angels Of Deception'.

When they first saw the film, CBS were reportedly unhappy with 'Out Of The Blue' because of its explicit content, and 'Twilight

Of A Champion' because of the revolver scene. Just how upset they were depended on who was talking, according to a September article in *SOUNDS* written by John Wilde. Stevo, Johnson and Tim Pope, who directed both videos, suggested that CBS were extremely unhappy with the graphic content, Pope saying that CBS in America were trying to sue him for being a pornographer. When Wilde spoke to Tony Woolcott at CBS, however, he seemed less flustered about the content itself but unhappy that it rendered the video less accessible to the public. He also refuted the idea that the label were suing Pope. Asked what he thought about the artistic merits of the film he refused to be drawn, suggesting it wasn't his job to be a critic. Considering that the initial storyboards presented by Pope suggested the videos would be more outrageous, the men in suits got off lightly. In an interview with *Melody Maker*, prior to any actual filming, Johnson had said he wanted 12-year-old prostitutes and dwarves dressed in Marilyn Monroe and Elvis masks driving through a small town in a Cadillac to re-enact the assassination of John F. Kennedy. In essence this spat was a classic case of the conflicting wishes of the artist and the record label. Johnson knew that CBS were in the business of making money and one suspects that he was very aware that, compared to most of his contemporaries, he had a very generous amount of artistic freedom. Woolcott, with an eye on the money, was naturally going to be unhappy with anything that might limit the return in any way, and accused Johnson and Pope of being self-indulgent.

The completed film was screened at the Electric Cinema in Notting Hill for an audience of family, friends and CBS executives. Linking sections, containing sound effects, superimposed lyrics and drawings, had been created in one week by Johnson and Christopherson to produce a more coherent whole. Pope recalls Johnson arriving in a Fedora hat, walking down the aisle with Eddie and Shirley. "I remember Matt talking to the projectionist beforehand and saying, 'Make it loud,' and when Matt wanted it loud it was deafening, ear-bleedingly loud. Too loud for me." In fact it was Stevo who had insisted on the volume, which upset Johnson as the sound was so distorted the audience couldn't hear the songs properly. Ian Pye, writing in the *NME*, was also numbed by the "ear busting volume" and noted that Johnson looked nervous and took "furtive swigs from a small bottle of vodka inside his coat", suggesting that the diet that had fuelled the whole project was still in effect. In one interview Johnson ventured that three years of marinating his vocal cords in vodka had given him the singing voice he was looking for. Though this may have been a tongue-in-cheek comment it is obvious that the time he spent on *Infected* was a personal journey of transformation as much as a creative venture. Fiona had sorted out his diet, thus improving his skin, and styled his hair. He also spent a lot of time working out and all this together amounted to a subtle but radical image makeover. Up until this point, Johnson, despite having a hip album on his CV, had looked rather uncool and slightly awkward in his own skin. Fans watching the video of 'Heartland' on television were no doubt surprised by this hip new image, and the inner confidence was obvious not just in the way he carried himself but also in the music.

The change wasn't just skin-deep, however. In the interview with John Wilde he had this to say: "I'm so glad to shed this image of the little introverted guy in the bedsit. That was me five years ago. I'm much more aggressive and confident now, very annoyed and frustrated." It was an odd combination of words which revealed that there remained unresolved issues within the inner life of Matt Johnson. If *Infected* was partly a purging process, some of the demons remained.

12

SLOW TRAIN TO DAWN

STEPHEN MALLINDER, AS ONE HALF OF CABARET VOLTAIRE, was no stranger to aggressive music, and the dynamic change in The The's sound and mood made a noticeable impression on him.

"*Soul Mining* felt like a personal one-to-one record, whereas *Infected* felt like a record that was a message to everybody. I remember going down to Portobello Road to the Electric Cinema and watching the film, and it felt like someone who was really confident, and going, 'I'm making another record, and I'm going to make a statement with it.' *Infected* was a really brave record and a dark record, a tough record. And it felt like the right record to make at that time, because when you look at '83 and *Soul Mining* and the period that record came out, there was a level of optimism, and youthfulness, but by the time *Infected* came out it had become darker. Even though Matt didn't deal directly with such specific political things, it reflected what was going on at the time, with AIDS emerging, with Thatcher, the miners, Falklands War, all those things, it felt like it was a record of its time, it reflected some of the dysfunction, and some of the tension that was underneath the surface for everybody. It felt a more significant record in some respects."

One notable aspect of the significance of *Infected* was that political dissent in music wasn't exactly mainstream. Various artists voiced their opinions on Thatcherism in song or in interviews but their music rarely sounded as angry as their sentiments. Billy Bragg sang with as much vitriol as he could muster, but armed only with a guitar there was no way he could match the sonic barrage that Johnson and Livesey created. Though he wasn't part of the mainstream pop world, Johnson now found himself under a significantly bigger spotlight, and, with various controversies surrounding lyrics and artwork, would also garner news in the pop columns of the tabloid press. His wasn't music for the masses but all of a sudden the masses were being exposed to his output. His antipathy to playing live led to a solution that meant he could reach an audience far larger than even a major tour could manage. The film project was not only part of his creative vision for *Infected* but also an appeaser to CBS, who needed to publicise and promote their product. Screenings of the film ultimately broadcast his music to millions; a gruelling tour of promotional interviews lasting nearly a year did the rest.

Because he lived on the same street as Johnson, Paul Webb had been privy to how the project had been shaping up for some time, and the contrast between Johnson's musical life as The The with his own, in Talk Talk, was sharp. "When he became my neighbour I was working on an album called *Colour Of Spring* and he was doing *Infected* and so I was hearing stuff from that before it was out and he was hearing bits and pieces of what I was doing. We were different. I was signed to a major record label who were pumping loads of money in and we were on that routine of doing an album, then going on tour, but he wasn't. I was intrigued by what he was doing because touring was way off the agenda with him. I was quite envious because I was doing the traditional tour while he was going out making these films across the world; that was how he was going to promote the record."

In one of many interviews he did in Australia, this one for *The Daily News* in Melbourne, Johnson estimated that he had already done six to seven hundred interviews to promote the album. "It's not natural," he told the interviewer, "to spend six months talking about yourself. You start to get selfish and self-obsessed. Everything gets very cloudy, you end up talking about your ideas and philosophies so much that they end up being worn out like a pebble on the beach. You get to the point where you don't believe what you're saying." Worn out by the same questions being asked over and over again, yet obliged to promote the record, it might have crossed his mind more than once that doing a live tour might not have been so bad after all, though when asked about playing he replied: "It's certainly not a case of stage-fright. I get offered a lot of dough now to do it. I could do with that. But I'm not interested – I'd be doing a tour just to sell records." He did, however, reveal that he had met up with Billy Bragg, who also happened to be in Melbourne, and over a drink suggested that maybe he would join Bragg on stage and, it being election year, sing 'Heartland', thus making it clear that his only motivation to appear live in any shape or form was in protest at politics back home. He felt there was no future in Britain, and now that the industry had been decimated and oil revenues had peaked he saw no reason to be optimistic looking ahead.

The trips to Australia were necessary when the album started to sell well there. Johnson found his promotional duties lonely and so, as they weren't having to fund a huge tour, CBS were happy to pay for Skinner to travel with him from time to time when he was in Europe. Though her boyfriend being away for long periods would ultimately cause the kind of problems not entirely unexpected of being a musician's girlfriend, she felt that lack of mental stimulation was a big drag. "It was hard work and boring and you have to answer the same questions over and over. They would always be short trips, but it was spread out over at least a year. That's why he would take so long between albums because it was hard for him to do any writing; he couldn't bounce ideas off other musicians. He would make notes when he found time to focus." As it was, and still might be, for many artists, the realisation that an artistically motivated creation becomes product once delivered to the record label often stuck in the craw, but the fact was that *Infected* was proving very successful as a result of his promotional approach, and the more successful it got the more he had to travel to promote it further.

The interviews may have become tedious but the compensations outweighed this. Johnson was spending most of his time away in New York, and his memories of these trips illustrate how far he had come from the days at Walrond & Scarman. No more last-minute stacks of mail to deal with. "I loved New York. Apart from the thriving live music scene and hanging out at legendary venues like The Ritz and CBGB I also loved going back to Alphabet City, where I'd lived for a week on my first visit to New York, as it always felt so edgy and vital down there, at places like the Pyramid Club on Avenue A and Save The Robots on Avenue B. I got quite addicted to the nightlife of New York and spent many late nights in clubs like Area and the Tunnel, though my favourite hang-out was Nell's. It was very dark, intimate and full of overstuffed sofas and old chandeliers. It quickly became the most fashionable nightclub in Manhattan and I became friendly with Nell the owner for a while. Whenever I'd find myself in New York I'd head down there and find myself rubbing shoulders with the likes of Mike Tyson, Prince, Susan Sarandon, Warren Beatty, Calvin Klein and numerous other film stars, musicians and artists. Bret Easton Ellis even later wrote about it in *American Psycho*. It was a period of extreme hedonism and narcissism and felt like being sat at the top of a world gone mad. As a contrast with this I would arrive back at our flat in grey and drizzly Stoke Newington and start to feel a bit claustrophobic."

Reviews of *Infected* in the English music press were uniformly positive. Many professed shock at just how aggressive, taut and muscle-bound the sound was in comparison to *Soul Mining*. The new maturity was duly noted, as was Johnson's ability to present a state-of-the-nation theme so succinctly. The *NME*, not the most reliable source of praise for The The, sat on the fence somewhat, the reviewer stating that after the initial shock had worn off, the album left him feeling at arm's length, but also admiring how "in just eight songs Johnson has freeze-framed a whole nation at a moment in time". Glyn Brown of *SOUNDS* was less doubtful and declared 'Sweet Bird Of Truth' a masterpiece. Paul Mathur of *Melody Maker* was another fan, singling out 'Slow Train To Dawn', extolling the lyric as Johnson's "most complete yet", and maybe he too was an admirer of its sound, the kind of almost danceable, soulful groove and crystal clear production that would a few years later echo in the music of bands like Happy Mondays. But the record was garnering praise in places that smaller acts couldn't reach, such as London's *Evening Standard*, women's magazine *Over 21* and *Tatler*. *What Hi-Fi*, who you would expect would know such things, declared that the "production is sharp and clear – nicely detailed in the treble but slightly lacking in bass". Veronica Lyons, who wrote the review, concluded by stating that the album "has a brilliance and a sense of purpose which is sadly lacking in 99.9 per cent of contemporary rock/pop music".

This last is a useful quote as, for those whose memories have clouded in the intervening years, or those who weren't there at all, it serves to remind us just how bland the music scene had become. Independent music was showing the first signs of running out of ideas and vitality by mid-decade. One only has to peruse the BBC chart archives to see how the diverse, original and exciting range of music of the early part of the decade had morphed into something bland and uninspiring. The emergence of more vital underground rock music, in the shape of Pixies, The Stone Roses, My Bloody Valentine and Nirvana was still some years away, and the real innovation and excitement was happening with house, techno and hip-hop. The mainstream middle ground was fast becoming a turgid wasteland populated by manufactured acts, many from the stable of Stock, Aitken and Waterman, and bands who sang in enormous stadiums that acted as echo-chambers for their own overblown vanities. The excitement of music – that manic pop thrill – had all but disappeared, unless you were in the right nightclubs.

Small wonder, then, that *Infected* felt like some kind of explosion when it appeared. This was everything that rock'n' roll had promised and pop music was supposed to deliver. Excitement, energy, a bit of anger and a dollop of controversy. Even after the sleeve of the 'Infected' single was altered so it wouldn't offend those of a delicate sensibility, the single still ended up being banned thanks to the lyrics. In the December 9, 1986 edition of *The Sun* newspaper celebrity gossip page, they ran a small article with the headline, 'Beeb ban "bad taste" AIDS disc', implying that the song was about the dangers of AIDS, and that the lyrics warned "teenagers of the risks of catching the disease from sleeping around". Not that a tabloid newspaper was remotely interested in accuracy.

The reason for the ban was the line *From my scrotum to your womb.* The BBC asked him to remove the offending line in an edit for radio play but when he acquiesced to their wishes they still refused to play the song, stating, somewhat ludicrously, that people could still buy the record. Johnson was understandably unwilling to give way to the suggestion by the BBC that if a version of the 'Infected' single without the offending line was made commercially available they would play it. With singles being a prime way to promote the albums they reside on, he wasn't having much luck, but was happy to lose out rather than compromise his integrity and bow down to the censor.

This decision was perhaps slightly easier to make because the biggest promotional tool for the album was due to be screened on the UK's Channel 4 in December on a Friday-night slot that guaranteed a healthy audience. *The Tube* had established itself as one place on television where cutting-edge music could be expected, the kind of stuff that was generally ignored by the more mainstream BBC and ITV channels. Indeed, Jools Holland, who had played the piano on 'Uncertain Smile', was one of the presenters. Showing the entire movie as a '*Tube* Special' was a bit of a statement from all parties, but then the concept itself was a bit of a statement.

MTV was still dominated by very mainstream music and most videos of the time were rather bland and functional; a far cry from what viewers were presented with for the first time that evening. When MTV later screened the film, the contrast with its usual output must have seemed stark.

Cabaret Voltaire had been making interesting videos for a number of years, many of them Burroughs-inspired visual cut-ups, so Mal Mallinder watched the film with particular interest. "The sheer ambition of that was brilliant, and to maintain the aesthetic through the whole thing was impressive. He translated who he was quite brilliantly through those videos. I don't think we ever wanted to do that, but more to the point we weren't ever able to do that." The last point bears thinking about because anyone watching was very aware of how expensive the whole film must have been, which lent it huge gravitas. It was a big statement of intent from both artist and label. The content itself, of course, did the rest. And the opening video made sure that everyone's attention was grabbed right from the very start. "Of course," says Mallinder, "'Infected' is the one you remember." The driving music, the visual references to *Fitzcarraldo* and the look in Johnson's eyes give off a sense of mania. The viewer is left to decide what is acting and what is real. The danger looks real, with this man strapped to some strange contraption on a boat, sailing down the Amazon. This is, very clearly, not the Matt Johnson of *Soul Mining*. This is a different person altogether.

As arresting as this was for those already familiar with The The, *Infected* was the point of entry for many more fans. This angry young man seemed to be voicing the disaffection that many were feeling now that Margaret Thatcher was at the height of her powers. More obviously, the film illustrated the power of television as a promotional tool for music. Not only was it screened for a second time on Channel 4 the following year, but it was also shown around the world, and this put the audience figures globally into the millions, rather than the thousands that a tour would have done. CBS would have been acutely aware of this and it was likely all along that this played a key part in their willingness to part with the huge budget in the first place.

Johnson watched the television screening at home with Fiona Skinner. Perhaps, away from the ballyhoo of a cinema packed with family, friends, journalists and industry insiders, it was harder to feel triumphant. Talking to Randy Bookasta several months later, he revealed the sense of anticlimax. "After it was over I just felt, so what? That was like the fruit of a couple of years' work and my soul laid bare before the night, and I just felt really empty." He added that it was now time for him to move on to a new project, though he was unaware that events in his own life would soon shape it. Now different paths were about to converge. One would see the demise of his relationship with Fiona Skinner, while another would sow the seeds for future live performances. In a strange way they mirrored his lyrical concerns: sex and love on the one hand, and social and political comment on the other.

Red Wedge was launched by Billy Bragg, Paul Weller and Labour MP Robin Cook in late 1985, designed to engage young people with politics. With the help of Labour Party funding a UK tour was arranged the following year, and other artists, including Johnny Marr, Jerry Dammers and Jimmy Somerville, soon came on board. It was always an awkward alliance; many music journalists and fans felt uncomfortable with the direct involvement of politicians, and not a few found the tone of Red Wedge a tad too worthy. It didn't mean that the conscientious objectors were fans of the Tories, but it was clear that the average punter wasn't convinced that voting intentions made the music sound any better.

Interviewed in 1986 and asked about politics, Johnson answered his own question about why he didn't get involved in Red Wedge by saying that he wasn't interested in token gestures and that to be a socialist required knowing what made the right wing tick. "Going on marches and listening to Billy Bragg", he suggested, wasn't enough. Perhaps Bragg was made aware of this comment because he later said in an interview that Johnson hid behind drum machines. This was a no-too-subtle dig at the authenticity of his music, and thus integrity. Bragg – basically one man and his guitar – was identifying himself with a long tradition of left-wing folk singers;

synthesizers and drum machines were presumably signifiers of something less worthy. He later claimed he was misquoted when the two men bumped into each other in Australia and, over drinks, they agreed that the possibility of The The appearing on the next Red Wedge tour could be seriously entertained.

As it happens Johnson was to appear on the Red Wedge stage twice, but only accompanied by Zeke Manyika on bass, and only to perform three songs – 'Flesh And Bones', 'Perfect' and, unsurprisingly, 'Heartland'. One concert took place at Islington Town Hall, a building where the red flag often flew in the days when Labour ran the council before the Blairite influence came to bear. He also played a date at Bay 63, formerly Acklam Hall, beneath London's Westway, where Ken Livingstone also appeared onstage. A *Record Mirror* review commented that "it was 'Heartland' that underlined the spirit of the evening so successfully. To hear the punters at the front sing 'This is the 51st state of the USA' in unison was quite extraordinary."

The dates were timed to coincide with the final run-up to the June 11 election, which the Tories won in such a convincing fashion it sent the Labour Party into a complete tailspin from which the traditional left couldn't really recover. The disappointingly low turnout of young Labour voters was a body-blow to Red Wedge, though not necessarily any endorsement of Margaret Thatcher and her government's policies. Apathy with the idea of change and disillusionment with Labour were equally to blame, whilst under the surface things were afoot that would lead many young people to sidestep traditional political engagement altogether.

Johnson remained sceptical. In the third issue of *Well Red*, the quarterly Red Wedge magazine that promised 'Pop and Politics', he was interviewed by Tony Fletcher. Fletcher pointed to the fact that CBS were one of the biggest multinationals around and that it might thus be deemed a surprise that he had such freedom to express his own political views in his songs, or on air, as he had recently done when hosting a two-hour MTV special. It wouldn't have been the first time that Johnson's attention had been drawn to this contradiction between his political stance and the nature of the label he was signed to. He said simply: "If something sells, they don't care whether it's communist, capitalist or Buddhist, they'll get behind it. It's pure business. There's no pressure from CBS on me." Later he said that he felt Red Wedge were preaching to the converted and for that reason he found it difficult to get fully behind them.

The MTV show that Fletcher referred to had seen Johnson talking about the themes behind *Infected*, and he pulled no punches when it came to sharing them with the viewers. Britain was spoken of as a nation in severe decline, now a mere aircraft carrier for American bombing raids on Libya. Seeing Coca-Cola baseball caps all over South America, whilst filming *Infected*, led him to compare the corporation to the Romans when it came to colonialism, and more pernicious American interference in Central America was also a target, the statistic that millions of dollars of US aid to Nicaragua led to the deaths of thousands of men, women and children was delivered to the camera as the MTV disclaimer scrolled across the bottom of the screen: *The content of this segment does not necessarily reflect the opinion of MTV Networks.* Seeing as Coca-Cola was one of MTV's sponsors it was no surprise that they wanted to distance the station from the views that were being expressed, though nefarious activities in Central America had already been highlighted by The Clash and Oliver Stone earlier in the decade.

Johnson, obviously not used to reading from an autocue, delivered his lines in a rather stilted fashion. Not as at ease with the television studio as he was with the music studio, his words lacked some of the authority that they possessed when sung to a musical backing, but the fact that he was able to air them in the first place, at a time when the BBC was censoring his views so heavily, was perhaps testament to the power of CBS. Without a tour to promote *Infected*, the best way to attract attention was to focus on the content of the lyrics and the themes behind th~

Thus Johnson was able to air his message and C~

were hoping, refill the coffers. The nature of N

channel would often be left running in the background as a kind of visual jukebox, so a fair number of viewers, used to the more usual diet of safe, sometimes inane video content, might have got a bit of a jolt when Johnson described *Infected* as he did. "Essentially it's about spiritual salvation but it has to be placed in context with the album's other themes: terrorism, trust, AIDS, lust, nuclear proliferation, holy damnation, infidelity, hypocrisy – in fact, all the things which constitute the problem of being human in the 1980s." Not exactly Rio dancing on the sand.

The MTV *120 Minutes* show had been broadcast in June 1986. A year later the personal impact of the three-year *Infected* project was about to culminate in the end of his relationship with Fiona Skinner. She was in the crowd at the Islington Town Hall gig on June 2, feeling somewhat conflicted. Her relationship with Johnson had been rather turbulent for around a year and his behaviour, when at home and, more pointedly, when away had led her to doubt whether he wanted to carry on. "I just didn't believe he loved me any more but he was too scared to tell me. I thought he was trying to push me to end it instead by being so awful!" Her life already seemed at some kind of crossroads. Growing frustrated with her job at Thames Television, especially under a new boss, she began learning how to use Quantel Paintbox, and with further encouragement from colleagues quit work to go freelance. As a leaving present they bought her airline tickets to New York. Watching him on stage that night she was agonising over what to do – stay or go. And if it was the latter then she was agonising over when to tell him and how. The fact that it seemed to be raining every day only served to increase the miserable mood in the air. How had it come to this?

Relationships often end because people change, and Matt Johnson had changed. He had gone into the *Infected* project one person and emerged three years later as another. Most of this change was wilful and he made no secret about the fact. In more than one interview he told interviewers how he was no longer the introverted young artist who sang songs of unrequited love. He was now the more experienced, more assured man who sang about politics and lust.

There may have been an insecurity lurking that made him feel the need to deny his former self, as he made clear to Randy Bookasta in 1987. "I think a lot of people viewed me from the *Burning Blue Soul* days as this guy sitting in a little room getting depressed, which is about five years out of date. With the *Infected* project I wanted to destroy a lot of those preconceptions with aggressiveness, confidence, and arrogance in a way. Hopefully I've done that and gotten rid of that last image." Having succeeded in his mission it dawned on him that his new persona was perhaps having negative as well as positive effects, but perhaps the arrogance that he referred to frequently, without any self-consciousness, was what stopped him from applying the brakes when needed. A steady diet of cocaine and vodka certainly wasn't helping. Nor, ironically, was success, which meant that not only did his lifestyle seem justified, but that he was obliged to talk about himself over and over again to hundreds of journalists. In this echo-chamber the ability to self-reflect was difficult. Drinking vodka when others were having their breakfast made it unlikely at all.

Johnson's very dry and mischievous sense of humour means that, sometimes, what he said in an interview might have to be taken with large pinches of salt. One in particular with Jon Casimir, of Australian magazine *Ram*, gave the distinct impression that excess was getting the better of him. Stevo being present undoubtedly led to a certain amount of naughty-boys-together behaviour but in print they came across as lecherous and somewhat sleazy, with Casimir finding it difficult to reconcile the man who "writes such jagged and inspirational songs" with the one who, alongside his manager, appeared to be so base. At the end of the interview when the journalist pointed out that the content of their conversation might make it difficult to get into print unedited, Johnson suggested he do just that: "I think you should. I come across too serious all the time. I think you should make it really disgusting."

What is striking about many of the interviews of this period is how honest Johnson was, though after several hundred journalists had asked essentially the same things, perhaps the urge to confess came as some sort of relief, and a way to avoid the monotony. He told *Biz* magazine that his drive and ambition made him a difficult person to live with and that he was, or had become, a selfish person. Tellingly he revealed to Kevin Fitzpatrick that Skinner found it difficult to accept aspects of their relationship appearing in his lyrics, and that cruder references within them might be mistakenly construed as being about her when they weren't. However, it was difficult to say that it wasn't you who had been *squealing like a stuffed pig*, when you didn't have the platform available to do so.

The blurred lines between art and life were always likely to lead to problems. As a fan of actor Robert De Niro, Johnson saw the idea of immersing himself in a certain amount of sleaze and danger as a form of method acting that would inform his music, a kind of artistic research, if you will. When Skinner found evidence of his infidelity in the laundry he had returned from the promotional tour of Australia with, she saw this as one bit of artistic research too many. She had been realistic about being in a relationship with a musician, and prepared to put up with a certain amount of infidelity in return for honesty. But there are always limits, and it was harder to forgive this new version of Matt Johnson. His behaviour was hard to defend, even if the lure of the sirens was understandable.

"*Infected*," says Johnson now, "was the simultaneous high and low point of my career. In a way it became a sort of personal morality tale. One of the themes of the album had been corruption, on a political and global level but also on a personal level. I'd been dreaming of 'sex, drugs and rock'n'roll' since I was a teenager in Roadstar and here it finally was, in spades." Travelling, mostly alone, from city to city across three continents, being plied with champagne, driven around in limousines, and surrounded by women – being the centre of attention everywhere you went – was almost inevitably going to lead to trouble. Deep down he knew it, of course. Talking a few years after this period he got straight to the point. "I had a relationship break-up because I'd turned into a pretty unpleasant person. The initial flush of success will do that to most people really. That mixed with some alcohol. I think celebrity is a toxin. Even minor celebrity. More often than not it changes people for the worse. It's an unnatural state of affairs and it turns people unpleasant."

He most likely knew it at the time but it took the end of his relationship to bring the realisation up from the depths. Until then self-awareness was not as straightforward. So Skinner was vacillating between stay or go, she was no longer tied to her job and in possession of an airline ticket that seemed almost fated to be used to both metaphorically and literally fly away. She convinced herself that Johnson no longer wanted this relationship, and rather than wait for him to pluck up the courage to end it, she would do it herself.

After the Red Wedge gigs the couple were due to holiday with Tim Pope and his girlfriend. Fiona was hoping that this would give her some time and space to think, and that if she was going to tell him it was over then it would be when they returned from the holiday. As it happened she never went on the holiday. "Matt had been so tense for so long I hoped a holiday would give us space to think, but one night I came home from work and he'd trashed the bedroom because he couldn't find his notebook – he was acting horribly and that was the final thing." She can't remember exactly what she said, only that she had ended it. She had expected him to be relieved, to admit that he too thought the relationship had run its course. What she hadn't expected was for him to fall apart.

Zeke Manyika remembers just how badly he took it. "I've never seen anyone so heartbroken. Basically I used to wake up in the morning and go hang out with him – I was that worried about him. I thought he was going to do himself in, I really did." The only thing that seemed to take his mind off things remained working on music, and if he wasn't in any kind of place to work on any of his own he was grateful for the opportunity of helping another's, as Manyika also recalls. "I was at his house one day, and he had this drum machine set up, and a keyboard there, and we did that track of mine 'Bible Belt'. I had this poem and I wanted to put it to music but it was too long and needed editing, but he was, bang! – up and straight into it and we started working on the track right away."

In the October 3 edition of *NME* was an article with the rather dramatic heading: 'Matt Johnson: My Darkest Hour'. The page lead continued in an almost tabloid fashion: "Not even the worldwide success of his *Infected* album could shield Matt Johnson from the twin body-blows he's suffered this summer. Thatcher's victory was bad enough, but worse, much worse, was to follow when Johnson's girlfriend of five years upped and left him." The article then begins with a quote from the man himself. "I've lost the only person I've ever really loved and it's devastating. Like a bomb going off in your life and you're running around trying to pick up the pieces." The rest of the one-page piece doesn't actually reveal much that a fan wouldn't already know, aside from the fact that Johnson was hoping to move to Shoreditch. He is quoted on politics and Red Wedge and little else. Unlike a typical feature there was no tour or record to promote and so it appeared to be one of those interviews that filled a space – either arranged by PR or an opportunistic freelancer. Three days later, its origin was revealed.

In the Ad Lib column of London's *Evening Standard* a short piece headed 'The The cheek of it' explained that Johnson had agreed to be interviewed for a book on socialist writers and artists. "Unknown to left-winger Matt," it continued, "one of Britain's most talented musicians, he was being secretly taped during a photo-session for the book. And his musings about his break-up with his girlfriend Fiona have been sold, not to one of the tabloids, but to the normally sanctimonious *NME*." Johnson was also quoted: "It hasn't helped the fact that I'm trying to get back together with Fiona."

The episode was an indication of the level of fame Johnson had reached. Though not on a par with the likes of Boy George or George Michael, he was nevertheless suddenly the target of gossip columns rather than musical analysis – never a good thing for anyone with any artistic integrity. Ironically, by the time the piece was published the couple were on their way to reconciliation, as the *Standard* article suggested.

The cat was, however, out of the bag, and Johnson chose to talk – openly this time – to G. D. Henderson of *Cut* magazine. He said he hoped that everyone who listened to *Infected* appreciated it because it had cost him his relationship. He also referred to himself as a "Lying, cheating, womanising drunk", though this analysis might have been offered by Skinner rather than his own self-reflection. As necessary as the realisation was, it came too late in the day. Johnson, whose music had once been referred to as existential blues, woke up on June 11 and his woman was gone. That *other* woman, meanwhile, was about to win another term of office. So Zeke and others rallied round.

Johnson was ready to woo Fiona back. While they had been apart he had taken to writing down his thoughts in a blue exercise book, a practice begun while he was in Crete, and he presented it to her when she returned. "Matt wrote down every emotion for that two weeks I was away, and I came back, and we met at Regent's Park zoo. He said, 'Let's just go for a walk,' and he gave me this book. I was allowed to read it once, on a bench. I knew he was watching me. I had to read it, and then give it back to him. And, it was everything – love, hate, pain, joy – and that was probably the thing that wooed me back. He was amazing really, did everything he could to show his love and regret for taking me for granted. He was sweet, he was thoughtful, then he was angry and hurt, then apologetic for being angry. He even bought me a bloody kitten. We didn't officially get back together until November. During all this upheaval my parents moved from a thirty-year life in London back home to Scotland. I was visiting them for Christmas and I remember calling Matt at his parents. That call was a turning point though. His mum picked up the phone and simply laid into me for about forty minutes. I held the phone to my ear and just took it. She was a lioness defending her son. Matt called me later; he knew we'd spoken but I didn't tell him what she said, just asked if he was willing to be with me even if his family no longer accepted me. Without hesitation he said 'Yes, absolutely.' He appreciated his mum saw him with a rose-tinted hue."

13

PSYCHONAUT

IN 1987, MUSIC BOX TV, A TWENTY-FOUR-HOUR CHANNEL available only in Yorkshire, broadcast a 'Making of *Infected'* special, consisting of the entire film, preceded by a programme where Sunie Fletcher interviewed Matt Johnson, Andrew Johnson and Peter Christopherson. At a time when Johnson should have been enjoying the acclaim that the film and album were gathering, instead he was feeling miserable. Just as everything was going so right, it seemed, something had to go wrong. Asked about what would be coming next he replied: "The next album is probably going to be less political in some ways, more personal, because *Infected* ruined my personal life basically. It created a lot of problems, because I've been so obsessed with my work, and I've neglected other areas of my life, and so the next album is probably going to be a love album."

Fletcher asked if this was "by way of an apology to someone?"

"Kind of, yeah," Johnson replied, then looked to one side, perhaps feeling a bit sheepish in front of a camera, before continuing: "Not necessarily an apology, but it certainly will be much more personal, and I've learnt a lot over the past five weeks; I've been through quite a traumatic time, and I've just realised that you may have gold records and critical reviews, but they mean nothing compared to other areas of your life. You can't consider yourself a successful human being unless you are successful in things that matter most, like personal relationships, and friendships and stuff, and there's areas of my life which I neglected."

In effect, when Fiona Skinner got on the plane and took off for New York, the *Infected* project was over and *Mind Bomb* was about to begin. Johnson had undergone huge life changes, and these, together with the hangover of filming and promoting the album and movie, had, as he admitted to many people at the time, and years later to good friend Johnny Marr, turned him "into a pretty unpleasant person". Life had become easy with a record label happy to fund his wildest dreams. When he wasn't shut away working on music or lyrics he could be found drinking cocktails with Paul Webb or Zeke Manyika. Webb was also his partner for many a late-night session at the New World Snooker Centre in Dalston, and the pair would also go running together in Victoria Park, sweating away the intoxicants of the night before. If he wasn't out with friends clubbing he would be at parties. Dave Dorrell, one half of M.A.R.R.S, who had reached the top of the charts with the hip-hop-cut-up hybrid 'Pump Up The Volume', would frequently throw parties, and in the loved-up vibe of such surroundings, amidst other people tasting success at a young age, notes of caution were thin on the ground.

The trouble with *Infected* – the flip-side to its global success and acclaim – was that it had dredged up things from the deep. Skinner called it his "angry record", and years later when interviewed on the occasion of its thirtieth anniversary he would describe it the same way. It wasn't just anger at Margaret Thatcher and the state of a nation in decline, marching in lock-step with American foreign policy. Inner demons had been released. Skinner feels the East End might have had something to do with it.

"If you come from that very male environment where issues are resolved by fighting, but you are a sensitive, artistic type, then that is hard. Matt saw someone come at his dad with a shotgun once. I think there is both an anger and the frustration of having to deal with this anger and the other emotions. He came from a very macho world."

Johnson acknowledges that his extended family were not only pranksters but quite pugnacious. "We would often be playing pranks on each other, making silly phone calls, etc. but on the other hand there was also quite a macho violent side where everyone would enjoy talking about fighting." This may have had a bearing on how he reacted to what he calls the toxins of fame and celebrity. Having to deal with this, he feels, contributed to much of his internal conflict. "The ego and fear begin to take command and can lead you into all sorts of places you shouldn't really go." Not only did he dislike what fame and celebrity did to him, changing his personality for the worse, but also what it did to the perceptions of others and how they acted towards him – either being overly sycophantic or, the reverse, offensive.

Maybe this is where some of the anger came from, or maybe it came from having to leave such an environment and go and live in the country, and then a small Essex town where he never felt entirely at home. Wherever it originated, Johnson decided that he didn't want to do another album riven with such levels of ire. Though he wasn't about to shy away from controversial subjects, he knew he had to heal some personal wounds – both those he had inflicted on others and those which he had inflicted upon himself. Getting back together with Fiona was a chance to establish a new beginning, to follow a different path, and, being the sort of person he was, this wasn't going to involve any half-measures.

Repairing the damage to their relationship was just one of the changes. Another, and one which he also used to entice her to come back to him, was purchasing a warehouse-style loft space. "It was one of the things that Matt used to woo me back," says Skinner. "It was our dream apartment. We had both fallen in love with Fran Duffy's apartment."

The space had belonged to photographer Peter Mackertich and video artist Chris Gabrin, who, along with artist Denis Masi and John Foxx, had bought the entire building in Shoreditch in 1979. Here was a chance to not only get a slice of New York loft-style living, but also return to Johnson's childhood memories of Spitalfields and Shoreditch. As well as this return to his roots he continued to reflect on where he had gone wrong in his personal life, and what direction he might take to put things back on a more positive path. As he was to say to journalist Sam King in a *SOUNDS* interview in May 1989, the end of his relationship had given him a "kick up the ass" and led to a period of intense self-reflection. He concluded, among other things, that he had been rather self-obsessed during *Infected* and now was the time to look outwards. This would inevitably, given his penchant for enquiry, lead to looking at things much bigger than the self, and in turn would inform the new album.

It was time to start writing. He described his process to Dave Henderson, for *OffBeat* magazine. "Where I work, I'm surrounded by reference books, notepads and my instruments. Everything is there and I have a very simple way of working, I like to be intense and I'm not very sociable when I'm working." His references this time would include the Bible, the Quran, the Bhagavad Gita, the I-Ching, the Kabbalah and other books on religion and spiritual matters, including Kahlil Gibran's *The Prophet* and the *Tibetan Book of the Dead.*

"I was also doing a lot of dream journalling and analysis. Many strange dreams and messages were coming through, even advice on what books and authors to read, such as Walt Whitman, Carl Jung and Friedrich Nietzsche. I was just searching for common threads between the major religions and philosophical systems." The blue notebook he had shown Fiona Skinner, with its lyric ideas and song titles, was also to hand.

Wanting to ditch the hedonistic habits he had indulged in during *Infected*, but not wanting to lose the intensity, he now opted for periods of fasting and strange diets, such as a forty-day grape and distilled water diet, designed to detox, purge and induce a heightened sensory state. Not quite relinquishing all drugs, he now switched to magic mushrooms, a natural stimulant more in tune with the mind-expansion he was aiming for. It was a heady cocktail, and this was the mind and body fuel behind *Mind Bomb*. An isolated month in a villa he had recently bought above a village in the Tramuntana mountains in Mallorca completed the writing process. Now it was time to think about getting into the studio.

James Eller remembers sitting in Ramport Studios in Battersea, south London, working on Julian Cope's 'Scottish album' as bass player. "The assistant came in and said, 'Somebody called Matt Johnson rang and wants you to call him back.' I said, 'Who's that?' and Dave said, 'Oh, that'll be Matt, from The The.' So I called him back. This was at the very end of '87, I think, and he said, 'Your name has come up a few times, and I'd like to talk to you about the possibility of putting a band together.'"

The Dave in question was Dave Palmer, also working on the Cope album. Eller, who had not long returned from the States, had only recently heard of The The, through watching the *Infected* film. He became an instant convert, so he was intrigued then excited about the offer. Johnson was working on pre-production with Palmer and Warne Livesey at his new loft in Shoreditch. It was Livesey who had suggested Eller as a bass player, having worked with him on Julian Cope's *Saint Julian* album.

"James is a really great bass player and he was the right bass player to have in that band, because he's technically very good, he's just into supplying what the song needs. He's got impeccable taste and impeccable timing. That's why I suggested him to Matt, because I felt that though there were a lot of great bass players, I felt James would have that sensibility of just 'laying it down'. He could come up with some great little flourishes where they were needed but he wasn't afraid to just sit on a riff, and I was pretty sure that he would work well with Dave Palmer."

Johnson contacted Eller and said rather than auditions he was going to have interviews, so Eller duly turned up at his flat and the pair spent a couple of hours chatting. Years later Eller tells me about the meeting and the man he has now known for three decades.

"The first time I met him, he had a huge flip-chart with lyrics on it… I believe he researches religions, Buddhism and stuff, and he gets really into it, so he's very knowledgeable as well. I think when I met him he was on a tomato-only diet, to see what it would feel like. Okay… he's funny, deep and funny. A bit eccentric, in a good way."

The next day he received a phone call to say he was in the band. It wasn't long before he was a victim of one of Johnson's practical jokes.

"When we were planning *Mind Bomb* he invited me round to his place. He was there with Warne. This was my first day officially in The The, and it was my turn to come round and work on the demos, and I walked in and Matt and Warne were sitting with their backs to the door, and I went, 'So, how's it going guys, what have you been doing?' And they played this sort of funky track, and it was quite good; drums and bass, a bit of Hammond and electric piano and stuff. So I was like, 'Ah yeah. That's really cool, that's great.' And I noticed from behind that they were hunched over, laughing their heads off. And what they'd done was, they had an eighties sound module and had played the built-in demo. So within one minute of starting in The The, that was my initiation."

It was like a crash-course into the mind of Matt Johnson for Eller: the predilection for practical jokes, the fastidious attention to detail that saw lyrics on flip-charts and the deep, or perhaps eccentric tendency to explore areas of the psyche that others barely knew existed. Maybe it wasn't tomatoes as Eller recalls but it's not like Johnson wouldn't have given them a go, just for the hell of it – to see what happened. Johnson's own memory is quite definite. "*Mind Bomb* was done on magic mushrooms; I had piles of books… I was meditating… doing all sorts of really deep, freakish things and getting into all this heavy Islamic stuff. Also Daoism, Buddhism, Hinduism, Judaism. I was trying to use consciousness as a type of microscope/telescope to delve deeper into the world around me. Ultimately, I did freak myself out a bit as I probably went too far but, in the end, everything seemed to simply boil down to love and fear and the realisation that all we see in this life is a manifestation of one of these opposing frequencies. I was also keenly aware, though, how the ego can pollute these kind of enquiries and mess everything up."

The interest in Islam was in one way a continuation of his interest in global politics and a growing awareness that tensions between the West and the Middle East were hotting up just as the Cold War appeared to be cooling down. If one wanted to be Orwellian about it, one could say that the Two Minutes Hate needed a new context. But Johnson was also interested in looking closely at religion at this time. As a self-confessed agnostic he was curious as to how religions could inspire so much hatred and how they could be abused by those in power. As his strange diets began to kick in, however, it seems his research also led him down another path in search of some meaning about life. These were big questions, deep questions, and it was clear from the very first recording sessions that *Mind Bomb* was going to be just as belligerent as its predecessor.

According to Eller, Johnson had *Mind Bomb* very well sketched out before they went into the studio. "He knew exactly what a lot of the drum parts would be, a lot of the bass parts. I mean some of them were exact. His guitar parts were all done, the orchestration I believe was all done."

Eller liked this exactness and thoroughness. Johnson ran a tight ship. "It was great being with those people, making records, Warne and Felix Kendall, the engineer. Everything was so easy. There was never any doubt; I mean I knew that when I plugged my bass in, and the bass rig was set up and mic'd up, that it would sound great. Everything was as it should be." Well set up. Always. From the beginning.

Which, recording-wise, was 'Armageddon Days', a song Johnson had written after digesting both the Bible and the Quran and coming to the conclusion that the religions behind both tomes had been distorted by those with vested interests; that prophets of

280

different religions said essentially the same things and it was the distortions that led to hate and war. Livesey was conscious that such a big subject was going to require big things in the studio. It wasn't going to be straightforward.

"He had a big vision for that track. I think there's an enormity in what Matt was saying in that song, that demanded both a lot of respect and real attention to try and convey, and it's interesting because with hindsight it is pretty prophetic. Although it was starting to happen, what that song is saying, this is now the world we live in. *Islam is rising, the Christians mobilising...* yeah, this is the way it's turned out. He saw that coming."

To temper the heavy subject matter of holy war, Johnson couldn't resist a bit of humorous pop-cultural theft and latched onto the idea of obliquely comparing the clash of civilisations to the sort of good old-fashioned ruck immortalised in Sweet's 'Ballroom Blitz'. While Dave Palmer utilised the same drum beat as the glam rock classic, Johnson appropriated the spoken introduction, only instead of asking band members if they were ready he asked if Jesus, Buddha and Mohammed were. Most of the reviewers would spot the in-joke and found it funny, but they were to be less generous when it came to the rest of the lyrical content.

With the tracking of drums, bass and guitar done it was clear that the song was going to need something big to elevate it. Perhaps because it was such a demanding track to record, Livesey has a good memory of the process. "We had these sessions with this thirty- or forty-piece male voice choir, and they are singing these lyrics... *Islam is rising, the Christians mobilising,* and they are all middle-aged gentlemen who are used to singing on operatic and classical records, and they were sniggering to each other as they read off the charts, but it was quite fun.

"There is a thing in the verses where the voices bend up in pitch, and there's a lot of instruments playing the same thing. The bass does it, the string section does it, and we had the bass singers in it, and we were doing this and thinking, 'That's really good,' and we said, 'There's not any way you guys could sing that an octave lower is there?' which is completely out of any sort of written range for them, and they said, 'Yeah, there's actually a technique we can use. It's difficult to do it and we can't do it with words. It's kind of like what the Tibetan monks do, a kind of faked octave.' And they did that and it sounded so great."

The track was a real collective effort, with over eighty performers on it. As well as the Ambrosian Singers there was the Astarti String Orchestra, and each person needed a Musician's Union form filled in. For Livesey it was a pretty intense start to the job. For Eller and Palmer it was beginning to feel that something good was coming together, so when Johnny Marr's name kept coming up in conversation it seemed like the obvious thing to do was give him a ring. In his autobiography, *Set the Boy Free*, Marr recounts that Johnson got in touch and they arranged to meet at an Iggy Pop gig. Talking to each other backstage, Iggy asked if they were working together, and if not then why didn't they? Some accounts have this as the moment Marr joined The The; Marr's book, not specific in chronology at this point, doesn't suggest otherwise. Johnson himself believes the Iggy Pop gig in question was in 1986 and that Marr was, at this point, still in The Smiths. What both are certain of is that when Johnson called to suggest he join the band, Marr went round to the flat in Shoreditch. Johnson remembers a long night. "After a few hours chatting at mine we went out to Heaven in Charing Cross Road, a famous gay club at the time and one of the few places you could find a very late drink in those days, then headed back to mine, and sat up talking for a few more hours." By which time Marr was, to all intents and purposes, a member of The The.

"It was an absolute no-brainer," according to Marr. "The The were my other favourite band. *Infected* was my favourite record other than my own. We stayed up all night drinking vodka, listening to his demos, which sounded great. At that point he had already recorded a few tracks with Warne that he wanted me to play on. He had a demo of 'The Beat(en) Generation'. I needed to know what was required."

His first day on the job was at Wessex Sound Studios in Highbury New Park. "It was a bonkers studio," according to Dave Palmer, "quite close to Islington. Johnny came over and he played on 'Beat(en) Generation', 'Good Morning Beautiful', and 'Kingdom Of Rain'. That was the first real session with Johnny, that was the start. When Johnny played on 'Beat(en) Generation' Matt had found his guy." Hardly surprising when you consider that Marr played his guitar part off the top of his head – and that was it, job done. Perhaps it is the atmosphere in the studio at that time that Palmer is referring to when he describes it as "bonkers" because Marr's own recollection of his first day includes Livesey sitting on a sofa at the back of the room, going, "Look at my hands, look at my hands, they're all red!" and Johnson retorting with, "Shut up Warne, there's nothing wrong with your hands." Marr sat there thinking, "Isn't anyone going to help that poor man?" But far from help, Johnson and Felix Kendall drew red spots all over their own hands and waved them in front of the stricken producer. All in a day's work with The The. To be fair, Marr's take on the situation was skewed somewhat by the fact that he had spent the previous three days dropping ecstasy, so the apparent lack of empathy on display probably did his comedown no favours; though when he admitted his intake, rather than chide him for a lack of professionalism, Johnson suggested they get back on one, and it was arranged for someone to deliver the requisite tablets to the studio. Soon all was well with the world again and everyone in it, including Warne, though he himself opted not to 'get on one'.

Livesey recalls this day as the culmination of the stress caused by success. Having been sent on a similar career trajectory as Johnson thanks to his work on *Infected*, he found that suddenly having what he had strived for was a rather disorientating experience. Now in demand, he fell into the trap of being scared to turn down all the work that was suddenly coming his way, work where bigger labels and bigger budgets were involved, thus bigger pressures.

"There was a particular time when we were at Wessex Studios, and we were recording with Johnny Marr and this was big pressure, this great guitarist we all wanted to work with, coming in, and I felt terrible, full of flu, but didn't want to take time off and was feeling stressed, all sweaty and a bit freaked out. After we got through that session I did take some time off; my wife and I and the kids went off to Italy for a bit of a break."

Livesey can't remember if the red spots he saw were real or not, but does recall that his experience was real and Johnson was, all joking aside, very helpful. "When I was freaking out he said, 'I've been through that' and he related the time when he had got so stressed he lost his vision for a day after *Soul Mining*. And this made me feel a bit better. You know… you are having this experience and then someone tells you they have been through something similar so you think, 'At least I'm not the only one – I'm not going crazy.' So I found him to be very compassionate and a nice person to have around while that was going on."

Ironically Kendall, partner in the hand-waving, would have his own meltdown later in the album's progress, perhaps as a result of Johnson getting him onto the grapes-only diet. Despite this he held it together enough to do a sterling job. Eller was well served in having a producer who also played bass and knew how to get the sound right, ensuring that it sat comfortably in the mix. This precision, and Eller's subtle playing, mean that the bass is prominent without ever drawing too much attention to itself, and as a rhythm section he and Palmer dovetailed effortlessly. Sometimes though, it would be Johnson's need to get everything just how he wanted it that would drive a particular session. Eller, recalling one such occasion, struggles to remember which song was involved, but has no trouble with the details of how Johnson got the sound he wanted.

"This is the length Matt goes to – I think he wanted an acoustic sounding bass on 'The Beat(en) Generation', or maybe it was 'Armageddon Days', I can't remember. So he basically hired every acoustic bass guitar he could find in London. In Livingston Studios there were fifteen of the things there, and we went through all these basses, going 'No, no,' or Felix would be going, 'No, that's too thin,' or 'I can't work with that,' and we actually went back to my bass guitar and tuned it down, and took all the top end out of it. It took all day, but it sounded great."

'The Beat(en) Generation' was the first track that Marr worked on, the lightness of which was tailor-made for his deft touch. The song, not the most popular among fans, took its name from a sign Andrew had written and stuck onto the door of his bedroom in the flat in Camberwell, a pun on the 'Beat Generation'. The Beats were considered the precursors to pop culture, and anyone who still carried a torch for literature as well as music couldn't help but identify them as the original teenage rebels. Adding those two letters made it clear where Johnson was going to be aiming his arrows in the lyrics. This track was going to be the first single, and for those who were expecting more of *Infected*'s industrial edge, the lightness and subtlety of 'Beat(en) Generation' was perhaps confounding. In fact the original plan had been to release 'Armageddon Days' as the first single, a harder-sounding track, but the Salman Rushdie affair meant that CBS decided against it. It had been intended to release 'The Beat(en) Generation' as the second single; Johnson feels it might have been better appreciated if this had happened.

It's all about the rhythm section, both of whom play impeccably. "I remember we went very tight on the kit," Dave Palmer recalls. "Warne didn't have many mics so we had kick, hat, snare, a ride cymbal, and that was it. There's no toms, no bleed, it's very focused." He also thinks Johnson had a clear idea from the beginning of what he wanted. "He wanted it to have that swinging kind of groove. I think we may have tried programming a brush track and thinking, 'That's the way it should go, we should have brushes on it.' We cut it really quick – three or four takes and it was done. It was kind of country, in a Johnny Cash kind of way. It's a cool song that one, I like it."

So too does Eller, though he is less sure about the opinion of others. "I was a big fan of country music, people like Johnny Cash,

Waylon Jennings and George Jones; that generation, the roots of country music, the tonality of which I really loved. I think I was the biggest fan of 'The Beat(en) Generation', I don't think the band liked it very much. I don't think Matt liked it very much but I loved that song. I love the sound of it. It's a very warm-sounding track. Dave's drums are superb on it... everybody is superb on it actually." Johnson did actually like it, although he doesn't consider it one of his better songs.

'Armageddon Days' was the first track recorded, and 'Beat(en) Generation' would be the first single, but the track that would appear first on the finished album was 'Good Morning Beautiful'. In his autobiography Marr mentions that before the key session on 'Good Morning Beautiful' he and Matt had been ingesting hallucinogenics. Just before they started in earnest Johnson asked him if he could play his guitar so it sounded "like Jesus meets the devil". In his altered state this may have seemed either an alarming or perfectly reasonable, even logical, request to make; who knows which way his mind was bending at this point? Johnson had of course also been on a diet of religious texts, and as far back as *Infected* was interested in the concept of the eternal struggle between good and evil. Maybe, when he made his request to Marr, he wasn't joking but actually meant it.

The title – 'Good Morning Beautiful' – came from egg boxes in New York, and it can be seen briefly in a fridge in the video for 'Twilight Of A Champion'. It next appeared, as far as The The goes, in the blue notebook into which Johnson poured out all his feelings when his relationship with Fiona Skinner ended. One imagines that in this context it might have been a romantic reference. By the time it became the title of the opening song on *Mind Bomb* its meaning was much less clear, but the song is certainly not about waking up next to the one you love. It begins – lyrically speaking – with a simple rhyme read by a child. *Satellite oh, satellite/Who sits upon our skies/How deep do you see/When you spy into our lives?*

This little vignette, a foretelling almost of our present surveillance society, at first glance appears to have little to do with the rest of the lyric, which deals with the theme of how the spiritual messages about absolute truth have been hijacked by the dogma of major religious faiths, subverted and twisted by those seeking power and control over the world population. Nowadays, when we have mass surveillance on a scale that even Orwell couldn't have predicted, we can see that one method of control has replaced another. Johnson was reading all manner of stuff and, through diet and drugs, altering his state of consciousness fairly drastically. Even if he wasn't making a conscious connection he was, to borrow some hippy parlance, feeling some heavy vibes. Just listen to the song and his 'voice of the devil' vocal and you can see where his head was at. Sure, it has a slightly hammy edge to it, but for all the accusations about being doom-laden, serious or po-faced that were constantly levelled at him, Johnson had a very healthy sense of humour. He seems to enjoy singing his apocalyptic lines in this way, taking the piss out of the Grand Guignol manner of fire and brimstone texts that are designed to strike fear into the little man.

Unlike the bombastic first tracks of his previous two albums, 'Good Morning Beautiful' is a much more subtle and slinky animal, without relinquishing any of the power that Johnson liked to open a set with. Dave Palmer is a big fan. "I absolutely love 'Good Morning Beautiful' because it is a beautiful, ambient-like, cinematic piece. I remember being there when Johnny was doing all that guitar. It was just amazing. It had that quality… it's got the trippy tablas, the voice at the start… it was really fucking special. And that set the tone for *Mind Bomb*. That's the first song and you think, 'Okay, this is gonna be an adventure. This is gonna be good.' On the *The The Versus The World* tour we would start off with 'Sweet Bird Of Truth' and end with 'Good Morning Beautiful'. That would be the closer, and we would stretch it out, it would be amazing."

The voice at the start is Warne Livesey's step-daughter; the keener-eyed will have noticed she gets a credit on the album's inner sleeve, albeit with the wrong surname. Her biological father was a bit upset about this, according to Livesey, and contacted the label to complain, but by then it was too late. For the record, then, better late than never, the girl who narrated the short poem is Esmé Whybrow. The tablas that Palmer refers to are played by Pandit Dinesh, and they join the slow build-up of instrumentation at the same time as one of Eller's insistent two-bar bass riffs, the rich harmonics of which add depth to the equally simple, but equally effective keyboard refrain. Add the tenor saxophones of Chris White and Phil Todd, and the electric harmonica of Mark Feltham and we are still waiting for Johnson's vocals and for Marr to do more than tease around with his FX pedals. The guitar, when it finally comes fully into play, is hard to discern half the time, sounding stretched, like the notes are made of elastic, distorted and warped. It is about as far away from The Smiths as it is possible to get whilst still being a pop record. No wonder Marr felt a sense of freedom. You can almost imagine him seeing the chords he strummed becoming visible and snaking around the studio before his eyes.

Johnson was as happy with it as everyone else involved. "There was a lot of synchronicity and happy accidents going on at those sessions. Fiona had been away to Indonesia and she brought me back a cassette I asked her to tape of some Islamic voices. It happened to be in the same key as 'Good Morning Beautiful'. It fitted straight in. So lots of little things like that were happening all the time on *Mind Bomb*. I just remember the sound, as we were working on that song, as brilliant. Just what I had in my head. A lot of credit has to go to Warne and Felix, our engineer, as well as the band of course. Everyone did a fine job." Felix Kendall was to win an award for his engineering on the track, given to him by George Martin, who could recognise studio wizardry when he heard it. The track, as Livesey recalls, was reworked quite considerably. "Our original version of 'Good Morning Beautiful' was three and a half minutes long, and when we got to mixing Matt came in with all of these new lyrics and different ideas and extra verses, and I was like, 'Well we don't have enough song!' So we ended up re-editing the song during the course of the mix. We used the same recorded section with different things muted, a new bit of vocal over it, and spliced that back into the sequence of the song. I think we spent five days mixing it, because we were actually reworking the track."

After this atmospheric opener the tempo, and temperature, is raised by 'Armageddon Days', which is followed by the equally pacy, but less strident 'Violence Of Truth'. The urgency of its simple Hammond organ refrain sets the pace and Palmer's drums take up the baton. Eller's bass has a rougher sound here, almost punky, a result of driving things to the edge in the studio. "I did 'Violence Of Truth' in Studio Two at Air with Roli Mosimann. It was in the autumn I think, across a period of a few months. He was trying to get a very distorted bass guitar, and he kept coming out and turning my amp up, going 'Nearly there, nearly there,' and he blew a quite expensive speaker cabinet I had, and I was like, 'Damn!' A 600-watt cabinet with two 15-inch speakers just exploded. I think they got the final take before the speakers went, so on 'Violence Of Truth' the bass sound is with the speakers about to give in." Johnson actually wrote the guitar riff on a keyboard, just like he had done with 'Infected'. In fact, it is basically the same riff speeded up and syncopated. When taking in the track-listing as a whole this matters less than it otherwise might because it acts as a slight relief from what has gone before and better serves the drop in pace that the final track of side one brings. Johnson would spend a lot of time considering the track-listing of his albums and with *Mind Bomb* his decisions – on the first three-quarters of the album – are spot on.

The track that would end side one of the vinyl album – 'Kingdom Of Rain' – has an atmospheric intro, like the album's opener, but then reveals itself to be a much lighter track that calms things down. The decision to use Sinead O'Connor on vocals was made when Johnson saw a video of a band called World Party, when he was in Boston. "The sound was muted on the TV but there was a girl singing backing vocals who I found mesmerising. I just had a feeling about her and knew I needed her to duet with me. It was a real bonus when I eventually heard *The Lion And The*

Cobra and found out how good a singer she was. It was through John Kennedy that we met. He represented us both by this stage." Kennedy passed a tape on to O'Connor of the track that Johnson wanted her to sing on. She liked it and agreed to work with him. The dynamic range of the track is fantastic, with swells of sound where the backbeat punches harder for a few bars, and Marr's guitar announces itself, before everything relaxes once more and Palmer's excellent stick work takes centre stage with its deft rimshots, and Eller's assured bass riff takes over. It is almost like a jazz performance, with each band member being given a solo of the briefest sonic duration before they fuse back into the mix; it keeps this up for nearly six minutes that fairly fly by until the song ends with the same thunder and rain sound effects and whale songs that it began with, ending side one as atmospherically as it had begun. In the days when an album's listening experience for most people still consisted of two parts, side one of *Mind Bomb* was hard to fault. This track, however, would not be one of the singles, let alone the first, much to the continued dismay of Warne Livesey.

"'Kingdom Of Rain' was the most obvious single, and with Sinead O'Connor being on it as well that was going to be a good thing. Unfortunately no one got her agreement for the track to be released in whatever form the label wanted, and because we hadn't negotiated up front she was allowed to have control on how the track was used. When *Mind Bomb* was being released she was working on her next album which had 'Nothing Compares 2 U' on it, and so she didn't want our song to come out as a single because she didn't want it to detract from her own, which is fair enough. I think it would have been different if we had been able to use it to promote the album, as the first single, rather than 'Beat(en) Generation'." Livesey is a big fan of 'Kingdom Of Rain' and Johnny Marr's contribution to it. "There's an incredible guitar part that Johnny played on 'Kingdom Of Rain' – a typical Johnny Marr arpeggiated picky part. I think he did one guitar part all the way through the song. I don't think there's overdubs. We worked on that part for the whole day, worked on the sound of it to get it just perfect. It sounds very simple actually but I've worked with good guitar players who go to that track and they know just how subtle it is. Even though it sounds like the same riff, each part is slightly different, it just moves round a little bit to work in and out of the vocals."

Most of this recording was taking place during the hot summer, and mild autumn, of 1988 when the country was at the dawn of a cultural revolution centred on the emergence of house music from America. After nine long years of Margaret Thatcher's cruel economics, and with no end in sight, the right combination of things came together and created a paradigm shift. Instead of the teeth-gnashing angst of fighting back through political protest, personified by Red Wedge, young people found that they could simply indulge in the teeth-gnashing experience of ecstasy and enjoy a kind of alternate universe. Using the type of entrepreneurial nous that Thatcher herself should have been proud of, a cultural network of music, clubs, raves, fashion, publications, record labels and thought mushroomed. Even if you weren't part of it, you couldn't escape the feeling that was in the air. The world, suddenly, felt ripe with possibility, after years of the opposite.

Many of the people involved with The The at this time embraced this change, and so Fiona Skinner, Johnny Marr and Dave Palmer would take frequent trips to Shoom and Spectrum to enjoy the vibes and get into the music. Palmer in particular seems to have taken to this new scene in a big way. "Oh it was all around us; my weekends were all about going to Shoom, sometimes going to the out of town things, Boys Own, you know, all those clubs. Thursday night behind Heaven, Spectrum, I did all of them. Sometimes Matt would show up and it wasn't really his thing, whereas I loved it. And at that time, 1988, I think people were just desperate to actually let their guards down and just fucking enjoy themselves, because we'd been through some dark times."

Marr, meanwhile, found that the spirit of the times was working its way into his playing. "I couldn't help but be part of what was happening at the Hacienda. So I was responsible for bringing a lot of that down the motorway with me and I think that was really healthy for the group. Matt was resolutely ignoring the house scene but I think that was him making sure he wasn't thrown off his course. I was in and out of the Hacienda but playing on songs like 'Kingdom Of Rain' and 'Good Morning Beautiful'. I had no kind of conflict there. I was still only 24, gobbling as many substances as I could and it was really good; it was great for the record."

Johnson claimed to hate house and techno but Zeke Manyika thinks he may have been somewhat duplicitous about this. "He used to take the piss out of the acid house thing; in fact he used to have a funny little dance he would do. But at home he would listen to lots of old soul and ska and stuff, so I was always puzzled by his reaction to the house scene. I think he might have been grandstanding a bit. He always had to have a reaction to everything, but I didn't trust his reaction to this, because we used to go to clubs, and be sitting around chatting." For someone who had embraced technology so much, it does seem a bit surprising that Johnson would dismiss house music. While it might be easier to see why he mistrusted the scene that sprang up around it, the good vibrations in the air definitely filtered into the studio, and while many journalists in the rock press would react sceptically at best and cynically at worst to his musings about spirituality, God and a higher meaning in life, here was a scene for which such lofty thoughts were bread and butter. They hadn't dubbed it the Second Summer of Love for nothing. In an interview with Roger Morton for *Record Mirror*, published on March 25, 1989, Johnson had this to say about his new album.

"Every day you're given choices, and the title *Mind Bomb* came about from what I would call splitting the moral atom, which is going so deep into yourself that you investigate the motive behind every desire, and trace it right down deep into yourself. It's essentially the struggle between light and dark that goes on in everybody." In fact the working title for the album had been *Psychonaut*, meaning a person who uses altered states to explore deeper meanings in life. The eventual title of *Mind Bomb* was taken from the Timothy Leary book *Politics of Ecstasy*, which Johnson had been reading on holiday in Spain with Fiona Skinner, after the album was actually recorded. It was easy, perhaps, to take the piss out of a club full of people shouting "Acieed!", especially when they were on a drug you had encountered years before, but Johnson had much more in common than he realised with the mindset that would take hold of the generation for whom acid house was a road to Damascus experience. The spirit of the times cares not whom it touches. As Marr says in his biography, "The mood around The The was really positive and forward thinking," and in 1988 everyone appeared to be going through a period of liberation, himself included. He didn't just feel physically free of The Smiths but free in every sense; with this came the freedom to think about different things and express himself in ways he hadn't been able to before. "I definitely felt a sense of freedom to go in directions I hadn't been in before as a musician, and I definitely felt a sense of being in the right place, with the right people at that time in my life, philosophically, and specifically with Matt."

In such a climate, the mind quest that Johnson had been busy pursuing was much easier for sympathetic minds to tune into, rather than simply disregard. Both he and Marr had read and soaked up Paul Brunton's *The Spiritual Crisis of Man*. Dave Palmer remembers that deep subjects of conversation were not uncommon, nor were they unwelcome. Speaking in 2017, when the utopian spirit of 1988 seems like ancient history, he says: "We would have many a philosophical debate, because Johnny is the same. That was the thing that really turned me on to be perfectly honest with you. The thing, I think, with Matt is this constant search. He's intrigued. It's a search of discovery for Matt, he's very curious. When he played stuff back he wanted you to feel something, he would look at you and it was like, 'Well, what do you think?' He would keep looking at you to see if it was hitting you emotionally. It's just my opinion but in every creative endeavour he's searching."

Of course, it wasn't like this twenty-four hours a day. Despite the intensity of his hunger for answers, and the intensity of the discipline and concentration that the studio sessions demanded, there was always room for light relief. In fact, because of the intensity involved, the relief when it did come was often typically school-boyish. Warne Livesey, who felt the pressure in the studio as much as anyone else involved, recounts how some of this pressure was relieved. "It was always a good laugh with Matt. We had loads of fun. A lot of it is just repartee and general cracks, but I think there were cream-cake fights and all manner of young-lad pranks." Then there were the possibilities that soft fruit presented. The market stalls of Berwick Street were nearby and the stallholders were about to get a temporary boost in trade.

"There were several rooms in Air Studios. The back room, where we spent the majority of our time, was right above the junction of Oxford Street and Regent Street, maybe four stories up. It's got big windows, and we were in there in the middle of the summer and it's warm. The windows had other windows constructed over them inside, to help with the soundproofing, which we discovered could actually be removed with the help of some tools, so we got the assistant to open these up so we could have some air when we had a break. I guess on one particular day, someone was eating grapes and lobbed one out of the window and there's all the passers-by a few stories below. The next time a couple of grapes go out, and next time someone's got a tomato and that goes out. Within a week or so this has escalated to the assistant being sent out to buy seriously big bags of squashy fruit to amuse ourselves with. Most of it just splatted on the pavement, but occasionally somebody would score a hit and the victim would be looking all around, trying to figure out what had happened. We would be chuckling away to ourselves and if anyone ever looked like they were going to look our way, would just duck back out of sight. So this was, to our state of mind at the time, quite hilarious, until one day somebody hit the wrong person, and she looked straight up and saw us. We all ducked back but it was too late. Several hours later the studio manager called through to the assistant on the phone and said, 'I've got a lawyer out here who claims that their client got hit by a tomato. I don't know what's going on in there, but get it sorted out quick because we're coming through in a minute.' So the assistant immediately puts the pane of glass back up, and screws it back in, so when this lawyer comes in and looks around we say, 'Look, you can't even open these windows, it's like a permanent pane of glass.' So they went away and we never heard anything about it again."

The whole thing had started because when Johnson finished his distilled water and grape diet there was a surplus. Rather than 'waste' the grapes by throwing them away they were used for this target practice. Johnson had also persuaded others to try this detoxifying diet. "I also put Dave Palmer and Felix Kendall on it too. Dave didn't last too long but Felix stayed on for quite a while – until he started hallucinating and saw rats running up and down the studio walls."

Problems with lawyers averted, the band returned to work and the daily takings on Berwick Street market returned to normal.

With all the songs about conflict out of the way, the pace slows on side two. After the sprightly 'Beat(en) Generation' comes what, for many observers, is the best track on the album. 'August & September' begins slowly, with the keyboard work of Paul 'Wix' Wickens and Johnson's vocals. Though the song is really a ballad, the skipping brushes of Dave Palmer give it a forward momentum that maintains the album's energy, assisted by the four-note oboe refrain played by Hilary Storer in answer to the simple refrain being played by Wix on the piano. At intervals we also get to hear some subtle effected guitar playing, but at no point does any of these instruments or players come forward to hog the limelight. This allows us to focus on Johnson's voice and lyrics. The song is about his break-up with Fiona Skinner (the title referencing the two months they were apart before they slowly reconnected) and the lyrics spell out the agonies he was going through, *when he was praying for the strength/To stop loving* (her), before deciding that he must win her back. *I started writing you the letter/Which turned into the book/Was gonna reach across the ocean/And force you to look/What kind of man was I?/Who would sacrifice your happiness to satisfy his pride?/What kind of man was I?/Who would delay your destiny to appease his tiny mind?*

The book referred to is the blue notebook, the contents of which inform *Mind Bomb*, written whilst Skinner was in America. Berating himself for the behaviour that led her to finally walk out he sings it in a voice that journeys from reasoned to tortured by the song's climax, where his pleas build up to a kind of *amour fou* and end on a slightly ominous timbre that suggests something dark about his soul that has perhaps been glimpsed earlier when he sings of going down on one knee: *With a glint in my eyes/And a rose between my teeth.*

Structurally the song is superb. Johnson is narrating a story here and he allows for musical pauses to fill in for elapsed time between each section of the story. With sublime playing throughout and a fantastic vocal performance it adds up to what might be his best song, and certainly the one where his own talents and the collective efforts of his collaborators come together in the most satisfying fashion. Dave Palmer remembers the fastidiousness required for the rhythm section: "I remember cutting that song. I think we kind of hit it every day over the course of a week, or maybe five days – it took us a long time to track that song, and it was because you couldn't really punch in on it; it was brushes and the brushes are constantly moving. We had to really nail it, and Matt was searching for something… he wanted it delicate, kind of humble, almost kind of falling apart. It took us a while." A while was, in fact, three days of drumming for Palmer, and right at the end he threw his sticks down and declaimed, "That's it! I'm done now!"

Johnson himself vividly remembers recording the drums of 'August & September'. "Dave Palmer was reduced to tears, we were working him that hard. It was a bit like a scene from the film *Whiplash*. But I knew just how good a drummer Dave was and I would never have pushed him so hard if I didn't think he had these incredible performances inside of him. I think his playing on 'Good Morning Beautiful' and 'August & September' are the best things he's ever done."

Because of all this, the track that follows seems meandering and loose by comparison, and suddenly the energy and momentum of the album is lost. 'Gravitate To Me' lacks the focus of what has preceded it and ends up sounding like a studio jam. Palmer's snares are panned at two and ten o'clock but the separation and reverb make his kit sound too wide; there's plenty of snap but not enough bottom-end. The band sound like they are enjoying themselves and with the clipped guitar they are obviously going for a funk vibe. The trouble is that, unlike the music of James Brown, who they were listening to a lot, they don't get it quite on-the-one. The lyrics too seem more generalised than usual. There isn't the sense that Johnson is singing from the heart here. That isn't to say he wasn't doing so, but it doesn't sound like he is singing about his personal life or the world he sees around him, and so there is no real narrative hook. Much of the energy missing is restored in the single edit, which lops off nearly half the running-time, and in doing so gives the track more clarity, and a definite increase in urgency compared to the eight-minute version on the album.

Maybe 'Beyond Love' should have been track three on side two. Certainly the briefest burst of flugelhorn by John Eacott at the beginning, echoing the way the oboe and clarinet are played on 'August & September', would have served as the perfect bridge to transition between two songs of different style. It is more sedate in pace, more akin to a soul ballad, but is well structured and nicely polished. It also possesses the kind of lyric on sex and love that listeners of The The are used to, with the jarring imagery of *the drops of semen/And the clots of blood*, lines that were hardly going to turn up in a love ballad sung by the likes of Alexander O'Neal. But we are okay with this because it is Matt Johnson and he isn't going to settle for the obvious. It is a love song but it reaches beyond the mortal soul, with an authentic plea to connect with something higher that he can't name. Knowing the themes of the album we can see, perhaps, why 'Beyond Love' is the finale. The last verse is his closing statement.

Looking back, Johnson thinks 'Beyond Love' is misunderstood. "It was an attempt at expressing a metaphysical idea more than it was a love song. Lyrically it is one of the most important songs on the album. I was trying to express metaphysical ideas about the world of illusion and duality we're trapped in, partly inspired by Plato's allegory of the cave. The line *So let us take off our crosses and lay them in a tin/And let our weakness become virtue/Instead of sin* is an invitation to leave religious dogma behind and embrace our true instincts and nature. In my 'mind experiments' making the album I'd reached the simple understanding that the two fundamental frequencies dominating all human behaviour in this dimension are love and fear, yet I was also keenly aware of something infinitely greater and benign. A source that was responsible for the creation and maintenance of our 'holographic' universe. So this song is simply a yearning to reach beyond love and the illusory world of duality and suffering we're trapped inside and *Up to something above*."

He took great pains with his lyric writing. They didn't necessarily come easily to him, so he would shut himself away for long periods as he worked and reworked them, agonising over each word. Then he would commit them to the recorded medium, and they were there for the critics and the fans to mull over or pick at, find solace in or deride. Now the work was done and he had to share it with the outside world.

Despite the pressure and the meltdowns, everyone involved has happy memories of recording the album. It was intense but also great fun, and the more the four worked together the more they felt like a proper band. For Johnson there was a real sense of satisfaction at the project's conclusion. "I remember at the end of it all, we'd just finished mixing, it was at Air Studios and it was late at night and we took all the windows out of their frames, and turned the lights off. There was this lovely breeze drifting in, and all the street lights from Oxford Circus below were making patterns on the walls, and we all just kicked back and cranked up the album at full volume, and enjoyed all the hard work we had put in. It was a wonderful moment."

14

THE THE VERSUS THE WORLD

LEE KAVANAGH WAS WORKING AT THE INTERNATIONAL Department of Phonogram Records when she came to the attention of Stevo. "He must have heard my name from somewhere and he wanted to get somebody in who was a bit more corporate, to placate Matt I suppose. In those days Stevo couldn't remember people's names so he used to call everyone 'Rabbit Ears' and he was like, 'Right Rabbit Ears, do you want this job or what?'" Coming from the orderly, corporate environment of parent company Phonogram to the madness of Some Bizzare took some adjustment but doubts she had about working for Matt Johnson were soon dispelled. "I was a bit scared. I thought he was a real militant, and miserable but when I met him I was completely amazed at how different he was from the public image. He and Zeke were always up to pranks, it was like being at school." The Some Bizzare offices were now on New Cavendish Street and there was an art gallery attached, called Discreetly Bizzare.

It was a good time to be working in the music industry. There was a lot of money, even during recessionary times, so bigger labels like Phonogram could afford to take risks and creativity had a chance to flourish. In such an environment Stevo had been able to indulge in his wildest whims, and more often than not did so, even if it was purely sartorial decisions. "He just didn't care," according to Kavanagh. "He used to say, 'All right Rabbit Ears, I'm going off to EMI.' Every Mistake Imaginable he used to call them, and he would take his trousers off, so he would have his brogues on, his socks, no trousers, Easter bonnet, because it was Easter, jacket. He had the best clothes; some posh designer jacket on, shirt and tie, and he would go off to EMI or Sony dressed like that."

When the times were good it was easy to ignore the negative aspects of Stevo's behaviour, and up until 1988 times had been very good, so good it might be easy to imagine that such a state of affairs could last forever. But with the high life comes complacency and over-indulgence, and if the fortunes of Some Bizzare appeared to be on the crest of a giant wave, Stevo may have been oblivious to any potential downward curve. The glossier end of the print media was filling its pages with a newer generation of bland artists, such as Curiosity Killed The Cat, Bros, Kylie Minogue and Jason Donovan. Intelligent pop music had rapidly become a rarity and the oxygen of publicity was diminishing for his label. His mercurial management skills, owing much to his eccentric and outlandish behaviour, were less useful when his more successful artists were sucked deeper into the corporate end of the music business. Independent success has a ceiling beyond which a different type of machinery is needed to elevate an artist to the mega-success that the major labels desire. Over-indulgence, more likely at the weekend, meant that Stevo's ability to manage things effectively and rationally was less likely. His anarchic style had got him this far but increasingly what was needed was professionalism. Either that or he was going to lose his influence on his roster of artists. All the acts on Some Bizzare shared the same idealistic streak as their boss but at some point idealism meets money head-on, as young artists start to think about the future. So far, Stevo had done all the right things for Johnson, both in terms of artistic control and success, but the bad contract that Johnson had signed with Cherry

Red was an immovable object that was limiting his returns, and the one that tied him to CBS was complicated by including Stevo as his manager. To make matters worse, the huge outlay on *Infected*, and in particular the budget for the film, meant that he would find it difficult to recoup. The business model of the major labels was based on debt, with the label as lender and the artist as debtor. Whilst happy to indulge in the creative whims of their artists, the bottom line was always about return on investment. CBS wanted their money back, and increasing sales was the way to go about it. In Johnson's case this meant a change in the way The The was marketed. Paintings of masturbating devils on record covers weren't the way to go about it. It was time for rebranding.

Success, at least on the level that a big label desires, requires visibility. Though the independent scene of the seventies and eighties might have produced creative and memorable record covers, very few of the biggest names could afford to get away with their faces not appearing on their product – even if it was the back of the sleeve rather than the front. Johnson knew this perfectly well, so he was now faced with a dilemma that on one level has come to define his career: the battle between success and recognition. Peer recognition wasn't the problem, and neither was critical recognition in comparison to the problems that public recognition might bring when it grew beyond a certain level. Apart from anything else, an increase in popular success creates an animal that needs feeding. As this level of success is often fleeting, the record company will demand that it is exploited as much as possible to keep the tills ringing. This means the sort of promotion that reduces things to an increasingly lower common denominator, and a creative career suddenly becomes something more akin to servitude.

He may have been star-struck when he first saw Marc Bolan on *Top of the Pops* but Johnson now had an adult appreciation of what fame meant and approached it with caution. His aversion to it was complex. On one level it came from growing up with an attachment to the ethos of post-punk which shunned the idea of 'selling out' or seeking fame over credibility; the role model was The Velvet

Underground – extremely influential yet, for the duration of their career at least, relatively unknown in comparison to their contemporaries – ditto The Stooges. Johnson, though, was serious about his art, and did know that the demands of success might distract him from his craft and require him to feed the machine with endless promotion and publicity, along with the possibility that he would have to dilute his music in order to appeal to a wider, less discerning audience.

But there was something else; something that led to him having all these dreams about losing control of himself, about selling his soul to the devil. It was as if he feared he had signed some kind of Faustian contract but couldn't recall it happening. In such a state of mind it was easy to get things out of proportion, like the time his car broke down in Soho and, fearful of being recognised, he simply leapt out and ran off, leaving Zeke and Fiona in the car as a thin trickle of oil made its way down the gentle incline of the street. It was why he admired Pink Floyd, who had managed to pull off the trick of invisibility despite huge success. Their record covers were more famous than they were. Prisms, floating pigs and burning men shaking hands were their public image. He said as much to Skinner: "Matt once said to me that the band he admired was Pink Floyd, because no one knew what they looked like. And that was one reason why he never wanted his face on the sleeve. He finally did it with *Mind Bomb*. I said to him it was time. 'You should be proud of The The. The The is you.' Even though really he is a solo artist he hid behind a band name. He's very private, but there's that dilemma... if you want to be well known, if you want people to listen to all your stuff then you can't be that private. You want fame but don't want fame. The sleeve was a big decision for Matt."

Johnny Marr also helped Johnson with his conflict over the cover. "He used to say to me, 'Why did you put your name at the bottom of the musician credits on *Soul Mining*? Why are you being so modest? Are you frightened of success?'" Another factor that led to this new approach to artwork for The The was that Andrew had delivered the artwork for the *Infected* sleeve late, resulting in the first 100,000 copies having to be printed with a still from *Infected – The Movie*. This caused a lot of tension between the brothers and Johnson decided they needed to take a break from working together for a while. As Fiona was an accomplished graphic designer – and had designed the typeface used for *Soul Mining* and the logo – she was an obvious choice for the design of *Mind Bomb*.

It was a band now, and CBS were keen to raise their profile. Having Johnny Marr in the group made pushing things to the next level much more feasible. Whether Johnson was conscious of the kind of thinking going on in the background or not, it is clear that the label wanted the sort of record sleeve that would more effectively promote the band, and make them identifiable. This was particularly important for the American market. Fashion photographer Andrew Macpherson was drafted in to take photographs for the sleeve; all of a sudden Matt Johnson's head was appearing giant-size on billboards. He had gone from invisible to unavoidable. If he had any reservations about appearing so boldly after years of record sleeve anonymity then his manager had no problems in expressing his own opinion on this change of direction, and it wasn't positive. Stevo saw it as a sell-out, but maybe he was seeing the writing on the wall. By the time the album was ready for release the relationship between Stevo and Johnson was effectively over. "For the *Mind Bomb* launch," says Kavanagh, "I remember going to The Crypt in Trafalgar Square. We had all the invitations with Matt's face on it – Stevo probably hated it… Stevo didn't come."

'The Beat(en) Generation' entered the UK chart at number twenty-six on March 26, 1989; four days later the band's performance of it for *Top of the Pops* was broadcast, DJ Gary Davis introducing it as their first ever appearance on the programme. The following week the single had crept up a modest eight places, a disappointing return after appearing 'live' the previous week. A week later it had slipped down to number twenty-five and proceeded to drop like a stone thereafter.

What Stevo didn't seem to acknowledge was that the methods that had brought such success for himself and his artists in the first half of the decade weren't as effective when the same artists needed to consolidate their positions in an increasingly corporate environment. His eccentric style of management had been part of the initial charm offensive at the beginning, but at that stage he held all the cards. The tolerance of such behaviour, however, wore thin with time. Inspirational ideas were one thing but what was increasingly needed was a clear head for business, and a reliability as a manager; he was coming up short on both counts. Stevo had often acted as if he was a pop star himself, rather than just a manager of pop stars, and indulged in the trappings accordingly. This was now getting to be part of the problem. Fiona Skinner recalls one incident that typified his behaviour. "Stevo was on an LBC Radio programme – a talk show hosted by journalist Gill Pyrah. Matt and I were living in Shoreditch then, and were listening to it and as soon as he started to talk we knew he was tripping. When they went to a break for some music they got rid of Stevo, and when they came back made up some excuse about him having to leave because he was ill. It was hilarious in one way, but when it's your manager it isn't funny at all." According to Johnson, things had reached breaking point as early as 1987, and his behaviour only grew more erratic and confrontational. Kavanagh was finding the atmosphere in the Some Bizzare office increasingly difficult. "When we were in New Cavendish Street he had the flat upstairs, the top flat, but it was awful… I would come in on a Monday morning and you just didn't know what condition he would be in coming down to the office, it was a terrible feeling. Sometimes he would be inspired, and other times he would be horrible."

The final straw for Johnson came in Germany when he was nearing the end of the promotion of *Infected*. One afternoon he was being interviewed in his hotel suite by journalist Sandra Maischberger, who would later become a well-known television talk show host. "There was an urgent banging on the door and I opened it to find Willy, my local CBS promotions manager, with tears streaming down his face. He was deeply shaken. He explained there had been an 'incident' with Stevo in the hotel reception soon after he had arrived from the airport. Stevo had flown in direct from a Soft Cell event in London and was 'tired and emotional', shall we say. Willy requested I come downstairs immediately to help sort it out. We then locked Stevo in his hotel room whilst I had to calm the situation down on the telephone between various CBS bigwigs in the UK and Germany. It was the final straw after a series of similar 'incidents'." To an outsider it must have looked like Stevo was the volatile artist, and Johnson his sensible and patient manager. Whatever patience the latter had with his manager's increasingly problematic behaviour was nevertheless now worn out.

"Parting company was not a capricious decision on my part as I'd sat down with Stevo on numerous occasions during those last few months to plead with him to change otherwise it would be the end of our working relationship. At one point even my accountant, Ronnie Harris, joined me and we both pleaded with him to change. He made endless promises but he wouldn't – or more likely couldn't – control himself. It was a very difficult time and very sad too as I was fond of Stevo on a personal level and there was a lot I really liked about him, but I was continually fighting fires and apologising to people so it was a very depressing and stressful period. When I eventually fired him I sat down with him face to face and told him as directly but as sensitively as I could. Consequently he wasn't involved in any way, shape or form in the writing, recording or promotion of *Mind Bomb*."

Johnson, like all the other artists on the label, needed a manager who was reliable and Stevo just couldn't deliver. Though Kavanagh had brought with her a professional attitude and a level of efficiency that had been sorely lacking, the cracks couldn't be papered over. "Matt just had to cut him off. Stevo saw it as a big betrayal, but there was just no way they could carry on working together. Stevo was brilliant but you ended up looking after him half the time. When Matt left, I followed, which was before *Mind Bomb* came out. Stevo didn't cope very well, drinking a lot, causing a lot of problems for the artists. He came in one day and it all just sort of blew up. He picked up the photocopier and threw it out the window, and that was my cue – I thought, 'I think I'd better go.' And so I said that to him, and he didn't like that. I said, 'Why did you throw the photocopier out the window?' And he said, 'You were being negative.' That was his reason. So I said I was going."

It wasn't an easy decision for people to make; to leave Stevo behind. He had, after all, made their jobs and careers possible, and the positive side of his complex personality blazed with such an intensity that it was hard to dislike him. They admired him too. Here was a dyslexic teenager from Dagenham who had taken on the music business single-handedly and built a mini-empire. When it was good it was very good. It's just that when it was bad it was, well, just too much. "I don't want it to sound negative when I was there," Kavanagh says, "because it wasn't, and when people say things about Stevo I always defend him, because you need people like him, otherwise everything would be boring and corporate, but it went too far. These things can never last can they? I did miss those days, there was never a dull moment." Johnson too knew he had lost a friend as well as a manager, though Stevo's reliability on both counts had been increasingly disintegrating. His close confidant now would be Johnny Marr, and after a period where he managed himself, Marr would have a role to play in who would free Johnson of this extra burden.

Kavanagh, having followed Johnson out the door, was asked if she wanted to work for him directly as a PA, an offer she accepted without too much thought. She could see from the outset that Johnson now had more control over what he was doing and was going to waste no time in pushing things forward in the direction he wanted. The most obvious difference was that The The, for the first time, was a real band. The more time the four members had spent together in the studio the more a sense of togetherness grew, the more the realisation that, working together so well, it would be ridiculous not to take things on the road. After nine years of existence, The The were finally ready to tour, and news of the prospect of it being a world tour was fed to the music press before the album was complete. It wasn't long before Kavanagh was helping to facilitate.

"Matt had a car then, a big old Rover we called Harold or the Matt-mobile. All of us used to squeeze in it, the band and me, and go off looking for rehearsal studios. He was excited to be separate from Stevo, and excited for *Mind Bomb*. You would think they had been in this band forever; everyone was in the right frame of mind, everyone wanted the same things. Matt was still the leader, if you like, but there were no problems, no arguments. You just knew this was going to be good."

One of the first things to do was find a keyboard player who could come on the road with them. Paul Wickens had been invited to do it, but Paul McCartney had made him an offer he couldn't refuse. Dave Collard, who had performed with The Subway Sect and JoBoxers, was one of the prospects who got the call to meet Johnson at his club in Two Brydges Place, Covent Garden. As Collard remembers it, "The first time I met Matt was at his club in London, clearly for a thinly veiled job interview, and his first and only music question was: 'You know the piano solo in "Uncertain Smile", can you do that?' I said, 'Yes.' He said, 'All right, you got the gig. Let's get some beers.'"

It was an astute choice, for not only was Collard an excellent musician, he was also ideal for the group dynamic, popular with everyone. James Eller felt he was just what they needed. "We added Dave Collard, and that was brilliant, he was laid-back to the point of being horizontal, very chilled, very experienced player and funny, so he was a perfect addition." With the line-up complete it was time for rehearsals. Some discussions for this, and the tour in general, also took place at Two Brydges, and as with anything Johnson set his mind to, attention to detail was thorough. It was this level of preparation, argues Palmer, that ensured a successful tour. "There was a lot of preparation, a lot of pre-production. I think we rehearsed at John Henry's for quite some time. We were taking out samplers and playing to tracks, playing to sequencers and stuff like that so technically that had to be worked out. There was a lot of thought about how can we recreate *Mind Bomb* but not be too bombastic, how do we translate this to a live situation? A lot of thought went into it, hence that tour was a really successful tour and totally fun, and that's captured at the Royal Albert Hall gigs." Johnson's meticulous approach was also appreciated by Eller, who was able to contrast his experience with previous tours that had been somewhat lacking in the preparation department. "At the beginning of '89 we started talking about rehearsing, which I think started in May. Rehearsal was in John Henry's by Pentonville Prison. Six weeks – Sundays off. And that was just fantastic. I don't normally like rehearsing but I really liked that. Attention to detail again – really wanting to get it right, every note, everything. It was just great."

It has to be remembered that Johnson had only played live a handful of times, the last occasion being back in 1983 at the Marquee. He had never done even a mini-tour before. The others had, and though this meant that they had the requisite experience, Johnson wanted to ensure that he didn't let them down as well as himself. If he was going to do this for the first time, nine years into his career, then he was going to make sure that everything went well. To this end, he sought the advice of Marr. Though he had never been on as extensive a tour as the one Johnson had in mind, Marr was nevertheless able to provide help in a number of ways. "He talked with me directly and very specifically about putting the crews together, the kind of gigs we were gonna do, how we were gonna do it, buses versus planes: he took on my management, and I'd been doing it relentlessly for five years so I knew a lot of things about what not to do. I brought on board a couple of crew guys who were very helpful." He also recalls how serious Johnson was about preparing for the stage. "We rehearsed the set at least twice a day and got to a place where just before we went out on the road any rehearsal was considered like a gig and Matt and I would have long phone conversations in the evening about the set. That is how I approach any live work with a band now."

Naturally, Johnson had to contend with his personal demons about playing in front of an audience, and such were his nerves that just before the tour he considered calling it off. But he wasn't the only one prone to doubts, as he found out during the rehearsals. "We were doing the rehearsals and Johnny and I were feeling uncomfortable; he's a great guitarist, Johnny, but we had this strange roadie who I don't think liked either me or Johnny. He had been a roadie for Dire Straits and he always gave us this funny look, and it got to the point where we would be rehearsing and we started to sort of clam up. We almost couldn't play. It started to affect our confidence to such a degree because we thought he was just sitting there, staring at us, judging us... which he probably was, thinking, 'They're not as good as Mark Knopfler.' Johnny said, 'This guy's freaking me out, I can't play properly, I can't do it.'"

Eller too found being on stage could often be a stressful experience. "Playing live is a weird thing. I don't particularly like it and I skulk around at the sides or the back. But with The The it was great because nothing ever went wrong because it was so well planned, so well rehearsed, and I probably felt less anxious with The The than with anyone else because it was so organised." Any anxieties were outweighed by the conviction of all involved that something significant was unfolding. Johnson was ready for this new challenge, had been working out, and had decided to stop worrying about his thinning hair and instead go for the shaved look. He felt leaner and meaner and free.

Mind Bomb entered the UK album charts at number four on May 27, 1989. It was the highest position The The had achieved thus far with an album, though it didn't rise any higher during its nine-week spell in the Top 100, half the number of weeks that *Infected* had lasted. Reviews were often schizophrenic. Ian Gittins in *Melody Maker* called it a "great record" but spent the bulk of his word count on questioning Johnson's intellect and mental state. He also offered the opinion that one of Johnson's crimes was that levity was beyond him, seemingly unable to spot it in 'Armageddon

Days' with its over-the-top approach and the obvious nod and wink to glam rockers The Sweet. Keith Cameron in *SOUNDS* was lukewarm in his praise; though he had no problem with the songs about God and religious war, he was less kind when it came to the autobiographical songs. Lee Kavanagh thinks that much of the UK music press had made their minds up before they even heard the album. "A lot of the press were waiting to crucify the album. I think it might have been a bit ahead of its time. I think the European press were much more understanding, especially in Germany. There were a couple of influential journalists in the English press who were negative and that tainted it. It was a kind of 'Who do you think you are' attitude from them."

Zeke Manyika also felt that many journalists had been busy sharpening their knives. "There were a lot of cynical comments from the music press around this time, about his state of mind. I think *Mind Bomb* is one of those albums where people have to wait a while before they can appreciate it. Matt was also dealing with his new status I suppose. He had just moved from being this well-respected cult thing, and because he had such firm views about things people were having a dig at him, accusing him of grandstanding or whatever... they got him totally wrong. He'd just found his voice and was very excited about it, and because he wasn't educated he maybe didn't know how to deal with journalists, who were mostly middle class. He was an easy target really. People really started having a go at him, for no good reason at all."

Manyika may have a point when he hints at the class divide between the self-educated working-class musician and the middle-class music journalist, but in talking about God, spirituality, karma and mysticism, and doing so in a very open and enthusiastic way, Johnson was laying himself open to abuse. Many writers probably felt that such subjects were either unworthy of serious consideration or beyond the ken of a working-class lad. Others simply had an axe to grind. The *NME* in particular had worshipped The Smiths and there was a sense that Morrissey-loving journalists blamed Marr for splitting up the group, and perhaps Johnson for ending any hope of a reunion. Marr was acutely aware of all of this, but also thinks that there was an air of inevitability about the reaction to the album. "Knowing what I know about the British music press, there would have been a backlash against him no matter what. But then throw in the fact that he was harbouring an ex-Smith, it was no surprise. Plus he was taking on concepts which were so ambitious and left him wide open to criticism from inane poseurs, masquerading as critics. I thought they were all wankers. I knew that what we were doing was good. In some ways it just galvanised us, we had an authentic reason to feel like outsiders."

When it came to the politics, Johnson was on firmer ground. Once again, like he had with 'Sweet Bird Of Truth', he had seemingly hit the nail on the head before anyone knew the actual nail was there. Though some journalists had found the lyrics to 'Armageddon Days' melodramatic, the Salman Rushdie affair seemed to vindicate him. In February 1989, months after the actual song had been recorded, never mind written, Ayatollah Khomeini of Iran issued a fatwa against Rushdie over his blasphemous book *The Satanic Verses*, effectively putting an end to the plan for 'Armageddon Days' to be the first single of the album. Rushdie had to go into hiding and in a stranger-than-fiction twist of fate one of the places he did so was the flat above Johnny Marr's own in Chelsea. The guitarist related the story to Johnson years later. "I'd go and get the mail in the hallway and I'd see all these letters for S. Rushdie, and I'd think shit, he's got to have a few words with his friends." Whether Marr was ever tempted to spook Rushdie by playing the song full blast beneath him isn't known but the whole affair was serious enough to prevent the release of the track until later in the year. As the situation had escalated, Johnson had felt obliged to make a public statement, saying that he sympathised with the Muslim position, but also suggesting that freedom of thought and expression was a God-given right. Beginning his statement with a line about how he was "both horrified and amazed to see another one of my songs burst into life on the world stage before my eyes" might have made him, as he later admitted, appear rather sanctimonious. As a result he received a fair amount of criticism, despite essentially saying the same thing most commentators had said in defence of freedom of expression, though more astute observers had pointed out that Rushdie should have known what he was doing. The whole affair brought the 'clash of civilisations' to the dinner tables of the chattering classes, none of whom, one suspects, had read the Quran, unlike Johnson. This was just one of the tectonic plates of global politics that was to shift in 1989. Before the year was out there would be the violent quelling of student protests in China's Tiananmen Square and an unexpectedly rapid end to the Cold War. As if to underline twelve months of violent change, on December 25 in Romania, Nicolae and Elena Ceausescu were executed. Amid such turbulence, *Mind Bomb* should have resonated more than it did, but while The The fans were largely in tune with the album's concerns, the critics were resolute in their indifference; it wouldn't appear in a single end-of-year poll in UK publications, ranging from music papers like the *NME* and *Melody Maker* to style magazines like *The Face*.

Johnson refers to the UK music press as having a schizophrenic reaction to the album. "One week *Melody Maker* likened it to Van Morrison's *Astral Weeks* whilst the next week they hated it. I was abroad a lot by this stage, in places like Paris, Berlin and Rome being interviewed by grown-up journalists about music, politics and religion for magazines and newspapers like *Libération*, *Der Speigel* and *La Repubblica*. Even *Time* magazine interviewed me in New York and devoted a whole page to a glowing review of *Mind Bomb*." In this context, the slagging-off from music papers like the *NME* seemed hardly worth bothering about.

In June MTV broadcast another *120 Minutes* episode with Johnson having to endure a rather banal interview, but this time there was no controversy. He talked about the incidents in China but the interviewer didn't seem interested. A month later, 'Gravitate To Me' was the second single from the album to be released, with

'The Violence Of Truth' on the flip. The 12-inch version had mixes by François Kevorkian and, more significantly as it would later turn out, Bruce Lampcov. It entered the UK chart at number sixty-four on July 22, took two weeks to move up one place and had disappeared entirely two weeks later. The 7-inch edit had injected a bit of energy into a song that was too laid-back for its own good but it was a curious choice for release. As disappointing as this may have been, the indifference of the record-buying public seemed hardly relevant when The The embarked on a huge world tour. They enlisted the help of Marcus Russell, who had been managing Johnny Marr. The tour was dubbed *The The Versus The World* and would include almost a hundred shows in twenty-one countries over the course of twelve months.

Johnson was in the strange position of being the leader of the band but the only one who had never actually toured before, and he was glad to have their collective experience to call upon. Talking to David Sly of the *Adelaide Advertiser* in an interview conducted over the phone from London he spoke about the forthcoming shows in Australia and New Zealand, which would kick off the tour after a couple of warm-up gigs in Portugal: "I have wonderful musicians in whom I have complete faith and confidence but the live arena is an untested forum for my work." Considering that he was also working with a new manager, the idea of a world tour was a bold move but, as everyone agreed, not to tour this band would have been almost criminal. The demand was there; it simply had to be met. The strength of the demand took the group by surprise from the very beginning, with the two dates in Portugal sold out, and almost as many fans locked out of the venues as the five thousand or so crammed inside. In an interview a few weeks later in Australia, Johnson described the shows. "They knew every word and stormed the stage. It was incredible." Keyboardist Dave 'DC' Collard (so named to avoid confusion with Dave Palmer), who had still been programming keyboard sounds during the final rehearsal before hitting the road, remembers that the band felt settled from the very beginning, though equipment gremlins did strike during the debut. "The first gig was in Portugal and it went so well, a huge crowd just digging every minute of it, that I think we all felt right at home and together as a band. I do recall one hiccup and it came when we were about to start the encore. I tapped the foot switch to start the sequencer for 'GIANT' and nothing happened. I looked at my keyboard technician who was feverishly checking my rack of modules but in particular the two Akai S1000s that held all the samples. He gave me a panicked shrug. I jumped down off the back of my riser to take a look, and I could see that one had crashed and the other was taking forever to load all the sounds. I rebooted them both and before long we were good to go, but it was an extremely uncomfortable five minutes!"

For Johnson, touring meant the extra burden of doing promotion, but at least the duty was sometimes shared by Marr, no doubt endorsed by CBS because he was also a prominent figure, one who would invite a few extra column inches in the press – even if this meant he had to endure more questions about Morrissey and The Smiths. Occasionally promotional duties would involve someone else, such as Dave Palmer, who found himself on Australian television with Johnson when they were due to play the Hordern Pavilion in Sydney on August 4. "Matt and I did a funny television show in Australia which was hilarious because we'd just been hanging out with John Lydon in the bar at the Sebel Townhouse in Sydney, and he'd got me and Matt wrecked. The interview was at midnight on live TV, so we were trashed, but it was actually a really funny interview. We were belly-laughing, it was that funny." This was the evening when Lydon offered his opinion that *Infected* was one of the most spiteful records he had heard in years, which Johnson took, quite rightly, as a huge compliment. He was also impressed with Lydon's drinking abilities.

"He was great fun to spend time with but he must have hollow legs because he drank the entire band and me under the table and then, surveying the damage, must have felt sorry for us as he insisted on paying for *all* of the evening's drinks. I was so drunk by then that I insisted Dave come along for a bit of moral support for the live TV interview but that didn't do me much good as he was even drunker than me and we couldn't stop laughing."

Having done a lot of promotion for that album in Australia, The The had a good fan-base and the concerts here were enthusiastically received. *On Dit*, the magazine of Adelaide University, decided that regardless of what was released in the remaining months of 1987, *Mind Bomb* was the album of the year. Simon Healey, who wrote the review, finished with: "*Mind Bomb* is a masterpiece. If you don't see The The live, you're crazy." Bruce Elder, reviewing the sold-out Sydney gig for *The Australian*, wrote, "This wasn't just a good concert. It was two hours of unique and vital music... In almost every case the live versions of the songs had a vibrancy and urgency which the recorded versions lack." A week later Michael Dwyer of *X-Press* magazine saw the band at Perth Concert Hall, the second of two dates in the city. He was mostly impressed, particularly with the first half of the set. "The The put in a show which will be hard to beat this year in Perth, in terms of both spectacle and musical excellence." The dates in Australia weren't without their problems, however, particularly in Melbourne's Festival Hall, where the venue's acoustics led to a swampy and uneven sound that inevitably threw a proverbial bucket of cold water over the atmosphere. Whilst in Melbourne, Matt was interviewed by Kevin Fitzpatrick, who was quick to remind him about the smut-laden interview he had given when last in town, while promoting *Infected*. Johnson talked politics, amongst other things, making the claim that the end of the decade would see the end of power for Margaret Thatcher – a fairly close prediction as it turned out.

After the Perth concert there was a five-day break that saw the band fly over to America for a three-date promotional stint. According to Lee Kavanagh, "Marcus would fly the crew in business class, and I was like, 'Marcus, you're spending a lot of money.' Matt had that love–hate relationship with touring and the cost of it, which he was having to fund. I tried to tell him, but I suppose if you're going to tour you have to do it properly."

315

Johnson was to rue his naivety, and years later is forthright about the financial implications of poor decision-making.

"To be frank, the management of the finances for *The The Versus The World* was disastrous. It caused arguments between Ron Harris and John Kennedy – my accountant and lawyer who could see my money dwindling away – and Marcus. Things like flying the entire crew to Australia business class was just one of the problems. There were dodgy merchandise deals, for which I would have to pay back tens of thousands of pounds out of my own pocket a full decade later! Everyone travelled in pure luxury, endless Four Seasons hotels, etc. I was just too inexperienced with touring to realise the massive damage inflicted upon my personal finances. It took years for me to get out of personal debt after that tour."

The first USA date was at the Roxy on Sunset Strip in Los Angeles, and while Mark Cooper, writing for *The Guardian*, found the performance disappointing, Dave Palmer remembers it as one of his favourites, describing it as "insane", suggesting that at least the band enjoyed it – and one suspects that the subjectivity of the fans was closer to the drummer than the journalist. Next up was the Paradise Theatre, Boston, where tickets for the show had sold out in half an hour. Here too acoustics caused trouble, with the vocals losing clarity during louder numbers, but reviews were full of praise – as was Craig Schmidt's review of the third date at the Symphony Space in New York, though he felt Marr was in danger of being under-used, contrasting the room he was given to showcase his skills during an understated performance of 'Beat(en) Generation' with other numbers where he felt the guitarist was being drowned out by the keyboards, though in truth this was more likely a problem at the mixing desk rather than with the arrangements themselves. The band were scheduled to return for a much more extensive itinerary Stateside the following year, and the next stage of the tour saw them returning to Europe. After a string of dates in Scandinavia, Germany and Holland they travelled through Italy and Switzerland before arriving in France to perform at Casino de Paris, in the French capital.

Johnson remembers the Paris date for two reasons. "The venue was packed and so hot that people started fainting. A group of Hells Angels were in attendance and I remember watching from the stage as they helped carry out some stricken audience members above people's heads. It was intense. But there was a young female journalist in attendance that the editor of the *NME* had obviously dispatched to carry out another hatchet job. After the show she came up to me and tried to play nice in order to get an interview. After months of snide campaigning against us I simply said I wasn't interested and walked past her. Obviously she couldn't cope with being snubbed so she just made up lots of lies about the venue being half full and with no atmosphere."

James Eller recalls the post-gig bash, when around ninety French journalists and television people were wined and dined at Les Bains nightclub, a bash that stretched out into the early hours. "There was an incident Matt had with a journalist in Paris. He didn't get on with her. I think she wrote for the *NME*, and they had an argument about something while all the crew and journalists were having dinner. I think he pissed her off, but honestly don't know how and I was aware there was a bit of a chill in the air with the *NME* after that for a while. The evening ended up muted. She had been sent to interview him and it hadn't gone well. I think he was widely admired but there was an element in the indie press where I think they thought he was a bit pompous, we were a bit supergroup-ish. Particularly with *Mind Bomb*." The journalist in question was Helen Mead, whose subsequent write-up was unsurprisingly lukewarm and included hints that Johnson's penchant for cruel humour didn't mix very well with alcohol. Perhaps the strain of touring was showing, or perhaps the singer was taking it out on a music paper he was at odds with. There was no love lost between himself and the *NME* and Mead was the unlucky person in the firing line.

It wasn't just the grind of touring and having to shoulder most of the responsibility, but also the constant need to be on call for interviews and promotion; a burden Johnson revealed when Marr asked him what it was like being band leader on tour. "It is a bit tiring because I'm not only doing the shows themselves and of course all the travelling, but also five or six interviews every day, phone interviews, face-to-face interviews, meetings with record company people and dealing with the politics of the band and crew members, and trying to keep the atmosphere buoyant. And of course all the other phone calls with management, and accountants telling you how much money you're losing, not to mention all the personal calls with family and friends." So maybe it was just the wrong day to be interviewing Matt Johnson at three in the morning, when he was tired and drunk.

Though the Paris gig had been a sell-out, in the days before Daft Punk and Air the French capital still lacked the coolness of other European cities when it came to music, such as Berlin, which for Eller stood out more than any other gig of the whole tour. "My favourite gig was the most difficult and it was in Berlin. We played in a kind of tent, about a month or two before the Berlin Wall came down. So all that was in the air, and what was interesting about Berlin was, before the wall came down, if you wanted to avoid the draft in Germany, you could go to University to study in particular fields, or you could go to Berlin because the West German government wanted to keep Berlin populated. So what that means is that you have lots of fairly anti-establishment people who are into music, so it was very, very cool at the time. All the cool West German kids were in Berlin. We were quite used to playing everywhere and it was like, 'Wow! The The at last!' From New Zealand to Detroit to Tokyo to Birmingham. Berlin was a bit different. There were four thousand young, uber-cool Berliners standing there, as if to say, 'Well, go on then...' We won them over in the end but it was tough. That's why I loved it, and we really did a good gig."

The problems the band faced were minor. The original backing vocalist didn't work out (an *NME* review of the Brisbane gig had described her as "slack") but this was remedied when they recruited Melanie Redmond, who had just completed a lengthy tour with Duran Duran. Tour manager Karen Krattinger, who had worked extensively with Prince, didn't really work out either and was also replaced. By the time the tour hit the UK, starting in Birmingham, the band were flying. Six more dates followed, including Glasgow's legendary Barrowlands, before four dates in London: Brixton Academy, Kilburn National, the Town and Country in Kentish Town and Hackney Empire. There was, according to Eller, a rationale behind the idea of doing four separate gigs. "I think Matt was offered Wembley, which was something like fifteen thousand at the time, but he said he didn't want to do it like that, which is why we did the four smaller venues. He thought doing Wembley was too straight, so we did four gigs instead; north, south, east and west. They're my favourite sort of venues as well... old faded theatres with two or three thousand people, preferably with velour seating. They feel great to play in." The venues were also symbolic, being four points of the compass, and this tour-within-a-tour was advertised as such.

Johnson appeared on BBC's *Late Show* arts programme, answering a few questions after a clip of the band rehearsing, and he talked about the disappointment of not being able to release 'Armageddon Days' when he wanted to. Two days after the Hackney concert it finally saw the light of day as a single and entered the UK charts. It would only spend two weeks there and reach no higher than number seventy. The *NME*, in retaliation perhaps for the way they felt Helen Mead had been treated in Paris, gave the single a scathing review and managed to damn the album at the same time. Johnson, and the band, if they had bothered to read it, might not have cared too much. Fans of the band clearly didn't care what the music press thought; by now there was even a The The fanzine, called *The Mercy Beat*, the fourth issue of which was on sale that October. All four London dates had sold out and it felt like a triumphant homecoming. It felt like nothing could go wrong.

A week-long break had been scheduled for the second week of October, after which the band were due to fly out to start the second, more extensive American leg of the tour. Johnson took the opportunity to fly out to Mallorca with Skinner and unwind at his cottage in the mountains. On the last day of their stay, after a pleasant day wandering the tiny streets of the village of Santa Maria, oblivious as to what fate had delivered, they returned to the cottage to find a note from a local friend, Toby Hogarth, who lived nearby with his girlfriend Sophie. The couples would often spend time together, sometimes going on boat trips along the coast. There was no phone at Johnson's cottage and so anyone wanting to reach him had to call Hogarth and leave a message. The message on the note said that Johnson needed to phone home as soon as he could. Johnson and Skinner walked the mile and a half to Hogarth's house, fearing that Matt's granddad Joe had died. "He was old and frail, and Matt was very close to him." With a heavy heart Johnson made the call home; what he heard made his world stop.

The phone call wasn't about his grandfather. Two days earlier, Matt's younger brother Eugene had been serving behind the bar of the family pub, The Woodman, and had gone upstairs to the room he occasionally slept in to get ready for a night out with his girlfriend, Karen. He was never late so when he hadn't come down, Karen asked the barman to go upstairs and see what was keeping him. He found Eugene on the bed, where he had lain down after his bath and suffered a ruptured brain aneurysm. It was this news that Eddie somehow managed to relate over the phone, his grief travelling down lonely wires from one country to another far away and into the ear of his disbelieving second son, who found himself collapsing under their weight. Shock set in immediately, as Skinner was witness to. "I remember Matt getting on the phone, talking to his dad and there was this physical sinking. It was awful. Our flight was in the afternoon the next day so I knew I had to do everything I could to keep him together until then. I just had to be there for him and had to get him home. He was broken. Devastated. Toby and Sophie were wonderful but after a while we had to go back to the cottage to pack our things. We were only two hours away but it felt like a million miles away, an eternity… that was the slowest of nights. We walked for ages round the village in the dark."

As morning broke, the valley beneath them was coated in mist. Skinner decided to get to the airport as soon as it opened, to try and get an earlier flight home. "It was torture, being only two hours away but unable to get back. We couldn't get on an earlier flight so we arrived back in London late afternoon. There was a driver we used all the time for the band, Colin, and I got him to meet us at the airport. I remember getting to his parents' home in Suffolk and it was awful. Losing a child is wrong on so many levels, it's not part of the natural cycle. It's devastating. I watched my own family go through it, and Shirley was such a controlled and quite controlling figure... this did not compute... this did not compute..." Shirley seemed to weather the storm of emotions better than the others, at least initially. Gerard, then only 16, is of this opinion. "She was very strong when it first happened, she was stronger than all of us, cos we all went to pieces, and mum was the rock." This, however, was achieved through some kind of monumental will; underneath the surface the devastation was waiting to manifest itself. Fiona Skinner had been through a death in her own family just a few years before she met Johnson, when her sister, June, died of a kidney disease; she used this experience to take on the role of support and carer.

"I remember Eddie just collapsing to his knees, and them all being in this complete state of shock, but without question I was welcomed back into the house. I took on the task of phoning a lot of Eugene's friends to give them the news, because nobody in the family could do it. I think I went into that mode where I just knew what to do, making lots of cups of tea, keeping them calm, feeding them, 'Just sit here, here's a film, watch television,' don't feel bad about laughing or forgetting for half an hour because you won't forget for the rest of your life. You're allowed these limits, these moments. But it devastated the family and his mum never recovered. The way Shirley coped with that death is she closed the shutters, and they rusted and they never opened again." The full impact hit Shirley at the funeral. Tim Pope was present. "I'll never forget when Eugene died, standing at the grave and I think the worst sound I've ever heard in my life was Matt's mum crying beside that grave... a mother crying for her boy." Gerard had lost the brother he had grown up closest too; it was to take him a decade to recover his equilibrium. But while he slowly recovered, Shirley was deteriorating. "Mum got very ill, little by little... a form of Alzheimers, but it was never properly diagnosed... it came gradually but it was brought on by Eugene dying, it affected her so much." It was as though the dementia was a way of coping, allowing her to hold memories of a little boy but not the recent memory of his death. It was the stress of this which seemed to have unravelled all her critical neural connections, because she was a strong woman and if her body wouldn't give up the ghost for her then her mind would have to do the job, in order to obliterate that awful day.

Eugene died in the middle of a recession, when interest rates had soared to an eye-watering 15 per cent. As if losing a child wasn't enough, Shirley and Eddie also lost The Woodman, and the family home in Steeple Bumpstead within the next three years. But life wouldn't stop, it had to go on and the family each had to find a way of coping. For Matt Johnson, it might have seemed that being in the middle of a world tour was the worst possible scenario, and he considered cancelling the rest of the dates. Fiona helped persuade him to carry on, though, and after a three-month break this is what happened. As difficult as this would be, carrying on provided some kind of solace. Performing allowed Johnson to escape himself at this time, though at first it all seemed pointless. And even before the tour was over he was to find the therapeutic value of songwriting some kind of comfort. Everyone was shocked by Eugene's death – band members, friends and all the people who worked for Matt Johnson. Eugene had been working with his older brother and was looking forward to the prospect of joining the second half of the tour to help out with merchandise. Dave Palmer recalls the impact on the band. "It was just unbelievable. Sometimes, things like that, you can't really fathom it out but you need to grieve and you need to take time off. And we were thick as thieves so when that happened it affected everybody. It affected the whole thing, it shook everybody up."

It also brought out the best in people, and it was this that kept Johnson from going under. "Fiona was truly amazing through this period. She'd had the experience of coping with June's death when just a teenager herself and so she was deeply empathetic. She was a true friend to me and my family and took care of us and helped us through a very difficult period. The entire band were wonderful too and gave me so much support throughout that period. I was also lucky to have a lot of support from close friends and business colleagues. It's in situations like these that you see just how good and kind most people are. In terrible circumstances the best of human nature often surfaces."

15

LOVE IS STRONGER
THAN DEATH

THOUGH *MIND BOMB* HAD FAILED TO MAKE ANY END-OF-year charts in the UK music papers or style magazines, it fared much better in America, making it into the influential Rockpool College Radio Chart, appearing at number six in the Top 100 albums for 1989, one place above the eponymous debut by The Stone Roses, who by now were the media darlings at home, as the *NME* finally found someone to replace The Smiths. Resuming their tour across the Atlantic, The The were embarking on a thirty-date journey through America and Canada. The Rockpool chart was a good indicator of how they might be received, and reviews of *Mind Bomb* in the American press had been much more positive than in England.

David Gottlieb was hired by Epic Records to set up an 'alternative music' department just months before The The were due to start touring the States. "Epic at that time wanted badly to break an 'alternative' act. Living Colour had just broken through, but that was mainly rock and MTV and was bleeding back to alternative radio. There was a desire to break a British act in the US who could live in the world of The Cure and Depeche Mode, etc., which had broken through in key parts of the country. The fact Johnny Marr was in the band now gave them even more incentive. It was an alternative supergroup. The The had always sold well in the States, around 150K–250K, which was a sweet spot for record labels at the time, who felt if you could get the next 150–250K, that's when an artist would take off and you'd reap benefits from selling the catalogue."

Hopes were high. There was definitely a sense that things could happen. The album cover was a sign that things were moving in a direction that would see The The move up a division. To break America, the image had to be more straightforward. The mystery that had existed up till now wasn't going to cut it. Marc Geiger, a young booking agent based in California, saw the recent changes as a positive. "I think over here it was a demystification of The The and who they were, and gave them a face." Geiger was an anglophile who had tapped into the heart of the English independent scene, and had represented The The Stateside since *Infected*, alongside many other groups on labels like 4AD and Factory. He knew what it took for an act to break in America, and mystery wasn't it. "When *Mind Bomb* happened, Matt's shit really started to come together. You have a band, you have a focused image, Stevo is out of the way – I don't mean that in a bad way – but it's no longer a riddle. Stevo managed through riddles."

One of Stevo's riddles might have been blowing a large raspberry down the phone when Geiger had first called Some Bizzare a few years previously, eager to make contact with Johnson. Not expecting this Bronx cheer, followed by the phone slamming down, he tried again, only to get the same result. Over and over again. He wasn't the sort of guy to be put off, however, and at some point either the phantom raspberry blower got bored or someone else answered the phone. "It was chaos trying to call there. It was pretty funny. Stevo was an interesting gatekeeper who was being bigger than the artist. He was crazier than Matt; Matt was the straight man."

With Stevo out of the way, things were doubtless more straightforward, the whole operation more focused. Though

Gottlieb feels that the momentum of the album had been lost due to the delay in starting the American leg of the tour, the fans who had discovered The The were more than ready to welcome them. It was just a case of getting down to work. For Geiger, who had plenty of experience in this, it was work that success ultimately boiled down to when it came to breaking through in America. "It's harder because it takes some work, but it's easier because the work is defined. But you've got to come over. You've got to remember that with those first two records he wasn't here at all, and there was nothing definable. Once he started to come and show himself, he was really competitive, it was really powerful, and the top artists and musicians recognised it, I mean he was an artist's artist."

It was difficult for Johnson to be back on stage. The experience wasn't always cathartic. Some nights he felt that being on stage with a guitar singing songs was pointless, a natural and understandable human response that the rest of the band could at least help him overcome. Other symptoms of his grief were less easy to deal with, as revealed to Michael Bonner of *Uncut* magazine twenty-six years later. "I had huge support from everyone around me at the time, but when we went back on tour again, it was awful because I kept seeing my brother's face in the audience." And with every interview and promotional appearance it can't have escaped him that he had called his album *Mind Bomb,* and that his brother had died of a brain haemorrhage. It was like he was being tested to see if his beliefs about the true nature of God and the soul were real. But he found the strength, and worked things out in his own head. As caring as those around him were, he was ultimately alone with his suffering, something that Dave Collard, for one, was acutely aware of. "Matt, when we were back together again, was still very engaged and fun but, I'm sure, suffering alone. I didn't notice any weakness in his performance, if anything it was more intense – but I can imagine at times it was a test of will."

Johnny Marr, who was closest to him, and had seen how he had made sure above all that he looked after his family first, saw clearly the inner strength of his good friend at this time. "The rest of us fully expected to not go back out on the road. From what I remember Matt's decision to do so was really out of professional responsibility. It was my first experience of bereavement really close to me, and I was really shocked not only by Eugene dying but what had happened to my closest friend at that time and its effect on him; but then I saw these things that he did that were incredible, his resolve and his determination to come to terms with it, which as everybody knows you never entirely do. I've never seen anyone so determined to try and make sense of it. I knew he was a big thinker but that was amazing what he went through."

Working their way through Atlanta, Washington and Philadelphia, the band arrived in New York. Ira Robbins, reviewing the concert at the Beacon Theatre for the *New York Post*, wrote that it had taken The The a decade to reach America but "it was worth the wait". The rest of the write-up was overwhelmingly positive, though other reviewers of the same concert were less enamoured. Regardless of journalistic opinion, this show, like nearly all others, was a sell-out. After gigs in Boston and Amherst the band played six dates in Ontario, Canada, before dipping back across the border to perform three nights at the Royal Oak Theatre in Detroit, and one date each in Chicago, Minneapolis and Denver. On February 26 they were back in Canada to play the first of three nights at the Commodore Ballroom, Vancouver. Tom Barrett, writing in *The Vancouver Sun*, began his piece by pointing out that despite receiving virtually no airplay locally The The had no problem selling out the venue three nights running. Dubbing *Mind Bomb* an "eloquent rant against organised religion" he clearly felt that the packed crowd got their money's worth. "Monday night they blasted the bejabbers out of the Commodore, setting up a rumble that made your nose hairs vibrate, even at the back of the hall. The sound was as thick as the smoke that enveloped the stage. Marr was particularly worth hearing, the most subtle and distinctive guitarist in rock today."

The final three dates of the American leg of the tour were in California, the third of these being in Los Angeles, where Johnson was interviewed by Edwin Fish Gould III, aka 'Jed the Fish', on KROQ-FM. It wasn't long before he got into his stride, talking about religious spirituality versus religious dogma, the American military industrial complex and the CIA. Gould, exclaiming that his guest was on a roll, could hardly get a word in as Johnson continued. "Mankind has invented God in its own image, this wrathful figure, and I believe religion is the ultimate blasphemy, because it basically uses God as a weapon against humanity rather than a liberating force. Nobody else is dealing with this stuff in a popular music format and it's hard to squeeze this information into pop music, which is why I'm trying to venture out into film and books…"

Gould can be heard laughing in the background, not at these words but the fact that they are being aired in the first place. He finally manages to interrupt: "Let me stop you for just a second. I think it's terrific that you are doing this. I sat around at high school thinking how come nobody in pop music addresses these issues?" You can tell Gould is enjoying all this, on a personal level and on a professional level. It certainly made for good radio, this level of enthusiasm and intensity. The interview also revealed to listeners that the just-released single, 'Jealous Of Youth', had almost made the cut when it came to the album but was left out in favour of 'Gravitate To Me' for musical and lyrical reasons. It was a particular favourite of Marr's. "We recorded 'Jealous Of Youth' in that climate of the clubbing scene. I had the demo of it and the master tapes of it in my house, and we recorded a lot of the guitars in a bedroom in my house. I played that over and over on loop and people were raving about it. It was one of the most romantic bits of music I had heard at that time. I really loved playing the guitar on it, one of my favourite guitar parts I ever played. Matt will tell you, I had a real thing for that song." The concert that evening, one of Dave Palmer's favourites, was at LA's Wiltern Theatre and was another sell-out. Like all other shows the audience were treated to songs from *Mind Bomb*, *Infected* and *Soul Mining*, with a rousing 'GIANT' to close the set.

America had been a good experience for The The and, despite his antipathy towards American foreign policy, Johnson's romantic attachment to the country, and New York in particular, more than likely grew stronger. While in LA he went guitar shopping with Johnny Marr on Sunset Boulevard and picked up a black guitar on the suggestion of Marr's partner, Angie, who thought it might suit him: a Gibson 345. Liking its action he got talking to the shop owner, who revealed that it had once belonged to Doors guitarist Robby Krieger. He forked out the couple of thousand dollars it was priced at and took up the proprietor's offer of a receipt showing a price some eight hundred dollars less, so he wouldn't have to pay as much tax on it when he returned home. From here it was onwards to Japan for three shows in Tokyo and one in Osaka, followed by a three-month break before the tour hit Europe for the summer and festival season. One such appearance, in Austria, lodged itself in the memory of Johnny Marr due to the weather and the fans of one of the other acts on the bill, as he reminded Johnson when he conducted a lengthy interview with him a decade later. "We went on before The Cure and although there were a lot of people to see us it was also a sea of Cure fans. The black hair all stood up, all the lipstick, the make-up. Anyway, into about our fourth song, it started to pour down with rain, and we weren't really digging the gig that much. It was daylight and we weren't really used to that. So by about four songs, after the rain started pouring down, you looked over to me and I looked out at the audience, and all the audience are just covered in make-up, running down their faces and all their hair all over the place, and we just looked at each other and..." Well, you could only laugh, and when you are playing in the rain and not really feeling it then any distraction is welcome.

On June 25 The The played in the Lycabettus Amphitheatre in Athens. Marr, who had been out in the sun all day, was suffering from sunstroke, to the extent that he was hallucinating. As he looked out over the audience he thought he could see the Acropolis but wasn't sure if it was actually there or just a figment of his fevered imagination. It got to the point where he had to ask for a second opinion, so he queried Johnson if it really was the famous monument he could see in the distance. A laughing Johnson assured him it was. The view from Lycabettus Hill was, to be fair, truly spectacular. This show is the one that sticks in the mind of Dave Collard. "My favourite gig, possibly my favourite gig ever, was the open-air amphitheatre overlooking Athens, looking down on the Acropolis and the next day taking a hovercraft to one of the islands where we spent the weekend playing football, swimming and drinking." The lengthy tour was nearing a close and the whole band had nothing but good memories of it. Marr found that he was free to play guitar in ways that The Smiths had never allowed him to, while Johnson was left wondering why he hadn't done it sooner. Dave Palmer, who has since done even bigger tours, still remembers this one with great affection. "What I noticed is the music really moved people. I saw fans completely losing it when Matt and Johnny walked on stage. It was great playing with people at the top of their game. It was a really wonderful experience to be a part of this band that everybody had so much respect for; fans, media, people in the business and the recording industry, people just showing up left, right and centre." James Eller considers this tour as the best he has ever been on, but also gives an insider view of what it is like to work with a man who most journalists deemed to be something of a misery, overly earnest, too intense. "People often ask me, 'What was it like touring with The The?' expecting it to be really serious, but it was the most hilarious five years I've ever spent. Everybody was really funny. Laughing all the time."

Marr too has good memories and found that so tight had the band become – helped no doubt by all the pre-tour rehearsing – that playing became rather transcendent. "It was really intense. Some nights we played shows where it felt like the audience were behind some kind of force field, and by that I mean it was great that they were there, but we were all listening to each other so closely we were really getting off on the music. We weren't feeding off the audience or adulation."

330

After more festival dates in Germany, Austria and Switzerland, the band arrived back in England on an early morning flight, ready for the final four concerts. Johnson was strolling through Heathrow customs with his Gibson 345 when he was pulled aside. The customs officers weren't experts on guitars, but they knew someone who was, and so their vintage guitar specialist was duly dragged from his bed by a phone call and asked a few questions. Johnson was held for some considerable time; funnily enough customs weren't in the least bit impressed by the fact that the guitar they were so keen to value was once owned by a member of The Doors. Couldn't give a shit in fact. And they weren't impressed when they found out its value was rather more than the receipt suggested, so they confiscated it. Johnson was now worried that he would end up with a criminal record. He was summoned back to Heathrow a few days later. John Kennedy couldn't come as he was getting married that day and so arranged for another lawyer to accompany Johnson. After some discussion the lawyer revealed that what the customs officers really wanted was an apology, and so a tired and contrite Matt Johnson stood there like a naughty schoolboy and said he was sorry, and he wouldn't let it happen again. Honest. They handed back Robby Krieger's customised Gibson 345 to its latest owner, thus allowing its warm and rich tone to be present all over the next album. Johnson then legged it to Knightsbridge and joined in the wedding celebrations at the Kensington Roof Gardens.

Any world tour worth its salt has a triumphal homecoming with one or more shows at the biggest venue a band feel they can fill. *The The Versus The World* was no exception and it was a measure of the confidence in the camp that they opted for three nights at the prestigious Royal Albert Hall in London. Johnson remembers creating an atmosphere to match the occasion. "We had these gigantic bowls of frankincense. We changed all the house lights to dark red, we had two gigantic 60-foot screens either side of the stage with projections of my brother's paintings, plus we had another gigantic projector showing the *Mind Bomb* videos on 35mm, and of course Tim Pope and his film crew running around. We turned it into a cross between a cathedral and a giant bordello. Wonderful shows packed out every night and a great way to end a few years' hard work. Back at the hotel after the last night I remember just lying back in a gigantic hot bubble bath. I was really exhausted after being on the road for a year but I just sat back with a nice contented feeling of a job well done."

Dave Palmer noticed how diverse the audience had become. "You'd got your really hardcore The The fans, you'd got your almost yuppie, banker type of people, but then you had rave kids there as well. It felt just like playing in a big-ass club. It was a party. We'd already done a couple of runs in America, we'd done Australia and New Zealand and we were on fire." Some of the intensity, but not the heady atmosphere of the incense, was captured by Tim Pope who, with a very basic set-up, filmed the shows for a concert film that was released a year later. Though he struggled with the low lighting levels, the footage is a good document of the band at the height of their powers. As intense as it was, James Eller was somewhat distracted. "My then wife was pregnant with our first child, and we were living in Bristol, so I was on tenterhooks. We played on Tuesday, Wednesday and Thursday, and Friday morning at six I got a call and my son was born that night. The last gig was at the Point, in Dublin, on Saturday night. I actually got the last seat on an Aer Lingus flight to Dublin, and just made it to the last gig. The Albert Hall was fantastic. It felt like some kind of culmination. We'd been everywhere, and everywhere successfully."

It is expected by most musicians that after a big tour there will be, along with the necessary rest, an emotional slump. The adrenaline needed to push through an extended period of stress is no longer required and the body doesn't know what to do with it. Moods swing. Wives and girlfriends often suffer as their partner gets used to the more mundane day-to-day existence that had seemed perfectly normal pre-tour. So Matt Johnson was going to experience this comedown anyway. It meant that his mind, body and spirit were at an unavoidably low ebb, and so it was now that the impact of Eugene's death really hit home. The full force of grief, though, would have a long tail. Essentially it would last for years. It would inform the lyrical content of the next album as well as strip him of the intensity of focus he had been able to muster up to this point. Despite this loss of focus, *Dusk* would turn out to be the album he was most satisfied with.

That the band would record another album was decided during the tour. In interviews Johnson had declared that The The would be the band of the nineties, and a quick follow-up album was both a wise move and a chance to break the habit of lengthy gaps between records. It turned out, however, to be the last album the line-up would work on, and by the end of it they would slowly disintegrate as the famous Johnson procrastination took its toll. This time there was at least a clear reason for the delay that was to put recording back a whole year. He had decided he didn't just want to use The Garden studio; he wanted to own it.

The last time he used The Garden as a client was to record two cover versions for an EP, titled *Shades Of Blue*, that would be released in February 1991. The A-side contained 'Jealous Of Youth', getting a second go at being heard after the initial release had come and gone without anyone really noticing. It was accompanied by a live recording of 'Another Boy Drowning', taken from one of the Albert Hall shows. The B-side meanwhile contained two cover versions, both mixed by Felix Kendall. The first was the jazz standard 'Solitude'. Originally written by Duke Ellington, it is the lyrics, penned by Eddie DeLange and Irving Mills, that had obviously struck a chord with Johnson, and give a clue as to how he was feeling when alone in those autumn and winter months after the tour ended. At night the solitude must have been amplified, given that Shoreditch was, at that time, still an evening wasteland. By accident or design the huge reverb tail on DC Collard's keyboards echoed the cavernous space of the room Johnson was living in, emphasising the emptiness. The only other performer on the track was Marr, and only he and Johnson performed on 'Dolphins', which was chosen on the strength of Tim Buckley's version on *Sefronia*. Here, the influence of Buckley on Johnson's vocal stylings is clear. It is another melancholic song and the mood of the music was reflected in Andrew Johnson's painting used for the sleeve. The figure depicted with a tattoo that has the initials E C J was an obvious expression of the anguish the family was feeling. The painting and the music contained on the B-side of the record were like a howl of grief.

The single and the concert film were premiered at the 'Eve of St Valentine's Day Massacre' at the Fridge in Brixton on February 13, along with an exhibition of Andrew's latest paintings called *Lonesome Monsters*, which were projected onto the walls and ceiling. DJ William Orbit played music before and between screenings of the video and Tim Pope's film. Paul Sexton, writing in *Select* magazine, called The The "a live music force to be reckoned with. They're likely to be bigger in 1991 than ever before." Clearly expecting actual live performances later in the year, and suggesting that Johnson had hinted an album would also arrive before the year was out, he was set to be disappointed on both counts. Reaction to the single was mixed, with *SOUNDS* declaring it 'Single of the Week' and, predictably, the *NME* delivering a scathing review. It entered the UK chart at number fifty-four on March 2 only to drop twenty-three places a week later before disappearing altogether. By this time Johnson was probably past caring about the fate of his singles, even if CBS weren't, and he was focused on writing new material for the next album whilst the protracted negotiations for the purchase of the studio dragged on. The delay was frustrating for the rest of the band but when he set his heart on achieving or acquiring something he had a dogged determination and patience. Whatever it took, and however long it took, he wouldn't be swayed. James Eller, now a father, didn't mind the down-time. DC Collard kept himself busy by working on sessions for other artists but Johnson also asked him to work on the first demos of the new material. According to Collard, "The final album was pretty true to those demos."

Lee Kavanagh was now working solely for Johnson, whose flat was the office. There were two large desks; one each. "There was loads to do. Even when a tour ended there was always follow-up. There was always interest in him, the phone would ring all the time. The requests I used to get most often were for him to appear on compilations, and he used to hate that. He would never go on any of those *Now* compilations. Never. A lot of requests. 'Would you like to be on an advert?' 'Would you like to come to Japan and advertise whatever?' He would never do it. So I spent quite a lot of time refusing a lot of different requests. He'd moved away from Stevo and been with Marcus and now he was with this big American, Steve Rennie, and now the label needed *Dusk*. By that time we had really good relationships with the record company. But he was never one for putting himself out there. It seemed like he was just going to ground, but he would be doing stuff, recording, working in the studio, there was always stuff to be done."

Despite Rennie being a Republican the pair got on well – for the time being at least – but if he thought he could hurry Johnson along better than anyone else had previously managed he was mistaken. "We were completely chalk and cheese," recalls Johnson, "and clashes down the line were inevitable. What I liked about him though was that he didn't have a hierarchical structure in the way he treated people. He was as nice to taxi drivers and cleaning ladies as he was to heads of corporations."

When the band were summoned to the flat to start work on the demos, another distraction was about to appear. Lee Kavanagh was hardly overjoyed: "Before *Dusk* what came through the door? A bar-football table. I ended up the taskmaster: 'Get downstairs, because you are supposed to be working on your album,' but there they would be, upstairs, playing on the bloody bar-football." So it was slow progress but, despite the distractions, the new album gradually took shape. For James Eller, the process, protracted as it was, didn't affect the efficiency of the music-making itself. "When he bought the basement studio we spent a long time meeting in his apartment. We did a lot of demoing of *Dusk*. He had quite a nifty 8-track portastudio. We did a lot of band arrangements. I would go and see him for a few days, then Dave would come round, and Johnny would be there for a couple of days. So we prepped it a lot then set dates to record. I think he had put aside two weeks to do that and we had finished the basic tracking by the first Friday." In fact the preparation was so good it often left relatively little to be done when they finally got into the studio proper. "Making *Dusk* was particularly great actually. I think Matt and Dave had some issues, but I remember it as a really constructive and positive time, and we demoed *Dusk* really carefully beforehand, so we knew exactly what we were doing when we went to record it. The tracking was incredibly fast, most of it in four or five days I think. Johnny's tracking ended up on the record; it wasn't ever replaced. The heart of those records was made with people playing together."

Always one for paying attention to detail, Johnson ensured that the studio had the required ambience, to which Palmer testifies. "Matt set up the vibe with incense and psychedelic lighting, working late into the night, and I do think the album captures that atmosphere." Everyone's mood, it seemed, was up. Johnny Marr, who had recently bought an Alfa Romeo Spider, was also enjoying the vibes. "I'd only just passed my driving test. I'd get up in the morning feeling really good and then drive down the Embankment with the roof down in the summer, and it's a beautiful sunny day, people are waving, I'm just like Dick Van Dyke with a real spring in my step, and then I'd get to the studio, which had been re-christened 'The War Room', and I would say goodbye to the day and my flash new sports car and go down the stairs into this dark basement with these dark red psychedelic oil wheels turning, and all these clouds of burning incense." To intensify the mood the heating would be left on, despite it being the summer, and it wasn't unusual for the band to strip down to their underwear in what was soon dubbed the 'Psychic Sauna'.

Johnson takes up the story: "It was Dave Palmer – who was a *very* funny guy – who dubbed the studio the 'Psychic Sauna'. Quite a lot of the recording of *Dusk* was done stripped to our underwear whilst pouring with sweat. It had started out as a joke that Bruce Lampcov and I played on DC. He was playing piano on 'This Is The Night' and we were genuinely hearing a rustle or squeak or noise of some sort, so we got him to remove one item of clothing after another, each time complaining that we could still hear the noise, until he was stark naked. It ended up like something from Monty Python. Bruce and I were in hysterics on the control room floor howling with laughter by this point. But, day after day in that sweltering studio, it wasn't long before we all followed suit – though most of us at least kept our boxer shorts on. I wanted an intense, sleazy vibe for this album so I ensured the studio was extremely dark and hot with incense burning and oil wheels slowly turning. We were all relaxed in each other's company and, as I wanted the album to feel more stripped down, it seemed perfectly natural to all strip off. I seem to remember Bruce and his assistant becoming overly enthusiastic and being fully naked at certain points too."

One of the things that particularly struck Marr about the sessions was how focused Johnson was. "You would descend into that basement and Matt would already be in there with Bruce Lampcov and they would be intensely focused on something that we had recorded, Matt perched on a chair or a bit of furniture, or pacing around, never ever relaxing. Even if he was on a chair he was squatting on it, always, always. Staring intently at the speakers. We would work on a track as a live band, all of us playing at the same time in the live room with Matt singing, until we got the right take, and that could take all day or it could take three days. That happened with 'Slow Emotion Replay'. 'Dogs Of Lust' happened very quickly because we needed that spontaneous free kind of atmosphere."

Johnson was looking for something different to *Mind Bomb*, something more earthy and organic. He had been listening to a lot of blues singers again: Robert Johnson, John Lee Hooker and Howlin' Wolf in particular. Bruce Lampcov, who had done a remix of 'Gravitate To Me' that appeared on the 12-inch release, had been asked to record some Detroit shows during the tour and the pair discussed ideas. Johnson, seeing how well the band had played together live, was looking to capture this on vinyl and Lampcov was regarded as the man who could facilitate this. Dave Collard thought he was a good choice. "Bruce was easy to work with, enthusiastic, hard-working and knowledgeable, a guy who straddled old-school and modern engineering." Lampcov has good memories of the sessions. "It was one of those records where everything seemed to come together exactly as it should. There was a lot of experimentation but we knew pretty quickly when something was right. Matt loved to push sounds to the limit and it was the perfect situation for a geeky sound engineer like me to try new things. We had a room at the back that must have been used to store coal in the early twentieth century; we called it the 'rat room' and used it for reverb and crazy effects. Remember this record was before plugins or Pro Tools so every sound had to be built from scratch."

The resulting album would be a departure from previous ones, where the studio itself had been used as an instrument. Johnson, having grown up with studio technology, had always welcomed its potential to shape sound, but now he wanted something stripped-back. Having frequently laid bare his emotions on record, now he wanted to also reveal the music in, more or less, its naked state. This may have had something to do with his inner state at the time. The pain inside came and went but it made its presence felt. He explained to Marr how this manifested itself one particular time. "I remember being in the studio and feeling quite spaced out, and I also remember Dave Palmer pulling me to one side and saying – it was a bit rich coming from Dave but – 'What's up Matt, you seem sort of spaced out, you don't seem yourself,' because he was used to me directing him very specifically; 'No that beat is not quite right… this beat is not quite right.' But I just felt really spaced out. Really, really weird. I just didn't feel like I had my feet on the ground or something. And I could really sort of feel that I was there, but not there, which was a very unpleasant feeling for me because I was having to fake it a lot of the time."

At other times he was the old Matt, as Eller recalls. "He loves a practical joke, the cornier the better. He went upstairs when we were making *Dusk*, and Johnny was downstairs in the basement, and he phoned Johnny from upstairs, pretending to be his bank manager. It was something along the lines of, 'Mr Marr, are you aware that thirty thousand pounds was withdrawn from your account this morning?'" And so his mood was up and down, he was there and then not there. Dave Palmer, meanwhile, was increasingly not there when he should have been there, and it was beginning to cause problems. Still very much partial to clubbing and raving, the recovery times from all-night hedonism were affecting his timekeeping, both in terms of turning up on the right day in the studio, and turning up on the right beat while drumming. Eller noticed the change; it was hard not to. "I think he was a couple of days late for a tracking session or something. 'Where's Dave?' 'Oh, I think he's in Italy.' Nobody really knew. He was jetting off everywhere enjoying himself and Matt was really disappointed, because the one thing Dave always had was precision. Matt could direct him and produce him and say, 'In bar fifteen, make it a bit squarer and by sixteen do a kind of loose sloppy fill,' and Dave would go, 'All right,' and nail it, time after time. And then he couldn't do that any more." Johnson was no puritan but when Palmer's intake began to affect his ability to perform efficiently he had no choice but to warn him, and when this didn't have the desired effect, sack him from the recording sessions halfway through.

Lampcov remembers that just as they were ready to record 'Dogs Of Lust' they were thus without a drummer. "It turned out that Vinnie Colaiuta was in town touring with Sting and we decided to try him out. He came down to The Garden after his show. Remember this guy is probably the best studio drummer in the world at the time. As we wanted the track to sound very raw we set up a very basic kit, something he wasn't used to. We worked for a long time to get him to loosen up and just play very simply, and his amazing sense of time and feel eventually come out. It's one of the best drum tracks I ever recorded." Drumming duties were subsequently shared by Colaiuta and Bruce Smith from The Pop Group. Part of the problem might have been the delay in getting into the studio, something that Johnson would later concede, and a point Palmer raises in his defence. "It had been a while. I was now living in America. Johnny was in Electronic. We were all kind of doing our separate things and when we all reconvened it felt different." In the end Palmer drummed on four of the ten tracks, and Colaiuta and Smith on two each; the other two tracks had no drums at all.

One of these was the album opener, 'True Happiness This Way Lies'. Employing samples of crackling vinyl and audience laughter from a sound-effects library, Johnson talks his way, perhaps even exhorts his way, through the first lines, slapping the body of his guitar before the guitar itself joins in and his voice turns more song-like. Musically the influence of the electric blues is clear, with subtle undertones of vaudeville via the laughter track. The use of a breathy, over-compressed close-mic style and samples would be explored years later in his Radio Cineola recordings. Lyrically he sets out his stall. Gone is the politics and in their place is soul-searching; not the angst-ridden soul-searching for a place in the world of *Soul Mining*, but the sort of soul-searching that life experience thrusts upon you. His interest in Buddhism had now become a quest for answers, though he was honest enough to show that knowing the philosophical wisdom didn't necessarily mean that any kind of real enlightenment had taken place. Thus the lines, *The only true freedom is freedom from the heart's desires/And the only true happiness… this way lies* are useless knowledge unless they can be acted upon. Therein lay the rub. In an interview with Ken Micallef he admitted that the problem the song lyrics concerned themselves with, was one he was still afflicted with. "Over the past fifteen years I've experimented with drugs, sex, alternative forms of health and medicine. They've all changed and added to me but I still have not found what I'm searching for." In another interview with *Details* magazine he added to this list acupuncture, therapy and flotation tanks, which he had tried with Paul Webb when they briefly became fashionably available. "But nothing seems to satisfy," he complained.

Though he had never shied away from this kind of self-reflection, it was the death of Eugene that had forced him to confront the big questions so openly. The centrepiece of the album tackles the biggest question of all, not why life? Rather, why death? And of course one answer is that without each there is neither, so the only thing approaching an answer is love, at least as far as any kind of healing goes. Johnny Marr had walked round the streets of Shoreditch one morning with Johnson when the latter returned to London after hearing about Eugene, an incident referenced in the first line of 'Love Is Stronger Than Death'. So moved was Marr during recording that his eyes filled with tears when he was playing his harmonica part. "There was no getting around the atmosphere put into that song, which we did live. It didn't take many takes, I think it was no more than the fourth take, if that, maybe the second take. I don't think we would have been able to do any more than four takes to be honest with you. It was too intense for me and I had to get out of the control room. We didn't discuss it but we all knew what the song was."

Though the song begins in subdued and melancholic fashion, Johnson singing the first verse over a minimal backing of guitar and keyboards, after a minute the mood is lifted by a chord change that sees Collard's Hammond organ suddenly soar and the introduction of Palmer's drums, as Johnson leads into the song's simple message: *Love is stronger than death.* Collard described playing Hammond on this track as an "emotional highlight".

His worth is also ably demonstrated on 'This Is The Night', where his bar-room style piano makes the track, leading a waltzing rhythm both wistful and world-weary. At dead on one minute extra piano chords, bass and drums drop in on the same beat as Johnson sings, *How many whores have walked through that door/Lain by my side and climbed in my mind/And taken me down to where the heat/Blisters the skin upon my feet.* If Jagger sang 'Satisfaction' in a way that suggested that, despite the lyric, he *would* actually get some, Johnson here sings as though he is Sisyphus, pushing his rock up the hill knowing it will roll back down the other side again. Lust only leads to some kind of damnation. Collard's playing is the only uplift, in a pour-another-drink kind of way. It is a song of experience that knows innocence is lost. The song was originally written in four-four time for guitar but it didn't feel quite right, so Johnson rewrote it entirely on the old Bell piano that had once been in the King's Head but was now in the corner of The Garden studio. He pushed drawing pins into the felt hammers and changed the time signature to six-eight to give it a bar-room feel. It was on this piano, painted bright pink, that Collard performed, recording the solo in one take. In his typical method way of doing things, Johnson made sure the atmosphere was just right when he was working on this track, as Marr can attest to.

"I went over to the flat where Matt lived, and we waited for it to get dark. We got into a very intense discussion about spirituality and the afterlife, and I got the feeling that Matt was trying to conjure up a certain atmosphere, which he did, and we had the street lights flooding the whole of the room through the windows. He engineered my guitar solo on 'This Is The Night' and it was first take. I was fully expecting to do it over and over, cos I would usually find ways of improving it, but he insisted that that was it. 'Don't do it again, you've nailed it.' It shows you why he's such a great producer. He did what was necessary. Afterwards he said, 'Right you've done that, now let's us cook up this song,' which became 'Lung Shadows'. He and I used to jam around that chord change. We were completely sober – no substances or alcohol or anything. It was very intense, very melancholic, and kind of trippy. We did it very quickly."

A running theme of the album is the age-old battle between physical lusts and spiritual yearning; Johnson was well aware of his blues and soul history, of the gospel music in the church versus the devil's music in the bar or the whorehouse. He spoke openly about his fascination with sleaze and in the *Details* interview is quoted thus: "I'm sometimes held [to] ransom by my biological urges." In 'Dogs Of Lust' he laments that *I keep reaching up/But they drag me back down*. It's the dogs of lust, not him. Johnny Marr doubles up on Johnson's wah-wah guitar riff with a blues-drenched harmonica solo, both instruments so distorted and rhythmically insistent that they barely need the rest of the instruments to kick in alongside. The riff itself had been inspired by the sound of an old-fashioned ambulance siren that Johnson heard on Shoreditch High Street when he was writing the song. Marr ices the cake with some deft funky guitar licks. Coming after 'Love Is Stronger Than Death' it seems somewhat incongruous, but 'This Is The Night' follows, as if to taunt because it doesn't matter *how many whores have walked through that door*, he isn't going to satisfy those lusts, or to put it another way, the action of those lusts isn't going to satisfy him.

'Dogs Of Lust' was chosen as the lead single from the album, released several months before; Johnson called in Tim Pope to provide a suitably swampy video that visually matched the sound and the subject matter. To help things along, he and Marr indulged in some mood supplements that the guitarist had brought along. "I believe we had a few tablets of 'medicine' and a couple of bottles of Tequila," the singer recalled when reminiscing several years later with his partner in crime. "Then we got the three aircraft-hanger heaters brought in and turned them up full blast. I remember James worrying that his bass guitar was melting. He was looking very concerned but I don't think he got dosed up. He was being sensible while we were off on another planet. Fantastic." Marr's own memory of the shoot tallies with Johnson's in regard to where their heads were at. "I was a bit sort of... erm... I'd forgotten that I even had my guitar on at that time." It was Johnson's favourite video. They had, by this time, spent a whole year recording the album, and now cranked the music up and attempted to capture the atmosphere of their live shows. Pope sprayed the band with glycerine during the first take to make it look like they were sweating, but this wasn't good enough for Johnson, ever the 'method' man, who then decided the heaters were the answer, because only real heat would do.

Side one of the album, after the preceding drama, finishes with the most upbeat and positive track, 'Slow Emotion Replay'. It is helped along its way by some lovely clipped guitar and the tremendously buoyant harmonica of Marr, who got so caught up in the exuberance of the music that he sang an impromptu harmony down his harmonica mic during the definitive take. For Johnson, a man too easily dismissed as doom-laden, it was a perfect riposte, and surprisingly, considering their track record, reviewers would spot an optimistic streak running through *Dusk*, and a lack of grandstanding. Even some of the axe-grinders would down tools and offer begrudging respect for this new work. It was a return, of sorts, to the introspection of *Soul Mining*, only this time the introspection had a more philosophical leaning, and the enquiry was more humble.

The more I see
The less I know
About all the things I thought were wrong or right
And carved in stone
So, don't ask me about
War, Religion, or God
Love, Sex, or Death
Because...
Everybody knows what's going wrong with the world
But I don't even know what's going on in myself.

For the naysayers these were the words of a man who was climbing down off his soapbox, while for admirers they were a sign of maturity. The angst may still have been there at times but the self-reflection was more penetrating, the acknowledgement that he didn't necessarily possess the answers to his own questions disarming in comparison to the declamations of the previous two albums. As more than one observer was to note, this was almost "chilled-out" for Matt Johnson. Perhaps the distraction of the bar-football table contributed to the more relaxed vibe, though the games – and there were plenty of them – were never short of competitive spirit, as Lee Kavanagh remembers it. "It would get quite violent. I would be working and they would be screaming and shouting in the background. But I didn't want it downstairs in the studio or we would never have got any work done at all." Johnson would tell the *NME* that without the football table, the 365 days it took to record *Dusk* might have been reduced to about four months, and the suspicion is that he may only have been half-joking.

Side two begins with 'Helpline Operator', which Johnson had apparently prepared for by spending hours on the telephone talking to the Samaritans. The resulting lyric is a strange tableau that speaks of the loneliness of the big city but manages to suggest something sexual, as if the Samaritans shared a party-line with a sex chat-line. Musically it sets up a sultry sound bed with atmospheric keys and strings and some trumpet by John Thirkell, before a snake-like guitar riff eases in, and some great bass-playing by Eller that pins the song to the floor. As good as the other playing is, it is the bass at the heart of the song, and Bruce Lampcov has to get a huge share of the credit according to Eller, who ranks the track as his favourite on the album. "Bruce is a fantastic engineer and co-producer. I was always impressed with any sound that he came up with. Bruce was particularly good for the bass on 'Helpline Operator'. We worked for ages on that. There's no guitar, it's all bass; it's played palm muted with a pick, the signal split and sent to a guitar amp, a Fender Twin I think, and to my normal bass rig. So what sounds like a doubling guitar is actually the same bass signal thinned out. We had the time and really explored all the bass sound possibilities on all the songs." The resulting bass is by turns thick without being flabby, and crisp. Eller's finger style and Lampcov's attention to detail leads to a lovely clipped yet full sound that never shows off, never draws attention to itself. Bruce Smith contributes some deceptively simple and crisp drums with just enough shuffle to push the beat along. Lampcov keeps the drum sound fairly dry and it is a good call, allowing all the instruments to share the sound spectrum without getting in each other's way. This was The The as unembellished as they had ever been in the studio. It is this unadorned sound on *Dusk* that serves as his acknowledgement and appreciation of the musicians he was working with and considered friends.

'Sodium Light Baby' is a fairly impenetrable lyric, though this hardly matters. It is set in the back of a taxi travelling through the city as dusk settles, Johnson looking up at the passing street lamps as the night creeps in. It reminded Marr of New York, and night-time cab journeys in that city naturally evoke the spirit of Travis Bickle. Johnson was a big fan of Scorsese, though unlike Bickle in *Taxi Driver*, who wanted to wash the streets clean of the sleaze and scum, Johnson was more interested in immersing himself in it, be it in New York or London. The amber glow of sodium lights would illuminate his flat at night, and the then-deserted streets of Shoreditch were as evocative in atmosphere as anything Scorsese captured on film, in terms of bleakness, decay and licentiousness hidden in pubs and clubs with plain doors and painted-over windows. At this period of his life Johnson was very much a nocturnal animal and *Dusk* is a hymn to the city after dark. "During this period I'd often get up at three or four in the morning and drive around London for hours listening to demos of the songs as I was writing them. There was a twenty-four-hour fruit and veg store on Essex Road in Islington in those days and I would drive there weekly in the wee hours to load up the boot with fresh vegetables for my newly acquired Champion juicer. I'd also often drive along the empty Embankment and spent much time wandering around St Paul's Cathedral and the empty backstreets there. London was so much quieter and emptier in the early hours of the morning, compared to now. Driving and listening, over and over again, helped bring the entire album into focus for me."

'Lung Shadows' maintains the mood but now it feels like much later at night. The track is an obvious nod to Johnson's love of soundtracks and consists of simple keys, bass and muted trumpet as a musical bed. Some whispered, spoken vocals lie deep in the mix and are joined by some equally low-profile guitar before the whole thing fades out. Dave Collard had originally written a horn arrangement for the track, performing it on French horn. Johnson decided to keep his notation but switch from horn to trumpet, giving a noir-like jazzy feel. It is the same taxi ride as before but this time on tranquillisers; witching-hour music. The journey through the night continues with 'Bluer Than Midnight', which sounds like it is being performed in some half-deserted bar in the dead hours before dawn when the sad and lonely are at their most vulnerable. The lyric starts with a simple refrain of *Save me*, repeated six times, and after stopping to mull over the problem of lust once more ends with Johnson asking why fear penetrates deeper into his heart than love? This track was the one that Collard was most pleased with performance-wise. "It was one take and we had discussed adding drums – no bass – after cutting the piano, so I played most of the song to a click track which would stop towards the end where I would build in volume and actually slightly speed up to give the track its contradictory feel of laid-back urgency, desperation." It's pretty bleak stuff but the final track of the album offers some kind of salvation.

Collard found 'Lonely Planet' another type of challenge, dealing with Johnson's implacable attention to detail. "Cutting the piano on 'Lonely Planet', I was just pulsing four beats to the bar throughout the chorus and then I'd add a simple Nicky Hopkins-type piano fill occasionally, which sounded great, but Matt wanted no additional notes at all, just the pulse: 'I want it relentless.' After he cut his vocal and added the strings, I had to agree with him." It is the strings that do the trick as well as some subtle but clever interplay of instrumentation and voices, with Paul Webb and Zeke Manyika helping out with the chorus, which provides some kind of answer to the soul-searching that has been going on throughout the album. *If you can't change the world/Change yourself.* Though some reviewers dismissed this as platitude they were missing the point; it was a personal reference to Tolstoy's quote that "Everyone thinks of changing the world, but no one thinks of changing himself," an admission that his own attempts at railing against the world with successive albums had effected no change and brought him no peace. Faced with something profound in his life he was now questioning things on a different level. He had given his thoughts away in the lyrics to 'Slow Emotional Replay', where he was making an honest admission, an acceptance of the scale of things and of perspective. And he refused to tie everything neatly together in a Hollywood ending by making it clear that, just because he knew that he had to change himself, this was something he knew he might not be able to fully accomplish.

Dusk is Matt Johnson and The The reaching a newfound maturity. By the time the band got round to recording it they were not as tight-knit as they had been on *Mind Bomb* and the world tour. They were growing up. James Eller wasn't the only one to become a father. "There were a lot of children born; my two were born during my time in The The, Johnny's were I think, Dave Palmer's was, Dave Collard, the keyboard player had his as well I think. So did Bruce Lampcov and Melanie the backing singer. It was like a baby factory, I think because we were all so happy." They were also geographically pulled apart. Marr was in Manchester much of the time working with Bernard Sumner on Electronic. Dave Palmer had moved to America and Dave Collard was in the process of doing so and had to record the album while his family went ahead of him. Johnson too was feeling the pull of America. He admitted to *MOJO* magazine in 2014 that "it didn't feel as much of a band effort as *Mind Bomb*. It's funny, though. It's one of my favourite albums, *Dusk*, I love that record. Everybody did a fantastic job, but at that point, I went on tour and the band had already fallen apart." Johnny Marr concurs, in his autobiography stating simply that "*Dusk* is one of the best things I've ever done." Eller goes even further. "The whole tone of it is interesting, the whole sound of it is very organic and warm, the whole process of making it was great. We demoed *Dusk* very thoroughly and diligently, so the sound developed very naturally, with Matt in overall control as usual. We also knew each other really well after a hundred shows, so I'd say that that record is the true sound of that band. It's also my favourite album of all time." Despite the slow disintegration of the band the five managed to come up with their best piece of work. There isn't a duff note on the whole album, so simpatico were they at this point. In a way it was their parting gift to each other.

16

FROM DUSK 'TIL DAWN

THE REVIEWS OF *DUSK* WERE, IN THE MAIN, OVERWHELMINGLY positive. Even the *NME* gave it 8 marks out of 10 in a review that, aside from giving Johnson's use of lyrical puns a thumbs-down, had nothing negative to say. Nor did it choose to get personal, calling the album a "rich and hugely rewarding experience which draws you to its cold bosom again and again". *Select*, *Spin* and *Rolling Stone* all gave it a positive reception and the *Independent* newspaper ended their review by stating: "At last, Johnson has made a record almost commensurate with his hype." *Time Out* went further, calling it "a minor masterpiece of major proportions". Style magazine *i-D*, meanwhile, decided that Johnson was "coming on like a post-Thatcher John Lennon". This reference to his hero might have pleased him, but others had noticed the Lennon influence and David Thomas of *The Times* was less kind, with a negative review and the opinion that the vocals were too breathy, and the singing style a poor imitation of the original Working Class Hero. David Bennun of *Melody Maker* was also firmly in the negative camp, writing that *Dusk*, though frequently absorbing, was "still inherently laughable as any other The The record". It seemed that *Melody Maker* had taken on the job of being down on

The The, as they had also dismissed 'Dogs Of Lust', saying, "It's way too clean and calculated and reeks of expensive lagers." The *NME* surprisingly published a wholly positive review of the single, calling it "a tingling, volatile, uninhibited near masterpiece". Masterpiece or not, the record only got as high as number twenty-five, entering the chart thus on January 16, staying there for one more week, before sliding away and out of sight. *Dusk* fared much better. It entered the album chart at number two in the first week of February, though the top spot eluded it and its stay in the chart was a meagre four weeks. Still, in terms of chart success and critical reception, this was a complete turnaround of fortunes compared to the way *Mind Bomb* had been greeted four years before. In fact this point was highlighted by a review of 'Slow Emotion Replay' in *Select* that April: "It must be great to be Matt Johnson now: all the snide twerps who dismissed him as over forever after the Great Mindbomb Disaster of 1989 are cowering with their copies of *Dusk* and backtracking like madmen." They thought the single was "wonderful". The *NME* were also positive, though in the space of a review consisting of three tiny paragraphs it was a feat of some linguistic dexterity that they managed to include so many backhanded compliments. The record itself, for all its zest, only made it as high as number thirty-five.

Johnson felt that *Mind Bomb* had suffered not just from journalists with an agenda, but also as a result of inexperienced in-house PR. To avoid the latter with *Dusk* he appointed an independent PR person in the shape of Rob Partridge. "I liked and trusted Rob. He ensured there would be no repeat of the *Mind Bomb* debacle. A former music journalist himself, he'd been head of Island Records' press department, before setting up as an independent. I was actually his second client after Tom Waits. Rob did a superb job throughout the *Dusk* campaign. We only missed out on a Mercury Prize nomination by one place." The *NME* also had a new editor, and while he didn't appear to be a big The The fan, Johnson thinks that Steve Sutherland gave him and his band a fair crack of the whip.

With a new album and accompanying singles to promote, Lee Kavanagh busied herself with interview schedules, and CBS, now owned by Sony, assigned a new person to the promotions role. "We did *Dusk* and then we met Maurice Schneider. He was fantastic. I think, like me, he didn't know quite what to expect when he met Matt. We met Maurice and we had this schedule, I think we must have been in Europe. I was sitting with Matt and Maurice looking at the schedule. The first five or six interviews were phone interviews, and I knew Matt so well by then and he said, 'Right, we don't need to worry about the phone interviews, because, Maurice, you'll be taking care of them won't you? Cos you know the album...' So I joined in. 'Yes, Maurice because, on promotional tours, with phone interviews, your predecessor would do them. They don't know it's not Matt and it saves time and energy, and Matt has got this whole schedule to do, so if you could just take care of the phone interviews that would be fine.' And he just didn't know what to think. 'They're winding me up. No, they're not winding me up.' So poor Maurice thought he was going to have to do all these phone interviews the next morning. I think we went to bed and the first phone interview was ten o'clock in the morning, and about half past nine he knocked on my door, and said, 'I can't do it, I can't do it.' And I was all innocent, 'What can't you do?' 'I can't do the phone interviews.' 'No Maurice, you don't have to do the phone interviews.' So he was like, 'I'm gonna get him!' I think he might have done one, for some German magazine or something, but we were standing beside him. There were always things like that going on."

"He definitely did one interview," Johnson says. "What made it even funnier was that he had a strong northern accent but I told him he had to put on a Cockney one in order to sound convincing, so I coached him on a few phrases. He sounded like Dick Van Dyke in *Mary Poppins* by the time I'd finished with him."

With the music press now offering praise, even if it was begrudging in some cases, there was once again the chance to promote The The via a film. Tim Pope was called upon, this time

Matt, Andy and Gerard Johnson – MJ's 40th birthday – Spain 2001. Photo: Johanna St Michaels.

Jack, Matt and Johanna – New York 2003. Photo: JG Thirlwell.

MJ Back In The USSA – 2011. Photo: Jack Johnson.

Matt, George and Helen – London 2012. Photo: Simon Mooney.

Eddie and Matt Johnson – Bishopsgate Institute event for *Tales From The Two Puddings* 2013.

Matt Johnson and JG Thirlwell – London 2013.

Marc Geiger, Matt Johnson, Earl Harvin – London 2015.

Matt, George and Jack Johnson – Croatia 2015. Photo: Helen Edwards.

Matt Johnson – Radio Cineola 2015. Photo: Jacob Sahqvist.

Radio Cineola's 'Midday To Midnight Marathon' – London 2015. Photo: Gerald Jenkins.

Meja Kullersten, Zeke Manyika, Matt Johnson – Performing live on Radio Cineola – London 2017.
Photo: Johanna St Michaels.

Johanna St Michaels, John Tottenham, Matt Johnson – English Premiere of *The Inertia Variations* – ICA, London 2017.

Matt Johnson and Tim Pope – Lisbon 2017. Photo: Helen Edwards.

Matt Johnson – London 2017. Photo: John Claridge.

working as sole director. Without the huge budget that had fed the *Infected* project the scope was to be less ambitious, though the same guerrilla filmmaking technique appealed to both Johnson and Pope. Working on the *Infected* videos in New York, Pope had put Johnson in different scenarios to see how he would react. He decided to continue with this philosophy. *"From Dusk 'Til Dawn* was what I would call an inadvertent documentary. I said to Matt and Johnny, 'Come to New York, and I will take you on a magical mystery tour.' They had no idea what they were ever going to step into. The basic idea was, 'How can I put the world right if I don't know what's wrong with myself?' That was the essence."

Using 16mm black-and-white film the result is a beautifully grainy picture that makes the end product look like an underground movie from the sixties. In New York, Pope and his cinematographer, Jamie Livingstone, trawled the streets posing questions to a variety of interesting-looking characters. "We just went from person to person to person. Some of the people we would just chance upon, others were sort of set up, like Annie Sprinkle, who was going to give herself an orgasm on camera. She was famous for doing these live transmissions from her vagina or something. Amazing people, who were found for me by this amazing woman called Barbara Nitke." Most of the film is edited footage of these encounters. Pope, asking the question, off camera, sometimes audibly, while Livingstone films the responses. The repetition gives the film an insistent rhythm that is at once compelling and frequently unsettling, adding up to a fine example of *cinéma-vérité*, and before you know it you have forgotten that this is supposed to be a film promoting The The. Only when the street filming is sequenced into the video for 'Slow Emotion Replay' do you register that you are watching a music video. Or maybe not. Like Bowie before him, Johnson saw the value in collaborating with artists of a different medium; for once he could relinquish control and enjoy the fruits of someone else's labour. Pope's film is best viewed as a vehicle inspired by music foremost and serving that music secondly. If you take away the music of The The it loses some of its context but still survives as a film in its own right.

Like *Infected* before it, the filming would often expose cast and crew to unbalanced situations that revealed the flip side to humdrum reality in, quite literally, stark black and white. Pope's camera mined the depths of people's emotions, capturing along the way the amused, confused and sometimes startled expressions of Johnson and Marr as the dark side and the crazy side was unfurled before them. The more extreme the situation, surmised Pope, the more freaked out would be the reaction he could capture on film. And so the vignettes become increasingly more unhinged. "We were putting ourselves into quite interesting scenarios; there was Danny the Wonder Pony who described himself as a sexual equestrian. You could hire him out for an hour as a woman and he had a dildo thing in his saddle, but the thing is, he also, without the dildo, clearly, hired himself out as a children's entertainer. We had been at this for two days and we would keep Johnny and Matt in the dark, waiting with their guitars in the back of this van, and they had no idea what was coming, and next minute they would be in with Annie Sprinkle and she would be having an orgasm. They would be out in the van, and I would whisk them out, they would walk into the room and I would have the cameras rolling. We ended up at this hotel... something dark had happened in this hotel. I don't think I'd ever had that sense about a place before. It was a dark place, and we all started getting the giggles. It was three in the morning, everyone was fucked, we'd been up for two days, Danny the Wonder Pony was coming down the corridor with the cow girl on his back, and it was just the most surreal thing... all these TV sets, and guns around... it was just a really odd and dark atmosphere." Pope wasn't the only person who picked up the dark vibes from the hotel. Producer Carol Heywood was quoted as saying that the hotel was disgusting and smelt of death.

When the camera wasn't focused on such extreme set-ups it would frequently – magically in filmmaking terms – alight upon extreme emotions, such as the time they came across two men in a bar one night. "It was Milano's Bar on Houston Street. We started interviewing someone else but he didn't want to know, and suddenly this guy came into the back of the shot, and I went, 'What's up with the world?' Clearly whatever had happened to him that day was something he wanted to talk about, and it was this really visceral moment where he just started falling apart. It was the only moment in my career where I thought, 'Should I be filming this? This is wrong.' But I felt he wanted to tell it, and the reason I used it was... if you read Matt's poetry, because that's what it is, that line I think is wonderful, *I'm just a slow emotion replay of somebody I used to be.* And in a way we found the characterisation of this completely accidentally. This man was the slow emotion reply of somebody he used to be. Once I'd got that moment I knew I'd got the film." The scene makes for uncomfortable but morbidly fascinating viewing. Marr described the awful internal breakdown as like a key turning inside the man as he started to weep.

Luckily, other encounters were not as emotionally raw. "One bit that cracks me up is Johnny's face when he's there with Annie Sprinkle because, again, they had no idea. They came into this room and I said, Johnny, Matt, sit there, and she's sitting there fairly naked, and starts with this vibrator, starts working herself up, which she was quite famous for doing as a performance artist, and there's a look on Johnny's face which is absolutely priceless."

To be fair to Marr, not only wasn't he expecting to be on the same bed as a woman bringing herself to orgasm but he wasn't in the best state to deal with the unexpected, or even the expected. Having arrived in New York from the Caribbean, and already recovering from a hectic schedule, all he wanted was to catch up on some sleep. "Matt told me that we were going to do something with Tim but he couldn't tell me what it was. Then when I got to New York and met him at the hotel, he still wouldn't tell me what it was, and we were shooting the next day. He said to me, 'Did you get any sleep on the plane?' and I said, 'No, I've been awake for about eighteen hours.' And he said, 'Great, cos you're not gonna get any tonight either.' Two phone calls were strategically made in the night from Tim's assistant to make sure I didn't get any sleep, so by the time the shooting started I was a bit tired and emotional. And still had no idea what the video was. The crew were all speaking in code so as not to tip Matt and me off as to what was going on." Looking back on it years later, and knowing Johnson's love of mischief, it occurred to Marr that his friend had been in on the whole thing from the start, as the pair were driven around New York and deposited at one bizarre location after another. "So we get out of this van and the cameras are on us and we walk into this studio where there is this live porno chat going on for this cable TV show, and we were asked all these questions about our sexual proclivities by some real weirdo guy, with the cameras in our face watching our reaction. Then we went to the apartment of the sex-guru Annie Sprinkles who had this dildo shrine, and who was actually a very kind and lovely woman, but we had to perform a song with her writhing around on the bed."

"She was doing it for real," Pope says, "and she did have an orgasm. And there's Matt sort of gloating in the background, with this dodgy smile on his face, and Johnny looking slightly, what-the-fuck-am-I-doing-here? It was hilarious, and I remember being on the floor crying with laughter."

The second half of the film centres upon 'Love Is Stronger Than Death' with filming taking place in and around New Orleans. Here there was a different kind of edginess. When they were filming in the swamplands, it was something more akin to scenes from Walter Hill's *Southern Comfort*. "We knew we were in trouble again. We were walking around in these waders and we were seeing moccasin snakes and crocodiles in the water, walking with some rather edgy guys. I walked into a bar with Matt in the middle of this Cajun thing, some guys were playing fiddle, and Matt and I walked in and the music stopped – just like in the films. This big guy who had been dancing with a woman stopped and said, 'I ain't never seen an angel before.' I'll never forget that moment. It was like, 'I'm about to die.' I thought, 'How the fuck am I gonna get out of this?' So I just went up to him and said, 'Hello, I'm Timothy from Enfield, can I buy you a drink?' And he said, 'Yeah, sure,' and the music started up and Matt and I got out alive." At the time Pope was going through a difficult relationship break-up. Having nursed Johnson through one a few years before in Greece, Johnson now returned the favour as they walked through the swamps, Pope with a broken heart, two Englishmen in the badlands, in a mist of heat and mosquitoes.

And Johnson was still coming to terms with the death of Eugene. In New Orleans, Pope filmed Oswan Chamani and Mary Robin Williams, Voodoo High Priest and High Priestess. The Voodoo High Priest said this: "In Voodoo we believe that the universe has a physical aspect. In Voodoo the teaching is that you are not the body. You only inhabit the body, and after you leave the body, which is what people call death, then you be living in the spiritual world. And to them it doesn't signify death at all, it just signifies a change of residence, universally, cosmically speaking." This might have helped.

* * *

Filming in New York was the last thing Johnny Marr did as a member of The The. He had not long been a father and wanted to spend more time with his family. A lengthy world tour wasn't something he felt he could commit to, especially when there was an alternative much closer to home, so he opted for working with Bernard Sumner on Electronic. In retrospect it is clear that the sound of The The changed after Marr joined, becoming less reliant on studio wizardry and synthesizers, and more geared towards classic instrumentation. It isn't that Johnson didn't desire for himself such a change – his and Marr's musical tastes had always been very similar and over the years they had cross-pollinated each other's record collections – it was more that Marr gave Johnson the confidence to move in this direction. Marr was the recognised guitar hero but Johnson's own playing, influenced by Syd Barrett, Michael Karoli, and for rhythm guitar, John Lennon, has always been underrated. Musicians like Marr and Collard were able to help him better deliver the sounds inside his head, while Eller and Palmer provided the bedrock.

Eller himself also had to make decisions at this point. Now a father, and perhaps therefore more conscious of the future, he was presented all of a sudden with an opportunity. "What happened was, we spent ages waiting to do *Dusk*, and then ages after doing *Dusk* waiting to work again, so I was sitting at home in Islington and I'd started writing, and ended up firstly with a publishing contract, and then a recording contract with Polydor, to make two albums. In the same week Matt phoned me to tell me the *Dusk* tour was ready, and two days later my manager called me and said, 'Polydor definitely want to do this. What do you want to do?' I said, ideally I would like to do both. And he said, 'I don't think you can do both.'" It was decision time. In the days before home-recording set-ups became affordable for pretty much anyone, the opportunity to make your own record was a rarity, particularly if you were a bass player. "I talked with Matt about it and it was really gut-wrenching. I thought, 'I'm going to make a record. I can always come back to The The later, if he'll have me.' So I made a record, and it initially went really well, but it was an expensive way to find out that I don't really like fronting things. I don't have the sort of personality to stand on stage and say, this is what I think about the world. I don't have that at all. The record never came out. I've kind of regretted it ever since."

Johnson now had an album to tour without a full band with which to do so. In an interview with Randy Bookasta for *Ray Gun* in March 1993 it sounded like he already suspected that Marr and Eller were going to be absent from any tour. "All of our lives have changed since I formed that group. I haven't had children yet, but they've had six children amongst them. If you are going to be away from home for a long time, it's really tough if you've got kids. It might be the right time to bring in a fresh, hungrier band." In fact, when it came down to it, Johnson was reluctant to tour at all, something that didn't come out at the time. "I was arm-twisted into it by Steve Rennie. He was only doing his job and he was right to insist I tour the album. Rennie and I would argue frequently and he could never get his head around the fact this strange Englishman would spend so much time, care and money creating an album but then seemingly try to sabotage all attempts to promote it."

The remaining members of The The relocated to New York for three months to audition members and rehearse a new band for the world tour, with Johnson deciding to give Palmer another chance after his wayward behaviour during the *Dusk* sessions. "I rented an apartment on 12th Street between 2nd and 3rd Avenues, and Dave Collard and Dave Palmer moved in with me. We rented rehearsal rooms at SIR at 25th Street and the three of us started auditioning musicians. The guitarist I wanted to replace Johnny at that time was actually Eric Schermerhorn. Dave Palmer was friendly with him and sang his praises to me. Eric and I first met in either London or New York, got on really well and knew we'd work together at some point. But he was in the middle of a project with Iggy and, quite rightly, didn't want to let him down. My next choice was Dave Navarro from Jane's Addiction. He was out of the band at this point and Geiger put us in touch. We chatted about it but he was also tied up with another project. So then the auditions began. We had quite a bunch of guitarists come in but none seemed right. We recorded all auditions onto my little DAT recorder and the two Daves and I would then carefully analyse them back at the apartment."

His eventual choice for guitar was Keith Joyner, who at the age of 24 would be the baby of the group. "What was strange with Keith," Johnson recalls, "was that his body language made it seem like he'd rather be anywhere on earth than standing on a stage.

He looked awkward to such a degree I'd actually discounted him from the job in my mind. But I wanted to give everyone a fair crack and when we listened back to the audition tapes there was no doubt Keith was head and shoulders above the other players. Keith almost seemed embarrassed by his own talents and his shyness on stage was to become a bit of a bone of contention, with me continually nagging him to liven himself up."

Also getting the call were bassist Jared Nickerson and harmonica player Jim Fitting. Nickerson had grown up in Dayton, Ohio, home of such noted funk outfits as The Ohio Players and Zapp. He had recently played with Bernie Worrell's band, and like the ex-Funkadelic keyboard player was equally at home with the funk and rock music. Roger Cramer tipped him off about auditions while nearing the end of a tour with Freedy Johnston. "He asked when would I be back in town and I told him the date and he said, 'Well that's too bad, Matt would be gone by then.' Fortunately for me there was a snow storm in New York that grounded all flights. Since we were travelling by van from our last date in Chicago I was able to get back to New York before Matt rebooked his flight, and made the audition at SIR. I walked in the room with Matt, DC Collard on keys and David Palmer on drums. The main audition song was 'Dogs Of Lust'. It's a funny song in that, as opposed to most of Matt's music, it had a behind-the-beat, laid back bass part. Very R&B. Also right up my alley. From what I heard later there were a bunch of bass players who auditioned as Matt had been at it for two weeks and I came in at the last moment aided by a snow storm, laid back on the bass line and got the gig. Matt afterwards said numerous times the fact that we sported the same hairstyle had a lot to do with it." With his little round spectacles and shaved head, Johnson thought Jared looked "like a 'black Gandhi'. He's a very smart guy and very funny as well as being a fine musician. He and I hit it off straight away."

Fitting, born in California but by then a Bostonian, had played with local outfit Treat Her Right, who played a blues-inflected rock, trying to get away from the standard kick'n'snare rock sound. He heard The The were auditioning through guitarist Stu Kimball but unlike Nickerson was familiar with Johnson's back catalogue. "I really liked that Johnny Marr had all these specific riffs and parts for the harmonica on *Dusk*. This was fun stuff for me to play. I had to experiment with a lot of effects to try and match the recordings, and find some nice nasty electric harmonica tone."

Jim was a real showman and, in stark contrast to Keith, loved being on stage. Johnson knew within seconds of his audition that the band had found their harmonica player.

It wasn't long before Johnson's concerns about Keith Joyner's stage presence were aired.

The Lonely Planet Tour was going to be a long one, ultimately taking in around ninety dates, so for the better part of a week, the band rehearsed daily in the venue where the tour was set to begin. Ever the perfectionist, Johnson wanted to make sure everything was taken care of before the band hit the road. His reservations about Joyner's static stage performance were aired at the soundcheck before the first show, as the guitarist remembers. "We landed in Linz, Austria for the start of the tour. For the better part of a week, the band rehearsed daily in the venue where the tour was set to begin. I recall the soundcheck before the first show. Matt stalked over to me at stage-right, and angrily denounced my lack of stage presence. *Can I move around or do something other than just stand there?* I was perplexed, as I wasn't in the business of performing to an empty room. I think I said as much, but I got it. I fully understood at the time the pressure that he was experiencing."

As it turned out, Jim Fitting had enough zest on stage to make up for any lack in the guitarist and this small bubble of pre-tour tension popped and was forgotten. The anxieties of the record label were quelled with a live performance by the band to a select audience of New York tastemakers at the Sony Studios, with MTV also in attendance. A recording was subsequently given away as a promo, dubbed *Live In New York (Yeah, It's A Bootleg)*.

After several dates in Europe the band played at Brixton Academy, garnering a curious review from Paul Moody, writing for the *NME*, who though suggesting that it was mostly fabulous, seemed intent on a character assassination of Johnson, thus continuing the simmering feud. From here the tour went to America and wouldn't return to the UK until the end of the year. For the first leg of the tour the support was supplied by The Cranberries, then one hit away from being huge, and Frank Black, who was flying solo after the demise of Pixies. Through June the tour moved up and down the East Coast, the band getting used to each other on stage and Johnson getting used to carrying more of the weight. Although Fitting helped draw audience approval with enthusiastic performances, Johnson often found the crowds too passive, urging them onto their feet in an attempt to generate a feedback loop of energy. Sandra Garcia, reviewing the concert at the Tower, Philadelphia, wrote: "big tours are still something new to Matt, and he's not quite into all this audience communication yet. He has to get over expecting the audience to offer total adoration, and offer up some of that quiet arrogance that threads through his work. Although, to be honest, that arrogance is largely missing on *Dusk*..." Whether she understood or not where that arrogance had gone she had identified a problem, in that much of the audience was still expecting the cocky Matt Johnson of *Infected* and *Mind Bomb*, and weren't ready for the more contemplative version.

In July the tour moved down to the Southern states and Dave Palmer, who had no doubt been ruminating over when to speak up, dropped a bombshell: he was quitting the tour. To go and play with Rod Stewart on *his* world tour. Both Johnson and DC Collard had seen adverts for the Stewart tour and were privately wondering whether this meant that Palmer would, quite literally, up sticks and go. He had after all played in Stewart's band the year before. With these fears realised, Johnson was understandably furious. Palmer had been unreliable during the recording sessions for *Dusk*, necessitating replacement drummers, but Johnson had decided to give him another chance and now he had thrown the tour into jeopardy. Nickerson recalls the first sign that trouble might be lying ahead. "At our first show in New York Dave didn't have any energy, as if he'd already spent it someplace before we hit the stage that night. Matt was livid after the show and didn't talk to anyone. That show might have been more telling than it appeared at the time because less than a week later Dave left us. I heard it was very touch and go as to whether the tour would be able to financially absorb the down-time and continue, and of course Matt was very disappointed. But I don't think he was caught off guard. The fact that Matt made it a point of contention early on, led me to believe he weighted Dave's leaving as a possibility. We postponed a few dates while staying in Atlanta for a week flying in and auditioning drummers."

The whole episode, according to Johnson, cost him "tens of thousands of dollars personally and almost derailed the entire tour". He threatened to sue the Stewart camp, but in the end made Palmer work a month's notice, which enabled the band to recruit another drummer. A week was lost, though this was a better state of affairs than might have been hoped for when Palmer first broke the news. Their friendship, however, came off much worse. That more or less snapped in half. In hindsight the whole affair could have been avoided had there been better communication, and for that Palmer has to shoulder the blame. Admitting from the start that he had accepted a lucrative offer to join Stewart's *A Night To Remember* tour might have solved the ensuing problem, but his reluctance to fess up early on made any subsequent justification sound much weaker. It was an offer he could ill afford to refuse; he just went about it the wrong way. Looking back, these two simple facts remain, as does Palmer's regret over the way he handled it. "Matt was extremely upset, and disappointed in me, but I was upset as well. I missed my friend, because Matt and I were really close, I mean, I would take trips down to London just to hang with him. We all have to make a living. I regret the way it went down, but it was the right decision for me; I'd just had a kid, I was paying child support and stuff like that..."

Though he no longer holds it against him, Johnson recalls the disappointment over what happened. "After I fired him from *Dusk* he pleaded to come back when we met up in New York and I played him the album. He loved *Dusk* and wanted to be part of the team again. I wasn't convinced he'd changed but I thought the world of Dave – as a person and a musician – and I wanted to believe he'd sorted his head out. I totally understand musicians having to earn a living and taking other work, especially as my records and tours are relatively few and far between. I never stood in the way of anyone else joining another band if they got a great offer. Wix joined Paul McCartney, Gail Ann Dorsey joined David Bowie. I just couldn't compete with the wages they were able to pay. On the other hand Eric Schermerhorn joined me from Iggy Pop. This sort of thing happens all the time in music. But you need to tell people upfront about your plans. Dave was supposed to be my friend but his behaviour almost derailed the entire tour and cost me at least $30K out of my own pocket in rearranged gigs, renting audition space, flying out drummers to Atlanta, and legal fees."

Andy Kubiszewski, introduced to Johnson by Trent Reznor, was drafted in to replace Palmer, in time for three dates in England. Like both Nickerson and Johnson, Kubiszewski sported a bald pate; when he took a shine to Johnson's black jumper with white skull and crossbones, buying one for himself, the singer saw fit to take advantage by occasionally shoving him out of the tour bus first in the hope that he could play his own role for autograph hunters. The ruse never worked, but mistaken identity was rather more common when it came to naive fans believing that Keith Joyner was Johnny Marr, which resulted in him being plagued for autographs and stories about Morrissey for the whole tour.

This was touring as a job, a necessity if you wanted to shift significant amounts of records. It was a seemingly endless round of long coach journeys, airport waiting lounges, hotel rooms and hotels that blurred together and after-show parties in every town where the promoter was keen to show off what they considered the hippest clubs. Luckily there were plenty of opportunities to inject fun into the proceedings, and ample opportunities to stray from the path if you wanted, as Dave Collard recalls. "Matt and I, along with Jared, crossed the border into Tijuana the morning of our gig in San Diego. We got word to one of the other band members to alert the tour manager that we'd been arrested by the Federales and quite possibly wouldn't make it back for the gig. Of course it was a ruse and we showed up minutes before show time to many quite unrepeatable expletives from our tour manager, Bucky."

On the dates supporting Depeche Mode it was hard not to have fun. Nickerson says the band would often join the Depeche Mode fans and watch the show after they had done their set, and that the touring machine of the headliners was on another level when it came to organisation. "Depeche Mode and crew were the Kingmakers of Fun. I'd never witnessed an organisation put so much time and effort in facilitating the party. They transported and constructed a recreation lounge with pinball games, football and a ping pong table at every venue. There was an after-show party organiser. On staff. With us right in the path of their well-oiled and fuelled party machine, we felt an obligation to play our part and have as much fun as possible. I think we held up our end of the bargain."

These support dates were in much bigger venues, a step up from the theatre circuit they had been used to, especially when they performed at Madison Square Garden, where Jim Thirlwell was in the crowd. It was a glimpse of the next rung of the ladder, and useful experience of playing to the people in the back row. There had also been a handful of support dates for New Order, another band who were making progress in breaking America. When they played San Francisco there was barely any time to soundcheck and when the show started the sound on stage was so bad Johnson walked off after a few songs. He had not been overly happy about playing the dates in the first place, which were festival-style affairs, but Steve Rennie had insisted. "We played when it was still light. We were not allowed a soundcheck at all for some reason. Rennie and I had a flaming row on the phone afterwards about me walking off. I sort of regretted it as I pride myself on being professional but we were lumbered with a complete halfwit as monitor engineer who didn't know what he was doing. I don't think my monitors were even turned on. I literally could not hear my own voice at all so I was caterwauling out of tune. I was just totally fed up at this point."

Jim Fitting was doubly disappointed. "I had a ton of family and friends in the audience so I was a bit bummed out about it. New Order weren't too happy either. When we opened for them at Chicago a couple of days later things were quite frosty backstage." The next day he was surprised to see two four-letter words scratched into his wooden harmonica case, the first being 'bald' and the second rather more subjective. "I still use that case and you can still see those words today." Johnson is of the opinion that it was the band's monitor guy who had carved the offensive message, after he had been fired from the tour. Though this was more of a war wound than a souvenir, at least Fitting survived the duration, unlike Bucky who was relieved of the obvious stress of dealing with a bunch of lefty-liberals and was replaced by Matthew Murphy, soon dubbed 'The Major' and fondly remembered by Nickerson. "He was wonderful, like your cool uncle from the other side of the family that you only see on holidays so he's always in a festive mood. I have to say… he kept us all very happy."

Johnson describes the contrasting figures of Bucky and Murphy. "I demoted Bucky to production manager after he had a rampage through the bus and attacked a couple of the band. He was a big guy, an old friend of Rennie and another Republican. He looked like John Goodman the actor. He loved talking about Harley D's and Micky D's. We teased him mercilessly one night by calling him Chucky, after the doll in *Child's Play*, and he ended up screaming "My name is BUCKY!" The angrier he got the more we all laughed. He ended up going on a rampage with his aluminium briefcase and attacked Keith, DC and Jim. He wasn't such a bad guy though and was just much happier travelling with the crew than being around the band. Matthew Murphy was introduced to me by Marc Geiger. I liked him instantly. With his penchant for wearing cowboy hats he was like a smaller version of Robert Duvall's Lt. Col. Kilgore in *Apocalypse Now*. We had a hell of a lot of fun together concocting vivid tales from his time as a Vietnam vet to gullible journalists."

So, while Johnson put a lot of work into the tours and felt responsible for the band, life on the road was, essentially, one of hanging out with the lads and being catered for in return for doing what you do best. It was like being in a bubble, albeit a very fine bubble. Outsiders coming into such a bubble therefore have a tendency to upset the inner equilibrium, even if the outsider is someone close, like your girlfriend.

Fiona Skinner's relationship with Matt Johnson, she now realises, had been drifting apart in that slow way where the tiny signs of disharmony, and their frequency, never quite register. It took a trip to see him on tour to bring home to her where they might be heading. "We hadn't seen each other for a month, which is the longest we had been apart, and I joined him in San Francisco, and they were going on to do a few more gigs in California. I got there first and so I had a night to myself in the hotel, we had this lovely suite, and I remember being really excited about seeing him, really looking forward to it. I was in reception when the tour bus pulled up and Matt and the band got off, and he hugged me, kissed me, and then he was signing in and he turned to Dave the keyboard player, and said, 'So what are you guys doing tonight, what's everyone doing for dinner?' And I thought, we haven't seen each other for a month and you're interested in what the band are doing for dinner. Okay. Enough said. And we went upstairs to our room and he'd had a bath or a shower and we were lying on the bed and he was moaning and moaning about England, 'The tour's going to be over soon, and I don't want to be back in England.' I just said, 'Do you want to be with me?' There was a pause, and I just thought the pause said it all."

Johnson's pause effectively signalled the end of their relationship. He recalls what happened next. "That night we decided we were going to separate. We went out and got very drunk and tearful on champagne. Whilst wandering the streets of San Francisco in the early hours we thought it would be a great idea to get 'divorce rings'. Only these would be rings through the navel. So, in for a penny in for a pound, I asked the young woman if she would also pierce my scrotum. Which she did. We woke up next morning completely hungover and with only dim recollections of the night before. But my navel piercing had somehow gone wrong and became infected and so I had to go back to the woman to get it re-pierced at a different angle."

Johnson had been quoted in many interviews around this time as being disillusioned with life in England, and suggesting he might prefer to be living in Spain or America. He had the villa in Spain and it was an idyllic setting, but America seemed to be the itch that had needing scratching ever since the family holiday back in '76, and every stay in New York, every new city on the road while touring there just made him more and more itchy. There was a sense that the grass might be greener across the ocean, that the people, certainly the music press, might be less cynical, that the outlook might be less pessimistic. Despite his distaste for American foreign policy the myth of the American dream was, compared to the broken dreams of Thatcherite Britain, still persuasive. Returning to English shores in the middle of another bleak winter might not have helped.

While the band had been away, 'Love Is Stronger Than Death' had been released as a single to mixed but generally positive reviews. Andrew Smith, writing in *Melody Maker*, provided a neat and concise summary of the relationship between the music press and Matt Johnson up to this point, before revealing the recent thaw: "Matt Johnson may have become an outcast as far as the music establishment is concerned (by which I mean us). He may have even brought it upon himself. Whatever. But listen. Listen with your ears and you'll find that the songs still speak for themselves.

You think I'm being facetious, that I'm setting Herr Johnson up for the big smart-arse pay-off in the last minute of extra time. Not so. He pens a melody, then lovingly imbues it with light and shade, like few others. 'Love Is Stronger Than Death' is excellent. No joke." The record only managed three weeks in the chart, however, its highest position being number thirty-nine in the last week of July. The same month *Burning Blue Soul* had been re-released, this time as a The The album at Johnson's request, so it could sit alongside his other albums in the record shops. Dele Fadele gave it a glowing review in the *NME* of all places, but in some ways the release only served to illustrate how much water had flowed under the bridge since 1981. Britain was a different place, for good and for bad, and Johnson, a dozen years wiser, had made up his mind that the bad outweighed the good.

In November Tim Pope's *From Dusk 'Til Dawn* film was released on VHS and, at the end of the month, the Jingle Hell tour was announced. It would include eight dates in England, with one each in Scotland and Wales. Fans in Glasgow were treated to a surprise addition to the line-up, and Joyner, having spent much of the last few months being mistaken for Johnny Marr, even pretending to be Johnny Marr when fans refused to believe he wasn't, now found himself on stage with the *actual* Johnny Marr. "Johnny made the trip from Manchester to Glasgow with plans to join the band on stage at Barrowlands. It was to be my first time meeting him, and I was quite nervous. The evening prior to the show, we were all sitting in the hotel lobby bar when one of the waiters, an older gentleman dressed in formal tuxedo, approached the table with two outrageous flaming cocktails on a tray. 'These are for Matt and Johnny courtesy of Mr. Big.' Matt and Johnny both appeared perplexed, no doubt scouring the room for a member of the local Glaswegian mafia. But I spotted them first at the far end of the bar; two grown men resembling large poodles in leather pants. I had to explain to Matt and Johnny that they were from an American hair metal band called Mr. Big. Apparently they were fans. God bless 'em.

"The following night we took a fleet of cabs to Barrowlands. The excitement was palpable. It was a sold-out show, and those in attendance had no idea Johnny was there. The room was set to explode. And I was overjoyed. Johnny was, and is one of my favourite guitarists. He joined us for about six or seven songs. I learned so much in that short span, and it's informed my style as a guitarist to this day. Here I was with this massive guitar rig, and Johnny shows up with a Fender Deluxe and a suitcase full of vintage effect pedals. A thumb pick and his bare fingers was all he needed, his signature sound sparkling effortlessly from the lone 12-inch speaker."

The tour returned to England for several dates, and one in Wales, before ending on December 20th at the Plymouth Pavilions. All that was left was end-of-tour japes, provided by Joyner and repaid in full by Collard. "I thought DC Collard would enjoy being pelted by large green grapes during his piano solo in 'This Is The Night'. He took the incoming fire admirably, never missing a note as the fruit gathered on his keys and rebounded off his forehead. Because his solo occurred before mine and he had to play throughout, I thought I was safe. Of course, I was wrong. When my moment arrived, he simply stopped playing and appeared behind me, proceeding to dry hump me for the duration of the solo, which was a complete mess."

The tour ended on December 20 as England was being dusted with snow, except for the south where it was just cold, wet and windy. This was the meteorological equivalent of the England Matt Johnson had described in despairing terms to various journalists while he had been away: the cynical, pessimistic, tight-lipped England that, though now rid of Margaret Thatcher, still lived under the yoke of Tory rule – a political party who had made great play of family values yet seemed to lurch from one sexual scandal to another, while worse ones festered underneath the surface, grim rumours, waiting to emerge in later decades. Fed up with the politics, with the music press and now at the end of his relationship with Fiona Skinner, it was obvious that things were going to come to a head. He and Skinner spent Christmas together but whatever festive spirit was present wasn't particularly healing and it didn't help that they went away together in the New Year, something Johnson now regrets. "We actually went to Telluride in Colorado with Geiger, Rennie and their wives and a few other couples for a skiing holiday in January. We'd already booked and paid and so, as we were still friends, we thought we may as well go. It was hard on Fiona though and perhaps we should have cancelled."

17

NEW YORK

TALKING TO JOURNALIST MARK SUTHERLAND ON THE EVE of the Jingle Hell tour, Johnson said he was looking forward to the shows but not to being back in the country. "I don't like Britain any more to be honest." He felt his career in his homeland was more or less over and that he "probably should have left after *Infected*". Home no longer felt like home. He was an outsider, an uncomfortable reminder of how he felt growing up in Ongar and Loughton. Having spent a lot of time in America, having had a calling for the country ever since he visited as a child, his next move was perhaps inevitable. All that remained was to tidy up loose ends.

The *Dis-Infected* EP was released at the turn of the year. The A-side included two versions of older The The tracks re-recorded at the War Room studios by the band who had toured *Dusk*. Renamed 'That Was The Day' and 'Dis-Infected', the two tracks were fairly faithful recreations of the live versions the band had performed on tour. The B-side was given over to two remixes, 'Helpline Operator' and 'Dogs Of Lust', the latter done by Jim Thirlwell, the former, a more radical reworking of the original, done by Bruce Lampcov and Johnson. The four tracks were included on an American CD-only release called *Solitude*, which also contained the tracks that had appeared on the *Shades Of Blue* EP. It seemed an odd decision to tread water in this way, though both the reworked songs of the A-side have their fans, with many rating 'Dis-Infected' much higher than its original incarnation. The single was one of Johnson's biggest sellers and saw his second performance on *Top of the Pops*. But revisiting his past was a way of closing the door on a chapter in his life, consciously or otherwise, and the video for 'That Was The Day', made by Fiona Skinner, was literally the end of one chapter in his life. "I filmed him and Dave Collard at Alcatraz prison. And that was the day we split. There's a picture someone took of us hugging and we decided we wouldn't tell anyone, nobody else would know, it was just our private break-up. I put together a collage of images and memories from Matt's childhood and our years together including Super 8 footage of our times in Mallorca and our last days as a couple in San Francisco – combined with live footage from Reading Festival that summer." The song and video thus became mutual farewell gestures.

If some fans were left wondering why he had chosen to release a single without any new songs then Johnson's next move would perplex them even more. Though the reasons for his eventual relocation to America were many, the chance to tap into the roots of modern popular music was one of them. After *Mind Bomb* he made a conscious decision to simplify his own writing style and once again he looked to singer-songwriters from the past for inspiration. He had been referencing blues singers like Howlin' Wolf and John Lee Hooker since the days of *Infected*, but now the two names that kept recurring were bluesman Robert Johnson and country singer Hank Williams. Johnson's original intention, as mentioned in several interviews when promoting and touring *Dusk*, was to record songs by both for a pair of EPs, but when it came to the prolific back catalogue of Williams he found it impossible to limit himself to four or five songs, and the decision was made to extend his ambition to an LP. The news was broken to fans first, via the second instalment of a newsletter to subscribers of a The The mailing list. The songs he chose did, he admitted to *Musician* magazine, veer towards "the darker side of Hank", which was perhaps an admission of how he was feeling when listening. He was also, no doubt, attracted to Williams' outsider status, having always felt a bit of an outsider himself, something that had been reinforced by the reaction of the music press towards his music and ideas.

Having narrowed down a list of possible tracks, he decamped to his villa in the Tramuntana mountains in Mallorca with Dave Collard. "I think he mentioned the idea to me on the *Dusk* tour in 1993. I was initially surprised but at the same time it made sense to me; after all, Matt at heart is a songwriter and Hank Williams is one of the best ever. We got together at his place in Spain and essentially rearranged/rewrote a selection of Hank's songs." After a few weeks in the sun working on the songs, Matt invited American guitarist Eric Schermerhorn over to join them; as Collard recalls, he was barely off the plane before he was coerced into a weary trek for some food. "On his first day, Matt and I tortured him, making him hike hills for miles and miles to get lunch immediately after he'd flown in from the USA. He was a trooper!"

Schermerhorn's gig prior to answering Johnson's call had been two years working with Iggy Pop, and prior to that he had worked for Tin Machine-era Bowie. The man had pedigree. "He called me in '93 or '94, to go to his studio in London. It was through friends that I met him; Michael Houseman, who knows Bruce Lampcov. We met and he said, 'Let's do *Hanky Panky*.' He said it was going to be all Hank Williams covers. I went to London, and I met the drummer, Brian McLeod, there and bassist, Gail Anne Dorsey. So we all went to his studio and at first it was daunting, but then I realised it was not going to be us trying to do country music." Schermerhorn liked the idea but had two initial reservations. The first was that he was still, technically at least, working for Iggy Pop. However, Iggy hadn't paid him a retainer and so the prospect of another musical venture was now slightly more appealing, particularly another one where he would continue to have creative input in terms of writing, which Johnson assured him he would. The second reservation was Hank Williams. As Schermerhorn succinctly puts it, "Whoah, that's sacred ground man..."

And then there was the chance to sample island life. "The other great thing is, we would go to Spain, his place in Mallorca; we'd fly there and we'd work in his little Spanish house in the hills, and I would be like, this is great... this is back when record labels would do that. 'Oh, you wanna rehearse in Spain? Sure.' Those days are over." So he left Iggy and agreed to help an Englishman cover an American icon. This would include all that hiking up hill after hill in searing Mediterranean heat in search of lunch directly after a long-haul flight. As introductions to a place go, it was arduous, but less surprising than when he first turned up at Johnson's Shoreditch flat at two in the morning. "He had said, 'Just come in the front door,' and it was like, two in the morning, so I knocked – nothing. I walk in, all the lights are off, and he's dressed as an Arab sitting in a chair with a gun, and he points the gun at me... and then he starts laughing." But having worked with plenty of Englishmen, from David Bowie to Richard Butler, and growing up where he did in Massachusetts, where taking the piss had been a sign of affection, nothing was going to faze him. He got Johnson's humour, and if this guy was crazy enough to tackle the back catalogue of a musical giant like Hank Williams then, hell, why not?

After the pleasures of working on tracks in the hills of Mallorca, the three returned to The War Room to start work on the recording of the chosen tracks. Johnson had recently started using Pro Tools, now an industry standard, but then a new piece of recording and arranging software that had a work flow in tune with the traditional hardware studio set-up. Like the Fairlight, Pro Tools allowed the user to do things in a fraction of the time. Instead of having to set up physical gear and manipulate physical tape, everything could be done with a few clicks of the mouse. And undone. As many times as you needed. There were no cost considerations, with the only real limitation being the processing power of the computer being used. Eric Schermerhorn watched with interest what Johnson and

Bruce Lampcov were doing with the new technology. "The first track on *Hanky Panky* is me playing Dobro. He cuts it up and does all these edits and it's like, this guy is still forward thinking... it was before Radiohead: Matt was ahead of the game, he was doing the digital Pro Tools early, doing these edits. So I would play stuff and he would loop it and mess with it. So the *Hanky Panky* thing was great because this is where I realised: 'This guy is a visionary, he's gonna take this stuff we did and mess with it,' and that was when I thought, 'I want to work with him more.'"

At this time Johnson was essentially managing himself, with Fran Muso, the wife of Steve Rennie, as caretaker manager for *Hanky Panky*. Roger Cramer would soon be administering things Stateside, and Johnson appointed Mitch Schneider to look after media for the album. A new figure would also enter Johnson's orbit at this time, one who was to play an important role over the next decade and more: Martin Callomon, aka Cally, who was working at Island Records as creative director. "Alex Sartore sat in the same office working for the Mango label and we become great friends. Alex took me to dinner one evening to meet Matt, as she thought I ought to art direct the Hank Williams project. I had just finished designing Chet Flippo's book on Hank and so was well versed in Hank's music. Williams was as unfashionable then as Patsy Cline was. Soon I was putting together the *Hanky Panky* visuals and ran slap bang into the 'Sony Way Of Doing Things', which were not really mine."

Johnson explained his approach to the songs when he was interviewed by Barry Stelboum for *The Island Ear*. "We initially put the songs down in the same tempo, structure and key as Hank. I would sing them exactly as Hank sang them. Then, I decided to change the key to suit me, and I changed the way I sang them. Most of the vocal melodies I kept the same, but I changed the music around so it changed the atmosphere of the song." More revealing was when he told Stelboum what had drawn him to Williams, seemingly identifying in him some kind of kindred spirit. "In reading these biographies about him, I grew closer and closer to him. What comes across about him is that even those that were very close to him didn't know him at all. He was very charming, a kind of good old boy, but in reality he was quite a loner. He was most intimate with his own songwriting; that's when he expressed himself and felt happiest. I could really understand that as a songwriter as well – that closeness you feel to your own work and you feel slightly alienated from others." Many observers were perplexed by his decision to release an album of covers but what he told Stelboum went some way to explaining his reasons. To an online question and answer session on AOL he added another. When asked directly by a fan if he was working with the words of another artist while he thought of a new direction in which to take himself, he replied, "I've had a certain amount of flack for doing a cover album but what people don't realise is that as a singer it is pleasurable and liberating just to sing someone else's words."

Two decades later he would talk to Michael Bonner of *Uncut* magazine about what had motivated him to steer his career off on such a seemingly oblique tangent. "Because I was taking so long writing, I thought, 'You know what, I just want to enjoy being a singer.' I don't think I even played any instruments on that album. It was almost like a vacation in terms of my songwriting. *Dusk* was a hard record to write, given the subject matter, but I wanted to keep working. There were a lot of raised eyebrows at the label, but at that point I think they were used to my behaviour. But they did get behind this record. It got fantastic reviews in America. Hank's daughter wrote me a lovely letter saying, 'My daddy would be proud with what you've done with his songs.' So it was an interesting project." Though Johnson, looking back, feels that Sony got behind the record, it is obvious that things at the label were changing and a new mindset was in place. David Gottlieb feels that there was a difference at this point between the Sony offices in the UK and the USA. "My recollection was Sony in the US being very into it, but I didn't get the feeling the UK company necessarily had the same enthusiasm. I think by 1995 both the label and the market in the UK had moved on from The The as a commercial enterprise and weren't sure what to do with *Hanky Panky*. I mean that was the time of the Britpop Blur–Oasis wars, so where would an artist whose best success had been a decade prior fit in, when they were doing covers of a long dead country & western superstar?"

In actual fact *Hanky Panky* might have been a completely different proposition had Steve Rennie not put his foot in it. Johnson outlines the story. "We were playing a warm-up gig at the 40 Watt Club in Athens, Georgia, and Michael Stipe came down to meet me. We spoke about possibly doing something together. I mentioned the Hank Williams project I was considering next. At that stage I was intending to only sing on one track and feature other singers across the album. Leonard Cohen had agreed and Marianne Faithfull – through my PR Rob Partridge – had also agreed. I was also about to make contact with Ute Lemper and k.d. lang. I thought Michael Stipe would fit well into this line-up, he seemed interested and I promised to update him on project developments. I always like to keep a very low profile on projects until they are completed and ready for release. And I would never mention the names of people I am intending to work with until everyone is comfortable. But completely behind my back Rennie wrote up and sent out a press statement that Michael Stipe, Leonard Cohen and Marianne Faithfull would be appearing on the next The The album. I was incandescent. I scrapped that idea for the album and decided to sing it all myself."

Though it can be seen as Johnson's own *Pin Ups* – and like Bowie's covers album it is equally air-brushed out of critical memory – it does make sonic sense when compared to *Dusk*. He might not have written the songs but he made them his own, and with Bruce Lampcov engineering and a continuing desire to return to classic songwriting and arranging, the two albums become siblings of a kind. Though the band – minus Gail Anne Dorsey, who was poached by David Bowie – promoted the album with a string of live television appearances in Europe and the USA, they didn't play any concerts together. Critics were somewhat nonplussed by the album upon its release, perhaps taken by surprise at a The The long-player appearing hot on the heels of the last one. Fans too gave it a lukewarm reception. Though Johnson made the material sonically his own – the sound was very identifiable as The The – it suffered the fate of the vast majority of covers albums that get released: a shrug of collective indifference. Do a good enough interpretation of an individual song and you can make it your own, but a whole album will always be a test of how willing a fan base is to dip into their wallets. One person who was impressed was Williams' biographer Colin Escott, who hailed the work as some of the finest cover recordings of Hank's classics. In America it was also voted one of the finest country records of the year. It did reach number twenty-eight in the UK album charts the week of release on February 25, 1995, but didn't linger. In all, Johnson spent three months on the pre-production and recording of the album. He also found time to play guitar on two tracks on the *Herd Of Instinct* album by 'O' Rang, a new project for Paul Webb and ex-Talk Talk band mate Lee Harris. But he wouldn't record any more music in England for well over a decade.

In one way *Hanky Panky* was an itch that Johnson needed to scratch. Flitting between London and New York while he was working on the album was part of the process that convinced him to scratch that other itch of his and move across the Atlantic Ocean to the place where popular music had been born. With his relationship over, there was nothing really to stop him fulfilling a dream that had seeded itself back in that bicentennial year when the Johnson family had toured around the Big Country in the hulking, overgrown camper van that had stressed Eddie so.

Though he had made his mind up, it probably helped that Dave Collard had already made the move and that he now had another good working foil in Eric Schermerhorn, who already resided in the Big Apple, having moved there a few years before. This next chapter of The The would thus start in America. He left his flat behind but, in what was to prove an astute move, did not sell it, choosing instead to rent it out, generating some income from this and The Garden studio, which he left in the hands of the team at Miloco Studios, who would run it as a commercial business. Nick Young remembers meeting Johnson in Hoxton and securing a handshake deal whereby Miloco would try and fill the studio while he was in New York and they would split the profit. Nick was part of a team that also included Pete Hofmann, Finnbar Eiles, Mark Allaway and Graeme Allen. When they took over they couldn't get a sound out of the mixing desk for four days; it turned out that when Tim Pope had shot the 'Dogs Of Lust' video all the chips in the desk had been blown. Cally would continue to work with Johnson, but would do so from England. It was Cally who had designed the fetching *Hanky Panky* belt buckle, displaying an artistic outlook that Sony appreciated but didn't fully understand.

Meanwhile – as the song goes – back in the States, Johnson was busy with promotion for what was to be the only single off the album, 'I Saw The Light', and in typical fashion had landed upon an idea for a video that would prove as challenging to complete as any he had done. In 1929, pioneering photojournalist Margaret Bourke-White had taken a series of photographs from the top of the newly completed Chrysler Building in New York, including what would become famous images of the silver gargoyles sprouting from the top of the skyscraper. Johnson, a keen observer of American popular culture, had become fascinated by these images and decided to emulate Bourke-White. Also in his mind was the final scene in Stanley Kubrick's *Dr. Strangelove* where the character played by Slim Pickens sits astride an atomic bomb, waving a cowboy hat, as it descends to earth. The image was seared into Johnson's mind after he first saw it as a youngster, and he felt it summed up America. Working on a video-script with Sam Bayer, he wanted to find a way of getting out onto those gargoyles, but soon encountered a problem. Insurance issues with the production company meant that there was no way he would be venturing onto as precarious a vantage point as a silver eagle protruding from three-quarters of the way up a skyscraper rising some 319 metres above the pavement below. For that they would need a stuntman. Meanwhile, a replica of one of the eagles was placed on the flat roof of a neighbouring skyscraper so Johnson could be filmed atop this with an authentic skyline behind him that included the Empire State Building. The shots that appear in the video are a mix of those done from the roof of the neighbouring skyscraper of Johnson and the rest of the band, and ones of the stunt-double that were filmed from a circling helicopter, as Johnson explained a few years later:

"We'd hired this Vietnam vet to circle closely round the spire of the Chrysler Building in his helicopter, and the tricky thing was that the Chrysler Building's management didn't know what we were really doing – we'd pretended we were just filming for an advert and we just wanted to film the view from the windows. And the security guard – I think it was the day of the Super Bowl or something – he just sat there chomping on his pretzels with his little outfit on and his feet on the desk watching the game on his portable telly… and he went, 'Yeah sure, go ahead,' and waved us past." The Vietnam vet was one of only a handful of helicopter pilots in New York who was licensed to fly close to buildings, and this is what he was now doing as Johnson and the others made it out onto the roof. "I'd actually sneaked out onto the edge of a gargoyle myself and nearly went over the edge, it was so cold and slippery. So in walks this stunt guy, dressed up in all my clothes, and he looked completely grey, ashen grey. Looking completely terrified. Like he really didn't want to do it, and I said to him, 'What's up, are you okay?' and he said, 'Well, actually I'm really nervous about this shoot.' I said, 'Yeah? But you must have done tons of things like this. You're a stuntman, you do this all the time?' And he goes, 'Yeah, but my speciality is fires… not heights!'"

Sony launched the album with a promo CD release in a branded wooden box containing the album itself as well as a CD EP single of 'I Saw The Light' and three other Hank Williams songs that hadn't made the cut for the long-player and were subsequently recorded in New York by Johnson and Schermerhorn. But neither the album nor the single sold well, something Sony may have been fearing, even expecting, so the label stopped promoting it. The music industry was at the beginning of a period of huge change, reflecting the increasingly corporatised world beyond the confines of the music business itself. Though Johnson may not have been conscious of it, the pressure would soon be on to deliver hits, something with which he had only had intermittent success previously. His bargaining position as a musical auteur had, in the rapidly moving world of pop, become weakened. Styles change as trends come and go. In Britain, the constant search for the next big thing meant that maintaining a successful career without the constant routine of tour-album-tour was incredibly difficult, as young blood came through and made established artists suddenly look old. Moving to America hadn't just been to escape what he saw as the cynicism of his own country but also to embrace what he felt would be the freedom and can-do attitude of another. It was in the main, however, a matter of the heart.

In Britain, after he was gone, a period of escapism would abound, with young bands singing like it was the sixties all over again. The Tories had been defeated and the impressionable, the gullible, and those merely happy not to think too hard about anything could celebrate as if change had finally come, when all that had come was a shape-shifter called Tony Blair. Johnson, who was by now consuming the writings of Chomsky, Howard Zinn and others casting a sharp critical eye on the continuing neoliberalisation of the West, would have choked on his own bile in such an illusory world, and so, ironically, being across the Atlantic in the belly of the beast would prove to be much more palatable. He would soon be frequenting underground bookstores, going on marches, and attending political events and lectures. Though he would find many of his Democrat friends often ignorant of what was being done in their name by their own government, he had an ally in Jared Nickerson, who on one occasion managed to secure tickets for the two of them to a lecture by Noam Chomsky at NYU. He would write some political articles himself, critical of NAFTA and the Telecommunications Act of 1996. In short he would find himself in his element. As Eric Schermerhorn sees it, "I think coming to America was like a re-tooling, like a rebirth."

As well as living in a new country, Johnson would be living with a new person. Johanna St Michaels was a model and actress, originally from Sweden, who had moved to America at the age of 15, on a sports scholarship. They first met in 1993 when St Michaels was living in LA. "It was an afternoon pool party in the Hollywood Hills. My friend Jane Sobo had invited me. She said the party was held for this cool English band that I never heard of. I happened to be seated next to Matt. He was very talkative, witty and quite mischievous. He contacted my friend later and invited me to his next concert a few months later. I went to the concert. I was blown away by his political lyrics and how emotional and sincere some of the songs were, especially 'Love Is Stronger Than Death'. I met Matt backstage afterwards, and he got me to promise that I would take him riding the next time he came to LA, so I did. We rented two horses at Sunset Ranch in Griffith Park." The ride was more com than rom with Johnson on a beginner horse called Elvis who ran off with the hapless singer on his back, and tried to remove him by rubbing him against a tree. "It was actually very funny. I think that broke the ice. We started to write faxes to each other. He loved to discuss politics and he had a great ironic humour. I had been living back in the States for six years then and I was starved of intellectual stimuli. We shared a lot of the same interests such as politics, art, photography and we were both adventurous. Neither of us wanted to live a regular life at the time."

The couple became an item, at the Chateau Marmont hotel, where Johnson would always stay whenever in LA, liking its then-faded glamour and whiff of old Hollywood. This time he avoided horses. "I rented a bashed-up old 1966 dark green Mustang convertible that I'd park in the Chateau's underground car park. We'd go off driving around the city at day, exploring museums, visiting the Griffith Park Observatory, whilst late at night we'd be swimming in the empty hotel pool and drinking champagne. Life felt very sweet indeed and I was happier than I'd been in years. The prospect of returning to grey, drizzling, negative Britain to live filled me with dread so it was obvious to me I would soon have to leave."

One lazy afternoon when Johnson was at the hotel, he was booked in for a series of telephone interviews and, rather than be stuck in his suite, decided to do them by the pool. Mobile phones not then being commonplace, he utilised the poolside telephone. "There was just an older guy and me by the pool that day. The phone rang and the older guy leapt up and quickly scuttled across poolside to grab it before I could move a muscle. 'Telephone call for Mr Matt Johnson,' he said in a mildly irritated tone. This happened about five times across the next two hours. Each time he'd leap up before I could move a muscle but each time it was for me. He gave me increasingly dirty looks as he begrudgingly handed over the phone. By the time the phone rang for a sixth time he remained slumped in his chair with a resigned look on his face as I got to it before him. 'Telephone call for Mr Helmut Newton.'"

Living in England meant that his new relationship necessitated transatlantic dating. They would meet in Stockholm, New York, LA and London. On one occasion they spent time in Mexico, visiting the Teotihuacan Pyramids and an artistic colony in the town of San Miguel de Allende. It even crossed their minds to relocate there, but in reality there was only one logical choice.

"I moved to New York simply because Johanna and I had fallen in love. She was in Los Angeles, I was in London and, after meeting up in various cities around the world, we decided to meet in the middle, as we also both loved New York. The fact that I'd visited the city at least twice per year since I was 20 years old also made it a completely natural move for me as I already had a lot of friends there and knew the city inside out. I'd simply grown bored in Britain, the weather got on my nerves, the political climate was depressing and the country was just starting to feel too provincial and claustrophobic. What better reason to escape than falling in love? But I would also realise later on that I was also trying to escape from the grief I still felt from the loss of Eugene."

St Michaels had grown up in a very left-wing family – her mother had even sent her to communist summer camps in Eastern Europe – so her un-American mindset didn't sit well with her environment. "It was all about which car you were driving and how you dressed, or how you looked, or who you were with, how much money you made, and it was so boring. I hated LA really." The chance, therefore, to move to New York and be with someone of like mind was very welcome. Johnson's relationship with Skinner was over and St Michaels had also separated from her husband, so the pair were free to start a new life together in an apartment at 395 Broadway, just below Canal Street, above a large five and dime store. From here, depending on their mood, they could walk a very short distance to either Little Italy, Chinatown, SoHo, Tribeca or City Hall. And so began the life irregular.

* * *

It was a pleasant surprise for Dave Collard to find out that Matt Johnson had decided to join him on the other side of the pond. Collard being only a couple of hours from New York, it wasn't long before they were back in the studio. "We did a few days of sessions in New York in the mid-nineties – I believe that was for *Gun Sluts*. It was very experimental. I spent most of the time on an old Moog, plus some Hammond work. The owners at the time were ex-porn directors and quite proud of it as I recall. I also got to play a Theremin. I'm not sure if Matt ever used those sessions on anything." The sessions, which contrary to Collard's memory actually lasted a few weeks, took place at Sear Sound, on West 48th Street, in 1995. Eric Schermerhorn remembers the early sessions. "We started working at Sear Sound, and it was still with the keyboard player, Dave. It was a kind of transition. And then I remember Matt coming to me and saying, 'I wanna do a record with you, Earl on drums,' and this guy Spencer, so it was kind of like a transition from the *Hanky Panky* guys and going to a four-piece, and that's where it happened, New York. He didn't want to do keyboards, he wanted to do more guitar-based stuff, for *Naked Self*. And then he moved to Tribeca, and I was living in the East Village and we would see each other every day. We hung out every day, he was like a brother. We wrote songs every day. I would go round to his house and show him stuff I'd been working on, he would sing, we would go and have a drink." By the time Collard was out of the picture Johnson was living only a ten-minute walk from Harold Dessau studios, on Murray Street, and it was here that they moved to in 1996, as Johnson recalls. "There was a lengthy and clear gap between the Sear and Dessau sessions. I had been quite unprepared going into Sear Sound, which was out of character with me really, and though I absolutely loved that studio we were just wildly experimenting and not really achieving many usable results."

It was the middle of the decade, and Schermerhorn was about to find out just how long-winded Johnson's working methods could be.

Back in England, Cally was being kept up to date with the progress of the pair's efforts. "Matt posted me cassettes of endless sessions he had conducted in a grubby white-tile-lined New York studio called Dessau. There followed email after fax: me enthusing as to how passage A could fuse with passage C, how there were whole songs struggling to get out and all that was needed were the lyrics." By this stage it was clear to Johnson that there was enough material for more than one album, but the first project that began to take shape was *Gun Sluts*. This was very experimental, without lyrics – which was perhaps due to his own struggle to write them – a struggle he had conveniently avoided with *Hanky Panky* – and contained tracks that in some cases stretched to sixteen minutes. This was most likely the stuff that Cally was getting on cassettes. It wasn't what Sony were expecting. Talking to Jonathan Bond of the *Phoenix New Times* a few years later, Johnson revealed the reaction. "We made this really unstructured, aggressive recording, a really great album. Sony sent some people over there to listen to it and they were horrified. They were like, 'Either change this or we can't

use it.' So I shelved the album and started work on *Naked Self*."
More recently he told Michael Bonner of *Uncut*: "They hated *Gun
Sluts*, it was my version of *Metal Machine Music*. I wasn't doing it to
break the contract. It's just where I was at the time, going in some
interesting new directions, listening to experimental music."

Only two tracks have seen the light of day. 'Diesel Breeze'
would find its way onto *Naked Self*, while the track 'Gun Sluts' was
produced as a one-sided CD single and sold on the *Naked* world
tour in 2000. A further track, 'Psychic Sauna', was included in a
Radio Cineola broadcast in 2010. The rest has become as mythical
with The The fans as *The Pornography Of Despair*, though one
imagines it is much more polished and fully realised. The work
remains in Johnson's vaults. Even Eric Schermerhorn isn't sure if
he has heard all of the finished tracks, though he is more certain
about their quality. "We did a ton of tracks at Dessau. He said to
me, we've got so much stuff we're going to do two albums. Same
people; Earl on drums… it's cool stuff, it's really gritty, it's great.
The stuff I've heard. The stuff he sent me." Several years later
Johnson would re-record some of the *Gun Sluts* material. "The new
recordings were actually a lot stronger than the original versions
from Sear Sound as I honed them down a bit and created some
structure to them, but they were still too experimental for a record
label to be interested, so I decided to put the project to one side."

With Sony rejecting *Gun Sluts* outright, the pair continued to
work at Dessau but it was obvious that without any lyrics the songs
would suffer the same fate. Johnson's tendency to stretch things
out when working on a project was now becoming very apparent
to Schermerhorn, and New York was awash with distractions,
such as an area they dubbed the 'Triangle of Filth', where old-
school strip clubs such as the Harmony Lounge, Baby Doll and
Blue Angel Cabaret were located. "It would be like, 'Oh let's work
for a while,' and then, 'Oh, let's go down and get a drink.' He did
have a work ethic but he would sometimes do everything to avoid
writing lyrics, and I would be, 'Come on, let's get to work.' I was
used to Iggy. Iggy would come, work, drink a beer then go. With

Matt, it was open-ended. I would be like, 'Hey Matt, what's going on?' and he would be, 'Oh, I don't know. Let's go down to the Triangle of Filth.' That was these three burlesque clubs. It was like Berlin in the thirties."

Johnson begs to differ. "*He* was the one who introduced *me* to the Harmony Lounge! In fact, on at least six occasions – when he was very late for recording sessions at Dessau – I had to go down to the 'Triangle' to retrieve him from 'the Lounge'. 'Triangle of Filth' was the name he and I gave to this little area due to there being three burlesque clubs in close proximity. These were nothing like the awful sort of 'bling' lap-dancing clubs for rich businessmen you see nowadays. These were seedy, dark and old school and the sort of place you were more likely to find Charles Bukowski propped up against the bar than see a Wall Street trader. The favourite was the Harmony Lounge on Church Street. Eric would talk breathlessly to me, Earl and Spencer about this place. It was like being trapped inside a David Lynch movie; open all day and night, unfathomably dark and hot and playing amazing music. It was owned and run by female lap dancers who refused to serve alcohol in order to keep drunken frat boys and Wall Street traders away. Eventually, I did become quite concerned as Eric repeatedly went missing during recording sessions. Luckily, I always knew exactly where to find him. I'd go down to the 'Triangle' and forcibly drag him out of the Lounge and all the way back to Dessau." And when the vibe in New York didn't feel right, Johnson would suggest a change of scene. "One time he said, 'We've got to go to Spain for two weeks.' He definitely wanted to create an environment. 'We gotta go to Majorca.' And I was, 'All right,' cos it's beautiful there and we would sit and play guitar, it was great. And drinking. He was drinking a lot."

To be fair, Johnson was taking a fairly holistic approach to life, so while on the one hand he would often be found in the Ear Inn at 5 a.m., drinking with Roli Mosimann, Jim Thirlwell and other friends and assorted locals, he would also find time to attend yoga classes with Johanna. They would also go jogging (St Michaels had represented Sweden at junior level at middle-distance running) round the pathways by the Hudson River and cycling in Central Park. He continued to meditate and it was whilst in New York that he discovered the writings of Buddhist philosopher, Alan Watts, the Indian Guru of nondualism, Sri Nisargadatta Maharaj, Noam Chomsky and theosophist writer and thinker Paul Brunton. and theosophist writer and thinker Paul Brunton.

Mostly he was enjoying New York, and it being the city it was, there was a lot to enjoy. He hooked up with Jo Murray, who had quit her job at CBS and moved to the city a decade earlier. She remembers visiting his loft apartment. "I remember it being a nice, spacious place, with a lot of nice old furniture and Matt's trusty antique typewriter. At that time, the area was still pretty interesting. Lots of nice old bars and we would sometimes meet at Walkers on North Moore Street, or the Liquor Store bar on West Broadway, and we did go to the Blue Angel, a gentleman's club, on one or two occasions for the fun of it! Tribeca still seemed to be quite desolate at night in the nineties, which made it a nice neighbourhood to live in at that time, but there were some fancy restaurants which drew the crowds. Places like Odeon, Teddy's, and De Niro's restaurants." They would sometimes go to Café La Fortuna at 69 West 71st Street, the coffee bar that John Lennon used to frequent, near the Dakota building. Lennon was, of course, Johnson's hero and he took to heart Lennon's quote about America being the Roman Empire and New York being Rome. This was, as he said to Schermerhorn, living in the belly of the beast. He talked about Lennon enough for Schermerhorn to gently remind him that his hero lost his life in the belly of the beast, but if the conversation got too deep there was always light relief in the Triangle, or another drink in the Ear Inn, or the Mars Bar, Max Fish or Cedar Tavern. Or some live music at the Knitting Factory or the Mercury Lounge, where he would later perform himself. Sometimes it was just enough to walk around and take in all the things that he had seen in films, like steam rising out of vents in the road, getting the same thrill at witnessing these sights as Schermerhorn would when visiting England and finding out that red telephone boxes really did exist. Schermerhorn was making money from doing session work, as well as spending time with Johnson. His sense of time was slightly different. "I had free time too, but he could get sidetracked really easily. Let's go get drinks, go to these clubs and hang out, and it was fun but at some point I could see what was coming – this record was going to take *forever*." But if distraction wasn't enough, next came responsibility.

In May 1997, Johanna St Michaels and Matt Johnson became parents when their son was born. They named him Jackson. Unlike Johnson's father, a measure of a generational shift, he was present at the birth of his son. "The day Jackson was born at St Vincent's hospital in Greenwich Village was one of the happiest days of my life. It was a long-drawn-out, painful labour and it was touch and go at times as the umbilical cord was wrapped around his leg so on the monitor we would hear his heart beat stopping and starting. It was awful. Labour was over twenty-four hours. But when he was finally born and I cut the umbilical cord it was such a massive relief and such a beautiful, unreal experience. I found it mind-blowing. I remember that morning – very early – I ran out to get some orange juice, coffee and bagels and it was one of those gorgeous blue-skied New York days and I felt as if I was walking on air, just like one of those cartoons you see about new dads."

Inevitably things changed. For St Michaels a big change was in terms of her career. "I got the main responsibility for Jackson so I could only do jobs in New York and not at night. Also I was 30 and I wanted to do something else, so I started to study photography. But it was a very happy period in our relationship when Jack was first born. Matt had a little room down in the financial district at Dessau studios. Jack and I went down there every lunch. Then we met up in the afternoons and when Jack was sleeping Matt and I played chess in City Hall Park." Eric Schermerhorn became a father at the same time and he and Johnson would team up when childminding duties arose. "We'd go to Washington Square Park, we'd got the kids in the stroller, six months old, and we'd play chess in the park. You can walk everywhere in downtown New York, so we would just walk, and I would always nudge him about the lyrics and he would be, 'Oh you don't understand…' He was his own torturer. He took forever. He's not lazy but…"

For Johnson, the problem was that the pair were working at different speeds. "It was a tricky one with Eric. He was a superb guitarist but I had also promised him some co-writing on the album. This was the first time I'd co-written so many tracks on an album and to be honest it was a bit awkward at times because writing the music is equally important as writing the words for me and I really prefer to work alone as I find the songwriting process deeply personal and meditative. But I was determined to honour my verbal agreement and so Eric was often over at my loft and bombarding me with dozens and dozens of his riffs and song ideas. It wasn't that they were bad ideas but many of them I didn't feel emotionally connected to."

So there was a lot of chess, and he and Schermerhorn would compare notes about this new parenting thing – the sleepless nights, the worrying about the future, paying for schools and all that business. And he still had this record to make and he still hadn't written any lyrics and it got to the point where the record label even contacted Johanna and asked if she could hurry him along.

Roger Cramer, then also managing Living Colour and Weezer, often found himself with little to do. "There was nothing going on. I remember going to meet him in his loft, it was kind of empty, and chatting with him, and he was playing me these huge instrumental tracks, and they were just so strong. I remember he had these little magnetic letters on a refrigerator or a board, and he said he used those letters to write lyrics. Mixing and matching these letters to make lyrics. I thought that was an interesting and unusual method. And Matt told me the tracks were all done and all he had to do was write the lyrics and the melodies, and I thought, 'Okay.' It sounded like an unusual process but that's what he was doing, and my memory is that a great length of time elapsed. There was nothing to do. I maybe helped him organise some recording sessions but he didn't really need that so much. Bruce Lampcov was producing and maybe I was in touch with Bruce, maybe I did Bruce's deal, probably worked on that with Matt's attorney." In fact Johnson was writing his lyrics on a Remington Rand Model One typewriter and using the magnetic letters to come up with song title ideas. But it was slow business. Tumbleweed kept blowing by.

In Harold Dessau, meanwhile, Johnson had built himself a new sonic arsenal based around vintage gear. Living in Chinatown meant he could root around in local stores, and he came across some old recording equipment. He told journalist Jonathan Kreinik how he ended up using it for the album. "Initially I just wanted to take some photographs of it for the sleeve, but I did some investigating of it. It was from some old radio station in, I believe, Shanghai the guy said. It was his father's equipment and he didn't want to sell it, but we took some of it down to the studio and I put a disclaimer on the sleeve because there's some of that distortion, but it gave everything this really interesting sound." The desire to return to old analogue gear was perhaps to counter Pro Tools. It was certainly a return to what he had grown up with at De Wolfe, a tacit acknowledgement that, as convenient as digital technology was, and as ripe with creative possibilities, when it came to the actual sound, nothing could beat the old ways. To retain as much of this analogue warmth as possible he decided to avoid diluting it with reverb, opting instead for the organic possibilities of tape echo. Judicious use of valve compression, particularly on vocals, was also a weapon of choice.

As well as looking for a new recorded sound, one a lot drier, he also made a radical departure from his existing sound-palette by opting to ditch keyboards, which in turn meant a new way of doing things when it came to writing the music. Schermerhorn, being a guitarist, now had a bigger part to play. "I was playing the baritone guitar, which is tuned for a lower pitch, for 'December Sunlight'. I remember saying to Matt, 'Check this guitar out.' Guitar became a big thing for him, baritone, twelve-string, we had all these different colours, and he got into that, using guitars the way he used to use keyboards. We had so many problems in the studio; the Pro Tools was the upgraded version, and it wouldn't talk to the computer and vice versa." The problems of working with new technology inevitably added to the delays. "There were days we couldn't do anything – there was a lot of wasted time."

For Johnson, the technical hitches were frustrating. "I remember one time Bruce was over and we spent weeks in 'down-time' whilst the team from Digidesign (then the owners of Pro Tools) pulled the system apart and tried to figure out why it kept crashing. The techno-boffins would be on the floor at my loft with pieces of my computer in their hands whilst Bruce would be horizontal in Johanna's and my bedroom, suffering one of his frequent blinding migraines. We had a powerful new computer, big hard drives, the latest software but the bastard thing just wouldn't work properly."

The delays were equally frustrating for Schermerhorn. "It was really productive at times, and sometimes it was a waste, we didn't do anything because Matt would be like, 'Oh, I don't feel like working today.' It was hard man. He has a work ethic but we could have done that record in six months and put it out. We started that in '96 and it didn't come out until 2000. All that stuff was down early on and it took forever because of Sony. It was definitely ahead of its time. Then when it came out the music business was in the dumper. It's just timing."

Naked Self began in earnest in 1997 when Johnson recruited two new band members. Drummer Earl Harvin was introduced via Marc Geiger. He had been working with MC 900 Ft Jesus, who were signed to American Recordings, where Geiger was doing A&R. "Earl is one of the best musicians I've ever played with," maintains Johnson. "Not only a drummer of the highest order but also extremely aware of everything the rest of the band are doing. He's also a very smart guy with a great sense of humour and has a very charismatic stage presence." To cover bass duties, Johnson brought in Spencer Campbell, who had been working for Kenny Rogers. He had already played in the *Hanky Panky* promotional band, after Gail Ann Dorsey left to join David Bowie. Campbell flew from Nashville for the recording sessions and he travelled light. "I brought two Fender basses. I recorded direct in a crappy little studio. Matt and Bruce had a huge bass tone, though I neither looked nor cared what they were using for that tone. Matt had the bass lines pretty much written. He knows what he wants, so the bass is always compositionally great for the song. I loved it. A killer tone. Great tracks. Fast, and off to NYC dinner. Just like we do it in Nashville."

The album opens with 'Boiling Point'. A long fade-in of a police siren, some skittering drums and reversed guitar makes way for a scuzzy, head-nodding drum beat, slow, heavy bass and heavily treated guitars, broody with menace, maybe even malice. It sounds like Johnson is revisiting *Burning Blue Soul*, only this time it is much darker. It's hard to tell whether it is the city that is reaching boiling point, or the narrator of the song, who is travelling on the New York subway. The mood is claustrophobic and full of dread. Halfway through, rather than let up, the sonic assault increases in its intensity. It's not unlikely that had *Gun Sluts* survived then it might have sounded as dark and twisted as this throughout. This kind of bleak soundtrack wasn't necessarily unusual in the nineties. Artists like Tricky, and Trent Reznor, in his Nine Inch Nails guise, had made it clear that beneath the glossy pop sheen of the decade, much darker undercurrents were flowing. Much of this music was possible because of new studio technology, particularly more powerful samplers, but Johnson was attempting the same soundscapes with only traditional rock instruments.

After this downbeat start comes 'Shrunken Man', which would be the only single from the album. Again the sounds are distorted, particularly the drums – overdriven and working that old valve equipment from China to the limit. It is a song of two parts – a melodic strummed guitar riff is twinned with a harsh guitar lead that, while it gives the song some energy, also threatens to overshadow the subtlety of what lies underneath. Despite the strummed guitar this is another downbeat track; the lyrics, speaking of feelings of vulnerability and numbness, are about a friend of Johnson's who was going through a torrid phase. The sound of sleigh bells at the end conjures up images of snowy New York at Christmas, but the overall feel is melancholic. Eric Schermerhorn hints at the working method behind this track. "I had the tube Echoplex tape machine at the beginning of 'Shrunken Man' and we did that at Dessau. That was just me and him, recording to Pro Tools at Dessau – tons of material to edit using the cut-up method." Schermerhorn, according to Johnson, is confusing two songs here. "'Shrunken Man' is just Eric on acoustic and me on electric. Eric is actually thinking of 'Boiling Point' here, which features tons of his beautiful Echoplex experimentations. We would sit for hours and jam on our guitars together down at Dessau and, with both of us also using looping pedals, I'd record it all into Pro Tools and then 'loop the loops'."

'The Whisperers' sounds more identifiably The The, with a lovely bit of simple, tightly strummed guitar and gentle drums. The production is so crisp you could snap it in half, compressed and up front; this would have been a better bet for a single. Johnson's vocal is confident, rising to falsetto without any effort. His voice has matured and this album sees it at its best. Earl Harvin does a great job here on drums, keeping it tight and simple with an extremely subtle touch. Again, the overall air is one of melancholy, the lyrics detailing loneliness and missed opportunity. Perhaps Johnson had watched the kitchen-sink drama of 1967 starring Edith Evans and taken not just the title but the downbeat atmosphere as well. The track was released in promo format for radio, though never released as a single.

'Soul Catcher' continues in much the same way, again with some gorgeous guitar work and Johnson's falsetto and harmonies accompanying his main vocal more prominent than in earlier songs. The mood now is more wistful, the lyrics reflecting, like many of the others, on a life lived, expressing regret in a self-punishing way. Johnson was now a father, and though he once said that it was impossible to write about the profound experience of the birth of one's own children, this song and lyric captures the mix of deep love and attendant fear that such a life change brings with it. In fact the song title came from regular Saturday morning trips with Jackson to the Museum of the American Indian, near Wall Street, where on one occasion they saw an exhibition of soul catchers.

Johnson had wanted *Naked Self* to be a political album as much as any of his others, and away from Britain and Thatcher's legacy he had been searching for new targets. Not surprisingly, living in the country that was the driving force of capitalism, his targets were globalisation and the kind of vapid consumerism that America championed, rather than American domestic concerns. He had written 'Global Eyes' in 1997 but by the time the album was released in 2000, the Seattle World Trade Organisation protests had brought global attention to an issue that has shaped our world and continues to do so. Naomi Klein's *No Logo* was published the same year as the Seattle protests and so, once more, Johnson was soundtracking paradigm-shifting events, and continuing to be inspirational for those who cared about, to borrow from Marvin Gaye, what was going on. Australian photographer Gerald Jenkins, who had been working on capturing the Aboriginal contribution to the opening ceremony for the Sydney Olympics in 2000, and was troubled by their continued exploitation, had been more or less forced into exile as a result of refusing to swallow the feel-good story that Australia was trying to promote about the Aboriginal place in Australian history and culture. He was listening to a lot of music with political comment and that included The The. "The Internet hadn't really taken off at that point, it was still very basic, and so I loved the lyrics to that song. I have always identified with his lyrics. His lyrics to me were Creole, like Gil Scott-Heron, like the man standing on the corner giving messages in rhyme; Matt was doing that."

The message was clear, and would be explored in detail in Joel Bakan's 2004 book *The Corporation*, which was made into a documentary film, with appearances from Chomsky, Naomi

Klein and Michael Moore, amongst others. Interviewed by John Fortunato, of *The Aquarian Weekly*, in 2000, Johnson explained his thinking behind the song. "I think we're facing a world of the corporation versus the individual. Corporations are becoming more powerful than entire nations." Saying that these unaccountable, and undemocratic, organisations should be broken up, particularly in light of advances in biotechnology, he sounded a dystopian science-fiction-like note, but two decades later those same corporations are even more powerful and just as unaccountable. The track includes Lloyd Cole amongst the backing singers. Cole was also using Dessau at this time and so the pair, over a cup of tea one morning, decided to contribute to each other's albums.

'December Sunlight' offers some welcome positivity lyrics-wise, from the female perspective at least, and the sound is upbeat to reflect the change in mood, with Schermerhorn playing the riff on his baritone guitar. For all Sony's demands for singles, one wonders if they failed to see the obvious potential for such here. The song would subsequently be reworked, with Liz Horsman accompanying Johnson on vocals. That version certainly had hit single written all over it but it would come too late, and though it appeared on the *45 RPM* compilation in 2002, was never released as an actual single. As well as missing out on single releases this was the first The The album not to appear on vinyl, the music industry having all but given up on the format by this time, vinyl being kept alive only by dance producers and DJs. As such there is no side one and side two, but we are halfway through now, so one can assume that the next two tracks belong on what would have been the flip side of a vinyl release. 'Swine Fever', an obvious comment on consumerism, is not Johnson's subtlest protest song, both lyrically or musically, being somewhat heavy-handed, though this was perhaps his take on the bombastic nature of advertising. In an interview with Dot Allison he commented on the corporate and consumerist nature of Western society, saying that it had got much worse than the 1980s. "You walk out the door and there's billboards bombarding you with commercials. Just to cut through people's numbness I suppose they've just got to keep notching it up a level. So it becomes incredibly aggressive and day-to-day life is utterly saturated with advertising. It's hard to get away from it." Though it is an angry song, strangely he doesn't inject any of this anger into his vocal performance, the guitars doing all that work for him – a simple riff that was apparently overdubbed fifty times to create its enormous sound. Underneath them we can hear some of the musical motifs of previous The The albums, and it is interesting to think how this song might have turned out had the no-keyboards rule been flouted.

'Diesel Breeze' follows and it is another heavy track, full of distortion and feedback that doesn't quite know what to do with itself. This is the only track from the *Gun Sluts* sessions that made it to the album, and is over almost before it has begun. The lyrics are a homage to Wire's 'The Other Window' from one of Johnson's favourite albums, *154*; the same lines appear at the end of both songs. Luckily it is followed by the most interesting track on *Naked Self*. 'Weather Belle' is the best evidence that this is an album that could only have been made in America. It isn't just the inspired use of banjo, but the overall feel, as the song sways drunkenly in fantastic fashion like rebel music from somewhere in the mountains, where defiance is interwoven with defeat. Lyrically it stays firmly in an urban setting, relating as it does the story of a couple who see each other in a bar. It is the first and last time they meet. Maybe this is autobiographical. The reference to drinking certainly suggests so, possibly explaining the lack of sobriety in the lurching rhythm. It reeks of a life where things happen and protagonists find it impossible to change the direction of their own fate, be this pouring another one, or being able to stop feeling as though they have a low locus of control. It is a song from someone who has taken life's blows; authentic blues music. Magnificent stuff.

Lyrically speaking, 'Voidy Numbness' continues with this theme, expressing as it does feelings of loneliness and seeking solution at the bottom of a bottle. Sonically, however, it has none of the subtleness of its predecessor. Perhaps the head-banging style is supposed to illustrate the anger of feeling that life has paralysed one's emotions, suggesting that some fight exists inside all the despair. The mood is changed once again with 'Phantom Walls' where we are back to reflection once more. Though it starts off rather downbeat and introspective, it soon opens up with more strummed guitar and the intimate vocal sound that both typify the production skills of Johnson and Lampcov. It is another great vocal performance and a return to the lyrical form of earlier albums, particularly *Dusk*, as it relates the acceptance of grief and the need to feel pain rather than avoid it. The song was written for his mother, who was seriously ill at the time, and serves as a loving tribute. It would have been a good place to finish the album but it is followed by 'Salt Water' and the mood is jarringly arrested. We are back in heavy guitar territory, with a sly and brief steal from the riff of The Beatles' 'Hey Bulldog' catching the ear. The rest of the song fails to grab attention. The lyrics, about addiction, are obscure and brief. It is a strange end to an ultimately uneven album.

As per usual, there were two sides to the recording process: the serious side that Johnson oversaw with his usual strict attention to detail, and the equally serious business of wind-ups, as Earl Harvin testifies to. "It's a wonder any recording got done. For example, at Dessau we would order food into the studio. Bruce Lampcov was really anal about keeping all the receipts; sometimes he would grab the receipt from the bag and pocket it before even looking at his food. So Matt would try and get the receipt out of the bag first while Bruce wasn't looking, just to watch him scramble through all the styrofoam cartons searching for it. One time Matt got it and Bruce chased after the delivery guy down the elevator and into the street for it, whilst we sat crying with laughter in the control room."

The attention to detail carried over into the artwork for the CD cover. Cally was called upon once more and applied his talents with the usual enthusiasm, as Roger Cramer notes. "He was part of the presentation of *Naked Self* and the packaging for that was brilliant. The music was beautiful, and the artwork and packaging was beautiful." Cally and Johnson had spent hours roaming New York and Hoboken, exploring subways and dodgy-looking alleyways armed with 35mm cameras. They reeled off shots, then swapped films so they could produce random double-exposures. Excited by the results, Cally flew back to England with the prints and negatives, where he was promptly mugged and badly beaten on the leafy streets of Chiswick. Quite what his attacker made of the photographs is anyone's guess but with him disappeared the original images for the CD booklet. Luckily, when the pair repeated the exercise back in New York, they were even happier with the outcome. The image they chose for the cover, of a naked light bulb in the ceiling, was a monochrome echo of the famous William Eggleston shot that appeared on Big Star's *Radio City* album. In its stark simplicity it was perfect for the album, visually and metaphorically.

It was finally done. After all the procrastination, the drinking breaks, the life changes, the daily soaking-up of what New York had to offer and the hassles with Sony over the early recordings, *Naked Self* was ready. And now the problems really began. Eric Schermerhorn, no doubt relieved that the album was finally finished, had mixed feelings. "There was a part of me that thought everyone is going to love this record, this is the shit, and then there was another part of me that thought this might go to the dustbin of history." At first it looked like this latter fear might be realised. No matter what the folk at Sony USA thought about things, the decisions were all made by Sony UK. They were invited over to New York to listen to the finished album and thought that it was still too aggressive, and that it lacked any identifiable singles. Roger Cramer describes the outcome: "I do remember Matt delivering the music to Rob Stringer. He had a good relationship with Rob, to my recollection, and Rob was a fan. It was like, 'I can't wait for the new The The album, too bad it's taking so long.' And then when he got the album I got a call from him and he said he couldn't release it, he didn't know what to do with it. I'm assuming he played it for his staff and they said, 'There's no singles here, what the hell?' And he'd spent a lot of money on it at that point and he could no longer support the project; it just wasn't commercial enough. If you think of the musical currents of the time, it was all about Backstreet Boys and NSYNC and all those insane sales figures that groups like that were enjoying. And my guess is they heard this music and they are thinking about how they are going to get it on Radio 1, and they thought, 'We can't do it,' and they called and said, 'We've got to drop him,' and I'm sure he said in so many words, 'Matt can have this record back, can take it somewhere else, but we can't release it.'"

Johnson, naturally, was angry. He felt that Sony had let him down, and in subsequent interviews bemoaned the fact that the label deemed his work not commercial enough to bother with. The fact of the matter was, however, that the industry had changed dramatically in all the time he had taken to deliver his record. For Dave Gottlieb, one of the key changes was the sheer volume of product on the market. "In 1991, there were 6,000 music titles released in the USA, across all labels, in one year. By the end of the decade that number was nearly 35,000 titles. So the marketplace was more crowded and the return needed to be quick." The days of labels allowing an artist to develop over a long period of time were disappearing, if not gone. The days of listeners returning to artists at the mature end of their career trajectory were in the future. Johnson was in a kind of historical no man's land. Grunge, hip-hop and R&B dominated the market now. Sony had more than once insisted that the album needed singles. Johnson consistently refused to budge. This battle had dragged on, the two sides at loggerheads. Eric Schermerhorn, though he was finding plenty of session work elsewhere to tide him over, was nevertheless frustrated by events. "I was like, 'Matt, just write a song, give them what they want. So we can get the thing out and we can tour. *Dusk* had great songs, give them one of those.' And he didn't want to. I wanted to keep it moving, we all wanted to go out on the road, and he didn't want to play ball with them, he was like, 'No, they want two more tracks.' I'm sure he looks back now and goes, 'Damn! I should have just done that.'"

Hindsight, of course, is a wonderful thing, but when the tectonic plates of change are in motion, existing ideologies find it hard to keep up with the pace. Johnson refused to budge on his principles. Sony meanwhile were only interested in the near future, in the market. The music industry, always conservative, was now at a point where risk was off the menu. Cramer, who concedes that the record suffered from having a lack of single material, thinks that the situation could have been resolved if Sony had taken what would have amounted to, in the grand scheme of things, just a little bit of a risk, and got behind the record. "Who would I fault? I would fault Rob Stringer for not sucking it up, dumping some more money into it and making it the best it could be. But he just turned around and bailed, said, 'Nah, can't do anything with this.'" What upset Johnson the most was that Sony sat on the delivered tapes for three months without comment. In the end he had to phone Rob Stringer at home, doing so very early one morning. A sheepish Stringer admitted that nobody had wanted the awkward task of telling Johnson that the label didn't want the album, that they liked and respected him too much to break the bad news. As excuses go it was pretty outrageous – equals parts compliment and insult, but mostly wasting three months when their artist could have been negotiating with someone else.

It was obvious that the relationship was over. There was only one way for Johnson to go, as he was later to concede. "It was a stalemate. So I just said, 'Look, if you don't like it then I really want to leave,' which of course I did, and in retrospect I don't know if it was the right move or not." By this point – on delivery of the album – Johnson had reached the end of his contract. Technically he was now a free man. It was time to renegotiate contracts, but he wasn't in the strongest of positions, as he concedes. "I was demanding a much better and more lucrative deal than the awful one I'd laboured under for the past eighteen years. But, after listening to *Naked Self* and hearing no 'hit singles' they just couldn't see the commercial potential or financial sense in re-signing me on a bigger and better deal. And they didn't want to release and promote an album with an artist who wasn't even on the label any more. I *would* have re-signed with Sony though as I liked the people there. I was just never happy with the poor royalties and advances. But I overplayed my hand when I should have been more modest in my demands, signed a short-term extension just to get them to release the damn thing and then left."

Sony's concern over singles was, on closer inspection, a curious argument, perhaps, and one that Johnson found hard to accept. "I had never really had hit singles in my entire career so why would I suddenly start having them now? It was absurd. I was always an album artist and I assured Rob that if Sony released it and gave it even modest support they would get their money back, plus it would be a nice long-term catalogue seller for the company like the rest of its siblings. But Rob was weak on this decision and fairly young in his job as Sony UK head honcho and so I think he wanted to prove to everyone he could make tough decisions. Ironically, *Naked Self* went on to have the best reviews I'd received for an album, so it was a critical success at least and Rob admitted to me a few years afterwards that he had made a mistake on this one and should have released it."

At the time, leaving seemed like the right move, maybe even the only move, but it was made much more viable by the fact that Sony were willing to hand over the master tapes of *Naked Self*, which in terms of how the record industry works amounted to a goodwill gesture. Roger Cramer was involved in the process. "We had a deal that we had to do to get the master back; they flew me to London to meet with Rob and the president. Rob was a consummate diplomat; he was basically smiling and apologising as the knife slid in. I was like, 'Yeah Rob, we understand,' but it just sucked for Matt. So they flew me to London and I laid out what we wanted, and we didn't get much. We got the master for *Naked Self* back. I wanted them to wipe out his un-recouped balance, and this and that, but it was stuff they were never going to agree to do." And so, that was the end of that. After over eighteen years signed to CBS/ Epic/Sony, Matt Johnson was now a free man. As disappointed as he was with Sony's reaction to *Naked Self*, he may have sensed that here was an opportunity to find a label that would get behind him, show the same belief that CBS once had. "It was a strange feeling for sure," he says when looking back years later, "a bit like leaving school. In fact I'd been at Sony far longer than I'd been at school so there was a sense of sadness and insecurity about loss and what the future may hold, but also a tremendous feeling of elation too – as if a weight had suddenly been lifted."

Cally was at this time working with Nine Inch Nails, through Island Records, and Trent Reznor made no secret of his admiration for The The. Reznor had signed to Interscope Records in 1992; part of this deal was that he was given, by Jimmy Iovine, his own boutique label, Nothing Records, run by himself and John Malm. Early releases, apart from Nine Inch Nails, included work by Pop Will Eat Itself and a new discovery, Marilyn Manson. Marc Geiger, who knew Reznor well, was able to connect the dots. "I'm the one who put him with Trent and really pushed it and forced it, and Trent was a huge The The fan, like me, and I was obviously very close to Trent and thought Nothing would be great for Matt from an image standpoint because Trent was putting forward at the time very interesting, difficult artists, he was almost the Some Bizzare of America." The deal, brokered by Marc Geiger, was negotiated by Johnson's UK lawyer, Andy Stinson. Roger Cramer was involved in the negotiations. "We got the master back and turned around and started shopping it, and up jumped Trent Reznor. I'm assuming it was a Geiger thing. He got us to Trent, who had a label, Nothing Records. And this takes so much time, the deal-making, but finally we did this deal." The advance was around half a million dollars, according to Johnson. "They were giving me an exact replica of the deal we'd asked from Sony plus the advances were to rise significantly for the following albums. I thought this showed commitment from their part – but little did I realise this was as good as it was ever going to get." In an MTV

News release from March 1999, Reznor is quoted as saying that Johnson's music was one of the main reasons why he had begun working on Nine Inch Nails. Johnson, meanwhile, said, "I'm feeling galvanised and extremely excited about the next few years." So far so good. Here was a hip new label who were going to ensure that *Naked Self* finally saw the light of day. Unfortunately, that would turn out to be the full extent of their efforts.

Roger Cramer knew something was up early on. "I remember going out to Interscope for a marketing meeting and thinking, 'These people are just going through the motions here.' They were a very powerful label at the time but they didn't support it. They did this deal and then basically under-budgeted everything. I don't think we ever even did a video for it. Interscope sort of dropped the record." There were a number of problems from the very start. One was the inevitable fallout from record company mergers and buyouts that were happening throughout the industry, the intricacies of which Johnson explains: "MCA had been bought by Edgar Bronfman Jr, from Seagrams, which was the booze company. Edgar Bronfman was like a wealthy sort of brat who wanted to be a songwriter, so he decided to buy a big music company. He then called it Universal. He then bought Polygram, so he was merging all these companies together, and then they were all taken over by Vivendi, the French water company. This was all happening in quite a short period of time and nobody in that company seemed to know if they were coming or going, so the people that would have been supportive of me got thrown overboard, no one could agree on budgets, it was a complete nightmare, and I would say the single worst experience of my entire career." The ultimate consequence of all this for Johnson was that funding was cut from numerous projects, including his own. Just as the album was being released he found the air supply was being switched off.

Well, apart from one small pocket of the Universal conglomerate – Motor Music, in Germany, who, according to Johnson, were the only ones interested. "They were wonderful people and hugely supportive. Every other territory we visited on tour we would literally have more people from Sony at our concerts than from Universal. Every country we visited the Sony staff would come up to me and say how much they would love to be working *Naked Self*. Yet there was barely any contact at all from Universal. A truly bizarre experience."

By now it was the year 2000 and, *Hanky Panky* not withstanding, it was seven years between albums. As Cramer bluntly puts it: "It just took him too damn long to put the music out, and his audience had moved on… seven years is a freakin' ice age in the pop music business." To put this into clear perspective it is worth pointing out that The Beatles had squeezed an entire recorded career into a smaller time span. Now, more than ever, Johnson was going to need someone behind him, to push The The back into the limelight. With all those record-label redundancies, most of his former allies were out of the picture. Now he needed label boss, and The The fan, Trent Reznor to step up to the plate. Only now was not a good time. Not at all. It was, as Marc Geiger points out, a question of bad timing. The good times of Nothing Records were over. "Trent went into a dark place. He was going through his own real issues, and they were pretty significant, personally." For Reznor and for the label, things were falling apart. The name of Nothing Records suddenly appeared horribly apt because nothing was being done by anyone to promote *Naked Self*.

Least of all, according to Cramer, Reznor. "I don't remember Trent being involved at all. I don't remember ever speaking to him. I spoke to John Malm, his manager, who was peripherally involved. Really it was just Interscope Records. It was up to the mothership label to fund it and do all the marketing and promotions, and I don't remember Nothing having any staff or anything – zero. At the time we were grateful. We felt rescued from the debacle that was Epic Records. And then it was just a stream of disappointments." Johnson puts the blame squarely with Interscope, rather than Reznor, who, before the signing, had told him how much *Mind Bomb* had meant to him. The only way Johnson and Cramer could see to salvage anything was by getting The The back on the road and doing a tour to promote the album. But this would be part of the stream of disappointments. "I remember having an argument with Tom Whalley, who was the president of Interscope at the time, about tour support, we asked for… the number $80,000 sticks in my mind. I remember being on a city bus, arguing with Tom on my phone, about tour support, saying something to the effect of, 'The least you can do is put the money into this tour. What else do you have to market the damn act?' He relented. It's not like they were broke. The bad times hadn't hit yet; they were sloshing around in fucking money, it was so ridiculous."

The label may have relented but the money that Cramer managed to crowbar out of them was never going to suffice for any kind of serious tour; when it ran out Johnson had to start paying for things himself. Eric Schermerhorn knew that a financial burden was the last thing his friend needed. "I felt for him because I knew he was the band leader, and the money wasn't coming in when we were on the road. We were getting paid, he wasn't getting paid; it's hard." If touring was an expensive enterprise then nothing brought this home quite like the concerts in an entire territory being cancelled. The tour was supposed to finish in Australia, but the fans there never got to see The The play, as Johnson explains years later.

"It was all booked up and we were ready to go and the promoter – he either cancelled or went out of business, and it cost me a lot of money, because I had everything lined up – crew, band members, hotels and everything." Cally was determined to claw some money back and so pursued the promoters, via agent Neil Warnock, who had been brought in by Steve Rennie, or directly, until they paid compensation. He then fell out with Warnock and fired him. This wasn't the only way Johnson suffered through lack of support from the label.

"I believed in the album so much I was just trying to keep it going, so I ended up providing the tour support out of my own pocket, because Universal had long lost interest, not that they had much interest to begin with. I was so determined to keep the album and the tour going, it was like the Charge of the Light Brigade really, throwing good money after bad; I didn't know when to give in, I wouldn't accept defeat. And it ended up costing me a fortune."

Even when the tour was running smoothly there were problems to deal with. "There was no one from the record company supporting us or even coming to the shows," Johnson was to tell Johnny Marr a few years after the events. "Hilariously, more people from Sony would turn up at the shows than from Universal. It was pretty sad really. But I kept the tour going out of my own pocket because I believed in the record so much. The record company wouldn't even send *Naked Self* to radio so we had the bizarre situation where radio stations in America were contacting us directly and asking for copies of the record; the record company just wouldn't give them copies. It was surreal." Johnson went on the attack. "I really let them have it then, over the airwaves and on the Internet, circulating some pieces I had written about the situation. Billboard ran the story three times." He appeared on several high-profile radio stations and was invited to talk on panels and television shows, but eventually decided that he didn't want to get bogged down with it all and opted out of being a spokesman for the ills of the music industry.

All of this was naturally having an effect on Johnson, but in truth, as far as his psyche went, things had been falling apart for some time, even when life in New York had been on a positive footing. "I often felt there was a kind of shadow hovering over me at times. I would often succumb to a terrible tiredness and fatigue and something just didn't feel right inside of me. I was pushing hard to break away from this feeling but at times I would become completely enveloped in a kind of 'brain fog' and feel completely spaced out and exhausted. I would have to lie in bed for days on end barely able to move and having to make excuses to people I was supposed to be working with. It felt as if my nervous system had short-circuited. Maybe all those years of intensity had finally caught up with me? During these 'attacks' I would try any and every alternative therapy going. I would be hooked up to intravenous vitamin drips, having acupuncture from my friend

Abdi, and I would also spend a lot of time at the Russian Baths. I'd been going there since Fran Duffy took me when I was 21. They had a selection of different rooms but I would always head to the 'radiant room' as it was like being inside a giant tandoori oven. Here you would be boiled pink and then beaten with oak leaves by a huge Russian. From there I would fall into the icy plunge pool, which was so freezing a sign beside it advised anyone over the age of 40 to discuss with their doctor before using!

"I wasn't sure if these attacks I was succumbing to with alarming frequency were purely physical and perhaps related to the terrifying episodes from the *Soul Mining* era when I had temporarily lost my eyesight and suffered various neurological disturbances, or if they had a psychological root and were connected to the bereavement my family had gone through with losing Eugene. Were these symptoms of undigested grief? So I began psychotherapy to try to untangle whatever was going on."

With all this happening, finally getting back on stage was some kind of relief – a reminder of who and what he was. Schermerhorn, sensitive to what his friend had been going through, could see what finally hitting the road meant. "He loved it, cos I think he knew that we had his back: me, Spencer and Earl. We rehearsed a lot and it was a force. He knew that and I think it was the first time he felt like that. It was never a bad night, the band was amazing; powerful and dynamic. He knew how to rehearse. We did festivals in Europe, they were great." Spencer Campbell's memory tallies with that of the guitarist. "The live gigs with Matt and The The were great. We had rehearsed for a month in NYC. The tour contained a good variety of different venues. Some of my personal favourites were the NYC dates at Mercury Lounge. We did lots of giant festivals; Glastonbury and of course Roskilde in Denmark, the one where the people died. We were on a different stage performing when Pearl Jam started their set. I remember looking over toward the monitor board and seeing our tour manager Reggie Griffith, with a look of horror on his face. Shortly after we were told about the tragic event. A horrible night for all of us. A very dark feeling indeed." Nine concert-goers died in the crush in front of the stage where Pearl Jam were performing, and another twenty-six were injured. It is also a dark memory for drummer Earl Harvin. "Goddamn, Roskilde was really tough. Of course with us and our audience being totally unaware of what had just happened only minutes earlier across the park, we walked off stage feeling elated from a wonderful set, to find the festival staff backstage all literally in tears. Still breaks my heart thinking of it today."

Roskilde was the one sombre note of an otherwise enjoyable tour. The band played a set that included most of the *Naked Self* album and a selection of 'hits' from The The's back catalogue. They were tight and powerful, relying on the attack of their sound and quality of playing, ignoring extravagant lighting effects or set design, aside from the industrial-looking microphone stand that Johnson and his lighting designer Kate Wilkins devised. "Kate Wilkins and I had decided to strip everything down to bare bones. In reference to the album sleeve we even had a large tungsten light bulb suspending over my head. I had usually sung with two or three different mics on a stand to capture the variety of tones I used on albums but for this tour I had a rusting industrial mic stand designed that looked like a trident that had been dredged up from the lower decks of the Titanic." Everything was stripped back and back to basics. The band played hard, and after the shows would sometimes drink hard. They were a tight unit, though occasionally, like on any tour, the booze loosened tongues more than they needed loosening. Earl Harvin recalls one such incident at the end of an American leg of the tour, in New York. "After the show we were celebrating the end of the tour and we were all extremely drunk. We ended up in a bar in the early morning hours called KGB, all sitting at a table drinking. Spencer exhibited some questionable behaviour that evening and Johanna, rightly, called him out on it. Spencer responded by telling her to 'fuck off' in no uncertain terms! Next thing I heard a big crash, looked over and saw Spencer lying on his back on the floor, with Matt on top of him, hands around his neck telling him not to speak to his partner that way. Matt got up but Spencer was so inebriated I don't think he felt any pain at that moment, so he just lay there, calmly collecting himself. Matt sat back down, then after a moment said out loud, 'Fuck's sake what'd I do that for?' And he pulled Spencer up off the floor and plopped him back into a chair. Another round was ordered soon thereafter."

Enjoyable as playing live again was, as good as the band were, it was too little too late. The problems at Nothing Records were ultimately heading towards lawsuits, as Reznor and Malm went to war, revealing how dysfunctional things had been behind the scenes. From there it was like a Russian doll of parent labels and the bigger they got the less they cared for The The and *Naked Self*. The lack of tour support, as Cally suggests, was the *coup de grâce*. "Financial tour support was pulled, Matt ploughed his own cash into it all and the tour manager made off with at least some of it. The shows, the band, the stage design were all magnificent. The band made a great and willing gang and the tour stretched on and on until the money ran out and the sales dwindled and thumbs were twiddled." And that was the end – when the money ran out.

18

RADIO CINEOLA: INERTIA VARIATIONS

FOR MATT JOHNSON, AMERICA WAS MORE THAN HOME from home. "Weirdly, I always felt more at home in New York than I ever did in London," he says, before making reference to a line from Wim Wenders' film *Kings of the Road*. Spoken by Hanns Zischler, who plays the character Robert Lander, he says, "The Yanks have colonised our subconscious." They did it through popular culture in all its forms, so even if you had never been there, the signifiers of America were ubiquitous. "When I arrived there at the age of 20 there was this overwhelming feeling of familiarity – was that from the films and TV I grew up watching or the DC and Marvel comics Andrew and I were addicted to as kids? Probably. I found it a very friendly place, I found I fitted in, it was very non-judgemental – coming from this very class-ridden, uptight, British society." Having been a regular visitor throughout the 1980s he was even more familiar with the country when he moved there the following decade, and being a foreigner enabled him to filter out the kind of domestic problems that he could never ignore in England. But things were changing in New York, in Matt Johnson's life, in the world itself as the globalisation project began to crush everything in its path. Johnson, of course, had been reading about this and writing songs about it. The protests in Seattle in 1999 were clear evidence of the paradigm shift underway, but smaller signs were in evidence everywhere. Johanna St Michaels, who had a less romantic attachment to America, saw the changes locally. "Our neighbourhood changed so much in New York when Matt and I were together. You could see it almost. Small stores were being bought up and sold out to chains, and small cafes used to disappear because the rent was too high. And also, during the nineties I felt like I was living in the shadow of the Empire, because we lived close to Downtown and the financial district, and it was all about money, how much money, and hedge funds and all that. It might have started long before I became aware of it, but it made me feel really sick." It was around this time, at the turn of the millennium, when the obvious differences between the social democracy of Scandinavia and the uber-capitalism of America became all too clear. Simply put – America had everything you could want, but only if you had the money to pay for it. "Matt lost a lot of money on his last tour, and there were a lot of strikes in the commercials industry, I did a lot of commercials to pay my bills... everything just disappeared, it was like living with a big black hole underneath you for ten or twelve years. And we paid lots of money into the system, like taxes. People think Sweden is so heavily taxed but it's only about 10 per cent more in Sweden compared to the States, but what do you get for your taxes in America? I think I got unemployment for six months and then all the health care and everything disappeared. And paying for schools for our son was like... it was just no way to live."

Johnson had not only lost money touring *Naked Self* but was still hugely out of pocket from previous tours, especially the first world tour where Marcus Russell's profligacy, and his own naivety, had cost him dear. Factor in an album that was released two years after it was finished and it is clear to see that financially he was in trouble. His advance from Nothing/Interscope helped

413

but by the time he had paid various commissions and payments for managers, advisors and lawyers, not to mention tax, there was a considerably smaller sum left to play with. He had a lot of people on his payroll and it seemed as though his main occupation was to write cheques, as money flooded out of his account at one end and only trickled in at the other. According to his accountant, Ronnie Harris, things had been looking precarious as far back as 1997.

In the autumn of 2000 Johnson spent time in a small weather-boarded house on the outskirts of Woodstock that belonged to a friend of his, Sam Kirby, who gave him her keys. He took a small 8-track studio and a Parker fountain pen that Johanna had given him, and would sit by the fire writing lyrics in notebooks, working on several tracks that would appear later – 'Pillar Box Red', 'Slow Rider', 'Mrs Mac' and 'Deep Down Truth' – interrupted only by visits from Johanna and Jackson. This retreat might have afforded him the space to write, but the reality of his financial situation was harder to escape. By 2001 Johnson had pretty much run out of money. Something had to give. "I was bringing in money from the UK and that was funding us. The problem was I was losing tens and tens of thousands from the tour. I then lost the Sony deal, and then I asked to leave the Universal deal. I was contracted for another album but I pleaded with them and thankfully they let me go. I was just broke. We bought the place in New York, but we had quite a big mortgage on it. Initially we rented out our apartment – we were going to move back.

"We left in the summer of 2001. The idea was to leave temporarily to cut costs and get our heads above water, the rental paying for the mortgage. I wanted to live in Spain but Johanna didn't want us to move there. I needed the rental from the building in London, so we lived in Sweden. But then of course 9/11 happened. We actually had tickets to fly back on the 10th of September, but what had happened is the people renting the apartment had decided to stay longer and signed a contract for a year, and after a while things started getting difficult in our relationship, and America started

414

to change, with Bush in power and the Patriot Act and all that nonsense. A lot of friends were leaving New York, the atmosphere had changed."

In Q magazine in December 1999 Johnson, talking about his habit of moving from one album to another in slow motion, said of the tardy arrival of *Naked Self* that it had been his longest gap between albums, but that the last ten years had been the hardest of his life. This period had begun with the loss of Eugene and ended with another loss, that of his mother. What made things worse was yet again being in a different country when it happened. Even years later, this still troubled him. It was Shirley who had instilled in him from an early age that blood was thicker than water and that you could never fully trust somebody outside of the clan.

"My mum had become increasingly unwell during the time I was living in New York. Her illness was a direct result of the deep, unrelenting grief she experienced after the death of Eugene. She just could not get over his loss. And despite all of us pleading with her not to forget the rest of us and to stay well for our sakes she lost the will to live. I spoke with her and my dad by telephone weekly and went back to England on the six-week 'European tours' Johanna and I took each summer and winter. I'd also head back for the odd week a couple of times per year too, and my parents came to stay with us a few times in New York. The happiest visit was soon after Jackson was born and although my mum was quite unwell at this time she was so proud to finally be a grandmother and was in her element holding Jackson. I know she was very proud of me and that I'd taken a big step in fulfilling a personal dream by moving to New York, yet I still felt guilty I was not seeing as much of her as I should have done." The quality Johnson remembers most clearly about his mother is her sense of fairness and it seemed so unfair that someone with such a sense of equity was gone, just as it had seemed so cruel that someone as gentle and kind as Eugene had died so early.

At Shirley's funeral, her eldest son, Andrew, finished his eulogy with a few lines that summed up how she played her part in making her boys feel secure enough to follow their different ambitions later in life. *Without fail she would always make us feel bigger and better than we probably were. She loved us, not for the people we tried to be, but for who we really were.* As bad as things were, Matt Johnson still had some way to go before hitting the bottom, and he would do it with such force that for a long time he wouldn't be able to pick himself up.

For St Michaels moving made perfect sense. "I had applied to do a Masters in photography at Gothenburg University and I got accepted in the summer of 2001. It seemed the right thing to do since there is free childcare in Sweden and you get grants to study. We thought we could catch our breath and maybe get back to New York." But, continuing the curse of recent bad timing, as soon as Johnson left New York the city exploded into life. Marc Geiger wonders what might have been had Johnson been able to stay. "What I think happened that really was sad is that Matt left New York when the city started to explode. In 2001 The Strokes and The White Stripes hit, and it just went on and on and on; that was the start of Brooklyn and Downtown. He left and New York was on fire for ten to twelve years. Matt just didn't plug into that scene, he was gone."

If New York was ablaze, Gothenburg felt, in the long dark winter at least, freezing. Maybe if Sweden had colonised Johnson's subconscious in the same way America had, things might have turned out differently. "One of the places we lived in in Sweden I really hated was a place in Paradisgatan. The apartment was at the top of a hill and had a really weird, dark energy. We were both financially stressed and arguing a lot. In the summer we'd spend time sailing around the archipelagos with Johanna's family and we'd also spend a lot of time up at her family's house in Värmland, which is isolated and situated amongst huge forests and lakes. I found the summers in Sweden beautiful – especially around midsummer – but the winters were just so hard, so that didn't help, and there were financial stresses and strains. We sold the apartment in New York in 2003 and bought a place in Gothenburg." Try as he might – though in truth he might not have tried as hard as he could – Johnson never got to grips with his new home. Cycling downhill on icy mornings to take Jack to school, with the sky still black, was something he was never going to get used to. For Johanna it was much easier; not only was she 'back home' but through her photography she found her life moving forwards, an attempt at a career change that would soon start paying dividends. She understands how it might have been different for Matt. "Sweden is very dark in the winter and I think you might have to be born there to be able to handle it. I also think when you don't speak the language you get very isolated."

In truth, the couple were going in different directions. While St Michaels felt at home and saw a future of possibilities and positive change, Johnson was out of sorts, depressed and could see no clear future in the music business that didn't include more of the problems that had stymied him over the last few years. The stress of moving, of losing family members, was added to the financial blows and it was no surprise that this was having an effect on their relationship. The problems had started in New York. Eric Schermerhorn felt there was a sense of inevitability about things. "With Johanna I'm not sure what happened, but Matt would say, 'Oh, we're stubborn. I'm stubborn.' They did fight. Cos she was strong and feisty and he was strong and feisty. They would have fights. She would be mad and... you know how it is, you have to compromise, man. It can all blow apart if you want it to. You've got to work at it. But he was like, 'I'm stubborn. She's stubborn.' Oh, that's gonna get you far. You have to learn to let things go. They fought. They fought about stupid stuff." The normal stuff that couples go through when things aren't working out. The serious stuff like money and then the stupid stuff that wasn't really stupid at all, signifying as it did that something had broken down. Things didn't get any better in Sweden. Their personalities meant that neither was likely to budge.

Johnson knew they were drifting apart. "I was spending more time away from Sweden as we were arguing a lot. I needed to find clarity in my mind and make some big life decisions. During this time I decided to place myself into a kind of 'solitary confinement' at the villa in Spain. Apart from a weekly telephone call to speak with Johanna and Jackson I didn't speak to anyone at all for almost seven weeks. It was a very, very intense period. I didn't drink alcohol or caffeine; I did a lot of meditating, walking and thinking. It ended up being an incredibly emotional experience as I ended up crying a lot for my mum as I'd been holding so much grief in. I was also crying for Jackson as I now knew Johanna and I would be separating imminently and I was worried about the impact this would have on him, both then and in the future." This was a period of deep soul-searching, and as well as concluding that his relationship with Johanna was coming to an end, he felt as if he was about to enter a period of great change; a shedding of his former skin.

The reviews for *Naked Self* had been good, with most observers pointing out that within its aggressive intensity lay moments of melodic delight, and above all another set of thought-provoking lyrics, perfectly in tune with the troubled times. As positive as the album's reception was, Johnson was in no position to start working on a follow-up. For one thing, all his music gear was nearly four thousand miles away in New York. And it was to here that he travelled with Cally to meet Rob Stringer, who had relocated to Sony's New York office, for a series of meetings to discuss a possible The The compilation album. Cally's recollections reveal the turmoil that the music industry was then in, with job security a thing of the past. "One meeting there saw Matt and I frisked downstairs, ushered up to the right floor only to see, as the lift doors parted, that no music was played in this record company; the only sound was that of executives unscrewing their gold discs from the wall, packing their U-haul boxes and quietly being led from the building by the same security guard that frisked us on the way up. Matt and I had meeting after meeting after meeting. Most of the American ones were hilarious as they were all 'huuugge fans of your The The' ('Which one is The?') but they were out of their jobs two weeks after the meeting." With careers being shredded faster than lines of cocaine had once been consumed, compilations and re-releases were perfect product for downsized times. To Stringer's credit he sanctioned some studio time so that a proposed singles collection could at least include a couple of new numbers. The feeling on both sides was that perhaps parting company had been a mistake. This project was a toe back in the water to see if both parties could still work together and, if things went to plan with the new recordings for the compilation album and the re-mastered catalogue, sign a new, improved deal and start afresh. So Clive Langer and Alan Winstanley were drafted in and for the first time since the early days of his career Johnson found himself out of the producer's chair. He revealed to Johnny Marr what it was like, after all this time, to be working with somebody else. "It was odd and I found it difficult to sit still, so I ended up jumping up and getting involved, but they were cool about that, they were nice guys to work with."

Acknowledging the fact that the aggressive style of much of *Naked Self* had hardly been a radio-friendly move, he reverted to a more melodic approach for 'Deep Down Truth' and 'Pillar Box Red', which, along with 'December Sunlight (Cried Out)', reworked from the original, made it onto *45 RPM: The Singles of The The*. The last of the three additions was produced by James Eller and featured the vocals of Liz Horsman alongside Johnson's own, an improvement on the original to many. This was a double CD release, vinyl having been abandoned by most labels with the exception of dance, electronica, hip-hop and R&B releases, which still served the preferences of club DJs. The sleeve, a bejewelled The The logo on a red velvet background, was designed by Cally and his wife, Jenny. A video for 'Pillar Box Red' was filmed by Tim Pope, who shot the interior scenes in the Palm Tree pub in Bow with a cast of Johnson's family and friends, including a fair few big men who were asked to put on lipstick. "What I did was I had a mirror in front of the camera, a bit like my favourite film, *Peeping Tom*, and I had to explain to these old friends of Eddie, 'Would you just put some lipstick on for us?' Luckily they all liked it, but I was the poor geezer who had to explain to them all what they had to do."

The lyrics to 'Pillar Box Red' saw a conflicted Johnson, trying to adjust to a country he recognised yet found vaguely foreign each time he had visited, before returning for good. It is a song about love and hate and how the past can be the heaviest of weights, where moving away in terms of geography and social class renders you rootless. While 'Heartland' was full of righteous anger, here it sounded like all the fight had been taken out of him. Though both new songs were full of uplifting melody and suggested a new direction for The The, fans were to be disappointed if they were expecting more to follow. They did get the opportunity to see The The live in 2002, when David Bowie, curating the Meltdown Festival, chose Johnson as one of the performers. With new songs and a concert it might have looked like business as usual but it was far from it, even if, in interviews of the time, Johnson suggested that he had a productive eighteen months ahead of him. Those same interviews also gave away his state of mind as he bemoaned the state of the music industry, the changing landscape of east London and his disappointment with New Labour, amongst other things.

The one-off concert for Meltdown was an opportunity to try something different and he asked Jim Thirlwell to accompany him in creating a set of reworked songs, using new technology. This was just the kind of approach one might expect from two performers who had never been shy of experimentation, but unfortunately things didn't work out as Johnson had hoped. Thirlwell points the finger at the tools, and for once the builders had a case for laying the blame. "That was a hard show because he had bought a bunch of new equipment and Matt was dead set on using this new stuff to create this set. I had this little iBook laptop that I used to travel with, but it wasn't my studio computer. It wasn't powerful enough to run this stuff and neither of us knew how to work the equipment, so it was a steep learning curve to figure this out. Plus we wanted to reinvent a lot of the songs. In the morning I would go into London and go to the Record Exchange and buy some records and find something and make a loop, and say, 'Here's a loop. Well, that could work for this song…' We were doing things like that, and so we made new backing tracks for familiar The The songs. I think we had two weeks to work on it and the time was ticking and it just wasn't coming together. We ended up creating stuff and then putting it on reel to reel. I was playing live along to this, and operating the multi-track, and we had films but it didn't work out as Matt had originally envisioned it, mostly because my computer was crappy. We had people coming in to help us and they couldn't figure out the equipment either. It's like those dreams you have when you're up on stage in a cold sweat and you're not wearing any pants or something."

Though Johnson might not have felt like he had been caught with his trousers down, he knew that the problems with equipment that wouldn't sync together had made for a disjointed performance. The audience response disappointed him. "Half the audience absolutely loved it, half absolutely hated it." His glass was half full. The audience, or at least half of them, seemed confused by the stripped-down and reworked versions of their favourite songs and were unmoved by the accompanying film made by Benn Northover. Alexis Petridis, writing in *The Guardian*, found the mood of the performance bleak, though interesting. "The show is intriguing and challenging rather than fun, which seems to disgruntle some sections of the audience. A few people leave, and the merits of Johnson's approach are hotly debated in the foyer. For all the set's resemblance to a rather stern lecture, it is different and provocative." Ian Tregoning, who had been in the audience, loved it. "It was fantastic because he was using his voice in a different way, he was singing falsetto, singing baritone… out of his range and doing it really well."

Johnson had wanted to take his audience on a journey but half of them didn't want to go. In many ways he was returning to his early days, exploring the experimental possibilities that technology offered. This time the technology was digital, most of it much smaller than the analogue gear of before, some of it only existing in a virtual world. He talked about buying a then-new piece of software called Ableton Live, but this kind of thinking set him apart from many of his fans. It was fine for Richard James, aka The Aphex Twin, to perform with software and laptops at the festival that week, but for The The to do the same was stretching it for half of his audience, a fact that clearly frustrated him. It hadn't been the most ideal of circumstances getting a show together in the first place, with no real base, and a relationship that was increasingly strained. In fact Johnson's relationship with Johanna St Michaels was such that the end surprised nobody, least of all themselves.

It was 2003 when things reached the point of no return. By now St Michaels was working on her first short film, *Best Wishes, Bernhard*, a macabre portrait of an old man who conducts an unsentimental relationship with dying. The dark mood of the film perhaps reflected the difficult period she and Matt were going through. "We were actually together when I started shooting, and we split up during that film. It was a crazy year 2003, we didn't have any money, and we split up and my sister got very sick, and a cousin killed himself, so yeah... it was a rough year. We are both very headstrong so it was a very volatile relationship at times. We were not very compatible in a lot of ways either. We come from very different backgrounds. I'm brought up with total equality when it comes to child rearing for example and Matt comes from a background where his mother did all the household work. We also had huge financial problems which is very hard on any relationship. That said I now see Matt as one of my best friends and as a family member. We actually often see each other with our new partners Jacob and Helen. Also we share our wonderful son Jackson and I'm very thankful we can be friends for his sake."

Johnson offers much the same summary. "It was tough, financially and emotionally. It was a horrible period for both of us, and not much fun for little Jack, I imagine. So though we were fighting, and rowing – obviously there were still deep feelings for each other, but it became obvious that we were better off as friends and artistic collaborators." The artistic collaboration would begin two years later in 2005 when Johnson provided the music for St Michaels' second short film, *Snapshots from Reality*. She had used his music in *Best Wishes, Bernhard* but now their relationship was purely as artistic collaborators. What came before then was a kind of unravelling, as the pressure of bereavement, financial setbacks, writer's block, a music industry turned upside down and the end of his relationship with the mother of his child broke the dam of his resolve. In retrospect it is surprising that the effects of this hadn't knocked him to the canvas earlier.

The final months before and after his relationship ended were particularly hard. "It was a very difficult time. I was coming to London drinking a lot, staying in hotels... going off the rails really, not doing anything creative. I didn't want to do anything creative. And then during the week I was staying at my dad's place. I love my dad but it was strange hearing him calling up, 'Matthew! Dinner ready!' I suddenly had that to deal with and then my belongings were still in storage after I had them shipped back from New York. So I was really living out of a bag with none of my stuff around me." The next three years were a period of instability.

"From 2003 to 2006 it seems I rarely slept in the same bed for longer than a week at a stretch. Not only was I flying back to Sweden a lot but also staying in cheap hotels in London, making trips back to New York to see my friends as well as escaping to Spain. I was like a man on the run, trying to escape from my own life. A friend of mine, the German actress Marlene Kaminsky, said to me, 'You have to make up your mind if you want to fool about flying here, there and everywhere seeing friends or if you really still have the urge to create.' This really stopped me in my tracks and gave me a long pause for thought. Though it would be a few years before I fully heeded her warning."

His belongings from New York, his earlier life in London, and his musical equipment were in three shipping containers on a farm on the borders of Suffolk and Essex. In 2006, having become friendly with the family who owned the farm, Johnson decided to rent a cottage and spent a year wading through these possessions, going through piles of paperwork and career-related detritus. He also discovered that the necks of vintage guitars had warped out of shape, strings had rusted and old synthesizers no longer worked.

"I was broke. It was a case of, 'How do I get out of this? How do I get on with my career on my own terms?' At this time there was the whole illegal downloading thing going on. The whole industry was in a state of flux, chaos. So it was a very, very strange time. The big question for me was how to make myself completely financially independent of the music industry. I was being offered plenty of recording contracts and offers to go back on tour but the money from touring in those days still hadn't improved much from a few years before and I couldn't afford to lose more money. Every recording contract I was being offered involved me handing over my copyrights in perpetuity, and I was damned if I was going to make that mistake again."

Though the publishing deal he had signed with Cherry Red had been disastrous he was at least earning some money from it. A different problem was the inflexible recording contract he had signed with Sony that meant he was seeing no return on his output, a situation that wasn't likely to improve. "I'm un-recouped with Sony because of their creative accounting practices," he says now, "and it being such a poor royalty rate and a bad deal where, for instance, they still charge 'breakages' on digital downloads. It's a prehistoric deal." The way out of his predicament, therefore, wasn't likely to include a return to the very model that had caused him so many problems.

Living in hotels, when he wasn't at his dad's, stuck in a kind of no man's land, and drinking too much, he vainly tried to plot a way out of his predicament. "It was tough after all that time, suddenly not having that support structure – management company, record company – it's a bit of a cocooned existence really where you exist between album and tour and in between there is that down-period where you seek inspiration. Suddenly there was this permanent down-period and it was a case of, 'What the fuck am I going to do?' So there was a sense of… it wasn't fear, more of a numbness, a sense of utter limbo."

In this regard he was merely resonating with the wider culture where, after the dot-com crash of 2000, the transition from one era to another seemed to have fallen into some kind of suspended animation. In New York, Marc Geiger had introduced Johnson to Josh Harris. "He was one of the big innovators on the Internet, the first guy to do any streaming video. He had an apartment that he had wired up; it was called 'We Live in Public'. There were forty cameras in the apartment, so he lived in public. I took Matt to the studio, which was attempting to be Warhol-like, and that started to get into Matt's head – the subversive potential of the Internet." Johnson never visited Harris's loft during 'We Live in Public', though he did see it from outside, passing it every day on the way to and from Dessau. For someone who struggled with the concept of fame, the very idea that Harris was promoting would have been anathema.

What intrigued him more about the possibilities of the Internet was Geiger's own web-based company, ARTISTdirect. Launched with Don Muller in January 1997, it was designed as a direct link between artists and their fans, therefore bypassing the record label. It was easy to see why Johnson might be interested, coming at a time when first Sony, then Nothing Records were failing him. ARTISTdirect went public in March 2000, but once again the curse of bad timing was to strike. A week later came the dot-com crash. Geiger's plans were thwarted and Harris saw his fortune wiped out almost overnight. Of course the crash was caused by foolhardy speculation, not the relative merits or failings of the Internet itself. The money men and dot-com entrepreneurs had just wildly misjudged its then capabilities. They were trying to fit square pegs into round holes. It wasn't that there was no gold in *them thar hills*, just that everyone was looking in the wrong place. It was simply a question of when someone would dig in the right places.

Johnson was in no frame of mind to be prospecting for the answer to his dilemma vis-a-vis the music industry, however. His life was in the middle of collapse. "The record industry was going through what I could only describe as a parallel collapse. A lot of people that I knew at Sony had either been fired or left their jobs. So it wasn't as if there was an obvious escape route back into my old life. The edifice was crumbling and the bridges were crumbling as well. But my main concern was this sense of numbness that was overtaking me. Obviously my personal life was difficult. I was living in a different country to my son, and that was causing me a certain amount of pain. I was drinking a lot and having a bit of a wild time, but not doing anything productive."

In truth he found himself doing all kinds of things but none of them was music. Instead he was travelling, photographing, writing journals, and reading copious amounts on geopolitics and more esoteric matters. "I had been involved in music since the age of 11 and since that time it had completely dominated my thoughts and my life. But my appetite for it began to dwindle. I was curious to see where this life without music might lead me as I was increasingly uncomfortable with the modern Western narrative that unless you are visibly 'doing stuff' – and continually bragging about it – it is as if you simply don't exist. I was coming under pressure from friends, family, my financial and legal advisors – as well as my audience – to just get back to music. But I just didn't feel like doing what everyone else wanted me to do. It didn't feel right. I had my reasons but in effect it looked like I was just playing truant from my own career." Though he was keeping busy, there were periods when he wasn't very happy. "I wasn't depressed but I was numb."

But not comfortably so. He was free but it was too much freedom, compounded by occurring at a time of uncertainty. It felt less like liberty and more like precarity. In this at least, as usual, he appeared to be ahead of the curve.

In 2003 Matt Johnson packed up his musical instruments and walked away from the music business. He didn't pick up a guitar for the next seven years. "This was at the low point, the nadir of my career I suppose. I was really rudderless, not knowing how to get out of this hole I was in. Financially I was fucked; I'd lost a fortune, had hardly any money, was heavily overdrawn and living on credit cards, no record deal, no publishing deal – nothing – no band. No desire, all my instruments locked away. It was the absolute low point. And all my friends, people like Jim, they said, 'Why don't you do another record?' I thought of it but didn't even know how to, I'd forgotten how to. There was that period of dismay and disgust with the music industry which had propelled me in this direction, but then I ended up in a place where I didn't even know how to get back even if I wanted to."

It's darkest before dawn, of course. Just as Johnson hit the bottom something happened, something that on the surface might seem barely significant. Jim Thirlwell sent him a book. The book was *The Inertia Variations*, a series of linked eight-line verses on the subject of doing nothing. As soon as Thirlwell had read it, one person sprang to mind. "I thought, 'This is Matt!' It's creating self-hatred out of procrastination. About not being able to get out of that cycle. I mean Matt, even when he was recording *Soul Mining* or *Infected* or something like that, he took a long time. He did like to fiddle around. It wasn't all work. He got a lot done but there was a lot of procrastination involved, and for many reasons. I got another copy of *The Inertia Variations* and sent it to him, and said, 'You've gotta check this out.'" Johnson, suffering from the very affliction the poem describes, recalls reading it for the first time.

"I remember sitting in the front room at my dad's place and reading it. Jim just said, 'It's from an old friend, I thought you would enjoy it.' I read the whole thing through in one sitting. And I was nearly falling on the floor laughing at one point, nearly crying at another point, then I was also thinking, 'Fuck! I should have written this. This is me! He's not only writing about me, this is me writing it.' I absolutely loved it. And I said to Jim, 'This is fantastic. Who is this?'"

The poem had been written by John Tottenham. Thirlwell had first met Tottenham in 1979 when the pair attended a weekend of gigs at the YMCA, off Tottenham Court Road, the same ones that Johnson himself had attended. They became friends and would hang out, spending many an hour at the Scala cinema. Both made their way to America in the early eighties, Tottenham to LA and Thirlwell to New York. They kept in touch, initially via Lydia Lunch, whom Tottenham had introduced to Thirlwell. Switching between painting and writing, Tottenham wrote *The Inertia Variations* in his early forties and it was published in 2004.

Though both he and Johnson were friends of Thirlwell, and though they had both stood in the same hall watching Joy Division, Throbbing Gristle and The Fall in 1979, they had never met each other. But somehow, Tottenham had unwittingly tapped into Matt Johnson's soul. Johnson told Thirlwell he wanted to get in touch with Tottenham because he wanted to do something – he wasn't sure what – with the poem. "So I wrote to John, and said, 'Look, I think I want to narrate it, or publish it, or do something with it,' and he was really gracious and said, 'Feel free. I'd love you to do something.'" If he had known at this point that his poem about the inability to do things was now in the hands of man who was suffering from the very same thing, he might not have held his breath; it would be a few years yet before Johnson did something. But the idea was in Johnson's mind and with beautiful irony, his state of inertia was going to be cured by a poem about inertia.

"I printed all the verses out, and started playing around with them on the floor, trying to make sense of it all. For me it started to represent not only the sense of inertia, but the chronic procrastination, loss of confidence, laziness; the time that I was wasting. But it was the magical properties in this poem that led me out of the inertia. It was like a lifeline was passed to me. I set up a little studio at my dad's house and started to narrate it, started to create soundscapes, and it started to breathe new life into me somehow. And it led me and lifted me out of my own inertia. And then through that I started to play around, and do some instrumental music, and one thing led to another."

One of the first things it led to was Sweden. He took the recording with him next time he visited. Johanna St Michaels came to the same conclusion as Jim Thirlwell, and Johnson himself. "He came over to Sweden and said, 'I've recorded some of this poem,' and I listened to it and it was Matt, this is like Matt, the inertia, the not doing anything... and being thoughtful, and hesitating and thinking, 'I'm not good enough,' and then thinking back on the good times. Nostalgia – that's Matt very much, and that poem is like nostalgia to me, you are thinking about all the things you didn't do, and Matt, to me, when we were together, it was always better in the past, and then we lived together for a few years and it was better when we were first together; it was always looking back, not living in the moment."

Now though, just when he needed it most, there was something, however vague, with which to imagine a future. Maybe it was at this point that St Michaels asked Johnson if he would provide music for her short film. It was only nine minutes long so here was a good way to dip a toe back in the water. Meanwhile he continued to mull over what to do with John Tottenham's poem. By this time Johnson had met Helen Edwards. She was living in the same building as Ian Tregoning, near London Fields. Tregoning was in the basement, while Edwards had a tiny space on the second floor. One night she threw a party and invited Tregoning, who in turn invited Johnson. Edwards had a boyfriend at the time, whom Tregoning had befriended. She knew who Johnson was but, not being a hardcore fan of his music, was able to see him for who he was rather than as Matt Johnson of The The. At first meetings were purely social. Alessandra Sartore, who knew Tregoning through Johnson, remembers meeting Edwards on a skiing holiday, though Johnson wasn't there. Not long after this Edwards left her boyfriend and started seeing Johnson, who was then still living in Suffolk with Eddie.

When they became an item Johnson found his focus changing. "We hit it off because she's very down to earth and very funny, so instead of going out drinking with lots of different people I was spending a lot of time with Helen. We were drinking a lot… probably too much, but we were having fun, out all the time going to private views, films, pubs, bars. This was when I was trying to figure out – do I want to do music? If I do, how do I do it on different terms? I was getting offers coming in from labels but I thought, 'What's the point?' So it was like an ego death, to go from a great loft apartment on Broadway in New York to suddenly, having lost a lot of money, being in a little bedroom in your dad's house." In a funny way it was just what he needed, though he was still struggling to find a way out, to break fully free from his inertia. Or, as Helen Edwards prefers, to stop procrastinating.

In fact Johnson had already found the answers to his predicament. In 1999 he took over a fan website that had been created two years earlier; this became the official The The website. Free downloads of tracks from *Naked Self* were offered to fans in an effort to do what Nothing Records had failed at, and get his music heard. Though he saw the dangers for artists in fans being able to get music for free online, he also saw the potential of the Internet to deal a blow to what he saw as the corrupt system of the music industry. Independence was the way to go, though at this stage he was still hesitating as to whether he should completely abandon the old model. He may have lacked control over the music that Sony owned, but there was plenty in his vaults that he could exploit – if he could work out a way to do it. This was partly a physical problem, as old magnetic tapes need restoring to rid them of accumulated moisture so they can be played without problems – a process known as 'baking'. "I've got hundreds of tapes and a lot of them aren't marked, and you know how analogue tape goes, you've got to bake it. And I did some and it was expensive, so I bought a machine, like a food dehydrator, that does it cheaply. But I haven't had the time. I don't want to release *Spirits* or *Pornography of Despair* without all the tracks on it, but I've got to go through hundreds of tapes. No one else can do it, cos they don't know what they're listening for."

At the Meltdown concert in 2002 fans had been given the opportunity to buy a limited edition promo double CD entitled

Film Music. The first disc was *Silent Tongue*, a collection of short instrumental pieces that behaved like soundtrack music, culled mostly from his archive of unreleased music alongside a handful of tracks from *Burning Blue Soul*, *Mind Bomb* and *Dusk*. It opened with that most atmospheric of The The songs, 'Lung Shadows'. It was released on Johnson's newly minted Lazarus label. Having failed in his attempts to buy the rights to his back catalogue he saw the only way forward was to be truly independent. This was hardly a new idea; for a decade and more dance and electronica artists had been running their own labels, but they had a network of DJs and clubs, in fact a whole scene geared towards just such a set-up. For more traditional rock and pop artists it was a different proposition. Breaking free of the corporate system offered freedom on the one hand, but on the other it meant losing out on the powerful machinery that, whilst exploitative, made everything happen, and happen on a potentially huge scale. This was perfectly illustrated in 2002 when Sony released the four-CD box set, *London Town 1983–1993*, which compiled The The's first four albums for the label starting with *Soul Mining*, along with a bonus disc containing a video interview between Johnson and Marr, and the video for 'Pillar Box Red'. This came with all the usual promotional support and distribution channels that meant it was everywhere at once, while the first Lazarus release was a limited edition, only available for one night at the Royal Festival Hall, and thereafter via the band's website. Promotion in the usual channels was out of reach. It was going to be a steep learning curve.

Johnson's only promotional tool was his website, and he used it to disseminate news, such as the fact he was working on a new album in 2002, planned to be released jointly by Lazarus and Sony in time for the twenty-fifth anniversary of The The two years hence. Whatever this was, it would not transpire. He also used it to promote his thoughts and ideas. In 2001 he published online *The The versus the Corporate Monster*, an attack on the music industry inspired by his own experiences and the 1993 article by Steve Albini, in which the financial exploitation of artists by record labels was clearly explained. Johnson summarised Albini, stating, "The artist pays for everything, yet owns nothing." Within his attack also lies an insightful view of how the future might look as he correctly points to the day when high-speed Internet connections and home entertainment systems that will be able to play higher quality digital sound files will cause a slump in CD sales. It was a case of ideas waiting for the technology to catch up. In 2002 Johnson sounded positive, if unsure of how he could make his freedom work for him. A year later, when his relationship with Johanna ended, this optimism seemed to have drained away. John Tottenham's poem was the spark he needed.

With most of his other belongings locked away, a curious thing happened. "All my instruments were in storage so I was away from my personal possessions but also my professional possessions. And I'd forgotten my professional persona." Matt Johnson of The The had effectively disappeared. There was nothing in his new relationship with Helen that involved that version of Matt Johnson. He was losing connections to his past. Not only was he no longer active musically, or signed to a record label, but he was also rootless in the sense that he couldn't live in his own home. And he was still coming to terms with the changes to not just the music industry, but London itself. For him it wasn't the past that was a foreign country, but the present. Layer after layer was being stripped away and what was left was inertia, procrastination, drinking; waiting for a solution. John Tottenham, meanwhile, waited patiently for Jim Thirlwell's friend to 'do something' with his poem, but all that Johnson had thus far done was to record himself narrating some of Tottenham's verses, using a rudimentary recording set-up at his dad's.

He still felt stuck. "I couldn't see a way out of things. I thought, 'I can't get back into my flat, I can't go on living out of a backpack. I've got to get my stuff out of storage.' I had just started doing the soundtracks and started warming to the idea of maybe doing music again... and then I went to see this life coach, to try to get myself out of this deep torpor and inertia, and open myself up. Fiona recommended her. She said, 'Look, she might be good for you.' So I went to see her in her office in the West End, and she started to get me to write things out, charts and what's important in my life? And is my life in balance? I started to write these things down, and obviously my life wasn't in balance, and she said, 'What do you really want?' And I thought, 'You know what, I need somewhere to work, I need a studio; I can't be working sitting on a bed in my dad's house, like I am twelve again.'"

The obvious step was to get back into his flat. He wrote apologetic letters to his tenants, one of whom was the actor Gael Garcia Bernal, giving them notice. This freed up two floors of the building, and he was able to move back into his home. Increasing other rents managed to offset the financial loss and he then built himself a small but well-equipped home studio, designed by Pete Hoffman and built by Miloco. With prized outboard gear from the likes of Neve, Massenburg, SLL, Urei, Manley and Eventide the whole studio cost over £125,000 and was funded by finally allowing some of his music to be used in adverts – on this occasion, in America. "Seeing that life coach was the turning point, because I was really treading water. I was drinking, having a good time, but not getting any work done. And I was feeling groggy and depressed but suddenly I had a studio and had somewhere to create, and then things started to pick up. I started doing more soundtracks. I still didn't want to sign a record contract or play live. It was baby steps really. I just started loving being in the studio again. This would have been around 2008 I think."

That year he completed the music for St Michaels' documentary, *The Track*, about a small race track in Värmland, Sweden, which was shown on Swedish television. At fifty-nine minutes it was a much longer film than Johnson had previously had to compose music for, and while the subject matter may have provided its own challenge it was a good experience of how to prepare a larger body of music for the screen.

By this stage Johnson had been more or less 'silent' for five years, releasing no records and not even doing any interviews.

In fact he would only do one interview between 2002 and 2014 – for a Dutch arts magazine called *200%* in 2007. Each annual edition concentrated on a particular theme, and art director, and editor, Thierry Somers settled on politics for issue two, offering the people he interviewed the chance to talk at length, without any editing, on their political views and their art. Somers had been a fan of The The since *Soul Mining* and was keen to include Johnson. "I knew that Matt talked in interviews about political issues and his music with political content, but became frustrated that these issues didn't make it into the final article. For quite some time he decided not to do any interviews. I wanted to do an entire story on what he is passionate about and interview him in-depth on pop music with political content. When I approached him with this idea he was a bit sceptical, but when I sent him over some of the topics I wanted to discuss with him, he agreed to participate."

Asked about issues deserving of a political song he came up with a long list that took in the War on Terror, surveillance society, corporate greed and the bastardisation of political vocabulary. Issues such as privatisation and the rise of Private Finance Initiatives were also mentioned. But he admitted that he didn't think political songs could save the world, and that writing political songs now would be more of a cathartic exercise, "to help temporarily ease a growing sense of political impotence". In this regard he was merely expressing the millennial angst of many, a fear that in a post-political world opposition to global capitalism has been obliterated to the extent that the only political choice left for the masses is the politics of identity. This general malaise would only increase after the financial crash that was just a year away. Johnson was once again tapping into the zeitgeist, one which would be summarised seven years later by Italian writer and theorist, Franco Berardi in his 2017 book *Futurability: The Age of Impotence and the Horizon of Possibility*. But Johnson didn't feel helpless, he told Sommers; far from it. "Contrary to popular belief I am an optimist and I remain convinced that we will somehow extract ourselves from this mess.

The world, by necessity, will need to be a very different world from the one we have grown up in. But that's okay."

The interview, as was intended, allowed Johnson to get it all off his chest and gave the reader a good insight into his continuing political concerns, but just as important, though perhaps less noticeable at first glance, was how he answered a question about the cathartic power of writing lyrics. "If I wasn't creating I think I would go mad. I think it's vital for everyone to have some form of creative outlet and self-expression. To make the inner world outer and make the outer world inner too, in order to make sense of one's life and what one sees around in the world. I think stifled creativity is what causes many people to suffer from depression or madness. And when I say creativity I'm not just talking about the arts as there are so many ways to create and to express ourselves. That's one of the main reasons we're in this life and on this planet I believe. To make the inner world outer and to take the outer world within." Here was a 'horizon of possibility' and a reminder that whilst he was a political animal, he was also a spiritual one, the latter beliefs being a way of dealing with the angst created by that sense of political impotence he admitted to Somers. He would be interviewed many times after 2014, but this interview remains the only one where he has been allowed, and felt willing, to speak in depth, and from the heart.

Though he had managed to set the world to rights, he was still struggling to finish projects, particularly when it came to writing music. Cally was essentially having to manage this lack of productivity. "Matt always had a problem in finishing things, he'd be the first to agree to this." Cally's solution to this problem was to utilise the opportunities presented by streaming audio technology on the Internet. Johnson had a nostalgic attachment, like many of his generation, to radio. "I would have been eight or nine when my Auntie Doreen bought me this little transistor radio in a black leather case. I would listen to it all the time; Radio Caroline, and Radio Luxembourg, and obscure shortwave radio stations from around the world, from Russia, China, South America or Eastern

Europe." He remembers the day he heard Cally's idea. "I was in my studio one day and I got a call from Cally. He was out in his open-topped car driving around the countryside, and he said, 'I've got this good idea. How about you do a little radio show, playing bits of the projects you are working on, just to put them out there and give you motivation?' Instantly I thought, 'Wow, what a great idea.' It was perfect. I started thinking about it. It was his suggestion, but I had to run with it a bit… think of a title. I'd had the name Cineola kicking around for ages. And then thinking about the content I thought that we had to have a cheesy musical ident, then figured out ways of treating the sound, phasing and distorting so it sounded like it was coming out of shortwave radio. Then the content… it could be interviews with collaborators or people I'm interested in, it could be tracks that have never been released before, rough mixes, upcoming releases… like a jamboree bag almost." As he recalls the memory, the sense of excitement he felt at the time is obvious. It was like a singing bowl had been struck. Clarity at last.

The pair eagerly set about exploring the possibilities of a radio environment that blended the physical and the virtual, Cally trawling the Internet, collecting radio call signals, talking about romantic radio figures, like Wolfman Jack. "Matt and I were immersed in a world of the analogue, anything that weighed a ton, had large knobs on, clunked when it opened and was made of nickel, leather and green baize. Matt created Cineola and a world was born. I discovered skeuomorph, the process of depicting a modern computer interface back into an old analogue counterparts: preferably the one it was digitally recreating. The The's shiny website became a newspaper, his studio filled with old gear, real and skeuomorphed."

This all took time of course, and whilst in the midst of it Johnson managed to complete a soundtrack for another of Johanna St Michaels' films, called *Going Live*, which was, again, broadcast on Swedish television. Gerard Johnson, meanwhile, having made a handful of short films – including *Mug*, about a day in the life of a London mugger, which starred his cousin Peter Ferdinando – had now managed to direct his first full-length feature film on a budget of just £40,000. This was about a lonely serial killer in east London, the eponymous *Tony*. Matt seemed like the obvious choice for soundtracking this film, having already provided the music for *Mug*. The soundtrack for *Tony* was released in 2010 on Johnson's new Cineola label, with the catalogue number Cineola 1, beautifully packaged, like a small hardback book, illustrated with his own photographs.

It was Helen, who had an MA in photography, who encouraged him to use his camera as a creative outlet. Johnson's interest in photography, inspired by having met Robert Frank in the mid-eighties, would now become something more productive, if only for his own enjoyment of the medium. The couple would travel all round Europe and beyond, always taking cameras. Johnson would take thousands of photographs over the next few years. They would visit the Paris Photo fair annually and he found the world of photographers and photography refreshing after years of music, musicians and record company politics. Helen curated exhibitions for many of the artists she represented and at one of these – *The One Ton Show* – both Matt and Andrew Johnson exhibited work. He would never consider himself a serious photographer, more of a serious enthusiast, and for a time a voracious snapper of shots. But somewhere within this process was an independence that he had been looking for, one that he could feed into his own label, as he had done with the release of *Tony*. Connecting the visual with the soundtrack was an interesting process, both in terms of matching his photographs to the mood of the soundtrack and in providing music simpatico with his brother's film.

The liner notes of the CD included a note from Gerard where he revealed how the music had originally been harder, more electronic, but as this didn't fit into the world of the lonely main character, his brother stripped it back, creating a sparse but melodic structure that complemented the mood of the film. Some of the darker electronic material was retained, as it fitted some of the more gruesome scenes in the film, but mostly this is Johnson playing delicate piano over subtle beds of sound. Soundtracks were keeping him busy as he also completed one for another of Johanna's films, *About Dina*. Newly energised and with a sudden flurry of activity, he realised he needed some help with organisation and so he asked Lee Kavanagh if she would like to work for him again. She came in time to help with the debut release on Cineola.

With the *Tony* soundtrack launching his offline label it was now time to launch Radio Cineola, the skeuomorphed radio show born of Cally's inspired idea. No doubt to try and eliminate the possibility of any further bouts of inertia, Johnson set himself a definite timetable. "I set myself the target of doing one a month throughout 2010, fifteen minutes a show, just to get myself working again. I was really having trouble getting back. I was out of the game so long. It's like being an athlete, and suddenly after not training for ten years you have to compete. You think you've forgotten everything you once knew. You are low on confidence. So this was a way of just finding my feet again, and giving myself a deadline. Sometimes I would make the deadline by seconds, and other times the show would be finished within good time in the month."

The fifteen-minute 'shows' were each introduced by an atmospheric, crackly ident and consisted, as promised, of spoken word interludes and music, some of it new, though most of it from his back catalogue – material that had never previously seen the light of day. There was plenty of variety and plenty of humour, and over the course of the twelve broadcasts an alternative The The career unfolded, as though a different The The had existed these past ten years in the virtual world. For the first instalment, as well as showcasing three tracks from *Tony* and 'Slow Rider', which had appeared on *Film Music*, Johnson also included two of his narrations of verses from John Tottenham's poem. The shows were also available to download from the website. He would include more verses from *The Inertia Variations* but still felt he wanted to do something more with it. As did Johanna who, inspired by her former partner's enthusiasm for this poem, was dreaming up ideas for another film project.

The soundtrack activity didn't stop here, and neither did the connections to people he knew. The photographer Steve Pyke had met Johnson in 1980 when he was sent by *SOUNDS* to take shots of him for a Dave Henderson feature on Some Bizzare. They got on well enough to become friends, and were often at the same gigs and political rallies in the early years of Thatcher's first term, when the majority of young people involved in the music scene shared an intense antipathy for Tory ideology. Eighteen years later and now a successful and respected portrait photographer, Pyke realised a childhood ambition to meet the astronauts who had walked on the moon and take their portraits for a *Life* magazine cover story. His then partner, Nicola Bruce, accompanied him to America and filmed these meetings. It took another decade for the funding to become available for Bruce to turn all her footage into a documentary – *Moonbug*.

Whilst looking over the footage she had been listening over and over to 'Lung Shadows', finding the atmospheric track an ideal accompaniment to her images. With Pyke and Johnson not only being friends, but also east London neighbours, it wasn't difficult for Bruce to meet with Johnson, discuss what she wanted, and offer him the job of providing a soundtrack. "I sent Matt notes like, 'What does space sound like?' and lists of instructions like, *evoke the sound of the solar wind, and creaking planets.* At the other end of the spectrum, this was an earthbound journey in a car across America. So there was a very different scale of themes. I remember, there were sporadic bursts of material arriving from Matt. I wasn't looking for songs, but stranger undercurrents of sound that could be embedded or drive the image, and propel the story forward. He managed to create a whole series of experimental tracks that were full of wonderfully rich and weird sounds."

Johnson also recorded himself and Pyke talking about the project, and though this wasn't used in the film, a transcript of one conversation would appear in the booklet of the soundtrack release on Cineola. By the time this came out in April 2012, Johnson had slowed down his Radio Cineola output. The one-a-month broadcast schedule had proven too taxing to sustain and instead he produced further shows when he could. The fact that Helen was now pregnant meant that 'when he could' wasn't so often. Significantly, when Helen found out she was pregnant, she naturally gave up drinking and Matt decided to do the same. Though his drinking had never got out of control, he realised that for a number of years he had been drinking more than was healthy, and that this drinking had also done him no favours when it came to being creative. It is easy to follow the romantic image of the artist and the bottle when you are young, but as middle age approaches the drink starts to win the battle. So Johnson was healthier than he had been for some time, his mind less foggy, his intentions clearer. It was good timing as this would prove a stressful year. "When Helen was heavily pregnant I was in the middle of a massive battle with neighbouring property developers that involved the police, local MP and Mayor of the borough."

Helen gave birth to a boy in April 2012 in Whitechapel; they christened him George in honour of George Orwell, George Best and Johnson's grandfather George Johnson. But before the joy at being a father for a second time had a chance to begin to subside came the terrible news that very same week that Andrew had been diagnosed with an aggressive type of brain tumour and had been given approximately six months to live. Worrying about his brother and having a new baby to look after diminished his creative output considerably but, remarkably, Andrew proved the doctors wrong and, though never fully recovering his health, would continue to defy their original prognosis.

Before Johnson could turn his full attention to plans that he had for Radio Cineola and John Tottenham's poem, he set up his own publishing imprint, called 51st State Press, and issued a paperback volume of Eddie's memoirs in the pub trade, *Tales from the Two Puddings*. Intended as an 80th birthday present, it now helped to distract Eddie from the terrible reality of Andrew's illness. The book was well received and attracted the attention of Rob West, who made a documentary based on it, with the co-operation of the Johnson family. When he was invited to be filmed by Rob West on the premises that were once the Two Puddings, but now barely resembled their former incarnation, the look on Eddie's face was a mix of resignation and bafflement.

The summer of 2012 saw the Olympic Games in London. The stadium and many of the other sporting venues had been built in Stratford on former railway land in often controversial circumstances. Matt was invited on to BBC's *Newsnight* programme to briefly voice the residents' opinion of the whole affair, though in typical television fashion he was given barely any time to say what he wanted. Opinions against the Olympic Games were generally unwelcome and when aired were very much curtailed. Johnson wasn't very satisfied with the experience. "It was just a local resident and me up against the Mayor of Newham, Sir Robin Wales. What was strange was that it was brought to my uncle Kenny's attention that the day after the interview Wales had dispatched his quislings around all the pubs in Stratford to find out information on my family and me. Of course this was all reported back to us immediately and made me highly suspicious. What was Wales afraid of? What had he been up to that he feared a loud-mouthed musician might discover and publicise nationally?"

By the time the Olympics had been and gone the skyline of Stratford had altered beyond recognition. For a nostalgic like Matt Johnson, the barely recognisable physical remnants of his childhood were probably hard to take, but proof, if nothing else, that our concept of home is as much abstract as it is material. His memory remained intact, even if the remembered environment hadn't. More problematic was that when it came to his current home the abstract and the material were intrinsically linked. His attachment to his building in Shoreditch was one bound up in memories that spanned a much greater expanse of lived time. The tide of corporate development sweeping in from the City has therefore been harder to accept. Seeing the physical landscape of

Shoreditch and Spitalfields increasingly, and permanently, altered was a more direct assault on his memories, and his daily life.

The changes to London that had disorientated him on his return were thus most noticeably felt in his own back yard. He quickly became involved, as a founder member, in a variety of campaign groups, such as Save Shoreditch, OPEN Shoreditch, East End Preservation Society and the East End Trades Guild, as well as being co-chair of the Shoreditch Community Association and sitting on endless committee meetings. He sometimes mused that maybe all this was displacement activity on a grand scale in order to avoid getting down to work. He met illustrator Lucy Rogers and artist Brad Lochore while part of a campaigning group focused on developments planned for Bishopsgate. Feeling that the group was being steered in a direction they didn't wish to follow they broke away. Johnson and Lochore subsequently became good friends, meeting regularly for breakfast, trying to balance the wish to continue campaigning with the need to spend time being creative. "Matt and I have suffered a lot over willingly taking on these campaigns – it's been a hit for both of us – so we have been discussing… how does one reconcile this creative life with putting on armour and going out to fight? So many of our conversations are about how to negotiate that, and also how to be creative in your fifties, which is different because what is important in your fifties is very different to what was important in your twenties. You start to think of summing up. I mean, the inevitable end is no longer over the horizon, it's something that is starting to shimmer mirage-like in the distance. You start to think, well what has it all been about?"

While some might have given up the fight and sold up, Johnson decided not only to stay, but to undertake the expensive restoration of the building he owned, an act of civic duty that contrasted sharply with the philosophy of those planning to transform the area with an aggressive array of high-rise towers. The stress of this undertaking would take its toll on his energies, distracting him from creative endeavours for several years. If an Englishman's home is his castle, then Johnson was under siege, whilst outside were the hordes of hipsters and boozers and the ever-encroaching behemoths of the globalised economy.

Speaking in 2013, before scaffolding and advertising wraps shut out the view through his windows and rendered the interior even more siege-like, he lamented the changing landscape. "When I first moved here in the mid-eighties there were fifteen licensed premises, which was fine; it was mainly artists, photographers, musicians… there were still cabinet-makers, and light industry. It was great because at night and the weekends it was deserted and under-lit and I loved it. Now, in Shoreditch alone, there are over three hundred licensed premises. The council just green-light the booze applications one after the other and although we try to fight… we had a conservation zone here, for what it's worth, but developers always find a way round it."

He had been taking part in campaigns with various groups since his return, but the more energy he spent fending off the exterior world, the less he had left to express his inner world. The outer was coming in so much he was trying to block it out, and the inner wasn't getting out at all. His balance was all out of whack. "I ended up serving a seven-year tour of duty with local politics and local campaigning – from handing out leaflets in the street, attending countless campaign groups, planning committees, licensing committee meetings, being interviewed in local newspapers, helping design slogans and logos, speaking to countless local residents to try and get them involved. It becomes all-consuming and, like pretty much everyone else who gets involved, you end up getting sucked deep into it because you feel so outraged at the corruption and incompetence of local government and the sheer unfairness of it all."

After giving a speech at the Bishopsgate Institute for the launch of the East End Preservation Society, along with Rogers, Lochore and other concerned parties that included Will Palin and Dan Cruickshank, he decided that he needed to retreat from these particular battles. The restoration of his own building, however, would continue to be a drain on his time, bank account and energy. It was now thirty years since *Soul Mining* had kick-started his career, and Sony took up the opportunity to mark the anniversary by reissuing the album. In the event they would be a year late in doing so.

On June 30, 2014 Johnson was interviewed on stage at Rough Trade East, in London, by Kevin Foakes, aka DJ Food, on the day that *Soul Mining* was re-released as a box set. In April, a limited 12-inch vinyl edition of 'GIANT' had been issued on Record Store Day, which included a remix by Foakes, as well as his 'remix' of the front cover artwork, on the sleeve's reverse. After the interview there was a Q&A session and fans, predictably, asked when there would be another The The album. Those who turned up at a second event organised for Classic Album Sundays, and hosted by its founder Colleen Murphy, would ask the same question, and receive the same patient answer.

The *Soul Mining* reissue had been re-mastered by Alex Wharton at Abbey Road Studios using the original masters, and was accompanied by a second disc containing five 12-inch single mixes and 'Fruit Of The Heart', which had appeared on the Australian release of the album in 1983. Alexis Petridis, writing in *The Guardian*, gave a five-star review, and Michael Bonner in *Uncut* was equally fulsome in his praise, even managing to squeeze into his review the strange fact that one fan had named a newly cultivated carnivorous plant after Johnson, who was invited to see his new namesake at the Chelsea Flower Show that summer, where it won the gold prize. As well as this horticultural appearance he was also invited to appear – bodily this time – on celluloid, albeit in a bit-part role, when J. J. Abrams contacted him to ask if he wanted to be an extra in *The Force Awakens*, the seventh *Star Wars* episode that he was then filming at Pinewood Studios.

The re-release of his first album as The The saw Johnson re-emerge publicly. Not only did he attend the above events but also began to grant interview requests, one of the first being for John Doran of online 'magazine' *The Quietus*. "*Soul Mining*, to me, is one of the all-time greats," wrote Doran. "I listen to it in the same way that some others listen to *Revolver* or *Pet Sounds*." Asked about the prospect of a new The The album, Johnson replied, "I do start to get a tingling when I think about it… especially with all the geopolitical stuff going on at the moment." Fans hoping for *Infected* to get the same anniversary treatment as *Soul Mining* were set to be disappointed. As Johnson was un-recouped with Sony – at least as far as they were concerned – he didn't make a penny from the reissue and Sony billed him for the remastering and packaging costs. He decided to put a block on any further boxsets until the financial issues are resolved.

In an interview with Doran he revealed he had been working on three more soundtracks. The first of these was for Gerard Johnson's film *Hyena*, about a corrupt police officer who gets caught up in a tangled-web moral dilemma involving East European gangs involved in drug smuggling and sex trafficking. The subject matter, and style of direction, called for a darker, heavier sound than the one Johnson had provided for *Tony*, so he had retrieved his old Minimoog and Roland SH-101 synthesizers from storage and set about recording a brooding electronic score, that in places gave a nod and a wink to the more abstract Moog pieces that Bernard Krause had contributed to the soundtrack of Nicolas Roeg and Donald Cammell's *Performance*. This time he was scoring to picture, Gerard sending over scenes as soon as he had shot them. *Hyena* would be the third release on Cineola in March 2015 and also appeared on vinyl, licensed by soundtrack specialists Death Waltz Recording Company. More than one observer, including Gerard Johnson himself, was to note that the last track of the album, 'Everybody Wants To Go To Heaven (but nobody wants to die)' sounded more like a The The track than anything else Johnson had done in his soundtrack work.

The other two soundtracks have yet to be released in any format. The first was for a Turkish film by Danish director Nikolaj Larsen, *End of Season*, which premiered in Istanbul in 2014. He had previously scored the soundtrack for *Je T'aime Infiniment* in 2010, which Larsen co-directed with Corine Shawi. The second was for

Johanna St Michaels' *Penthouse North*. This required a jazzy score that took Johnson out of his comfort zone and he struggled to get it completed on time, much to St Michaels' discomfort. "I was a nervous wreck, because we got into Hot Docs, Toronto and we didn't get the soundtrack until the day before we had to make the DCP to deliver the film." In actual fact Johnson was involved in another soundtrack that year, though this one was much shorter and altogether more abstract.

Denis Masi, a sculptor who had once lived in the same building as Johnson, remained in Shoreditch and the two developed a friendship. In 2014 Masi asked him to add some music to his contribution for a group exhibition organised by filmmaker Jim Hawkes, which required each artist to provide 100 foot of film. Masi chose footage of his 1970 body art film, *Lip Smear*, a conceptual piece about the distorting lens of television, whereby he had filmed himself distorting his face against an 'invisible' sheet of glass. Johnson added a correspondingly distorted, abstract soundtrack, punctuated at intervals by the sound of a crowd laughing and whooping, and the piece was renamed *Face Smear – Reality TV*. The film, clocking in at just under three minutes, is at time of writing on the homepage of Masi's website. He says, "The way he saw that piece was, for me, absolutely fantastic, because it was like late nineteenth century, early twentieth century carnival; it was like a freak show, like Elephant Man. This guy is doing a performance for these people and they are responding to it, so I felt it was absolutely perfect for the piece."

Masi has followed Johnson's career, and his involvement in local issues. "He doesn't tell me everything, but he's a very concerned person. He's concerned about the kind of society we live in, he's concerned about capitalist mechanisms and how exploitative they are, not just from his own experience but in a general sense, so from that point of view he's politically motivated and that's why he probably sees the best way to operate is to have your own messaging, don't rely on anyone else to do it. And to be concerned about local issues. Local issues lead to larger issues."

In the past Johnson's 'own messaging' was his music and the print media where he was able to get his message across. Inevitably, given the subjective bias of editors and journalists, and the constraints of a word-count, this message was sometimes distorted or ignored entirely. The Internet, and Radio Cineola, gave him the power of editing rights. With one problem thus solved it was a case of overcoming the problem of distributing this uncensored message. Though the Internet offered freedoms, it relied on old-fashioned methods of promotion to exploit some of these freedoms. The medium may still have been the message, but if the message was lost in the vast expanse of the web then transmission was being lost in virtual space. Johnson was now ready to use Radio Cineola in a more ambitious way than he had done so far and, specifically, to use it for a political message that linked local issues he had been directly involved in with larger issues, on a national and global scale.

He had by now been forced to be more proactive in his own affairs due to first Cally, and then Lee Kavanagh, having to quit their roles as manager and personal assistant, the former for personal reasons, the latter due to being offered a job closer to home. Johnson had been managing himself for nearly two years and, on recommendation from Lucy Rogers, had enlisted the help of Gillian Glover, who by coincidence had spent time working at Dessau studios in New York as well as in Gothenburg. Glover helped set up a new infrastructure and worked tirelessly to ensure it worked. Other members of the new team included engineers at Studio Cineola, Finnbar Eiles and Mark Allaway; Martin Lewis, who took on artwork for the Cineola label; Modo, who would handle manufacturing, and Steve Phillips and Joe Mallott, who handled press and radio PR respectively. Distribution was taken care of by Essential. Family continuity was maintained with legal work undertaken by John Kennedy's nephew, Kieran Jay, whilst Ron Harris's daughter, Charlotte, took care of accountancy matters. This was the independent set-up that Johnson needed, though he was still feeling his way towards a new way of regaining his former role.

Speaking in January 2015 Johnson said the following: "I just haven't found the key in this new world... not that I particularly found the key in the old world, cos I always felt, even when I was on Sony that the albums did relatively well, but never as well as I wanted them to. I always had that sense of failure after every record. The sense of disappointment, anticlimax, which is a natural feeling I think after the creative process. I never felt that any of them did what I wanted them to do." Feeling this way about things that, by any standards, had been a success, it is easier to see just how much he was now afraid of failing in his endeavours. Radio Cineola, though, provided a kind of safe haven. "It's quite playful, and about finding another vehicle, one that doesn't involve standing on a stage or necessarily putting records out. It's finding new ways to express, and I feel I'm only just scratching the surface, it hasn't reached anywhere near its potential yet. I'm hoping this next project is going to make it something more tangible. And it could possibly develop into something that could include a live performance."

The "next project" that Johnson was referring to was a documentary that Johanna St Michaels had been thinking about ever since her ex-partner had brought a copy of *The Inertia Variations* to Sweden with him. She was as enamoured with Tottenham's verses as Johnson was, and decided that his idea to sew them into the fabric of his early Radio Cineola broadcasts would make a good subject to explore. She had been wrestling with the idea over time, discussing it with Johnson. "We first thought we would do an art film, and I sought money for it and we got a 'no' on every application – I don't know how many applications I did, because I believed so strongly in this idea. And then we wrote down ideas. We were going to build the tower, Matt was going to present the poem and then it was going to be the art film. We started getting funding for it, and we started spinning this idea – there would be the film and the radio station. And then we get funding from all the major art institutes in Sweden, from everyone, they were saying, 'We don't understand it, but this is a great project.' And so then I thought, 'What is the story? What is going to carry this film?'"

The first steps into this collaborative *Inertia Variations* project were tentative. The Radio Cineola mast, which appears in the ident for the 'station', was turned into a nine-metre-high steel sculpture by architect Jacob Sahlqvist and blacksmith Lars Lincoln, inspired by the design of Moskow's Shukhov Tower, which was commissioned by Lenin as the first radio tower to transmit across the Soviet Union. In December 2014 it was temporarily installed on the roof of Röda Sten Konsthall in Gothenburg, and illuminated by lighting designer Kate Wilkins, who had worked with Johnson on many of his live shows in the past. This installation was accompanied by recordings of Johnson narrating verses from John Tottenham's poem, and his own soundscapes. Visuals filmed by St Michaels were projected onto the ground. Somehow, from this art installation, an idea for a film needed to emerge – a story.

Johnson suggested that they combine the *Inertia Variations* project with a live Radio Cineola broadcast. Johnson had taken Tottenham's poem and edited it down, presenting it within a time span of twelve hours. St Michaels took this idea and suggested a Radio Cineola broadcast lasting twelve hours. As well as political content she wanted music, ideally performed by Johnson himself. He was less keen on the idea, preferring to fill up the screen time with others performing his songs, a concept that he had been toying with as far back as 2000. "That was another standalone project as well – *The End Of The Day* – an album of other people interpreting my songs, and this had been going on for years because I hadn't found the right device... I mean you can't release your own tribute album, which is what it would look like. How that idea started was with a track called 'Shrunken Man'. Instead of getting people to remix it, Cally and I asked people to do different versions. Jim Thirlwell, John Parish and DAAU all did versions. So it was continuing with that idea really." They bounced the idea back and forth but felt like they were hitting a wall. Johnson reveals the breakthrough. "Johanna and her assistant Karin Blixt went off to these scriptwriting workshops. I was supposed to go but didn't have the time. One was in, I think, Croatia, and one was in Norway." The workshops taught them that what was missing from the early draft of their script for the film was any kind of dramatic tension.

"The final piece of the jigsaw was when Johanna came back and said, 'Okay, we film live on election day, the whole broadcast.' Suddenly that put everything into focus. And suddenly it was a case of, this fits, that fits, this fits. My passion for geopolitics and what are sometimes disparagingly called conspiracy theories... it all fits in. And so leading up to the few weeks before the show I'd appointed my friend Pam Esterson, an ex-BBC producer, to be our line producer for the first broadcast, contacted various people, like geopolitical analyst William Engdahl, mind control expert Neil Sanders, journalist Neil Clarke, David Edwards from Media Lens... these are people that I read regularly anyway. A combination of those and friends and associates, like Brad Lochore and Lucy Rogers to speak about local politics, John Kelly, Zoe Hepden, who is a professor of philosophy and teaches politics to young kids, Marian St Laurent, who's an expert in semiotics, spiritual healer Abdi Assadi. So the two weeks before I'm sitting up till the early hours, researching, reading books, preparing all the questions, but I found it fantastically stimulating. And for the actual show itself of course, we needed to get the crew sorted, the cameramen and soundmen set and whatever. Then there were technical issues to be solved, for instance, running an Internet radio show – nobody seemed to know anything about it, and it took us a couple of weeks to find out how to do that – to get the right software, to get the right Internet services to do it – so that was a bit of a challenge." No inertia here then. But no music either. The interviews are all recorded and Johnson explains that he intends to do something with them, possibly release them on his label. Some interviews were conducted via Skype calls whilst others took place in the makeshift studio as people dropped by at various points of the day; Tim Pope, Lucy Rogers, Brad Lochore, Neil Maskell and Zeke Manyika all took their turn in the chair to be interviewed by Johnson and discuss a variety of political issues, local, national and global. Despite the sometimes depressing nature of topics being discussed, the atmosphere in Johnson's flat was warm, an antidote to the inevitable bad news to come.

As disappointed as anyone present when the results started to come in towards the end of the broadcast on May 7, 2015, nothing could disguise the fact that Johnson was, whilst physically exhausted, brimming with mental energy. "I really felt in my element to be honest," he tells me three weeks later. "It was how I often felt in the middle of a tour." In a sense he had been 'on stage' for twelve hours, live and direct. It was a shot in the arm for sure, and a relief for Helen to be able to see him express himself at last to an audience, sitting at his desk, taking Skype calls, interviewing people, playing recordings, segueing segments together with audio idents, like a cross between a conductor and a film director. And all the time St Michaels was directing her small film crew, amassing twelve hours of footage. Commenting on what the film might capture, she mentions something that Johnson had himself said. "I think Matt put it the best. It is the interior of him and the exterior of him, in the film; the radio station being the exterior and the poem being the interior."

The documentary now had a working title of *Radio Cineola: The Inertia Variations* and it would be this and the restoration of his building that would increasingly occupy him. Later in May he was invited to talk at the Fireside Sessions, an event that was part of the Alternative Escape, the official fringe of the Brighton Festival. Interviewed onstage, he was asked whether he agreed that there was a lack of political music compared to the 1980s. He replied that he didn't know but that he thought music wasn't a good medium any more for political messages, that documentary makers were now the ones making political statements. Talking about playing live in response to a question from the audience, he said that whilst he disliked the idea of being away from his family for any length of time, he did miss getting goosebumps from when the audience would sing a song back to the band. The interviewer pointed out that he hadn't had those goosebumps for thirteen years. "Actually

I did last week," he replied, mentioning the Radio Cineola election day broadcast. "I was high as a kite after that."

On September 28 he was invited to another Classic Album Sundays event, this time at the Cafe Royal on Regent Street, to talk about his favourite soundtracks and his own soundtrack for *Hyena*. He was full of a cold and seemed distracted at the event, having to answer the inevitable questions from fans about the possibility of a tour or a new album. What nobody knew was that Andrew Johnson's health had taken a sudden turn for the worse. Matt would spend the next few months travelling back and forth between London and his dad's home in Suffolk, feeling numb, bracing himself for the pain to come. He was with Andrew when he died on January 18, 2016; though he had known what was coming, the shock was still devastating.

(OUTRO – THINGS FALL INTO PLACE)

Then indecision brings its own delays,
And days are lost lamenting over lost days.
Are you in earnest? Seize this very minute;
What you can do, or dream you can do, begin it;
Boldness has genius, power and magic in it.
> – Goethe, *Faust* (as translated by John Anster)

AFTER SPENDING YEARS WHERE IT APPEARED HE HAD been doing nothing – though in fact he had actually been doing something – Matt Johnson suddenly decided to do everything all at once. On September 18, 2017 there were four announcements on his website. The *Inertia Variations* documentary would have its UK screenings that month; the *Radio Cineola: Trilogy* box set would be released; he would appear at a Classic Album Sundays event at the Royal Albert Hall to launch the release and talk about the triple album, as well as his love of soundtrack music; and The The would be playing live the following summer – the first such shows for sixteen years.

It was, of course, the last of these items that caught everyone's attention. The initial UK date was a return to the Royal Albert

Hall and tickets sold out in several minutes. A second was then added at Brixton Academy, which also sold out, and a third was then announced at the Troxy, a venue in Limehouse, London. For those with deeper pockets a fourth option to consider was The The's headline show at the Heartland Festival, in Denmark. It was actually this date that instigated what would soon turn into a mini-tour with further concerts announced at intervals in Stockholm, Dublin and a headline slot at Festival No 6 in Portmeirion, Wales. These dates were just the start, and by April 2018 Nottingham, Leeds, Birmingham, Newcastle, Bristol, Glasgow, Belfast, Boston, Toronto, Chicago, Detroit, New York, Los Angeles and San Francisco had been added to the list.

The catalyst for this sudden burst of activity was another Radio Cineola broadcast that had been filmed by Johanna St Michaels for the *Inertia Variations* documentary. This took place over three hours on May 14, 2016 in Johnson's flat to a select audience of family and friends, many of whom were either performing or part of the film crew. This time the set-up was geared towards the music, rather than the radio show. Tom Bright, Thomas Feiner, Liz Horsman, Meja Kullersten and Colin Lloyd Tucker performed their interpretations of 'Love Is Stronger Than Death', 'This Is The Day', 'December Sunlight', 'Slow Emotion Replay' and 'Bugle Boy' respectively. As well as singing, each of the five were interviewed by Johnson and, to tie in with the theme of the documentary, each was asked about inertia. Horsman, who sang the song she recorded back in 2001, revealed that she could relate to it easily. "I said that I felt like fear is the mother of inertia. For me that's what keeps me from the studio – fear of not being good enough. So that event was a reassurance that I'm not alone."

Johnson had contacted James Eller in February to ask him if he would get a band together but Eller had a long wait before he heard from him again. "He called me a week or so before and said, 'I can't think about it yet, but next Monday, I'll be on it.' Monday morning nine-thirty the first email comes in, and it's super detailed – these are the artists, this is the track they are going to do, I want so and so to do this. And then emails kept coming, the phone calls, and it reminded me of what it was like being in The The."

Eller had spent some time planning how he wanted the band to line up and who he wanted to be in it but when he outlined his ideas, Johnson immediately vetoed them and said, "What I want is, like a jazz trio. So it'll be you, a drummer and a keyboard player." Eller chose Chris Whitten (drums), who he played with in the Julian Cope band, and Ian Berryman (keyboards: Florence & The Machine), and the trio started the tricky work of arranging stripped-down versions of the songs each of the singers had chosen. At this point Eller expressed the same idea to Johnson that Johanna had done. "I said, 'It would be really brilliant if you appeared in the last five minutes, singing something unannounced, because it would freak people out.' And he said, 'I'll think about it.' And then he phoned me a week later and said, 'I've got a song.' He emailed it to me on the Sunday night beforehand – it was that close to the show, and I actually paused before playing it, because I thought, 'He's done lots of music, for soundtracks and stuff, but it's been years since he's sung anything. What if this is terrible? It puts me in an awful position because I have to tell him then that we can't do it.' I played it. It was like close to midnight on the Sunday beforehand, and I called down to Sarah and said, 'You have to hear this.' She's not even a The The fan really, and she just went, 'Wow, that's quite something.' And we happened to be going to my in-laws the next day, and their house is noisy because they've got kids, but the whole house went quiet when I played it to them, so I thought, 'This is a good sign.'"

From the outset it wasn't certain whether Johnson would actually sing the new song. He was having second thoughts about performing, not having done so since he left the stage of the Royal Festival Hall some fourteen years before. With the cameras rolling he was understandably anxious. Even some of those closest to him were unsure what he was going to do, and the band themselves were left wondering, as Eller recounts. "We didn't know that he actually would until the moment he walked to the mic to do it. It

455

was pretty tense! He completely nailed it. The whole event was euphoric actually."

The online response to the broadcast was hugely positive, in no small part due to the fact that those who had tuned in heard the first new The The song for sixteen years, whilst those who had missed it cursed their luck. Johanna St Michaels was obviously both relieved and overjoyed that she had got what she had wanted to make her film resonate. With the song acting as the narrative pay-off to the documentary there was some concern about people putting recordings of the show online, whilst all those present were under strict orders not to do the same with footage recorded on their mobile phones.

Fans became aware of the documentary when a trailer for *The Inertia Variations* was screened, alongside *Infected – The Movie*, at the ICA in London over three nights that September. Director Tom Wilcox hosted a Q&A session after the screenings with Johnson, who was accompanied on consecutive nights by Johanna St Michaels, Tim Pope and myself, discussing various aspects of the film and album. As usual the audience were invited to ask their own questions and as usual they asked about the prospect of new material or live performances. Johnson gave his usual patient replies, saying that anything was possible.

In January 2017 he finally got round to listening to the song he had recorded the previous May. That same week he was visited by Johnny Marr; as soon as the guitarist heard the song he said he would play on it if he was considering releasing it. So pleased was Johnson with the result of Marr's contribution that he scheduled a release of the song for Record Store Day, and on April 18 an announcement was made on the official The The website that a new single, 'We Can't Stop What's Coming', would be available the following week as a one-sided 7-inch single in a limited edition of 2,000. The sleeve contained an image from one of Andrew Johnson's many sketchbooks, and another illustration was etched into the flip side of the vinyl record. Such was the response on the day that many fans were unable to secure a copy and expressed their disappointment online, especially when some of those who did manage to buy a copy then listed them on auction websites at inflated cost. To combat this, further copies were made available online, only for the website to crash as fans rushed to buy it. Facing criticism at the limited supply, Johnson decided to release a second edition of the single in June, this time on buttermilk vinyl, minus the etchings.

'We Can't Stop What's Coming' was for and about Andrew but for Johnson the lyrics served a dual purpose. His brother's death had led him to question again what life means, especially in the dark times we currently find ourselves in. "It's also a lyric about cycles of life," he explains. "I use a lot of nature imagery. First of all, Andrew was a real nature lover; he loved birds, and animals, so I was using that as a device, but it is also about powerlessness and letting go. All of us are dangling by a thin thread that separates life and death, and really there's nothing to do but follow nature's lead and embrace life, and allow it to lead us where it will. I really wanted to do a song I was proud of, for Andrew, and I wanted it to have a deeper meaning so it could help other people as well."

The reaction to the single made him take stock, and he realised that as much as he believed in making a stand against the corporate development of Shoreditch and east London, his energies were best directed into doing what he did best – music. Johanna's film served as the impetus for this decision, and became the document that recorded it. The deaths of Eugene and Andrew were like bookends to a period of his life that he was only just coming to understand, and the film was able to capture this process. Johnson explains the negative and positive significance of both these points in his life. "Eugene's death caused this protracted period of inertia and some sort of creative paralysis, because of the grief and the sadness. And also, everything seemed so trivial, especially show business. Then when it happened to Andrew there was the realisation that life is very brief." Quite simply, the inertia, the procrastination, the fear and the doubt was coming to an end.

The Inertia Variations had already been premiered by this time, at the Gothenburg International Film Festival in February, and subsequently in March at the Stockholm Tempo Festival and CPH:DOX in Copenhagen. The UK premiere was at the Edinburgh Film Festival in June alongside the *Radio Cineola: The Inertia Variations* art installation and a reading – directed by Gerard Johnson – of John Hopkins' 1968 play *This Story of Yours*. The English premiere was announced for October 20 at the ICA in London, with further screenings at Home in Manchester, Watershed in Bristol and Showroom in Sheffield. By then the live dates were public news and sold out. Johnson invited John Tottenham to attend the screenings and participate in the ensuing Q&A sessions. Now for the first time there were no questions about when The The might play live again, only about the possibility of more dates being added. Though those close to Johnson had been increasingly speculating that he may in fact return to the stage at some point, no one had been prepared to say when this might be, or even if it would ever happen. When it came to The The performing live, nothing had been certain throughout his career after all.

Paul Boswell, who had been Johnson's agent from 1982 to 1988, and then started working for him again in 2002 – thereby neatly missing out on any live performances of The The – knew not to invest too much hope in persuading him to consider getting back on stage. Nevertheless he would routinely ask Johnson each time they met for their annual lunch saying it was time, that good offers were coming in. And he routinely came to expect the same negative answer. So when they met for lunch in the summer of 2017 he wasn't expecting anything different. Johnson describes his response to Boswell's usual opening gambit. "He said, 'Matt, we've had a fabulous offer from the Heartland Festival in Denmark,' which is apparently named after one of my songs. 'They want you to headline it, they're really keen.'

"So I leant across the table, shook hands with Paul and said, 'Let's do it.'

"He said, 'Really?'

"I said, 'Yes. Let's do it.'

"And then he said, 'Okay then, how do you feel about doing the Albert Hall?' And I was a bit apprehensive, and I said, 'Oh, I don't know, I don't know if there's the interest there, I really don't know how I feel about that.'

"He said, 'Well, I've got a good feeling about it.'

"So I said, 'Okay.'"

The reason for Matt Johnson's change of heart was threefold, involving Johanna pushing him to write a new song for the film, Andrew's death as the event that convinced him to do so and, finally, noticing something in the film when he watched it for the first time. "There's that wonderful scene where Jack is watching me rehearse, and there's a voiceover and he's talking in Swedish, saying, 'I think it's really good my dad is making his comeback in dedication of Andrew.' And the first time I saw that, I just thought, 'You know what, this comeback has got to be more than just a one-off single for Record Store Day. It's got to be more substantial for it to be the turning point, to mean something.' Jack saying that triggered something in me." It was shortly after this that he met Boswell for lunch and the deal was sealed. Johnson, always adept at keeping things under his hat, wasn't in a hurry to let anyone other than Boswell know. "I didn't tell anybody about these shows. I kept it very quiet. A lot of my friends were very surprised. I wanted it to be a bolt out of the blue for everybody, and it was. I didn't want word getting out. Helen didn't find out until just before the time."

Marc Geiger, who maintains that had Johnson toured America for a third time in the mid-nineties he would have broken into the circuit on the same level of success that acts like The Cure and Depeche Mode had enjoyed, was thus one of many surprised to find out. "I was pressuring him for years, I didn't even know Boswell was doing this, I was thrilled he did. When I heard about Heartland Festival and the Royal Albert Hall, I was like 'Fuck, yeah!' This is what is going to put him back in a creative place." Almost immediately, as his American agent, he started thinking about the possibility of securing dates in America for his friend.

The excitement generated by the announcement of live dates had overshadowed the announcement of the release of *Radio Cineola: Trilogy*, the triple album that tied together long-held plans to release Johnson's readings of John Tottenham's poem, the versions of The The songs by other artists, soundtrack music from the documentary plus selections from the interviews that had been broadcast in the May 2015 Radio Cineola election-day broadcast. True to style these were lavishly packaged, with an accompanying booklet, in both CD and vinyl format. It was the closing of a circle he had started at the beginning of the century, thus ending a chapter in time for a new one to begin. Releasing such an album in risk-averse times was a glorious, almost eccentric statement, and a defiant one, evoking as it did an age when spoken-word albums were commonplace and often of the most obscure and eclectic nature. It was well received by reviewers, some of whom even understood the value of its extravagance.

All that remained to be done now was assemble a band. Of course Johnson had been giving this quiet and careful consideration for some time. "I have one member from each of the three tours," he tells me. "I've given it a tongue-in-cheek title – *2018 Comeback Special* – as a reference to Elvis's '68 Comeback Special, though I won't be wearing a leather outfit! It's nice to have one member from each of those three bands, and then a new member for this one. I'm delighted with the group I've put together. I want it to be a summary of my career, but maybe with one or two new songs. It's just a case of stripping the songs down to their essence and reworking them through this line-up. I want to make sure I do the songs justice, and I've got to reconnect with them. I don't want to do songs I don't like. I don't really listen to my back catalogue so I'm hoping its going to be new and fresh for me as well."

James Eller was one of those to get the call-up. "He called me once he'd decided to play live again and asked me to be involved. Of course I agreed straight away, The The is my favourite band of all time and to be in it again makes me happy." On drums the nod went to Earl Harvin, now living in Berlin. "I've said to Matt for years now that I'd be very keen to play should the opportunity arise," he says. "So I was very happy when he contacted me saying he was thinking of doing music with a band again. It's exciting because it's been a long time since we've made music together, and we have all grown since that time. I certainly have more musical experience than I did when we last played, and even though Matt hasn't been on stage as a front-man per se, he has been continuously making music with all his soundtracks. So he has a fresh musical perspective as well." Keyboard duties were allocated to DC Collard, which just left a guitarist to find.

An obvious candidate was Johnny Marr, but though Johnson ran the idea past him he said he couldn't do it as he had his own album due and would be out on the road at the same time. Whilst talking, Marr said he knew who should join on guitar: a friend of his called Barrie Cadogan. By coincidence Johnson had not long before used the 'Shazam' app to find out who had written the theme song to the television show, *Better Call Saul*. Little Barrie was the three-piece band responsible and Cadogan was on guitar and vocals. The next day Marr arranged for Cadogan to visit Johnson and the final member of the new line-up was thus recruited. Preparation and rehearsals were scheduled to begin in March 2018. The band, according to Eller, were raring to go.

Journalist Tom Doyle, who interviewed Johnson for *Q* magazine in June 2017, and as a fan met him in Dundee in 1985, is not only glad to see him returning to action but also feels a much needed re-evaluation of his position will take place as a result. "A voice like his is much needed in a time when most contemporary music has become so safe. You only have to look at the social media responses to The The's return to see how much he's been missed. When the stories of the eighties and nineties are written in music mags, The The are often overlooked, in favour of the usual suspects – The Smiths, Blur, Oasis, etc. But I think that with Matt's return to activity, he'll get his rightful credit as an innovator and important artist." Marc Geiger, whose working relationship with Johnson goes back to the 1980s, remains a huge fan and thinks he can return gracefully. But he wants to see more than just a live band, as he told me over the phone in December 2017. "As a fan I need that music, I need some depth, I want somebody to write stuff that means something. I want to see him play live, that's the start, but ultimately I want him producing, I want him creating, there's not many people who do what he does, not with the depth he does. So, we'll see."

Discounting the one-off appearance at Meltdown, this will be the first time The The have played in the UK since 2000, when Johnson's time living in America was coming towards an end. When he first arrived in New York, Johnson used to carry around with him a quote from Goethe's *Faust*. The quote in fact was a somewhat free and poetical translation by Irish poet John Anster, but the words, about the pivotal moment of making a commitment, resonated with him. "Reading that quote would often give me the courage to leap off the side of the cliff and, incredibly enough, you do find these unseen forces coming to your aid, and things *do* fall into place." While he didn't seem to heed the words when he was abroad, he found that all these years later they were ringing true. He had been afraid but others gave him the courage to make the leap.

The fact that the shows announced had sold out so quickly lifted a huge weight from Matt Johnson's shoulders. At the back of his mind, whenever he had contemplated returning to the stage, there was the fear that the interest wouldn't be there, that nobody would care. As Marc Geiger describes it, "It's a long, slow walk back." Within seven minutes of the tickets for the Royal Albert Hall going on sale this fear had been eliminated. "I was very surprised, pleasantly surprised because they sold out in minutes. We probably could have done three nights in the Albert Hall, like I did in the past but the other nights weren't available. So I really credit Paul's persistence; he wasn't hassling me, he was encouraging me, in a very supportive way. Also Johanna, who was pushing me to get back into the creative swing of things, and then of course there was Jack's comment, and obviously Andrew. With him going... it shook me to my core. I thought, 'If I don't do it now then I'm never going to do it. What am I waiting for?'"

Before long it almost seemed easy. He was back in his old skin. He had seized the very minute, and found there was power and magic in it.

In our accelerated times the idea of taking time out and indulging in *vita contemplativa* is such an alien concept that anyone engaging in it might be deemed to be simply doing nothing, might even feel guilty about not doing something. While John Tottenham used the term inertia in the title of his poem it is tempting to consider the possibility that his irony concealed a deeper truth. Ivor Southwood, in his book *Non-Stop Inertia*, argues that the modern predilection for appearing to be, or actually being, perpetually busy in fact conceals a real paralysis of thought and action. It is the impulse to be busy with something that in fact leads to inertia.

Matt Johnson's own period of inertia was, more than anything perhaps, a natural, psychological response to a series of what were, for him, catastrophic events; the natural response to a sustained period of stress. More recently, however, it would be more correct to say that he was in an artistic hiatus, one that was complicated by a fear of re-emerging as an active performing artist, only to find that nobody had turned up to welcome him back. Those nagging fears aside, he would be the first to admit that it was a good life, one free of the necessity of compromise. He re-emerges now with his reputation intact.

So what next? Johnny Marr wasn't surprised by his friend's long silence, but for him, as much as anyone else, it was about the music. "People would always be asking me, 'When's Matt Johnson putting a record out?' Constantly. One time it happened after one of my shows and Fiona was with me, and I turned to her and said, 'See?' I would ask him, and it got to the point where it sounded like I was just trying to be nice to him or just trying to encourage him. But I told him, 'Matt, people all over the world are asking me, all the time, *When's Matt Johnson gonna put a record out?*' It didn't concern me though because Matt is his own man and no one is gonna get him to do something he doesn't want to do. I think he could put out a great record at any point he wants."

He probably will. But action can only take place now, never tomorrow. So I guess he will start today. Things will fall into place.